PRICE THEORY

PRICE THEORY

Nobel Laureate in Economics

MILTON FRIEDMAN

ALDINE PUBLISHING COMPANY, New York

About the Author

Milton Friedman is a Senior Research Fellow at the Hoover Institution (Stanford University) and is Paul Snowden Russell Distinguished Service Professor of Economics, University of Chicago; a member of the research staff, National Bureau of Economics Research; a past President of the American Economic Association; and a fellow of the Econometric Society, the American Statistical Association, and the Institute of Mathematical Statistics. The recipient of the Nobel Prize for economics in 1976, he is the author of many journal articles and books. Among his best known works are *Essays in Positive Economics, Studies in the Quantity Theory of Money, A Theory of the Consumption Function, A Program for Monetary Stability, Capitalism and Freedom, Dollars and Deficits: Inflation, Monetary Policy and the Balance of Payments, The Optimum Quantity of Money and Other Essays, A Monetary History of the United States* (with Anna J. Schwartz), *Monetary Statistics of the United States* (with Anna J. Schwartz), *Money and Economic Development, There's No Such Thing as a Free Lunch, Free to Choose* (with Rose Friedman), and *Monetary Trends in the United States and the United Kingdom* (with Anna J. Schwartz).

First published 1976 by
Aldine Publishing Company
200 Saw Mill River Road
Hawthorne, New York 10532

ISBN 0-202-06074-8

Library of Congress Catalog Number 76-1397

Printed in the United States of America

Third printing, 1981

Table of Contents

Preface

Shortly after the initial edition of this book was published, I shifted for nearly a decade from teaching price theory to teaching monetary theory. Three years ago, I resumed teaching price theory. Next year (the academic year 1975–76), I plan to teach it for the last time. Hence, if I were ever to revise substantially the provisional version that was published in 1962, now seemed the time to do so.

I cannot pretend that the present version is the finished treatise that I had in mind (or in youthful dreams) in the earlier years of teaching the course. But it is a much expanded and, I hope, improved version. I have filled in four of the six gaps that I enumerated in the preface to the initial version. The two I have not filled in are industrial organization, for reasons given at the end of chapter 6, and the theory of general equilibrium, because there are such good extant expositions of the classical Walrasian general equilibrium approach and I am not competent to present a succinct yet faithful exposition of the more recent general equilibrium developments, particularly in the field of growth models. In addition, I rather suspect that these developments are as yet in a preliminary and unsatisfactory state.

In addition to filling in the designated gaps, I have added a discussion of personal probability to complete the utility analysis of choices involving uncertainty and have inserted a largely expository lecture on the Phillips curve, which I gave in September 1974 in London. This topic may seem to belong in monetary theory rather than in price theory. However, I believe that it belongs in both, for reasons that I trust the text makes clear.

I have included in this edition, as I did in the initial version, my class reading list and a collection of the problems that I have assigned to the class to work on at home. I have been gratified at the professional attention attracted by the problems in the initial version. However, I have not kept track of the articles and notes that they have stimulated, so I cannot provide comprehensive references. I have retained in this edition all the problems from the initial edition and have simply added the problems that I

vii

have assigned since then. My heaviest debt for problems remains to Aaron Director and George J. Stigler, but I have continued to borrow from other colleagues as well.

In preparing this edition, I have benefited from criticisms and suggestions of a number of readers, including teachers who have used the book in their courses. Marshall Colberg was particularly helpful. To him and the others who sent me comments, my sincere thanks. I am deeply indebted also to my secretary, Gloria Valentine, who, in preparing the manuscript for this edition, continued her unbroken record of displaying a degree of efficiency exceeded only by her good cheer.

I cannot end this preface without recording the great personal satisfaction that I have derived from teaching price theory to successive generations of able and enthusiastic graduate students. The formal structure of price theory has an aesthetic quality that has always reminded me of the famous last lines of Keats's "Ode on a Grecian Urn":

"Beauty is truth, truth beauty,"—that is all
Ye know on earth, and all ye need to know.

Milton Friedman
Ely, Vermont
August 3, 1975

Preface to Price Theory: A Provisional Text

It is now more than a decade since the contents of this book were first mimeographed and used in classes in price theory at the University of Chicago. Throughout that period, I have been extremely reluctant to have these notes offered for general sale. The reluctance has derived from my dissatisfaction with their scrappy nature, from my intention to use them as a basis for a fuller and more satisfactory treatment of price theory, and from my optimistic belief that I would be able to turn to the preparation of the fuller treatment momentarily. As an empirical economist, however, I cannot neglect the evidence that has accumulated in that decade. Clearly, I must reject the hypothesis that a fuller treatment is imminent. Moreover, it has not been feasible to keep the mimeographed notes from getting fairly wide circulation. Hence, despite my continued dissatisfaction with them, it has seemed best to make them generally available.

These notes had their origin in the entrepreneurship of David I. Fand when he was a student at the University of Chicago. He induced Warren J. Gustus to collaborate in preparing summaries of lectures in a two-quarter course in price theory that I have given at the University of Chicago since 1946. I went over the summaries, revised them in detail, wrote alternative versions for some, substituted previously written but unpublished material for others, and inserted, both then and at intervals since, published material that seemed particularly relevant. These notes would never have been brought out but for Fand's and Gustus's work, and I am much indebted to them.

In the present version, the reprinted material includes an article on "The 'Welfare' Effects of an Income Tax and an Excise Tax," a revised version of an article that first appeared in the *Journal of Political Economy*, reprinted here from my *Essays in Positive Economics*; a few pages on statistical cost curves from a comment of mine in *Business Concentration and Price Policy*; part of an article of mine that appeared in David McCord Wright (ed.), *The Impact of the Union*; and an article on "Choice, Chance, and the Personal Distribution of Income," reprinted from the *Journal of Political Economy*. I am indebted to the University of Chicago Press, Princeton University Press, and David McCord Wright for permission to reprint.

In teaching the course on price theory since these notes have been available, I have found that the chief gaps in them, which it is necessary to supplement by class presentation, are in respect to (1) the theory of the division of income between current consumption and the accumulation of wealth; (2) industrial organization, with special reference to problems in the economics of the individual firm; (3) fact and theory about the size distribution of income; (4) the theory of profits; (5) capital theory—the final section of the notes on this topic have turned out to be too succinct and condensed, particularly with respect to the arithmetic of the relation between income streams and capital values and the stock-flow analysis embedded in that section; and (6) the theory of general equilibrium.

I have added to this version of the notes two appendixes that may help to fill these gaps as well as supplement the notes. Appendix A gives the reading list that I have used in my course. Appendix B gives a collection of some of the problems that I have assigned to the class to work on during our so-called reading period. The problems are in two parts, those in part 1 having been assigned during the first quarter and those in part 2 during the second quarter. For want of any better sequence, I have listed them in each part simply in the chronological order in which they were assigned. I have used the part 1 problems primarily as a means to fill the gap numbered (2) above; hence, these deal mostly with the interpretation of industrial practices. The answers to some of these problems can now be found in the literature, but I have made no attempt to give references. As every teacher knows, class problems and exam questions are almost community property. I cannot myself trace the source of most of the problems given, except that I know my heaviest debts are to Aaron Director and George J. Stigler, from whom I have borrowed shamelessly.

Milton Friedman

1

Introduction

These notes deal with price theory. The larger part is devoted to the pricing of final products; the rest, to the theory of distribution. The reason for devoting more attention to the pricing of final products is that the theory of distribution is a special case of the theory of pricing, concerned with the pricing of factors of production. Hence, the principles that explain prices in the product markets also explain prices in the factor markets.

Meaning of Economics: Economic Theory

Economics is the science of how a particular society solves its economic problems. An economic problem exists whenever *scarce* means are used to satisfy *alternative* ends. If the means are not scarce, there is no problem at all; there is Nirvana. If the means are scarce but there is only a single end, the problem of how to use the means is a technological problem. No value judgments enter into its solution, only knowledge of physical and technical relationships. For example, suppose given amounts of iron, labor, etc. are available and are to be used to build an engine of maximum horsepower. This is a purely technical problem that requires knowledge solely of engineering and of physical science. Alternatively, let the objective be to build the "best" engine, where the concept of "best" involves not only horsepower, but also weight, size, etc. There is no longer a single end. No amount of purely physical and technical knowledge can yield a solution, since such knowledge cannot tell you how much power it is

1

"worth" sacrificing to save a certain amount of weight. This is an economic problem, involving value judgments.

This concept of an economic problem is a very general one and goes beyond matters ordinarily thought of as belonging to economics. For example, according to this conception an individual is dealing with an economic problem when he decides how to allocate his leisure time between alternative uses. Indeed, strictly speaking there is hardly any problem that is purely technological. Even in the cases cited above, the engineer building the engine will have alternative ends, thinking about other things, making his work pleasant, etc., and these will affect his decision about how hard to work on the stated technological problem. This concept of an economic problem is also broad in the sense that it covers equally the problems in a Robinson Crusoe economy, in a backward agricultural economy, or in a modern industrial society.

Economics, by our definition, is not concerned with all economic problems. It is a *social* science, and is therefore concerned primarily with those economic problems whose solutions involve the cooperation and interaction of different individuals. It is concerned with problems involving a single individual only insofar as the individual's behavior has implications for or effects upon other individuals. Furthermore, it is concerned not with the economic problem in the abstract, but with how a *particular* society solves its economic problems. Formally, the economic problem is the same for a Robinson Crusoe economy, a backward agricultural economy, a modern industrial society organized on a communistic basis, and a modern industrial society organized on a capitalistic basis. But these different societies use different institutional arrangements to solve their economic problems. Thus there is need for a different economics—or a different chapter in economics—for each kind of society. There turns out, in fact, to be much that is common to the various chapters, but this cannot be required in advance; it is, rather, one of the conclusions of economic science.

Our definition of economics can be viewed as something of a compromise between a completely general definition of the economic problem and an opposing desire for concreteness of application.

How does this definition of economics distinguish it from other subjects of study?

The emphasis on "alternative" ends, which introduces *value judgments,* distinguishes it from the technological and physical sciences, which are concerned with the relation between scarce resources and single ends. The acceptance of the ends as *given* distinguishes it from psychology, which deals with the formation of preferences, and from ethics, which deals with the evaluation of preferences.

The most difficult line to draw is between economics and political science. Certainly governmental institutions of the kind studied by political science are means whereby a particular society uses scarce means to satisfy alternative ends. The title of a well-known book by Harold Lasswell is *Politics: Who gets What, When, How.* Replace *politics* by *economics* and the title would clearly be equally appropriate—yet the book so labelled would be altogether different.

Or consider Alfred Marshall's definition of economics: "A Study of mankind in the ordinary business of life; it examines that part of individual and social action which is most closely connected with the attainment and with the use of the material requisites of well-being." In the Great Britain of Alfred Marshall's day, this definition may have served rather well. But today, when the government plays so large a role in the attainment and the use of the "material requisites of well-being," it too does not distinguish between economics and political science.

More fundamentally, Marshall's definition implies that the fundamental difference between the two disciplines is in the character of the ends pursued, that economics is concerned with the "material requisites" and other disciplines with the "immaterial" requisites. But this is not a satisfactory criterion. Economics has as much to say about the use of resources for art, literature, theater, schooling, and other aspects of the "immaterial" requisites as for the material requisites. And clearly, governmental agricultural policies deal with "material" requisites.

A more satisfactory criterion is the means of organization studied, economics being mainly concerned with market mechanisms of purchase and sale as devices for organizing the use of resources. Political science is mainly concerned with mechanisms involving commands, whether by a constituted authority or by explicit voting. But even this distinction is much less than fully satisfactory. Economics has much to say about the consequences of different sets of commands; political science has to encompass governmental interventions into market arrangements.

This difficulty in drawing a dividing line has had consequences. One of the most stimulating developments in the two disciplines since the early 1960s has been the use of economic tools to analyze political arrangements. This merging of the two disciplines has been the work of both economists and political scientists: Downs, Dahl, Stigler, Buchanan, Tullock, to mention just a few of the most prominent names.

Four Economic Sectors

To return to the emphasis on "a particular society" in the definition of economics that I have given, differences in the institutional arrangements that are used to solve economic problems can be illustrated by reference to our own society. One may think of our society as consisting of four sectors, each using a conceptually different arrangement: the government sector, the household sector, the sector consisting of nonprofit institutions, and the market sector.

In every society, whether the U.S. or the U.S.S.R., a substantial fraction of all resources, probably more than half, are used in the *household sector*. The major resource in all societies is human productive capacity—*human capital* as it has come to be called—and most of our time and energy is spent, not in productive activities organized through the market or by the command of governmental authorities but in activities within the household. In addition, much physical capital—from owned homes to kitchen equipment to clothes—is utilized within the household sector. Most of these uses of resources raise no social problem, at least not for economics. Yet there are many interactions between the household sector and the market sector.

One of the important interactions arises out of shifts of activities to and from the household. Such shifts affect, among other things, the validity of estimates of national income as measures of growth. For example, the steady decline in average hours of employment has meant that the growth of measured national income understates the growth of total output because it excludes the value of the additional leisure. On the other hand, the transfer of many activities, such as food preparation and laundering, from the household to the market has had the opposite effect.

In recent decades, there has been an increasing use of economic analysis to interpret behavior in the household that was traditionally excluded from the realm of economics. Gary Becker's pioneering work in this direction deserves special mention.

The principle of organization operating in the household is similar to that employed in a collectivist society—central authority. The major difference is that participation in the household is voluntary for adults. But even this difference does not exist for children.

The *government sector* has clearly been growing rapidly in the U.S. and in most other Western countries. In the U.S., spending by state, local, and federal governments, after being roughly stable as a percentage of net national product for a century or more except for major wars, has risen from roughly 10 percent of net national product in 1929 to 20 percent in 1940, to 23 percent in 1950, to 30 percent in 1960, to 35 percent in 1970. These numbers in some ways overstate the role of government, in others, understate it. They overstate it because much of the expenditure simply transfers control of resources from some people to others (e.g., welfare expenditures) rather than uses resources directly (e.g., highway construction). They understate it because governmental actions that have significant effects on the economy may involve negligible expenditures (e.g., import quotas, minimum wage rates, I.C.C., antitrust).

Because so large a fraction of the government's activities are carried out through the market or impinge on the market, the growth of the government sector has not reduced the relevance of the price theory presented in this book. Indeed, this theory has proved highly relevant not only to the government sector in a "mixed" economy like the U.S. but also to the operation of a supposedly wholly government economy like the U.S.S.R. In practice, even though the basic organizing principle of such an economy may be central authority, every such economy has found it necessary to put extensive reliance on market mechanisms for organizing resources.

The *nonprofit sector* is the smallest of the four sectors in the U.S. economy. It consists of such institutions as universities, churches, museums, nonprofit hospitals, but also of mutual insurance companies, mutual savings banks, cooperative grocery stores. The characteristic feature of the nonprofit sector is that the persons in charge of such institutions exercise authority not as agents for "owners" or as representatives of the body politic in general but as "trustees" either for a purpose (as in a university or church) or for a self-constituted group (such as policyholders of an insurance company). Of course, in many cases the nonprofit form is simply adopted as a tax-evasion device. In any event, the nonprofit sector operates, at least in Western countries, primarily through the market.

The *market sector* thus overlaps all the other sectors. The fundamental principle of the market sector is the use of purchase and sale to organize the use of resources.

In a "pure" market economy, cooperation among individuals is achieved entirely through voluntary exchange. In its simplest form, such an economy consists of a number of individual households—a collection of Robinson Crusoes, as it were. Each household uses the resources it controls to produce goods and services that it exchanges for goods and services produced by other households, on terms mutually acceptable to the two parties to the bargain. It is thereby enabled to satisfy its wants indirectly by producing goods and services for others, rather than directly by producing goods for its own immediate use. The incentive for adopting this indirect route is, of course, the increased product made possible by division of labor and specialization of function. Since the household always has the alternative of producing directly for itself, it need not enter into any exchange unless it benefits from it. Hence, no exchange will take place unless both parties do benefit from it. Cooperation is thereby achieved without coercion.

Specialization of function and division of labor would not go far if the ultimate productive unit were the household. In a modern society, we have gone much farther. We have introduced enterprises that serve as intermediaries between individuals in their capacities as suppliers of services and as purchasers of goods. We have introduced money to facilitate exchange and avoid barter, thereby enabling the acts of purchase and sale to be separated into two parts.

The introduction of enterprises and money does not change the fundamental principle of a market system, but it does introduce complications that are the main subject matter of price theory and also monetary theory. A more fundamental change is introduced by the mixing of the market sector with the other sectors, particularly the governmental sector. Many of the most subtle and interesting applications of price theory involve analyzing the effect of various governmental interventions.

Both Russia and the United States can be described as *enterprise money exchange economies*. In both countries, the bulk of the resources outside the household sector are used in enterprises that acquire the use of resources by purchase for money and distribute the bulk of the output by sale for money. The key difference is that in Russia almost all enterprises are *public* or *governmental;* in the U.S., most are *private,* in the sense that the residual income recipient—the body or persons entitled to receive or required to pay any differences between receipts from sales and expenditures on the purchase of resources—is the body politic in the U.S.S.R., identifiable private individuals in the U.S.[1]

The difference I have stressed between the character of the enterprises is not identical with the difference that is often regarded as critical—that there is "private property" in the U.S., "public property" in the U.S.S.R. In both countries, the bulk of property, defined broadly to include human productive capacity, is privately owned. Neither is the difference between the U.S. and the U.S.S.R. that individuals, including managers of enterprises, act in their private interest in the U.S. and in the public interest in the U.S.S.R. In both countries, individuals act primarily in their own interest, fairly narrowly defined.[2] The difference is that the character of the ultimate residual income recipient alters the rewards and sanctions associated with various actions and thus changes what it is in the self-interest of people to do. To illustrate in a dramatic way: the manager of both a U.S. and a Russian factory must take into account the possibility of being discharged for alleged mismanagement, but the Russian manager must also take into account the possibility of being shot.

Private enterprise exchange economies also differ widely. Perhaps the key difference for purposes of price theory is in the conditions that must be met for establishing an enterprise. At the one extreme, establishing an enterprise requires government permission that is more than a formality (as, for example, is true in the U.S. in banking, generation of power, and

1. Even this statement is oversimplified. With a U.S. federal corporate tax rate of 48 percent on income over $25,000, the U.S. government in effect owns 48 percent of all U.S. corporations and is a residual income recipient to that extent.

2. This qualification is put in to keep the sentence from being a pure tautology—whatever induces men to act is what they regard as their interest.

many other areas). At the other extreme, anyone is *free* to establish an enterprise without special governmental permission (as, for example, is true in the U.S. for most retail trade, manufacturing, etc.).

The notion of free in the term *free enterprise* should be interpreted as the freedom to set up an enterprise rather than the freedom to do anything one wishes with his enterprise, including preventing others from setting up enterprises.

Distinctions in Economic Theory

Economics is sometimes divided into two parts: positive economics and normative economics. The former deals with how the economic problem *is* solved; the latter deals with how the economic problem *should be* solved. For example, the effects of price or rent control on the distribution of income are problems of positive economics. On the other hand, the desirability of these effects on income distribution is a problem of normative economics. This course deals solely with positive economics.

Within positive economics, the major division is between *monetary* theory and *price* theory. Monetary theory deals with the level of prices in general, with cyclical and other fluctuations in total output, total employment, and the like. Price theory deals with the allocation of resources among different uses, the price of one item *relative* to another. The division between the two main branches of theory is not dictated by *a priori* considerations but reflects the empirical generalization—which is at least two centuries old—that the factors determining the level of prices and of economic activity can be regarded as largely distinct from those determining relative prices and the allocation of resources. Of course, the two sets of factors overlap, but for most problems the overlap is treated as sufficiently small to be neglected.

Professional jargon has come to designate monetary theory as *macroeconomics*, price theory as *microeconomics*. This usage is unfortunate because it gives the misleading impression that monetary theory is concerned with things in the large *(macro)*; price theory, with things in the small *(micro)*. Both branches of theory are concerned primarily to understand things in the large: for example, "the" price level, for monetary theory; "the" relative price of wheat or copper, for price theory. Both branches of theory analyze things in the small to further their understanding of things in the large: for example, the demand for cash balances by the individual holder of money, for monetary theory; the demand for bread or coffee utensils by the individual household, for price theory.

This book deals entirely with price theory.

Economic theory, like all theory, may be thought of in two ways. It may be thought of as a language or filing system, or it may be thought of as a set of substantive, empirical propositions. With respect to theory in the

first meaning, the relevant question to be asked is usefulness and not right-
ness or wrongness. The proposition that price is determined by the interaction of demand and supply forces is merely an attempt to set up a useful
filing system within which there can easily be placed under the headings
"demand" or "supply" any one of the forces affecting price. The usefulness of this filing system will in turn depend on the substantive fact,
whether a listing of the forces operating on demand contains few elements
in common with a listing of the forces operating on supply. Economic theory as a set of substantive propositions contains propositions that are, in
principle, capable of being tested because they attempt to be predictive.
The definition of a *demand curve* is "theory as language." However, the
statement that the demand curve slopes downward to the right is theory as
a substantive empirical proposition. It has empirically observable consequences, whereas the definition of a *demand curve* does not. Theory as
language coincides with Marshall's *engine of analysis*. The objective is to
construct a language that will be most fruitful in both clarifying thought
and facilitating the discovery of substantive propositions.

The Operation of the Price System

As Knight points out in his *Economic Organization,* the economic problem may be subdivided into five interrelated problems. Every society must
make some provisions for the handling of these five problems:

(1) fixing standards,
(2) organizing production,
(3) distributing the product,
(4) providing for economic maintenance and progress, and
(5) adjusting consumption to production over short periods.

As already implied, there are fundamentally only two principles of organization that can be used to handle these problems: centralized authority (command) and the market (voluntary exchange). Most actual
complexities arise out of the widely varying mixtures of these two principles that are employed in different countries or in different sectors for any
one country.

There is little of a specific nature that can be said about the pure ideal
type of a command economy. The image is that of an army with a com-
manding general giving orders that are transmitted down a rigid hierarchy
and that govern every detail of behavior of the lowliest foot soldier. All
five of Knight's problems would be resolved in the process. But in any society or organization that encompasses a considerable number of persons
and is dealing with problems of any complexity, this image is highly misleading. It is literally impossible to run such a society or organization by
the pure command principle. The person at the center cannot possibly

have the information required to operate in this way or the capacity to transmit and enforce such detailed instructions. To illustrate in a trivial way, one widely used tactic in labor disputes is to "throw the book" at management or "work by the rule," i.e., to operate only in accordance with printed rules or orders. The result is to bring production to a halt. In practice therefore, "command" is always supplemented by voluntary cooperation.

The pure ideal type of a free-enterprise money exchange economy requires more discussion to show how prices of different kinds play a key role in the resolution of each of the five problems.

The existence of alternative ends implies that there must be some way of rating these ends and reconciling conflicting evaluations of these ends by individuals within the society. In a free-enterprise exchange economy, this task is accomplished essentially through voting—voting in the market place with dollars. In effect, this is a system of effective, proportional representation that permits every group in the society to express its wishes to the extent of its dollar votes. The votes of the members of a free-enterprise exchange economy are manifested through prices, which, in turn, reveal the standards of the society.

Given these standards, there must be some machinery to translate these values or choices into productive activity. Production must be organized both among and within industries. This is accomplished by the price system through the interaction of two sets of prices: prices of products and prices of resources or factors of production. Prices of products in relation to the costs of producing them determine the distribution of resources among industries; the relative prices of resources, in turn, determine the coordination of factors within industries.

Every society must provide some means of dividing the total product among individuals in the society. In a free-enterprise exchange economy, this task is accomplished by the price system. Individuals in such a society separately own the resources used in production. They get a claim on the product by selling their services on the market for a price. The total claim of any individual is determined by the quantity of resources he owns and the prices at which he is able to sell the services of these resources. Factor prices or the return per unit of time per unit of resource together with the distribution of ownership of resources thus determine the distribution of the total product among the individuals in the society.

Prices serve as guideposts to where resources are wanted most, and, in addition, prices provide the incentive for people to follow these guideposts. The use of factor prices to distribute the product makes it possible for other prices, namely product prices, to serve the functions of fixing standards and organizing production. This connection is crucial. The great difficulty with the attempts by collectivist countries to rely more heavily on market mechanisms arises from their trying to separate the distribution of the product from the use of prices to transmit information and organize production.

Problems 1–3 above deal with the adjustment of production to consumption. These are the only economic problems with which the members of a static society would have to be concerned, i.e., the organization of existing resources and their utilization in known ways. However, the members of a changing society also face the problem of affecting the volume of resources and changing the ways in which they can be utilized. This is, of course, problem 4, the problem of economic maintenance and progress. The relevant price for solving this problem in a free-enterprise exchange economy is the interest rate, which provides an incentive for owners of capital to maintain their capital or to add to it.

In any short period of time for which the amount of a product is relatively fixed, there must be some way to adjust consumption to production, to ration the limited amount available among potential consumers. Rationing may be by favoritism, bribery, chance, or by prices, but one way or another it must be accomplished. When people are allowed to bid freely for goods, prices will adjust to a level such that the quantity people want to buy *at the market price* is equal to the quantity available.

Prices, therefore, do three kinds of things in solving the above five problems. They transmit information, they provide an incentive to users of resources to be guided by this information, and they provide an incentive to owners of resources to follow this information.

There are two main difficulties with a summary description such as the preceding one: oversimplification and the danger of confusing description with justification. The problem solved by a price system is an extremely complicated one, involving the coordination of the activities of tens and hundreds of millions of people all over the globe and their prompt adjustment to ever-changing conditions. The price system is an extremely subtle and complex device for solving this problem. Casual observation of the world leads to an underestimation of the complexity of both the problem and the devices used to solve it, because insofar as the price system works we are hardly conscious of its workings. The complexities are brought to our attention only when something goes wrong. A summary description necessarily involves oversimplification, emphasis on the highlights, and neglect of not unimportant details.

In any normative judgment of the price system on the basis of the preceding description, several things must be kept in mind. First, the description implicitly supposes the existence of effective competition in translating consumer wishes into productive activity. It is assumed that people can affect their incomes only through use of their resources and not through interference with the price system. There is freedom to compete but not freedom to combine. Second, the controlling force is pecuniary demand; voting is in proportion to the number of dollars a person has. This is not obviously "just." The basic inequality, it should be noted, is inequality in the ownership of resources. What the market does is primarily to determine the return per unit of resource, and there is no reason to believe that the market aggravates the inequality in the ownership of resources. Moreover, any given degree of inequality is much more serious in an economy that is governed largely by status or tradition than in a market economy where there is much chance for shifts in the ownership of resources. Historically, the fundamental inequality of economic status has been and is almost certainly greater in economies that do not rely on the free market than in those that do.

Every actual society uses a mixture of the two ideal types, though the mixture differs greatly from one society to another. The command element may be introduced in various ways and at all levels. For example, a tax on cigarettes introduces a "command" element into the setting of standards, making cigarettes appear to be more costly in terms of other goods than they are on a purely technical level. I.C.C. regulation of the operation of railroads introduces a command element into the organization of production. Welfare payments and the income tax introduce command elements into the distribution of the product.

These are examples of command elements introduced deliberately through explicit political channels. But command elements are also introduced by difficulties of assigning credit for benefits or assigning responsibility for costs. For example, in the classical case introduced by Pigou, if smoke from my chimney dirties your house, and it is not feasible for you to require me to compensate you for the cost imposed on you, then a command element has been introduced. You are in effect paying part of the cost of heating my house. You would be willing to do so if appropriately compensated. But as it is, you do so not as a result of a voluntary exchange but by my being in a position to "command" you. It must be stressed that this is an extremely complex question, and this example simply illustrates the possibilities without providing an analysis of the problems it raises.

2

Theory of Demand

The Concept of Demand

Wants are to be taken in our analysis as givens or data. However, it should be recognized (as in Marshall, Book III, Chapter 2) that wants can be both the cause and the result of action. There is the "work-to-live" school, who treat wants as the primary ends, and the "live-to-work" school, who treat activities as the primary ends. In many ways, this classification is very fundamental and is a key to an economist's position on many issues. For example, one who (implicitly, perhaps) belongs to the "work-to-live" school, like Alvin Hansen, is likely to stress existing wants, take the consumer as the dominant economic entity, regard the consumption function as stable and as the key to understanding the economy, and can readily adopt the idea of stagnation. On the other hand, one who belongs to the "live-to-work" school, like Schumpeter, will regard the producer-innovator as the dominant economic entity, stress innovation (even though it may come in waves), and be led to a theory of dynamic economic development.

The relativity, i.e., nonconstancy, of wants has a number of important implications. In the first place, it directly affects the allocation of resources, since it means that a fundamental want is for more wants, which leads to the employment of people to teach music appreciation, art appreciation, etc. In the second place, and more important, it means that the complete satisfaction of all wants—a literal economy of abundance—is impossible. Satisfaction of all the wants existing at any point of time would mean the emergence of a new series of wants. By the standards of 150 years ago in the U.S., or of some less-developed parts of the globe today, the current

American standard of living would seem like paradise. A corollary is the impossibility of defining a minimum standard of living in absolute terms. There is a widespread misconception that such a standard can be determined "scientifically," by which is typically meant in terms of physical and biological laws, and without reliance on "subjective values." This is clearly contradicted by a comparison of different standards constructed at different times or for different societies. The differences are large and clearly represent differences in customary standards. Similarly, it is contradicted by examination of the food component of such standards. It has been shown that the nutritive requirements imposed could be satisfied for one-quarter or less of the amount customarily allotted to food by persons who have attempted to construct minimum-cost diets. The rest must be considered as designed to satisfy a desire for variety or for good-tasting food, i.e., to satisfy wants that cannot be evaluated objectively.

Despite these qualifications, economic theory proceeds largely to take wants as fixed. This is primarily a case of division of labor. The economist has little to say about the formation of wants; this is the province of the psychologist. The economist's task is to trace the consequences of any given sets of wants. The legitimacy of and justification for this abstraction must rest ultimately, as with any other abstractoin, on the light that is shed and the power to predict that is yielded by the abstraction.

A basic distinction in the theory of demand is between "demand" in the *schedule* sense and "demand" in the sense of *quantity demanded*. The harm that can be done by confusing these two senses of the term *demand* is suggested by such statements as: (1) "The price went up and therefore demand went down," and (2) "Demand went up and therefore price went up." Each statement separately seems sensible, yet the two are clearly contradictory if the word *demand* is supposed to have the same meaning in both. Of course it does not; in (1) it means "quantity demanded," in (2), "demand schedule." Subsequently, the word *demand* will be used only when reference is being made to the demand schedule; and the words *quantity demanded* will be used when reference is being made to a particular quantity.

To bring out the distinction more clearly, consider the following proposition: "A change in the price of butter may affect the demand for oleomargarine; it does not affect the demand for, but only the quantity demanded, of butter."

A demand curve of a particular group for a particular commodity can be defined as a locus of points, each of which shows the maximum quantity of the commodity that will be purchased by the group per unit time at a particular price. It represents an attempt to relate a rate of flow to a price at an instant of time. For many problems, it is useful to conceive of a demand curve as a boundary line separating two spaces, the space to the left of the demand curve representing points that are attainable under the given conditions of demand, in the sense that demanders would be willing to buy the indicated quantity at the indicated price; and the space to the right of the demand curve representing points that are unattainable in the sense that demanders would not be willing to buy the indicated quantity at the indicated price (see Figure 2.1).

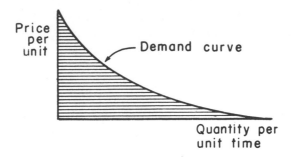

FIGURE 2.1

The demand for any commodity or service may be a *composite demand,* compounded out of the demand for a number of different uses: e.g., the demand for leather is a composite of the demand for leather for shoes, for pocket books, etc. A product may be jointly demanded with some other products: e.g., there is a *joint demand* for tennis rackets and tennis balls, automobiles and automobile tires. More generally, the demand for any product is always a joint demand for the resources used to produce it. The demand for a commodity or service may be *derived* from the demand for some final good: e.g., the demand for carpenters' labor is derived from the demand for houses.

Consumer demand for final products is the ultimate source of the derived demand for resources. For short periods, however, the demand of dealers can vary independently of the demand of final consumers. The demand of dealers, in turn, may be strongly influenced and affected by expectations concerning future prices, a factor that generally plays a much smaller role in determining consumer demand. For this reason, the usual tools of demand and supply may not be very useful in a study of day-to-day fluctuations in this type of market. Of course, formally they could still be used for this purpose, but major attention would then have to be placed on changes in them rather than movements along them. Another way of putting this point is that demand and supply are useful concepts when the forces affecting demand are largely distinct from those affecting supply, as they are in general when consumers and producers are being dealt with. In this case, the demanders are in general a different set of people from the suppliers, and so the forces affecting demand are likely to be distinct from those affecting supply. However, in a traders' market, the same people are both demanders and suppliers, frequently shifting from one side of the market to the other. In this case, the filing system of supply and demand is not very useful.

When the demand curve is conceived of as a boundary line, under given conditions, a point on the demand curve represents the maximum quantity that buyers would purchase per unit time at a given price. To be precise, one should specify the alternatives considered open to the demanders. As generally drawn, the demand curve supposes that demanders are free to buy either the indicated quantity or any smaller quantity at the indicated price. A different demand curve is obtained if the demanders are supposed to be faced with an all-or-nothing decision, i.e., with the alternative of buying either the indicated quantity or nothing at all. In general, an all-or-nothing demand curve would be to the right of the usual

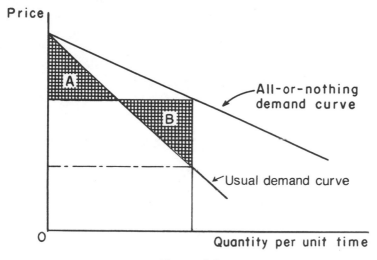

FIGURE 2.2

demand curve (as in Figure 2.2). In a special case, it will be determined by the condition that the cross-hatched area B equal the cross-hatched area A.[1] More generally, it can be expected to be between the usual demand

1. The special case is that for which the total amount spent on the product in question is sufficiently small that changes in the amount spent do not appreciably affect the value that the consumer places on a unit of income. In this case (Marshall's "constant marginal utility of money"), the price shown by the usual demand curve for any quantity can be regarded as the maximum amount the consumer would pay for an additional unit of the commodity, whether he has paid the same price or a higher price for the prior units. The integral under the demand curve is then the maximum total amount he would pay for the indicated quantity, and that amount divided by the quantity, the maximum average price he would pay on an all-or-nothing decision. The condition that the cross-hatched area B equal the cross-hatched area A is equivalent to the condition that the price times the quantity on the all-or-nothing curve equal the area under the usual demand curve. It will be seen that an all-or-nothing alternative is equivalent to perfect price discrimination.

curve and a curve determined by this condition. The all-or-nothing demand curve is useful in analyzing certain problems, but our main concern here will be with the demand curve of the usual type.

Three different roles are played by "time" in the demand curve. First, the horizontal axis measures quantity per unit of time: e.g., pairs of shoes per month or per year. This use of time enables one to draw a continuous curve even for items such as pianos or houses, where purchases are made in discrete amounts. Second, the various points on the demand curve should be thought of as *alternatives* as of a moment in time. The demand curve is a snapshot at a moment in time and represents the maximum quantities that would be purchased at alternative prices. In this sense, "time" is used as a synonym for "under the given conditions." Third, the demand curve will depend on the period of adjustment. The purpose of a demand curve is to facilitate analysis of the effects of changes in supply. The effects of any given change in supply will, in turn, depend on the period of adjustment allowed for in the demand curve. In the shortest of all runs, where conditions are allowed to vary very little, one would expect the demand curve to have the least elasticity. As the range of conditions that are allowed to vary is widened, one would expect the elasticity of the demand curve to increase, as indicated in Figure 2.3.

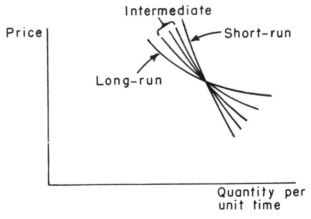

FIGURE 2.3

The Concept of Supply

In analyzing supply, as in analyzing demand, it is necessary to distinguish between the supply schedule and the quantity supplied. The supply schedule separates those price-quantity combinations that are consistent with the conditions of supply from those that are not. In general, the *supply schedule* will be defined as showing the minimum price at which a given quantity will be forthcoming. This definition also covers the case of a forward-falling, negatively sloped supply curve, as will become evident subsequently. For many problems, it is not so much the supply curve itself that is important but rather the area that it bounds. The supply curve, like the demand curve, involves the use of time in three different senses. There is time in the sense that the horizontal axis measures quantity per unit of time. There is time in the sense that the various points on the supply curve are to be interpreted as *alternatives* at a moment in time. Finally, there is time in the sense of allowance for a period of adaptation included in the drawing of the supply curve. This last use of time enables one to generate short- and long-run supply curves.

We can now put together the two tools of supply and demand and examine summarily the so-called law of supply and demand.

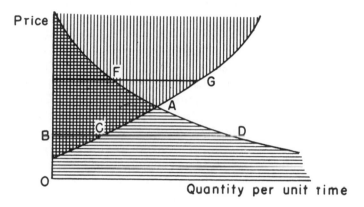

FIGURE 2.4

The demand and supply curves limit the pertinent or observable price-quantity relationships to the triangular, cross-hatched area in Figure 2.4. For a more precise statement it is necessary to make some assumptions concerning institutional arrangements. In a free market, the point of intersection of the supply and demand schedules in Figure 2.4 (A) is of particular significance. At this particular price, and only at this price, will the desires of demanders and suppliers be simultaneously satisfied. At any other price, either demanders will want to buy more than suppliers want to sell (a "shortage") or suppliers will want to sell more than demanders want to buy (a "surplus"). At point A, the underlying forces of demand and supply, not demand and supply themselves, have established a price that equates the quantity supplied and the quantity demanded.

If a free market does not prevail, the price may not be at A. For example, suppose a maximum price of OB is established by government and effectively enforced. In this case, demanders would want to buy BD, suppliers to sell BC. A complete description will have to specify how these conflicting desires are reconciled. Somehow or other, BC will have to be "rationed" among demanders eager to buy a larger amount of BD. CD measures the size of the rationing problem and the pressure on the maximum price. If this is handled by some method other than subsidizing suppliers, the final point will be at C. Similarly, suppose OE is established as a minimum price and effectively enforced. Demanders would want to buy only EF, suppliers to sell EG. The problem is now to ration suppliers, and FG measures the size of the problem.

Two examples may serve to illustrate the usefulness of these concepts. Consider, first, the case of automobiles during and shortly after World War II, when automobile manufacturers maintained list prices below the price at which the quantity supplied would have been equal to the quantity demanded. The result was that most consumers could not buy cars at the nominal list price; they paid higher prices in the form of premiums to dealers, lower allowances on used cars traded in, or bought essentially new cars at uncontrolled prices as "used" cars. The price consumers actually paid was indeed higher than it would have been if manufacturers had charged a higher list price. If manufacturers had charged a higher list price, the quantity of cars supplied would have been higher, since the higher price would have induced them to push their production farther despite the higher costs this would have involved. But clearly a larger quantity of cars would have meant a lower free market price for consumers, since the conditions of demand would have been the same whichever policy the manufacturers followed. "Low" prices at the manufacturing level thus resulted in fewer cars, a higher price per car to final consumers, and a redistribution of income from laborers and consumers to automobile dealers. Diagrammatically, the process is indicated in Figure 2.5. If the forces underlying supply and demand had been allowed free

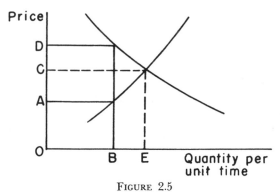

FIGURE 2.5

play, then the equilibrium quantity would have been OE and the equilibrium price would have been OC. With a nominal "list" price of OA, the quantity supplied was OB but consumers were willing to pay OD for this quantity OB. Thus various indirect forms of paying this price arose. The price finally paid (OD) was above the equilibrium price (OC), and the quantity supplied (OB) was less than the quantity (OE) that would have been supplied at the price OC.

A second example is union action on wage rates. The ability of unions to set wage rates or to fix minimum wage rates (which are presumably above the equilibrium rate) is the fundamental restrictive action. Because the union sets the wage above the equilibrium wage, the number of people willing to work at this union wage as given by the supply curve exceeds the number of people that employers are willing to hire at this wage as given by the demand curve. Therefore, much of union activity is concerned with rationing the available jobs among the job-seekers. This is the real economic function of such practices as high initiation fees and featherbedding.

The concept of an equilibrium price has been employed in the above analysis, and perhaps some elaboration of this concept of equilibrium is in order. An equilibrium position is one that, if attained, will be maintained. Three different types of equilibria may be distinguished: stable, metastable, and unstable. A stable equilibrium is one such that if a small displacement occurs, there will be a movement back to the original position. For example, for a negatively sloped demand curve and positively sloped supply curve, if price should rise above the equilibrium price, quantity supplied will exceed the quantity demanded and this will set forces in motion that will drive the price back to the original equilibrium level. The meta-stable case occurs when given any displacement there is no tendency for further movement. This would be the case if the demand and supply curves were coincident. The unstable case is that which occurs when an original displacement sets up forces leading to further displacement. This third type is exemplified by a case where a price rise results in a quantity demanded in excess of the quantity supplied, causing the price to rise even more.

The Concept of Elasticity

The concept of elasticity of demand is used to describe a particular property of a demand curve. To speak in general terms, it describes the effect of a change in price on quantity demanded—the extent to which quantity demanded "stretches" when price changes. Changes in quantity and price are generally measured as percentage changes, in order to have an elasticity measure that is independent of the units in which price and quantity are expressed. More specifically, elasticity of demand is the ratio of the percentage change in quantity demanded to the percentage change in price that is responsible for this change in quantity demanded when "other things" are given and when the change in price approaches zero.

In mathematical terms, elasticity of demand is equal to $\frac{dq}{dp} \cdot \frac{p}{q} = \eta$, where q is quantity demanded and p is price. For a demand curve, the range of values for η will generally be from 0 to $-\infty$ inasmuch as quantity and price move in opposite directions. Often an attempt is made to estimate elasticity over an arc, given the two points that the arc connects, and the formula $\dfrac{q_2 - q_1}{q_1} \cdot \dfrac{p_1}{p_2 - p_1}$ is at times used. With this formulation, however, the answer depends on which point is taken as a starting point. In general, there is no one, unambiguous way of measuring elasticity over an arc. There are a large number of formulas for estimating and approximating arc elasticity. The concept of point elasticity is for this reason, among others, more useful.

The concept of elasticity can be applied to any function, i.e., the elasticity of A with respect to B given C. It is, thus, a property of any two variables related functionally. In the general case, elasticity would therefore be $\left(\dfrac{\partial A}{\partial B} \cdot \dfrac{B}{A} \right)_C$. However, in the case of demand, when only two variables are being dealt with, it is possible to state the formula for elasticity as $\dfrac{dq}{dp} \cdot \dfrac{p}{q}$. Mathematically, elasticity is simply the logarithmic derivative of a function, i.e., $\dfrac{d \log q}{d \log p}$.

One of the most important reasons for employing the elasticity concept when dealing with demand curves is that it provides a very convenient method of indicating the behavior of total receipts. The change in total receipts depends on two factors: the change in price and the change in quantity. For a negatively sloped demand curve, these factors have opposite effects on total receipts. A decline in price tends to reduce receipts, the associated increase in quantity tends to increase receipts, and conversely for a rise in price. If the percentage change in price is equal in absolute value to the associated percentage change in quantity, the two effects offset one another and total receipts do not change. But in this case, as is obvious from its definition, elasticity of demand is -1. This is generally described as unit elasticity of demand. If the percentage change in price is larger in absolute value than the associated percentage change in quantity, then the effect of the change in price will dominate, so total receipts will move in the same direction as price, declining when price declines and rising when price rises. In this case, the elasticity will range between 0 and -1, and demand is said to be inelastic. If the percentage change in price is smaller in absolute value than the associated change in quantity, then the effect of the quantity change will dominate, so total receipts will move in the same direction as quantity and in the opposite direction from price, so total receipts will rise when price declines and decline when price rises. In this case, the elasticity will range between -1 and $-\infty$, and demand is said to be elastic.

Geometrically, the above relationships are illustrated in Figure 2.6. Ana-

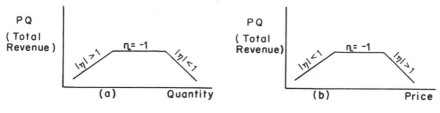

FIGURE 2.6

lytically, let there be a change in price, Δp, and a change in quantity associated with this change in price, Δq.

$$\text{Total Receipts at New Price} = (q + \Delta q)(p + \Delta p)$$
$$= qp + q\Delta p + p\Delta q + \Delta p\Delta q.$$

As Δp approaches zero, $\Delta p\Delta q$ will generally tend to be very small compared to the other terms and can be neglected so that

$$\text{Change in Total Receipts} = \Delta(pq) = p\Delta q + q\Delta p.$$

Divide the expression $p\Delta q + q\Delta p$ by Δq to get

$$\frac{p\Delta q + q\Delta p}{\Delta q} = p\left(1 + \frac{q}{p} \cdot \frac{\Delta p}{\Delta q}\right) = p\left(1 + \frac{1}{\eta}\right) = \text{marginal revenue,}$$

which is defined as change in total receipts per unit change in quantity. If demand is elastic, η will be between -1 and $-\infty$, so $\frac{1}{\eta}$ is between 0 and -1, and the expression $1 + \frac{1}{\eta}$ will be positive (between 0 and 1). Marginal revenue will therefore be positive, and total revenue will rise as price declines. If the elasticity is unity (-1), the expression $\left(1 + \frac{1}{\eta}\right)$ will equal zero; marginal revenue will be zero; and total revenue will be constant. If the demand is inelastic, the expression $\left(1 + \frac{1}{\eta}\right)$ will be negative; and total revenue will decline as price declines.

It is now possible to indicate some uses to which the elasticity concept may be put. The more inelastic the demand curve, the greater will be the fluctuation in price due to a given change in quantity supplied. In the case of agriculture, the demand curves are supposedly inelastic. This means that every change in quantity supplied will bring about relatively greater changes in price per unit of product. In addition, every increase in quantity supplied means a reduction in total revenue.

Consider the case of a monopolist. Without any knowledge of his cost curves, one can immediately conclude that he never would be operating in the inelastic part of his demand curve. In such a part, the receipts would be less than at a higher price, while total costs would clearly be no less, since it can in general not cost more to produce a smaller than a large quantity (he could always produce the smaller quantity by producing the larger and disposing of the excess). However, if one could choose which industry to monopolize, he would want to choose one for which the demand curve was highly inelastic at the competitive price. Once a successful monopoly had been established, price would be raised so as to operate in the elastic portion of the demand curve (the exact point in the elastic region will, of course, depend on cost conditions).

Another case to consider is that of a monopolist whose cost of production is zero. A monopolist will not operate in the inelastic portion of his demand curve, for here he can always gain in total revenue by increasing price. Likewise, this monopolist will not operate in the elastic portion of his demand curve, for here he can always gain in total revenue by decreasing price. Hence, he will operate when the demand is neither elastic nor inelastic, hence, of unit elasticity. At this point, total revenue will be at a maximum.

It is sometimes asserted that *luxuries* and *necessities* may be classified by the elasticity of the demand curve, a necessity having an inelastic demand and a luxury having an elastic demand. This definition of a luxury and a necessity leads to some odd results. For example, it classifies cigarettes as a necessity but white bread as a luxury. Actually, it is very difficult to define the two terms in any meaningful manner. A consumer is only in equilibrium when he regards himself as getting the same "value" or "utility" or "satisfaction" for a unit of money spent in one use as for a unit of money expended in any other use; otherwise, why doesn't he subtract the unit from the one use and spend it on the other use? It therefore follows that on the margin everything is equally necessary or equally unnecessary. As we shall see later, the term *luxury* is now more generally defined in terms of the effect of a change in income rather than in price.

The elasticity of demand depends primarily on the availability of substitutes. Consequently, the more narrowly defined is the commodity in question, the more substitutes will be available and the greater will be the elasticity of demand for the commodity. Thus the elasticity of demand for white bread is greater than the elasticity of demand for bread.

Ceteris Paribus

The demand function has been defined as the locus of points showing the maximum quantities that will be purchased at various prices, given that other things remain the same. A moment's reflection will indicate that if a demand curve is defined with *all* other things remaining the same, there cannot possibly occur changes in quantity or price, and there would be no use for a demand curve. As a slightly less extreme example, consider the following, each of which is sometimes included in ceteris paribus:

(1) prices of all other products,
(2) quantities of all other products,
(3) money income or money expenditures of consumers.

If all three were included in ceteris paribus, then since the prices and quantities of all other products are held constant and since the amount of money income or expenditures is held constant, the amount of money left for expenditure on the commodity in question would be given. Consequently, the demand curve would have to be of unitary elasticity. Clearly, it is not very useful to define a demand curve in such a way that all demand curves are of unitary elasticity.

The purpose of ceteris paribus is methodological and not substantive. The question at issue is not the factual one of what things will or will not remain constant, but rather what principle shall be used to select the things that will provisionally be assumed to remain constant. As will be seen later, it is useful to hold constant provisionally some variables that will necessarily undergo change (those variables that affect the variable in question and are, in turn, affected by it) for the very reason that it is desired to analyze the changes that these variables will undergo. For example, consider the effect of the removal of a tax on oleomargarine on its price and output. The removal of the tax means a change in the supply of oleomargarine, and the problem becomes what kind of a demand curve to draw for oleomargarine. The shape of the demand curve for oleo will depend on what is being held constant with respect to butter, as Figure 2.7

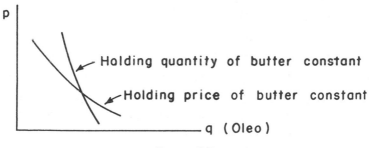

p

Holding quantity of butter constant

Holding price of butter constant

q (Oleo)

FIGURE 2.7

indicates. If the supply of butter is completely inelastic, then the ideal demand curve for oleo is the one that is constructed holding the quantity of butter fixed. If, on the other hand, the supply of butter is completely elastic, then the ideal demand curve for oleo is the one that is constructed holding the price of butter fixed. In fact, both the price and the quantity of butter are likely to decline in response to a decline in the price of oleo. In this case, the problem is most conveniently handled by means of successive approximations. If it were true that the supply of butter were either infinitely elastic or completely inelastic, then a demand curve could be constructed that would yield the answer directly without resort to the method of successive approximations.

In analyzing the effects of the removal of the tax on oleo, let us draw the demand curve for oleo holding the price of butter constant. If the supply of butter were completely elastic, then the price of oleo would go down, the quantity of oleo would go up, and the quantity of butter would go down. The assumption has been made in Figure 2.8 that the supply

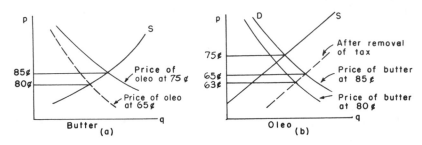

FIGURE 2.8

curve of butter is not completely elastic. When oleo declines in price from, say, 75¢ to 65¢, the demand curve for butter will shift and the price of butter will decline from, say, 85¢ to 80¢. However, when the price of butter declines from 85¢ to 80¢, the demand curve for oleo will shift and the price of oleo will fall to 63¢, again causing a shift in the demand curve for butter, etc. If this process is continued long enough, the solution of a system of simultaneous equations will be arrived at.

	Butter	Oleo
Supply	$q_b = q_b (p_b)$	$q_o = q_o (p_o)$
Demand	$q_b = f_b (p_b, p_o)$	$q_o = f_o (p_b, p_o)$

The last example should make clear the distinction between holding something constant on a curve (with ceteris paribus) and assuming that, in fact, it will remain constant. In this example, the price of butter was held constant precisely in order to analyze the changes that it would undergo.

One may ask, why not solve the simultaneous equations directly instead of going through the process of successive approximations just described? The answer is that we seldom in fact know the simultaneous equations explicitly. We use our conceptual apparatus to organize a largely qualitative analysis. The process of successive approximations makes it clear at each point what information is needed and makes it possible to carry the analysis as far as the available knowledge will permit or as far as it is worth carrying in light of the accuracy of information available and the precision required in the answer.

For the analysis of demand and for other purposes, it is useful to classify the "other things" to be held constant into three categories:

(1) those "things" that significantly affect the variable under study and that are in turn significantly affected by it, e.g. the price of butter in an analysis of the effect on the price of oleo of removing a tax on oleo;

(2) those "things" that significantly affect the variable under study but that are not significantly affected by it, e.g., income in an analysis of the effect on the price of oleo of removing a tax on oleo;

(3) those "things" that neither affect significantly the variable in question nor are significantly affected by it, e.g., the price of feathers in an analysis of the effect on the price of oleo of removing a tax on oleo.

The variables under (1) are held constant in order to study the changes they will undergo; they are held constant only as an intermediate step in the analysis. The variables under (2) are held constant in order to fix the analysis, to separate the particular relations under consideration from other (independent) changes going on. The variables under (3) are ignored. Consider the demand for oleo. The variables that are included in (1) are the prices of or quantities of closely related commodities, i.e., substitutes or complements. The variables that are placed in (2) include tastes and preferences, money income, the average price of all (or all other) commodities, wealth and distribution of income. Everything else in the world is included in (3). Of course, just where the line is drawn between these categories cannot be specified once and for all; it depends on what effects are regarded as "significant" for the purpose in hand and on empirical knowledge about the relevant factors and their effects.

The demand function with the above classification in mind may be written in the following manner:

$$(1) \qquad q_x = f(p_x; p_y, p_z; I, P_o, W, T, \ldots \ldots),$$

where p_y and p_z are the prices of commodities closely related to x, P_o is the average price of other commodities, I stands for income and its distribution, W for wealth and its distribution, and T for tastes and preferences.

If one goes to the limit of regarding any conceivable effect as "significant" and is unwilling to put anything into category (3), then it would be necessary to include the price of "every" other commodity, the income and wealth of every individual, and the like.[2] Such a demand curve is used by mathematical economists and is frequently written as follows:

$$(2) \qquad q_x = f(p_x, p_y, p_z, \ldots \ldots; p_a, p_b, \ldots \ldots),$$

The first set of prices are the prices of products; the second, of the services of factors of production. This "Walrasian" function does not indicate ex-

---

2. "Every" is in quotation marks in order to emphasize the ambiguity in the concept of a commodity and the impossibility of getting an exhaustive list of commodities once and for all and independently of the problem.

plicitly all of the variables held constant. It includes explicitly only prices. Implicitly, however, the quantity of resources of various kinds owned by different individuals is supposed fixed, and so a particular set of factor prices is taken as determining the income and wealth of every individual. Similarly, tastes and preferences are also regarded as fixed. This Walrasian demand function may, as already suggested, be regarded as a limiting form of a function like that of equation 1. It is clear, however, that its value is for a very different purpose. It is an extremely useful abstract conception to bring out the logic of the interrelation of the price system; it cannot be used to analyze a concrete problem.

To return to the demand curve with which we are primarily concerned, let us concentrate attention on the variables whose precise treatment raises the most difficult problems: the price of the commodity in question, the average price of all other commodities, and money income. If we concentrate on these variables, we can write equation 1 as:

$$(3) \qquad q_x = f(p_x, I, P_o),$$

remembering that the variables we have omitted are to have given values.

Equation 3 gives the impression that the quantity of x demanded is to be regarded as a function of three separate and independent variables. However, this is not the case. The demand curve is primarily used to analyze relations among parts of the economic system, to analyze the influence of changes in the "real" underlying circumstances. If all of the variables in the parenthesis (p_x, I, P_o) were multiplied by a common factor, this would not change any of the "real" possibilities open to the consumer; it would simply involve a change in units, e.g., the substitution of "penny" for "dollar." Consequently, it seems appropriate to regard the right-hand side of equation 3 as a homogeneous function of zero degree in p_x, I, and P_o; i.e., a function that has the property that

$$(4) \qquad f(p_x, I, P_o) = f(\lambda p_x, \lambda I, \lambda P_o),$$

where λ is any arbitrary number. This is equivalent to saying that p_x is a function not of three variables but really only of two.

This corresponds very much to a rather common-sense view that there are two kinds of forces that will affect the quantity of a product demanded by an individual: (1) changes in the general range of goods available to him—changes in "real" income or general command over goods and services, and (2) changes in the terms on which he can substitute one commodity for another—changes in relative prices.

The problem now is how to express this distinction in terms of the demand curve, how to "collapse," as it were, the three variables p_x, I and P_o into two in such a way as to give meaningful results when either of the reduced variables is held constant and the other varied.

The usual solution is to make λ in equation 4 equal to $\frac{1}{P_o}$ so that the demand function becomes:

(5)
$$q = f\left(\frac{p_x}{P_o} ; \frac{I}{P_o}\right)$$

This is generally described by saying that money income and the price of "other" commodities are held constant when the effect of a change in price is being considered. This is a mathematically simple and convenient way of reducing p_x, I, and P_o to two variables, but unfortunately it does not correspond to the distinction drawn earlier between changes in "real" income and in relative prices. If this particular way of collapsing the function is chosen, real income will vary as we move along the demand curve. Assume that the price of commodity X declines. Since money income and an average price of all other commodities are being held constant, the individual can buy the former quantity of all commodities and still have money remaining. This would indicate that with the price decline in commodity X, the individual's real income has increased, in the sense that the range of alternatives open to him is greater. This has been recognized and has led to a further subdivision of the effect of a change in one price: the effect attributable to the change in the range of alternatives open to him, and the effect of the change in the relative prices alone—the so-called income effect of a change in price and the so-called substitution effect.

Thus, replacing the three variables P_x, I, and P_o by the two $\frac{P_x}{P_o}$ and $\frac{I}{P_o}$ does not really produce a two-way classification of forces affecting quantity consumed. It still leaves a three way-classification: (1) the "substitution" effect, (2) the "income effect of a change in price," and (3) the "effect of a change in money income." However, (2) and (3) are logically and conceptually the same. The distinction between them arises only from the accidental form taken by collapsing the three variables into two. For an illustration of this point, consider Table 2.1.

The change from line 1 to line 2 is the kind of price change encompassed by the usual demand curve, and these two points would be plotted on a single demand curve of the usual kind. This change is regarded as composed of two parts: one reflects the increased range of alternatives open to the individual and the second the change in relative prices. Consider now the change from line 1 to line 3 and then to line 4. The end quantity is obviously the same as on line 2 since line 4 involves simply multiplying the price and income entries on line 2 by 1.01. ($\frac{I}{P_o}$ and $\frac{P_x}{P_o}$ are the same.) The movement from line 1 to line 2 is thus equivalent to a movement from line 1 to line 3 plus a movement from line 3 to line 4. The movement from line 1 to line 3 involves a change in "real" income roughly equal to that involved in the movement from line 1 to line 2, since \$1 is the extra money that would be available to the individual at the lower price of X if he bought the same quantity of X (namely, 10) as he did before. Thus the movement from line 1 to line 3 is identical with part of that involved in going from line 1 to line 2, yet it is classified very differently, namely as the income effect of a change in income, not as the income effect of a change in price.

TABLE 2.1

	q_x	p_x	P_o	I
(1)	10	1.0	1	100
(2)	11	0.9	1	100
(3)	10.1	1.0	1	101
(4)	11	0.909	1.01	101

An alternative way of collapsing the three variables, p_x, P_o and I, into two in a way that corresponds more closely to the two-fold distinction suggested by economic considerations is, first, to replace P_o by the purchasing power of money in all uses and then to use this as the λ in equation 4. More precisely, let

$$(6) \qquad\qquad P = W_1 p_x + W_2 P_o$$

or a weighted average of p_x and P_o where the weights may be taken to be proportional to the quantities of X and of other things consumed in the initial position (so that P is conceptually equivalent to the usual cost of living index number). Then we can write equation 4 as

$$q_x = f\,(p_x, I, P_o) = f\left(p_x, I, \frac{P - W_1 p_x}{W_2}\right),$$

or setting $\lambda = \dfrac{1}{P}$, as $q_x = f\left(\dfrac{p_x}{P}, \dfrac{I}{P}, \dfrac{1 - W_1 \dfrac{p_x}{P}}{W_2}\right)$

or, more generally, as

$$(7) \qquad\qquad q_x = g\left(\frac{p_x}{P}, \frac{I}{P}\right).$$

It is clear that in this case, a change in the price of X relative to all prices with $\dfrac{I}{P}$ fixed does not involve any "obvious" change in "real" income. If to fix our notions we think of I (money income) as fixed, then a decline in p_x must be accompanied by a rise in other prices if P is to stay the same, which tends, as it were, to use up any funds released by the decline in price of X. This can be further illustrated with the simple numerical examples cited above. These are reproduced below in Table 2.2, with some additional calculations. By the usual definition, lines 1 and 2 are on the same demand curve. By the alternative definition in equation 7, they are not, since, as shown by the last two columns, lines 1 and 2 differ in two respects: first, the price of x is lower on line 2 than on line 1, and second, real income as measured by $\frac{I}{P}$ is higher. The change in real income is the same as that involved in going from line 1 to line 3; the change in price is the same as that involved in going from line 3 to line 4. Lines 3 and 4 are on different demand curves by the usual definition and on the same demand curve by the alternative definition.

TABLE 2.2

	q_x	p_x	P_o	I	$\dfrac{p_x}{P_o}$	$\dfrac{I}{P_o}$	P	$\dfrac{p_x}{P}$	$\dfrac{I}{P}$
(1)	10	1.0	1	100	1.0	100	1	1	100
(2)	11	0.9	1	100	0.9	100	0.99	0.909	101
(3)	10.1	1.0	1	101	1.0	101	1	1	101
(4)	11	0.909	1.01	101	0.9	100	1	0.909	101

(NOTE: $P = .1\, p_x + .9 P_o$, since $q_x = 1/9$ of q_o for (1).)

To summarize, general considerations suggest the desirability of having two functions. One function should be so defined as to summarize the forces affecting the demand for the commodity in question operating via relative prices. In this function, real income should be held constant. The other function should be so defined as to summarize the forces affecting the demand for the commodity in question via real income. In this function, relative prices obviously should be held constant. A function of this latter type is the Engel curve, which relates quantity demanded and real income. The ordinary demand function is intended to provide a function of the former type but does not do so, because changes in real income are not rigorously excluded. A demand function in which real income, in the sense of money income divided by the purchasing power of income, is held constant does yield the desired function.

Statistical Demand Curves

The objective in estimating a demand curve statistically is to derive a Marshallian demand curve for a particular commodity under specified conditions. Two kinds of problems must be faced in deriving demand curves statistically: the first involves the data themselves and the second is the problem of transition from the data to the demand curve.

Generally, there are two kinds of data: time series data, prices and quantities of the commodity in question at different points in time; and cross-section data, prices and quantities for different units or groups at one point in time.

With respect to data, some of the problems are as follows: (1) An enormous number of prices exist for almost any commodity or service. Shall retail or wholesale prices be used? Those in New York or Chicago? As of January or December? Rural or urban? How are different qualities to be treated? If an average is to be used, how should the average be constructed? (2) What quantity should be used? The quantity produced or the quantity available for domestic consumption, i.e., how shall we treat imports and exports? How will stocks be treated? Generally, the quantity purchased for final consumption is taken as the relevant quantity. (3) Is the time unit to which the figures refer the same for price and quantity? The geographic unit?

Suppose that all these and other relevant decisions concerning the data have been made. The next problem is to use the data to derive a demand curve. In formal terms the answer is relatively straightforward. It is desired to put the data in such a form that they relate to a single demand curve. Corrections should be made for all factors that have differed for the different observations in order to approach as closely as possible a set of given conditions. However, a dilemma exists here. If conditions could, in fact, be made identical, then only one price and one quantity would be observable. Therefore, what is really desired is to have the conditions affecting demand unaltered and at the same time to have a maximum of change with respect to the forces affecting supply. Alternatively, if the forces affecting demand have varied, and the forces affecting supply have remained unchanged, the data could be used to generate a supply curve. Generally, however, there will be variations in the forces affecting both demand and supply. If this is the case, the only hope of deriving a demand curve lies in the hypothesis that the forces affecting demand and the forces affecting supply are different. If the same forces have been affecting both demand and supply, then correction for changes will ultimately yield only a point, not a curve.

To illustrate how corrections may be made for changes in forces affecting demand, changes in population might be allowed for by computing quantity per capita, changes in the general level of prices by dividing the price of the commodity in question by a general price index. For some variables, for example, real income (money income divided by the price index), a more complicated technique will be required.

For example, consider Figure 2.9. After adjustments in the data have been made for population and other changes, a scatter diagram a is obtained. Now it is desired to see whether a demand curve will be generated by adjusting the data for changes in real income. Suppose every point on scatter diagram a that is associated with a high income is labelled +, every point associated with a medium income is labelled O, and every point associated with a low income is labelled −. Then if diagram a yields a pattern similar to that of diagram b, it may be inferred that an attempt to hold real income constant would yield a point. In this case, it appears that real income has affected both demand and supply. However, if diagram a yields a pattern similar to that of diagram c, then it seems not unreasonable that changes in real income have affected primarily the demand curve and that a demand curve can be estimated from the scatter of points for each income level. Another way to state the results obtained in diagram c is that the slopes of curves fitted to three clusters of points show the effects of relative prices, the positions of the three clusters the effects of income. It may be that the effect of relative price is approximately the same at different income levels. In this case, evidence on the price elasticity of demand can be obtained from observations for all levels of income. In effect, by "correcting" for income differences, the various clusters in diagram c can be brought together in a single cluster. If the effect of relative price is not the same at different income levels (i.e., if there is no simple scale in which the clusters in diagram c display approximately the same shape), the situation is more complex; in effect, the price elasticity must be calculated as a function of real income. The actual techniques are those that come under the heading of "multiple correlation" and need not be considered here.

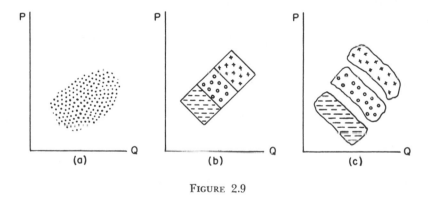

Figure 2.9

In certain cases, the same data may be used to derive both demand and supply curves. This is possible, for example, when some reactions can be taken to be lagged, as in the so-called cobweb case, in which it is assumed that the quantity supplied this year depends on the price of the preceding year. Prices of last year will affect short-period quantity supplied but not demand; hence a demand curve can be generated by taking this year's price and this year's quantity. To generate a supply curve, this year's price and next year's quantity would be taken, since quantity supplied is assumed to be a function of last year's price.

Consider now the possible uses of contemporaneous data. One kind of contemporaneous data consists of family budget data giving the income and expenditures of a group of families. Unfortunately, there are no variations in conditions of supply with respect to these families and hence no price differences to estimate the demand curve. It is not possible to get a price-quantity curve, but an Engel curve may be derived giving a relationship between income and either quantities purchased or expenditures on a particular category of consumption.

One such statistical construction to which much attention has been paid is the relationship between total expenditures on consumption in a given period (usually a year) and what is regarded as total income in the same period. We may use this relationship to illustrate the problems in interpreting such data.

What is desired is the effect on a family of a specified change in its circumstances. What is available are data on differences between different families in different circumstances. This raises a problem of correcting for differences in circumstances other than the one of immediate interest (namely, differences in money income). But more important, for our purposes, is the meaning of such a curve as DE on Figure 2.10. In this figure,

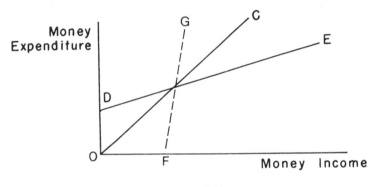

FIGURE 2.10

money income in a particular year is measured along the horizontal axis, money expenditure along the vertical axis. The line OC bisects the quadrant and therefore indicates the points at which money expenditure is equal to money income. The line DE represents the average expenditure of families in different income classes, computed from a particular family budget study. Its position is roughly the same as the results actually obtained from such studies—it shows dissaving among low income classes, saving among higher ones; it shows the percentage of income saved as increasing with income. A naive interpretation of these results would suggest (1) that the rich are getting richer and the poor poorer and (2) that the percentage of income saved in a country would tend to be higher, the higher the per capita income. But other data contradict these conclusions: inequality of income has not tended to increase over time and the percentage of income saved has been roughly constant in this country for at least the past fifty years.

The explanation is that the money income by which the families are classified does not represent or measure their permanent income status; it is the amount of income received during a particular year and thus reflects all sorts of random and temporary effects. This introduces a bias into a figure such as Figure 2.10. Consider, for example, the lowest income group. Insofar as the incomes of people in this group have been affected by random influences, they have clearly been made lower than usual—to put it differently, no one can be in this lowest income group because his income was accidentally *higher* than usual. On the average, the "normal" income of the people in this group is higher than their income during the particular survey year; to some extent, they adjust their expenditures to their normal income; hence their expenditures will appear high relative to their average income in the survey year. Conversely, at the top of the income scale, the average income in the particular year of those with the highest income in that year tends to exceed their average normal income, so expenditures appear low relative to average income in the survey year. This effect is obviously present in the intermediate classes to a smaller degree. Classes below the middle income tend to have average incomes for the survey year below their normal incomes, and conversely. In consequence, even if expenditures were a constant percentage of "normal" income, a survey would yield a relation like DE in Figure 2.10 between average consumption expenditures and income, for families classified by income.

But the same data might well yield a very different relation like the line FG if the families were classified by consumption expenditures and average income were plotted for each such class. This reverses the bias. Families with the lowest expenditures are likely on the average to have expenditures below "normal" and conversely. What this example illustrates is the well-known "regression bias."

Another kind of contemporaneous data consists of data for different spatial units, such as different states or cities or countries. The problem of constructing a demand curve from such spatial data is essentially similar to that already considered for time-series data. To construct a demand curve, it is essential that conditions of supply vary considerably, conditions of demand very little. But for any product that has a national market, conditions of supply are about identical except for transportation costs for different states or other subdivisions of the United States. It follows that a demand curve can be constructed readily only for products that have a local market, which would imply that conditions of supply are different. Then, however, it is necessary to correct for differences in conditions of demand, which can to some extent be done by allowing for size of market, degree of urbanization, per capita income, etc.

The possibility of using spatial data is fairly limited. At the same time, when they can be used, they have the great advantages that factors varying considerably over time are automatically eliminated and that additional data for testing or extending any results become readily available.

An enormous amount of work has gone into attempts to estimate demand curves from both time series and spatial data and Engel curves from family budget data. So far as I know, no one has attempted any summary judgment of the success of these efforts. In some, perhaps many, cases they have clearly been attended with success, in the sense that the results are consistent from one body of data to another and that predictions based on the calculated demand curves are better than alternative predictions. In many, perhaps most, cases they have been failures. It would be extremely valuable to have a study classifying the statistical results by degree of success and attempting to find out the circumstances under which success is most likely.

Of course, the usefulness of the concept of the demand schedule does not hinge on the success with which quantitative demand curves can be estimated. Its major value is as a means of organizing knowledge and thinking about a problem and as a guide to qualitative answers about the direction of effects. At the same time, quantitative estimates of demand curves would extend the range of usefulness of the concept by enabling it to be used to get quantitative estimates of the effects of various changes.

Utility Analysis of Demand

The purpose of this section is to go behind the market demand curve. To begin with, a market demand curve can be broken down in two different ways. (1) At any given price we can subdivide the total quantity demanded into the quantities demanded by individual consumers. By doing this for various prices, we can express the market demand curve as the horizontal sum of the demand curves of the individual consumers. (2) Alternatively, at any given price, we may be able to subdivide the total quantity demanded into the quantities demanded from the various sellers. By doing this for various prices, we may be able to express the demand curve as the horizontal sum of demand curves for the products of the individual producers. The reason for saying "may be able" for 2 but "can" for 1 is that if the products of different producers are literally identical, consumers will be indifferent about the producer from whom they buy the product. Hence the amount demanded from each will be indeterminate. The division of the total among producers will depend entirely on conditions of supply. In both cases, the subdivision supposes that the price is the same for all units considered—either all buyers or all sellers. It is this supposition that permits us to add the quantities for individuals to get the sum for the market.

This supposition raises no problem for demand curves for individual consumers, since it is in general appropriate to regard all as paying the same price—to regard the price as outside the control of the individual consumer. As we shall see later, it does raise a problem for demand curves for individual producers, since it is often desirable to ask what would happen to the quantity demanded from an individual producer if he varied his price while other producers did not. Demand curves designed to answer this question will not be additive.

Our purpose in investigating the demand curve of the individual is to learn more about the market demand curve. If the demand curve of one individual depended critically on the behavior of his neighbor, we could learn little about the market demand curve from analysis of the behavior of an isolated individual; the essence of the phenomenon would be precisely mass reactions, and we would do better to stick to the market demand curve. The analysis that follows, therefore, takes it for granted that this is not the case, that the individual's demand curve depends on his own relatively fixed preferences and on his objective circumstances, not immediately or directly on what his neighbors are doing. "Keeping up with the Joneses" is not eliminated as a factor affecting his preferences; it is eliminated as the proximate determinant of his consumption behavior.

The goods that an individual can buy are, of course, limited by his resources—his income and wealth—and by the prices or terms at which goods and services are available. Subject to these limits, the individual decides somehow or other what goods and services to purchase. These decisions can be regarded as (1) purely random or haphazard; (2) in strict conformity with some customary, purely habitual mode of behavior; or (3) as a deliberative act of choice. On the whole, economists reject 1 and 2 and accept 3, partly, one supposes, because even casual observation suggests more consistency and order in choices than would be expected from 1 and more variation than would be expected from 2; partly, because only 3 satisfies our desire for an "explanation." Accordingly, we shall suppose that the individual in making these decisions acts *as if* he were pursuing and attempting to maximize a single end. This implies that different goods have some common characteristic that makes comparisons among them possible. This common characteristic is usually called *utility*. Utility is sometimes confused with *usefulness*, which is a misunderstanding of the concept. We observe that people choose; if this is to be regarded as a deliberative act, it must be supposed that the various things among which choice is made can be compared; to be compared, they must have something in common. Because we name this common characteristic *utility*, it does not follow that the common characteristic is to be identified with *desirability*. The function that enables us to predict how a consuming unit does behave is not necessarily the same as the function that would tell what is desirable.[3]

Let X, Y, Z, etc. stand for the quantities of various commodities. Then the notion that these commodities have some element in common and that the magnitude of this common element, utility, depends on the amounts

3. To avoid the misleading connotations of utility, Vilfredo Pareto invented the word *ophelimity* as a substitute. Unfortunately, it never caught on.

of the various commodities can be expressed by writing utility as a function of X, Y, Z . . . . This function gives "total" utility. An important additional concept is "marginal utility," which is defined as the rate of change in total utility as the quantity of one commodity is increased while the quantity of other commodities is held constant. For example, the marginal utility of X is the rate of change of total utility per unit change in X for given values of Y, Z, etc.

Marginal utility is not, as is sometimes supposed, the utility of the last unit; otherwise, the following paradox would occur. Assume X refers to oranges and that all oranges are alike. Since all oranges are alike, the utility of each orange must be the same. If marginal utility were the utility of the last orange, it would equally have to be the utility of every other orange; therefore, total utility would be equal to the product of marginal utility and the number of oranges. Clearly this is not a useful way of defining marginal utility. Total utility is equal to the product of the *average* utility and the number of oranges—i.e., this is a definition of *average utility* consistent with our usual use of the term *average*. *Marginal utility*, defined as "the rate of change of total utility," is the utility of the last orange plus the change in utility of the preceding oranges when one more is added. It is the rate of change in total utility per unit change in quantity and is not the utility of a marginal unit.

More important still is the concept of "diminishing marginal utility." The classical writers (Smith, Ricardo, etc.), in seeking an explanation of value, came to the conclusion that demand and utility could not be a determinant of value. This conclusion was intimately related to the diamond-water paradox. In arriving at the conclusion, they reasoned that water is more useful than diamonds, yet diamonds are much more expensive than water; therefore utility could not explain value. In rejecting utility as a measure of value, they arrived at a labor cost theory of value, wherein utility was regarded as a condition or prerequisite of value but not as a measure of it.

The fundamental confusion here was an inability to separate total utility from marginal utility. A less fundamental difficulty was a failure to specify units. Obviously, there exists an amount of water that would be more expensive than a given amount of diamonds. The problem of units aside, what the classical writers did not see and what the theory of diminishing marginal utility brought to the surface is that the decisive factor in price determination is the addition to utility from having a little more water or a few more diamonds. Hence, the marginal utility of diamonds can be very high (because diamonds are very scarce) relative to the marginal utility of water (because water is very abundant); and in consequence, the price of diamonds can be high relative to the price of water; and yet the total utility of water can be much greater than the total utility of diamonds. This is illustrated in Figure 2.11.

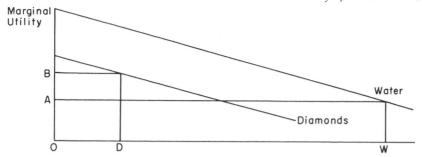

Figure 2.11

The solution of the diamond-water paradox enabled the neoclassicists to bring in demand as a determinant of price. However, the triumph of marginal and diminishing marginal utility has, in a sense, been carried too far. While it is true that diminishing marginal utility can account for lack of specialization in consumption, it by no means follows that we must have diminishing marginal utility to explain or rationalize this observation.

We shall now show how a demand function can be obtained for an individual from his utility function and budget constraint. Assume that there is some function U (X, Y, Z, . . .). Without a budget constraint, the individual would continue to increase his consumption of X, Y, Z, . . . until their marginal utilities became zero. To simplify the problem, let us assume that the individual has already decided how to distribute his resources (e.g., labor power) and thus already has an income to dispose of. Further, let us assume that the individual is facing given prices, P_x, P_y, P_z, . . . , and that his money income is I. From this it follows that the budget constraint

$$XP_x + YP_y + ZP_z + \ldots = I,$$

where X, Y, Z, . . . are the quantity of each commodity, summarizes the limitations of the individual's resources. Given that U (X, Y, Z, . . .) is to be maximized subject to the constraint of $XP_x + YP_y + ZP_z + \ldots = I$, the method of the Lagrangian multiplier may be employed. Therefore we write

$$U (X, Y, Z \ldots) + \lambda (XP_x + YP_y + ZP_z + \ldots - I).$$

Differentiating this expression with respect to X, Y, Z, . . . and λ we obtain

$$U_x + \lambda P_x = O$$
$$U_y + \lambda P_y = O$$
$$U_z + \lambda P_z = O$$
$$\cdots \cdots \cdots \cdots \cdots$$

$$XP_x + YP_y + ZP_z + \ldots - I = O$$

From this it follows that $\dfrac{U_x}{P_x} = \dfrac{U_y}{P_y} = \dfrac{U_z}{P_z} = \ldots = \lambda$. The economic meaning of this is that marginal utility per penny's worth of commodity X must equal that of commodities Y, Z, ... This common marginal utility per penny is equal to λ, which is Marshall's marginal utility of money.[4] Another way to state this result is $\dfrac{U_x}{U_y} = \dfrac{P_x}{P_y}$ The interpretation of this is

that $\dfrac{U_x}{U_y}$ represents the rate at which the individual is *willing* to substitute

Y for X, while $\dfrac{P_x}{P_y}$ represents the rate at which he *can* substitute Y for X on

the market. The equilibrium condition is that the rate at which the individual is willing to substitute Y for X be equal to the rate at which he can substitute Y for X, since if he were willing to substitute fewer units of Y for one unit of X than he can get on the market by giving up one unit of X, then it will pay him to do so, and conversely.

This result can be illustrated diagrammatically, as in Figure 2.12. In

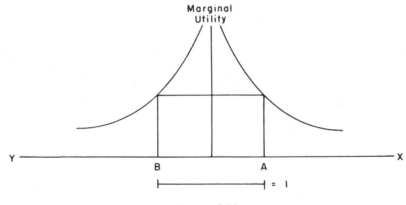

FIGURE 2.12

this case, we assume that the marginal utility of X is independent of the amount of Y; i.e., that the utilities of the two commodities are independent. The unit on the horizontal axis is a penny's worth of X or Y. The bar equal to I represents the individual's income. The consumer is in equilibrium when he has so allocated his income that he receives as much utility per penny's worth of Y as he receives per penny's worth of X. From this diagram, it would appear that without diminishing marginal utility the

4. This term, despite its ancient provenance, is misleading. It would be better termed "marginal utility of income" to avoid confusion with the utility derived from holding cash balances.

individual would either specialize in the consumpton of X or Y. This is valid but only because of the fact that we have assumed independence.

Figure 2.13 represents a case of dependence. In this case, even with increasing marginal utility, we do not necessarily get specialization in consumption.

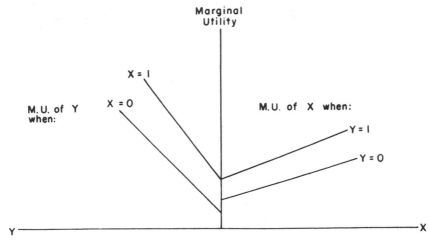

FIGURE 2.13

Diminishing marginal utility will provide a negative slope for the demand curve, but the fact that the demand curve has a negative slope does not require diminishing marginal utility.

To illustrate the derivation of a demand curve, consider the following utility function: $U = \log X + \log Y$. Assume that P_x, P_y, and I are given. The condition for maximization is that $\dfrac{U_x}{P_x} = \dfrac{U_y}{P_y}$. Now, $U_x = \dfrac{1}{X}$ and $U_y = \dfrac{1}{Y}$. Therefore, $\dfrac{1}{XP_x} = \dfrac{1}{YP_y}$. From this it follows that $XP_x = YP_y$. However, the budget constraint is $XP_x + YP_y = I$. Then $2XP_x = I$ and $X = \dfrac{I}{2P_x}$, which is the demand curve.

We have just seen how, from the utility function, $U = \log X + \log Y$, the demand function, $X = \dfrac{I}{2P_x}$, has been derived. This demand function has the property that the amount of money spent on commodity X is a constant sum. The demand curve is thus an equilateral hyperbola. It will also be noticed that this utility function is one where the marginal utilities of X and Y are independent. The marginal utility of Y depends on the quantity of Y alone, and the marginal utility of X depend on X alone. The above utility function also has the property of diminishing marginal utility for each commodity.

Suppose now that the utility function is $U = XY$. In this function, the marginal utility of X is equal to Y ($U_x = Y$), and the marginal utility of Y is equal to X ($U_y = X$). Diagrammatically this can be shown as in Figure 2.14. In this function the marginal utility of X remains constant if X is increased, and the marginal utility of Y remains constant if Y is increased. This function differs from the former in two senses: there is no longer diminishing marginal utility and there is dependence. However, the demand function generated by the utility function is the same, $X = \dfrac{I}{2P_x}$.

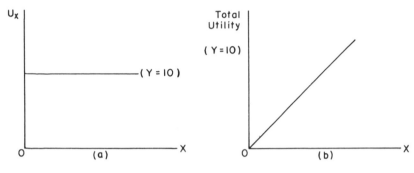

FIGURE 2.14

Now consider a third utility function, $U = X^2Y^2$. In this case the marginal utility of X (U_x) is equal to $2XY^2$, and the marginal utility of Y (U_y) is $2YX^2$. In this function there is dependence and increasing marginal utility for both X and Y. Solving for the demand function we obtain $X = \dfrac{I}{2P_x}$, which is again the same as was obtained in the two previous instances.

In the three preceding functions we have had independence and decreasing marginal utility, dependence and constant marginal utility, and dependence and increasing marginal utility. Yet in each case we end up with the same demand function. This seeming paradox can be stated in another manner. We notice that people spend one-half of their income on commodity X, which is the case when the demand function is $X = \dfrac{I}{2P_x}$. Yet there are three different utility functions that rationalize this observed phenomenon. Let us construct a table indicating how different baskets of goods will be ranked by these utility functions: Function I: $U = \log X + \log Y$ (the numbers are for natural logarithms); Function II: $U = XY$; Function III: $U = X^2Y^2$; and let us add a fourth function, Function IV: $U = \sqrt{X} + \dfrac{\sqrt{Y}}{2}$.

From Table 2.3 it may be seen that utility functions I, II, and III all rank bundles in the same way, while IV does not. The different utility functions assign different numbers to these bundles; but when considering any two bundles, if function I indicates the one bundle has a higher utility than the other, functions II and III will do likewise. Since in ordinary market behavior, i.e., behavior under certainty, the individual indicates only whether he prefers one basket to another but never by how much, it should not be surprising that these three utility functions yield the same demand function. Functions I, II, and III are all functions of (XY), and thus if we call $U = XY$ one utility function, the other two can be written down as functions of U, namely $F = \log U$ and $G = U^2$. Function IV, however, cannot be made a function of U. This may be generalized by saying that if some $U = f(X,Y)$ is consistent with the individual's behavior, then so is any other function $U^* = F[U(X,Y)]$ providing that $\dfrac{dU^*}{dU} > 0$. These two conditions guarantee that the various utility functions generated will rank baskets in the same way. In the terminology of the next section, these three utility functions would have identical indifference curves even though they attach different numbers to the curves.

TABLE 2.3

X	Y	I	II	III	IV
1	1	0	1	1	1.5
1	2	.693	2	4	1.707
1	3	1.099	3	9	1.866
2	1	.693	2	4	1.914
3	1	1.099	3	9	2.232
2	2	1.386	4	16	2.121

Indifference Curve Theory

The indifference curve apparatus is another device to summarize tastes succintly. Consider any commodity space, XY, and consider any bundle of X and Y labelled P in this commodity space. This commodity space may be divided into four quadrants as in Figure 2.15. Let us assume that the

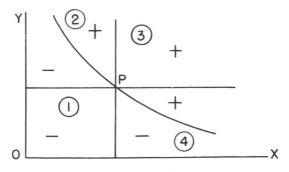

FIGURE 2.15

individual prefers more of each commodity to less. Then any point in the region labelled 3 is clearly preferable to point P, since it represents either more of X or more of Y or more of both. By similar reasoning, P is clearly preferable to any point in the region labelled 1 inasmuch as P represents either more of X or more of Y or more of both. With respect to the points in quadrants 2 and 4, we can think of asking the individual whose preferences we are determining how he ranks each point relative to P. If he prefers the point, we can label it +, if he prefers P, we can label the point −. In this way we can attach + or − to points in regions 2 and 4. There will be some boundary line between the −'s and the +'s; the points on this boundary line represent combinations among which he is indifferent, and this boundary line we may call an indifference curve. Our assumption that more is preferred to less means that the indifference curve cannot go through quadrants 1 and 3. Hence, the indifference curve can never have a positive slope but must be negatively inclined at all points in the economic region. Given that the indifference curve is negatively inclined at all points, there is still the possibility that it may be either concave or convex to the origin. On grounds that will be shown later, it is reasonable to assume the indifference curve to be convex to the origin. By starting with a point other than P, we could in the same manner generate a different indifference curve. In principle, an indifference curve goes through every point. The set of indifference curves is a map of the individual's tastes.

With respect to the individual's opportunities, they may be represented geometrically as in Figure 2.16. The individual is assumed to have a money

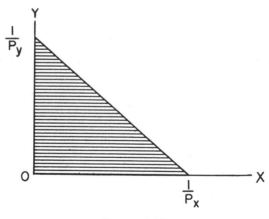

FIGURE 2.16

income I, which he spends on commodities X and Y. If he spends all his income on commodity Y, he can purchase $\frac{I}{P_y}$ units of Y. If he spends all his income on commodity X, he can purchase $\dfrac{I}{P_x}$ units of X. The slope of this

line with respect to the X axis is therefore $\dfrac{P_x}{P_y}$. Economically this means

that if the individual purchases one unit less of X, he saves an amount of

money equivalent to P_x. With this amount of money he can buy $\dfrac{P_x}{P_y}$ units

of Y. $\dfrac{P_x}{P_y}$ therefore represents the rate at which commodity Y can be substi-

tuted for X. The shaded area in the diagram represents the area of attainable combinations.

Superimposing the two boundaries obtained, we see that the individual
will never stop within the area of attainable combinations but will en-
deavor to end up on the boundary line. The condition of equilibrium is
that the individual select that point on the line of attainable combinations
that is on the highest indifference curve. The rationale for the assumption
of convexity of the indifference curve with respect to the origin may now
be seen. If the indifference curve were everywhere concave to the origin,
then the point of equilibrium would be on one of the axes, i.e., we should
expect to find people specializing in consumption. We, therefore, rule this
out. If the indifference curve were somewhere convex and somewhere concave to the origin, the individual would never be in equilibrium at any
part of the indifference curve that was concave to the origin. Therefore,
the economically relevant part is always the part where the indifference
curve is convex. If the indifference curves are convex to the origin, the
point of equilibrium is a point at which the line of attainable combinations is tangent to an indifference curve.

As shown above, the slope of the line of attainable combinations is

$\dfrac{P_x}{P_y}$, or the rate at which the individual can substitute commodity Y for

commodity X. Similarly, with the indifference curve, if the individual
gave up one unit of X, he would lose approximately U_x units in utility.
Therefore, to keep the individual on the same indifference curve, it is

necessary to give him $\dfrac{U_x}{U_y}$ units of Y. $\dfrac{U_x}{U_y}$ therefore represents the rate at

which he is willing to substitute Y for X. The tangency condition for

equilibrium requires that $\dfrac{U_x}{U_y} = \dfrac{P_x}{P_y}$, since $\dfrac{U_x}{U_y}$ measures the slope of the

indifference curve with respect to the X axis. Another way of stating this
equilibrium condition is to say that the rate at which the individual is
willing to substitute Y for X must equal the rate at which he can substitute
Y for X.

We are now in a position to see why the three utility functions in the
previous section yielded the same demand curves. All three utility func-

tions yield the same indifference map. For example, if $U = f(X,Y)$ is the utility function, then the indifference curves generated by this utility function will have the slope of $-\dfrac{\dfrac{\partial U}{\partial X}}{\dfrac{\partial U}{\partial Y}} = -\dfrac{U_x}{U_y}$. If we take any function of U, say U^* where $U^* = G(U(X,Y))$, then the slope of the indifference curve given by this U^* function will be $-\dfrac{\dfrac{dU^*}{dU} U_x}{\dfrac{dU^*}{dU} U_y} = -\dfrac{U_x}{U_y}$. Thus, we see that all these utility functions will have the same indifference curves. This holds even if $\dfrac{dU^*}{dU} \leq O$. The condition that $\dfrac{dU^*}{dU} > O$ is necessary to guarantee that the ordering is in the same direction.

As we have just seen, the indifference curve is a boundary line separating two areas, one containing bundles to which the bundles on the indifference curve are preferred and the other containing bundles that are preferred to the bundles on the indifference curve. The slope of the indifference curve is the rate of substitution in consumption. The slope of the budget line represents the rate of substitution in purchase. The budget line does not have to be a straight line. In a Robinson Crusoe economy, the indifference curves would be the same as those described above, but instead of a budget line there would be a transformation curve. The slope of this curve would represent the rate of substitution not in the market but in production.

The objective of the indifference curve apparatus is to derive a demand function for, say, commodity X in terms of the price of X, the price of Y, and money income. However, it is clear that if all prices and income were doubled, the individual's opportunity line would remain unaltered. This means that it is not the absolute levels of P_x, P_y, and I that are important but rather the ratios, such as $\dfrac{P_x}{I}$ and $\dfrac{P_y}{I}$. There are really only two independent variables. If we assume relative prices unchanged when income increases, we can obtain the quantity of X and Y demanded as a function of real income.

For example, in Figure 2.17 the line ABCDE is supposed to be the locus of points at which lines of attainable combinations parallel to those shown are tangent to indifference curves. In the segment AB, the quantities of both X and Y increase as income increases; from B to C, the quantity of X increases and the quantity of Y decreases as income increases; from C to D, the quantities of both X and Y increase as income increases; from D to E, the quantity of X decreases and the quantity of Y increases as income in-

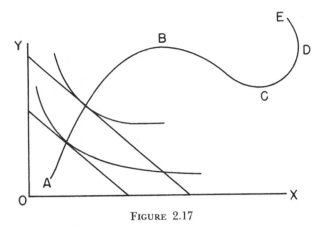

FIGURE 2.17

creases. A good is said to be a *superior* good if the quantity consumed increases as income increases and an *inferior* good if the quantity consumed decreases as income increases. In the above diagram, X and Y are both superior goods between A and B and C and D; X is a superior good and Y an inferior good between B and C; X is an inferior good and Y a superior good between D and E. These same results can be plotted in the form of an Engel curve as in Figure 2.18. The behavior of quantity with respect to

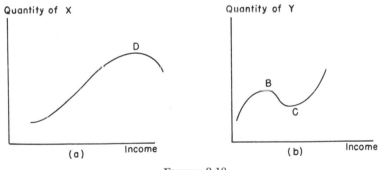

FIGURE 2.18

income can be described by the elasticity of quantity with respect to income (generally called *income elasticity*) or $\frac{dq}{dI} \cdot \frac{I}{q}$. If $\frac{dq}{dI} \cdot \frac{I}{q} > 0$, the good in question is a superior good; if $\frac{dq}{dI} \cdot \frac{I}{q} < 0$, the good is an inferior good. If $\frac{dq}{dI} \cdot \frac{I}{q} < 1$, the percentage of income spent on the good in question decreases as income increases; if $\frac{dq}{dI} \cdot \frac{I}{q} = 1$, the percentage of income remains constant; if $\dfrac{dq}{dI} \cdot \dfrac{I}{q} > 1$, the percentage of income spent on the good increases as income increases.[5]

As we have noted, income elasticity is frequently used to define the terms necessities and luxuries. A good is termed a "necessity" if its income elasticity is less than unity, a "luxury" if its income elasticity is greater than unity.

Unit income elasticity for all commodities would mean that the income-expenditure path on an indifference curve diagram would be a straight line through the origin. From the definition of income elasticity, it follows that $k_x \, \eta_{xI} + k_y \, \eta_{yI} + \ldots = 1$, where k_x is the fraction of income spent on X, k_y on Y, etc.; and η_{xI} is the income elasticity of X, η_{yI} of Y, etc.

The Three-Fold Classification Implicit in
Indifference Curve Analysis

The analysis of consumer behavior in terms of indifference curves implicitly classifies all factors affecting consumer behavior into three categories: (1) goods—these are the axes of the indifference curves, (2) factors determining opportunities—these are summarized in the budget line, and (3) factors determining tastes—these are summarized in the indifference curves.

The important thing about this classification is that it is not given, once for all. It is a classification the contents of which are to be determined by the problem at hand, so that the same factor may for one purpose be treated as a good and measured along the axes, for another as an opportunity factor, for another as a taste factor.

To illustrate, consider regional location. For a person considering where to settle, it is clearly a good, to be measured on one of the axes. Once he has settled, it is an opportunity factor, since it will affect the prices he will have to pay for various goods and services, and also, a taste factor, since it may affect the importance he attaches to winter coats versus bathing suits, or heating versus air-conditioning.

As a formal matter, all these aspects can be handled by treating regional

---

5. The proof of these statements is as follows:

$\dfrac{XP_x}{I}$ is the percentage of income spent on X.

$$\text{Now} \quad \dfrac{d\left(\dfrac{XP_x}{I}\right)}{dI} \;=\; \dfrac{P_x I \dfrac{dX}{dI} - XP_x}{I^2} \;=\; \dfrac{XP_x\left(\dfrac{I}{X}\dfrac{dX}{dI} - 1\right)}{I^2}.$$

From this it follows that $\dfrac{d\left(\dfrac{XP_x}{I}\right)}{dI} \gtrless 0 \quad$ according as $\dfrac{I}{X}\dfrac{dX}{dI} \gtrless 1$,

which is precisely the proposition stated above.

location as a good measured on one of the axes. Corresponding to each regional location, there is a cross-section of the multidimensional surface of attainable combinations and indifference surfaces. The cross-section for one regional location may correspond to different opportunities and different tastes than the cross-section for another. But while this is entirely correct formally, it does not alter the shift of emphasis according to the problem.

Another interesting example is number of children in a family. In part, parents make a deliberate decision how many children to have. For this problem, children are objects of choice, a "good" to be measured on an axis. But once the children are present, they clearly affect opportunities (the cost of going to the movies, for example, will be raised by baby-sitter fees) and tastes. An additional and very fundamental complication is that an additional set of indifference curves comes into the picture—the indifference curves of the children.

The Derivation of Demand Curves from Indifference Curves

It is now possible to show how demand curves may be derived from indifference curves. If we hold money income constant and allow the price of X to change, the price ratio line will rotate about a pivot on the Y axis, as in Figure 2.19. For different prices of X, we obtain different quantities of X demanded, and a demand curve can be generated in this way, which is, in fact, the usual way. However, in this kind of demand curve, real income changes as one moves along it.

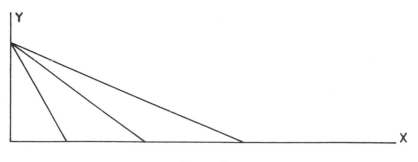

FIGURE 2.19

It is possible to construct a different kind of demand curve. Consider a bundle of goods, X_o, Y_o, and draw a budget line through it. The line can be rotated around this point. This is a device to try to keep apparent real income the same. The equations of these lines will be $P_x X_o + P_y Y_o = I$. Diagrammatically this second method appears as in Figure 2.20. For fixed money income, this is equivalent to holding the purchasing power of money constant. The usual way of constructing a price index is to compute it as the (relative) cost of a specified bundle of goods. For example, if the bundle of goods consists of (X_o, Y_o) and if prices under two situations (two time units, two geographic areas, etc.) are (P_x, P_y) and (P'_x, P'_y), then the price index in the second situation relative to the first is $\frac{P'_x X_o + P'_y Y_o}{P_x X_o + P_y Y_o}$. But if I is fixed, this ratio is obviously unity for all the budget lines going through the point (X_o, Y_o), since both numerator and denominator are then equal to I.

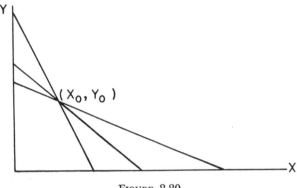

FIGURE 2.20

The points of tangency of these lines to indifference curves generate a demand curve for which "real income" is constant, in the sense that money income divided by a price index computed as just described is the same.

Still another kind of demand curve could be generated by considering the set of budget lines tangent to a single indifference curve. The corresponding quantities and relative prices would give a demand curve for which "real income" is constant in the sense of utility.

The relationship among these various constructions can perhaps be brought out best by considering the so-called income and substitution effects of a change in one price with all other prices and money income unchanged. In considering these, we shall want to distinguish between the "Slutsky" effects, which correspond with rotating budget lines about a point $(X_o Y_o)$, and Hicksian effects, which correspond with considering the set of budget lines tangent to a single indifference curve.

Consider Table 2.4, and Figure 2.21. Table 2.4 brings out the difference between Slutsky's measure of the income effect and the Hicksian measure. The difference between (a) and (b) is that the price of X is lower while the price of Y and money income are unchanged. The consumer is obviously better off since he is consuming more of both X and Y. Situation (c) is what Slutsky would have called a *compensated* change in price from situation (a). Income in (c) is less than that in (a) by just enough so that at the lower price for X the individual could, if he wanted to, buy the same amount of X and Y as previously. Fifty units of X would cost $25.00 now instead of $50.00 and he has $25.00 less income. In Slutsky's terms, his *apparent real income* is unchanged, but at the new price, the individual does not buy fifty of X and fifty of Y; he buys sixty of X and forty-five of Y. Since he deliberately chooses the latter bundle instead of the former, we must suppose him to prefer it; in consequence his "real" real income is higher for (c) than for (a); he is on a higher indifference curve. For Hicks it would be necessary to take away enough money to keep the individual on the same indifference curve. We may suppose this would require taking away $28.00, as shown by situation (d), which describes a budget line tangent to the same indifference curve as that to which (a) corresponds. Situation (e) is identical with (c) except that instead of a changed income to "compensate" for the decline in relative price, it shows a changed price of Y — a constant "purchasing power of money." Situation (f) is similarly identical with (d) and shows a constant "purchasing power of money" in a slightly different sense.

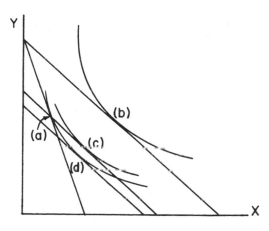

FIGURE 2.21

TABLE 2.4

	I	P_x	P_y	X	Y
(a)	100	1	1	50	50
(b)	100	1/2	1	80	60
(c)	75	1/2	1	60	45
(d)	72	1/2	1	58	43
(e)	100	2/3	4/3	60	45
(f)	100	50/72	100/72	58	43

The advantages of the Slutsky measure, even though in one sense it is an approximation while the Hicks measure is not, is that it can be computed directly from observable market phenomena and behavior, namely, prices and quantities purchased. The Hicks measure cannot; it requires knowledge of indifference curves. The smaller the price change, namely the closer P_x is to 1 in the table, the less significant the difference between the Slutsky measure and the Hicks measure.

The Hicks and Slutsky measures give two different ways of generating demand curves that have the property of keeping real income constant. We can generate a demand curve by using Hicks's measure of the change in real income; this would be the equivalent of scalloping an indifference curve. Or we can generate a demand curve by using Slutsky's measure of the change in real income, which is equivalent to rotating a line about a point. It might be said that the Slutsky method is a way of keeping apparent real income constant. Figure 2.22 indicates the relationships among the three types of demand curve discussed: (1) the ordinary demand curve, along which all other prices and money income are the same and, as a consequence, real income changes; (2) the demand curve where real income is kept constant by keeping the individual on the same indifference curve (following Hicks); and (3) the demand curve where apparent real income is kept constant and where the individual is always enabled to buy the original bundle (following Slutsky).

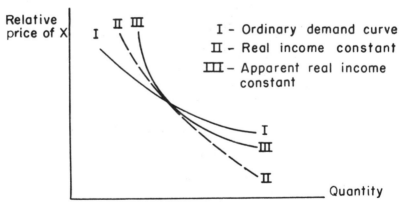

FIGURE 2.22

The differences among these three demand curves will be more clearly seen by reference to Figure 2.23. As a result of a change in price of commodity X, we have a movement from P to Q or from X_1 to X_4. This movement from X_1 to X_4 is the movement included in the demand curve as ordinarily defined. However, this movement from X_1 to X_4 as a result of a change in price is a compound of an income and a substitution effect. As explained previously it may be desirable to restrict the demand curve to the substitution effect alone. We can break up this movement from X_1 to X_4 in two different ways. We can, following Hicks, say that the movement from P to S or from X_1 to X_2 is a result of the change in the terms of trade or the substitution effect. The movement from S to Q or from X_2 to X_4 is the result of an income change. Therefore

$$\begin{array}{ccccc} Total\ Effect & & Income\ Effect & & Substitution\ Effect \\ (X_4 - X_1) & = & (X_4 - X_2) & + & (X_2 - X_1) \end{array}$$

This approach is formally neater than the following one but it does not deal with observable quantities.

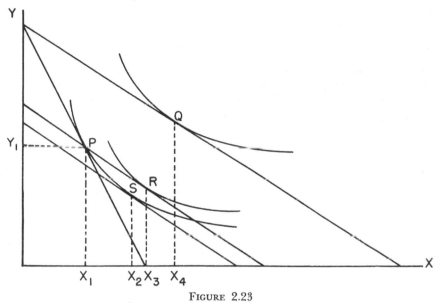

FIGURE 2.23

Alternatively, we can try to separate out the income and substitution effects in terms of observable quantities by following Slutsky. When the individual was at point P, he consumed X_1 and Y_1 and spent on them his whole money income I, at prices P_x and P_y. If the price of X changes from P_x to $P_x + \Delta P_x$ (in the case diagrammed, ΔP_x is negative) and P_y does not change, it would clearly take $I + X_1 \Delta P_x$ to buy the same bundle as before, i.e. to buy X_1 of X and Y_1 of Y. We may, therefore, regard an income $(I + X_1 \Delta P_x)$ and prices $(P_x + \Delta P_x, P_y)$ as a compensated change in price from the initial situation, i.e., a change in price where the real income effects of this change in price have been offset by a change in money income. With such a compensated change in price, the individual would move from

P to R or from X_1 to X_3. Following Slutsky, we may call this the substitution effect, and the movement from R to Q or from X_3 to X_4, the income effect. Therefore:

$$\begin{array}{ccccc} \textit{Total Effect} & & \textit{Income Effect} & & \textit{Substitution Effect} \\ (X_4 - X_1) & = & (X_4 - X_3) & + & (X_3 - X_1) \end{array}$$

It will be noted that the difference between the Hicks and Slutsky approach is $(X_3 - X_2)$. The fundamental proposition given by Mosak is that as ΔP_x goes to zero, the term $(X_3 - X_2)$ approaches zero more rapidly than any other difference. It is, of course, true that as ΔP_x goes to zero, Q, R, and S all tend to converge to point P. This means that $(X_4 - X_3)$, $(X_3 - X_1)$, $(X_4 - X_2)$, and $(X_2 - X_1)$ as well as $(X_3 - X_2)$ all go to zero as ΔP_x approaches zero. However, $(X_3 - X_2)$ is different from all these other quantities in that it approaches zero more rapidly, in the sense that the limit of $\dfrac{(X_3 - X_2)}{(X_4 - X_1)}$ as ΔP_x approaches zero is zero, but the limit of, say $\dfrac{(X_4 - X_3)}{(X_4 - X_1)}$ as ΔP_x approaches zero is not necessarily zero. This has the implication that the Slutsky measure of the change in money income needed to keep real income constant is a good approximation to the ideal change in money income. We can now write these discontinuous difference equations in continuous form:

(1)
$$\frac{\partial X}{\partial P_x} = \frac{\partial X}{\partial I}\left(-\frac{\partial I}{\partial P_x} \right) + \frac{\partial X}{\partial P_x} \qquad \text{(Hicks)}$$
$$\begin{array}{ll} I = I_1 & U = U_1 \quad U = U_1 \\ P_y = P_{y1} & P_y = P_{y1} \end{array}$$

(2)
$$\frac{\partial X}{\partial P_x} = -X_1\frac{\partial X}{\partial I} + \frac{\partial X}{\partial P_x} \qquad \text{(Slutsky)}$$
$$\begin{array}{ll} I = I_1 & P_y = P_{y1} \\ P_y = P_{y1} & I = I_1 + X_1\,\Delta P_x \end{array}$$

where for equation 2, $X_1 = \dfrac{\partial I}{\partial P_x}$, since the change in I required to compensate for the change in price is $X_1\Delta P_x$ and per unit change it is $\dfrac{X_1\Delta P_x}{\Delta P_x}$ or X_1.

The term on the left side of both of these equations is the movement from X_1 to X_4 divided by the change in price; i.e., it is the change in quantity per unit change in price. The first term on the right side of both equations is the income effect which is gotten analytically by taking the change in quantity per unit change in income and multiplying it by the change in income per unit change in price implicit in passing from the original indifference curve to the new indifference curve. The second term in both equations is the substitution effect, and it states the change in quantity per unit change in price when either the individual is kept on the same indifference curve or he is given a compensating change in his money income (see Figure 2.24).

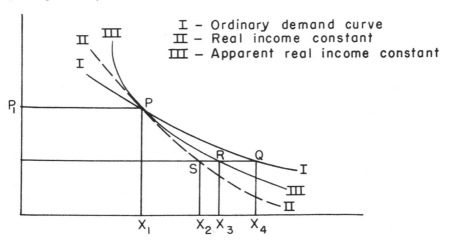

I – Ordinary demand curve
II – Real income constant
III – Apparent real income constant

FIGURE 2.24

We might take note of one other fact: $\dfrac{\partial X}{\partial P_x}$ is the slope at point P of

$$I = I_1$$
$$P_y = P_{y1}$$

the ordinary demand curve. Therefore, if we take the Slutsky expression and multiply every term in it by $\dfrac{P_x}{X}$, we obtain:

$$\frac{P_x}{X} \frac{\partial X}{\partial P_x} = - \frac{\partial X}{\partial I} P_x + \frac{\partial X}{\partial P_x} \frac{P_x}{X}$$

$$\begin{array}{c} I = I_1 \\ P_y = P_{y1} \end{array} \qquad \begin{array}{c} P_y = P_{y1} \\ I = I_1 + K_1 \, \Delta P_x \end{array}$$

The left-hand term of this equation is nothing more than the elasticity of demand of the ordinary demand curve at point P. We shall label this η_{xp}. The term $- \dfrac{\partial X}{\partial I} P_x = - k_x \, \eta_{XI}$ where $k_x = \dfrac{X P_x}{I}$ or the fraction of income spent on X, and $\eta_{XI} = \dfrac{\partial X}{\partial I} \dfrac{I}{X}$ or the income elasticity of X. The last term,

$$\frac{\partial X}{\partial P_x} \frac{P_x}{X}$$

$$P_y = P_{y1},$$
$$I = I_1 + X_1 \, \Delta P_x$$

is the elasticity of demand at the point P of a demand curve drawn so that real income is constant. We shall call this $\bar{\eta}_{xp}$. We, therefore, obtain the following:[6]

$$\eta_{XP} = - k_x \eta_{XI} + \bar{\eta}_{XP}$$

Utility Analysis of Labor Supply

Up to this point, we have been treating income and total expenditure for consumer services as identical, or, to put it more generally, we have been examining the allocation of a fixed sum among alternative consumption services without asking how that fixed sum is arrived at. The sum allocated to spending is itself the result of two sets of decisions to be regarded as arrived at to maximize utility: (1) the decision about how much of the resource services at the disposal of the consumer unit to devote to productive activities, and (2) the decision about how much to spend on current consumer services and how much to add to or subtract from accumulated wealth. In principle, the whole set of decisions is to be regarded as arrived at simultaneously, but it is analytically convenient to consider them separately. We can regard the decision how a hypothetical sum would be distributed among alternative consumer services as determining the utility attached to that amount of consumption, this utility then entering into the other decisions as a single dimension.

For some resources owned by the consumer unit, he is indifferent how they are used. This is generally the case for property (nonhuman capital). For such resources, maximizing utility from their use is simply equivalent to maximizing the payment received for their services. For other resources, particularly for productive services rendered by an individual personally, his human capital, it matters to him not only how much he is paid for their use, but how they are used. Work entails utility or disutility, and the utility or disutility may depend on the kind and amount of work that is done. In effect, the provision of human productive services must be regarded as a joint act of sale of productive services and consumption of the associated amenities of the productive activity pursued. We shall consider this choice further in chapter 11 on "The Supply of Factors of Production."

Here, it will be enough to illustrate the utility analysis of the allocation of human capital by examining the simple case of the choice of how many hours of homogeneous labor per unit time to offer on the market, neglecting the possibility that there are different activities, involving different

6. You will find it instructive to demonstrate for yourself that the curves in Fig. 24 are in the correct order for a superior good but not for an inferior good, and to draw a corresponding diagram for an inferior good.

sets of working conditions (nonpecuniary advantages and disadvantages), available to the individual.

Figure 2.25 plots a hypothetical set of indifference curves for an individual. The vertical axis measures consumption, or the total value of consumer services per unit time. As noted, a maximization process is implicitly supposed to be behind each value of consumption: consumption is assumed allocated among alternative services so as to maximize utility. The horizontal axis measures the number of hours of work per week. There is a vertical line at 168 hours a week, because that is the maximum physically available. The indifference curves are drawn as first declining then rising as the length of the work week is increased. The declining segment implies that some work is a "good," i.e., that the individual would be willing to sacrifice some consumption in order to be able to work, that if he had an alternative source of income, he would be willing to pay in order to work. Beyond some number of hours, however, Figure 2.25 assumes that additional work is a "bad," that it involves disutility and individuals will not be willing to work additional hours unless they are com-

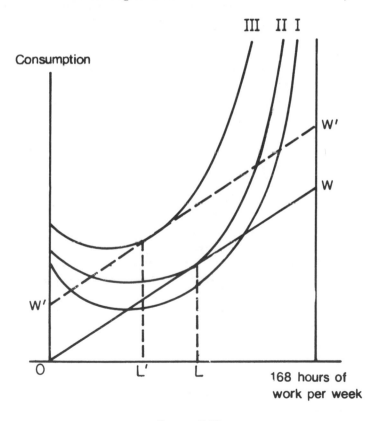

FIGURE 2.25

pensated by getting additional consumption. The indifference curves are shown as ultimately asymptotic to the physically maximum limit of 168 hours per week. The higher the indifference curve, the higher the utility— i.e., for a given amount of labor, the greater the consumption the higher the utility.

Obviously, the declining segment may not exist; work may be regarded as a "bad" regardless of how short the work week. The declining segment is included here to illustrate a general point, which is particularly evident for labor services, namely, that whether a particular service is a "good" or a "bad" is not a technical phenomenon dependent on its physical characteristics but a market phenomenon depending on consumer preferences and on market supply and demand. The same physical item may be a "good" or a "bad" depending on circumstances. If the market price is positive, it is a good; if negative, a bad. To illustrate in a trivial way, the kind of singing that is done by a rock star is obviously a "good," since the public is willing to pay a high price to listen to it; the kind of singing some of us do is a "bad," since we would have to pay people to listen to us. As musical tastes change, what was at one time a "good" may become a "bad," and conversely. To illustrate in a more fundamental way, in modern advanced societies, almost the only hard, back-breaking physical labor that can be observed is done by people for sport and they typically pay for the privilege of engaging in such labor. What has for millenia been a conspicuous "bad" has become a "good."

The straight lines OW and W'W' in Figure 2.25 are lines of attainable combinations, or budget lines. The line OW corresponds to the case in which the individual has no source of income other than payment for labor services, so it starts at the origin. The slope of the line is the wage rate per hour (net of taxes, etc., so that it shows the amount available to add to consumption). The point of tangency gives OL as the amount of labor that will enable the individual to obtain the highest indifference curve. Note that it is the "highest" and not the "lowest" indifference curve because the curves are concave upwards, which is the fundamental justification for drawing them that way.

The line W'W' corresponds to a case in which the individual has a nonlabor source of income of OW'. As drawn, he is thereby led to reduce the length of the working week to OL'. This result is not of course inevitable. It simply reflects the particular set of indifference curves, though it does seem like the result to be expected, at least for nonlabor income above some minimum.

The kind of analysis used in the preceding section to derive demand curves from consumer indifference curves can clearly be used here to derive supply curves of labor for different combinations of wage rates and nonlabor income, and the earlier analysis of income and substitution effects can be carried over here. You will find it useful to do so.

Utility Analysis of Savings

Let us turn now to the decision about how much of current receipts from the sale of resource services to spend on current consumption and how much to add to accumulated wealth, or alternatively how much to subtract from wealth to add to current receipts for spending on current consumption. (This analysis will be used and expanded further in some directions in chapter 17.) It is tempting to try to incorporate this decision into utility analysis by the same device as we have just incorporated the decision about how many hours to work, namely, by adding another axis to the indifference diagram on which is measured savings, or the number of dollars per year added to accumulated wealth. Indeed, Leon Walras succumbed to this temptation in the latest edition of his great book, *Éléments d'économie politique pure,* published in English translation under the title, *Elements of Pure Economics,* after having resisted it in earlier editions.[7]

The difficulty with this apparently simple extension of the utility analysis to cover saving can be seen by supposing it to be followed by measuring consumption on one axis and the rate of saving on the other, both measured as number of dollars per year. What is then the price ratio that is relevant? Clearly it is 1: a dollar per year can always be added to savings by subtracting a dollar from consumption. In his desire to include a substitution effect, Walras defined the variable to be measured along the saving axis not as the number of dollars per year devoted to saving but as a commodity E, equal to the permanent income stream purchased with the saving, i.e., the permanent income stream, r, yielded by one dollar of wealth, where r is the rate of interest. The price of one unit of E is then $\frac{1}{r}$ or the reciprocal of the interest rate (if r = .05, it costs \$20 to buy \$1 a year). However, this makes the two axes noncomparable: consumption is a flow, dollars per year; E is a rate of change of a flow, a second derivative, dollars per year per year. With a properly specified utility function, the indifference curves remain the same over time regardless of which point on them is attained, so long as the basic underlying conditions are the same. Not so with indifference curves for consumption and the Walras commodity E. A positive E adds to the stock of wealth so as time passes, the individual becomes wealthier and wealthier. For the same level of consumption, the rate at which the individual will be willing to substitute still further additions to wealth for further additions to consumption will decline. The indifference curves so defined will change.

The difficulty with the simple approach is that saving is not another commodity like food, clothing, etc., which offers utility in accordance with

7. Milton Friedman, "Leon Walras and His Economic System," *American Economic Review,* 45 (December 1955): 900–909.

the rate of saving. Saving is a way of substituting future consumption for present consumption. For a satisfactory analysis of saving, we have to take account of its basic role, not simply add an axis to an indifference diagram. It is essential to consider more than one time period. Accumulated wealth, unlike saving, may have certain characteristics that make it in part a good like other consumption services, insofar as it provides a reserve against emergencies. This service can be measured along an indifference curve axis, and part of income regarded as used to purchase it. The income used to purchase it is the difference between the (anticipated average) maximum return that can be obtained from the wealth and the actual (anticipated average) return from holding the wealth in a form that provides greater utility as a reserve.

If we neglect this role of wealth, the case that it is easiest to present on an indifference diagram is one that Irving Fisher analyzed: the hypothetical case of a finite period, most simply, a two-year period. This case is given in Figure 2.26. The vertical axis measures consumption in year 1, the horizontal axis, consumption in year 2. The diagonal line shows equal consumption in the two years. Let R_1 be receipts in the first year, R_2 receipts in the second, and r the rate of interest, and assume that the individual to whom the figure applies can borrow or lend any sum at the interest rate r that he can repay or make available out of his receipts. The maximum amount he could then spend on consumption in year 1 if he spent nothing in year 2 would be

$$(3) \qquad W = R_1 + \frac{R_2}{1+r},$$

because $\frac{R_2}{1+r}$ is the maximum amount he could borrow and repay with his receipts in the second year. W is his initial wealth and defines the intercept A on the vertical axis of the line of attainable combinations. The maximum amount he could spend on consumption in year 2 if he spent nothing in year 1 is

$$(4) \qquad (1+r)\,W = R_1\,(1+r) + R_2.$$

The line AB thus is the line of attainable combinations. The rate of substitution in the market is such that the individual can add $(1+r)$ dollars of consumption in year 2 for each dollar reduction in consumption in year 1. As drawn, the equilibrium point P shows a choice involving higher consumption in year 2 than in year 1, but that is of course a result of the particular set of indifference curves and the particular interest rate.

We can use this simple model to illustrate the concept of time preference —the rate at which individuals are willing to substitute future consumption for present consumption. The rate of time preference is thus the slope of the indifference curve and hence varies from point to point in the

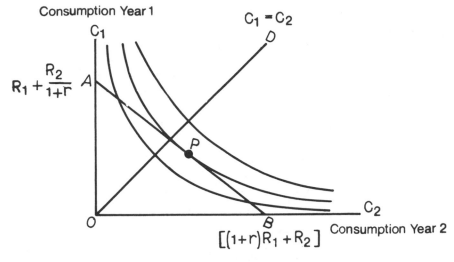

FIGURE 2.26

diagram. At a point corresponding to high consumption in year 1, low consumption in year 2, the individual prefers additional future consumption to present consumption, i.e., he would be willing to give up more than $1 of current consumption to add $1 to future consumption. Conversely, at a point corresponding to high future consumption, low present consumption, the individual prefers additional current consumption to future consumption, i.e., it would take more than $1 of future consumption to compensate him for giving up $1 of current consumption. The rate of time preference is therefore a variable, depending on the levels of present and future consumption. At point P, the rate of time preference is equal to the market rate of substitution $(1 + r)$ because the individual adjusts his time pattern of consumption to bring about that equality.

It is common to say that individuals "underestimate the future" or have a "preference for the present over the future" or "discount the future." One way to assign a meaning to such expressions is to define them in terms of the rate of time preference on the diagonal line in Figure 2.26. Along this line, future consumption is equal to present consumption. It seems reasonable to say that an individual is neutral between present and future if the slope of the indifference curves for points on this line is unity, or more generally if the indifference curves are symmetrical about this line. An individual underestimates the future if the indifference curves for points on this curve are flatter than the − 45° lines and overestimates the future if they are steeper. More generally, we can say he underestimates the future if the indifference curves are asymmetrical about the diagonal line in such a way that a point to the left of the diagonal is on a higher indifference curve than its mirror image to the right of the diagonal.

To return to the determinants of consumption and saving, we are back in a familiar situation. It appears that the pattern of consumption depends on three variables: R_1, R_2, r, yet it is clear from Figure 2.26 that only two variables are important: $W = R_1 + \dfrac{R_2}{1+r}$, and r, namely wealth and the interest rate:

$$(5) \qquad\qquad\qquad C = f(r, W).$$

If we interpret R_1 and R_2 as measured incomes in the two years, consumption in each year depends not on income but on wealth (or "permanent income"). On the other hand, if we define savings as the difference between measured income and consumption, savings does depend on income, because

$$(6) \qquad\qquad S_1 = R_1 - C = R_1 - f(r, W).$$

In this model, there are two motives for saving: to "straighten out the income stream," that is, to make consumption steadier over time than receipts—this motive causes R_1 to enter into equation 6; and to earn a return on savings, this motive causes r to enter into equation 5. W in equation 5 can be regarded as playing a dual role as a measure both of available opportunities and of the consumption service of a reserve against emergencies.

A special case of equation 5 arises if the indifference curves in Figure 2.26 are similar in the sense that all indifference curves have the same slope along any ray from the origin. Equation 5 then reduces to

$$(7) \qquad\qquad\qquad C = k(r) \cdot W$$

or, to include other factors that might affect consumption not included in our simple representation:

$$(8) \qquad\qquad\qquad C = k(r, u) \cdot W,$$

where u stands for these other factors. In this special case, we could define the consumer's numerical rate of time preference by the common slope along the diagonal. If he has neutral time preference in this sense, then for any positive rate of interest, future consumption will exceed present consumption. If he discounts the future, then for some positive rates of interest current consumption will exceed future consumption.

The simple time period model can also be used to illustrate the effect of a difference between the rate of interest at which the individual can borrow and the rate at which he can lend. This difference may arise simply from the costs of financial intermediation between borrowers and lenders or from the difference between human and nonhuman capital that makes human capital generally less satisfactory as collateral for a loan. Let r_B be the rate of interest at which he can borrow and r_L at which he can lend, with $r_B > r_L$. Then the budget line will have a bend as in Figure 2.27 at the point corresponding to receipts (R_1, R_2) in the two years. There is then no unambiguous measure of wealth, and the final outcome may depend on the initial position, depending on where it is and the shape of the indifference curves.

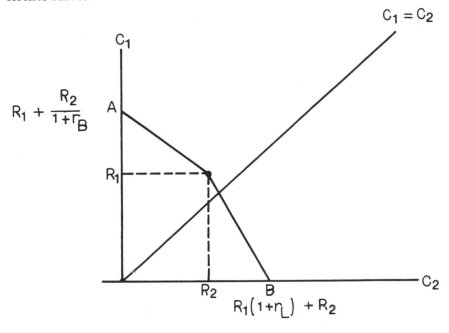

FIGURE 2.27

Generalizing this analysis to an indefinite time period is easy to do formally, hard to do in two-dimensional graphs. The formal generalization is that the economic agent is regarded as having a utility function that is a function of the whole future pattern of consumption:

$$(9) \qquad\qquad U = F[C(t)],$$

where $C(t)$ represents the flow of consumption at time t, and t extends from the time period in question to the indefinite future, say t_0 to ∞. He also is regarded as having an opportunity set

$$(10) \qquad\qquad G[C(t)],$$

that summarizes the alternative time patterns of consumption that are available to him. He is then regarded as maximizing the utility function in equation 9 subject to the opportunity set of equation 10.

This generalization is perfectly general and perfectly empty. To give it content, it is necessary to specialize equations 9 and 10. For example, equation 9 can be specialized by supposing that there exists some internal rate of discount, say ρ, such that a particular form of equation 9 can be written

(11) $$U(t_0) = \int_{t_0}^{\infty} f[C(t)]e^{-\rho t}dt$$

in which case, of course, any monotonic transformation of equation 11, say

(12) $$U^* = F(U),$$

will also do provided $F'(U) > 0$. Equation 10 can be specialized by supposing that there exists some market rate of interest r such that any pattern
of consumption is available for which

(13) $$W(t_0) \geq \int_{t_0}^{\infty} C(t)e^{-rt}dt,$$

where W is the similarly discounted value of the individual's anticipated
stream of receipts in the future. There has been much analysis, especially
in the literature on growth models, using such specializations but no such
specialization as yet has reason to be singled out as deserving particular
confidence.

One way to present an indefinite time period in a two-dimensional
graph is to specialize the opportunity set in equation 10 by supposing that
the only alternatives available to the individual are two-dimensional: a
rate of consumption of C_1 for one time unit, say a year; a rate of consumption of C_2 for the indefinite future thereafter. For this to be at all reasonable, we must suppose the individual to have an infinite life with unchanging tastes. This may seem absurd but in fact is not. It simply is a way of
representing the observed phenomenon that the family, not the individual, is the basic consumption unit, and that in deciding on current consumption versus future consumption, the person making the decision
takes into account the utility that his descendants will derive from consumption as well as his own. The infinitely lived and unchanging individual thus represents the long-lived family line. Though highly special,
the two-dimensional representation brings out one important feature of
the saving-spending process concealed by the two-period example.

Let R_1 be the rate of flow of receipts in the first year, R_2 the assumed
steady rate of flow indefinitely thereafter, and r an assumed constant rate
of interest over time at which the individual can borrow or lend. Then his
initial wealth is

(14) $$W = R_1 + \frac{R_2}{r},$$

where r enters into the denominator of the final term rather than $1 + r$ as
in equation 3, because R_2 is here a perpetual income stream rather than
simply a one-period receipt. This initial wealth defines the point A, the
maximum consumption in the first period if consumption thereafter is
zero. The maximum consumption after the end of the first year is R_2, the
perpetual receipt thereafter plus interest on the first year's receipt if con-

sumption in the first year is zero, or rR_1, so $rW = rR_1 + R_2$ defines point B, and the line connecting them is the line of attainable combinations. Its slope with respect to the C_2 axis is $\frac{1}{r}$, or the number of dollars of current consumption that must be given up to add \$1 per year to all future consumption; with respect to the C_1 axis, the slope is r, or the number of dollars that can be added to future consumption by giving up \$1 of current consumption. Figure 2.28 is drawn for an interest rate of .20 in order to make it possible to distinguish the different points.

P_1 is the equilibrium position, involving as the figure is drawn, lower consumption in the first year than indefinitely in order to raise future consumption. Let us now move one year ahead and look at the situation again, again assuming that the only alternatives are a rate of consumption of C_1 for one year and of C_2 thereafter (this is the unsatisfactory element of the analysis because, of course, we would expect the individual at time 0 to choose a whole future pattern of consumption and not proceed in this step-at-a-time fashion). The indifference curves are the same, since we have assumed the individual to have unchanging tastes, but the opportunity line is different because saving in year 1 has added to his wealth. The new opportunity line (A′B′) will go through the point on the diagonal corresponding to the abscissa of P_1. The new equilibrium is P_2.

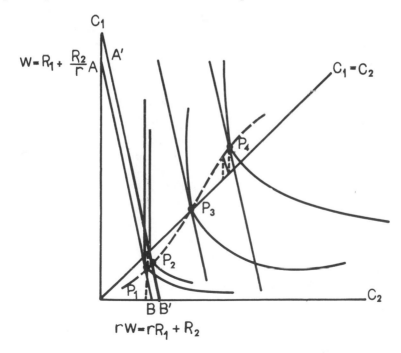

FIGURE 2.28

The dashed line is the locus of such points of equilibrium in successive years and defines the individual's future consumption path. As drawn, the dashed line cuts the diagonal at P_3. At this point the rate of time preference of the individual as defined earlier (for a constant level of consumption) equals the rate at which he can substitute current for future income. This is a point which if attained will be maintained.

Suppose we had started the individual with a wealth such that P_4 is the equilibrium. Then the individual would have dissaved in the sense of reducing wealth to add to current consumption. He would have followed the path suggested by the zigzag line down the dashed line until again he arrived at P_3.

The advantage of this construction is that it brings out the difference between the equilibrium stock of wealth (desired wealth) and the equilibrium rate of approach to that stock of wealth. The wealth corresponding to point P_3 is the equilibrium stock of wealth. If the individual does not have that stock of wealth, he will move toward it. There will be an equilibrium rate at which he will want to move toward it that will depend both on how far he is from his desired wealth and on what his current wealth is. The considerations determining the desired stock of wealth are different from those determining how fast he wants to move toward it, though this distinction is blurred by the two-dimensional representation in Figure 2.28.

In that figure, in order for there to be an equilibrium stock of wealth, it is necessary that the slope of the indifference curves become flatter along the diagonal line as wealth increases; that is, that it require larger and larger increments in future consumption to compensate for giving up $1 of current consumption, or, alternatively, that the preference for present over future consumption increase with wealth. This seems intuitively perverse. It seems more plausible that if anything the reverse would occur.

If the indifference curves were similar in the sense that they all have the same slope along any ray from the origin, the dashed line would, unlike the dashed line in Figure 2.28, never cut the diagonal. It would be rather such a ray. If below the diagonal, it would imply indefinite accumulation of wealth; if above, indefinite decumulation. But in both cases there would be an equilibrium rate of accumulation or decumulation. For modern progressive societies, there is no inconsistency between observable phenomena and a representation implying indefinite accumulation.

This is a very incomplete treatment of a very complex problem. Its purpose is to illustrate how the apparatus we have developed can illuminate such problems.

3

The "Welfare" Effects
of Taxes

This chapter discusses the relative effects on welfare of an excise tax and an income tax. It demonstrates that an alleged "proof" of the superiority of the income tax is no proof at all, though it has repeatedly been cited as one. It then outlines a "correct" analysis of the problem.

The explicit content of the paper is, however, only indirectly related to its major aim, which is to show by example the difference between two approaches to economic analysis. From this point of view, the present paper is an extended footnote to an article in the *Journal of Political Economy,* in which I contrasted two definitions of the demand curve— the usual one, which supposes money income and money prices of other commodities the same for different points on a single demand curve, and an alternative definition, which I attributed to Alfred Marshall and which supposes *real* income to be the same.[1] I argued that the usual definition has arisen out of, and reflects, an essentially arithmetical and descriptive approach to economic analysis; the alternative definition, an analytical

This chapter is reprinted from my *Essays in Positive Economics* (University of Chicago Press, 1953), pp. 100–13, by permission of the publisher; copyright 1953 by the University of Chicago. The figures have been renumbered and the footnotes differently designated to conform to the rest of the book. This chapter is written in the spirit of the "new" welfare economics, because the technical problem it deals with has been considered primarily in those terms and despite serious doubts about the acceptability and validity of this approach to normative economics. The value of the general approach is a separate and broader issue, not considered here, except for the parenthetical comment in note 4.

1. Milton Friedman, "The Marshallian Demand Curve," *Journal of Political Economy,* 57 (1949): 463–95.

and problem-solving approach; and that the usual definition is in consequence less useful for most purposes. The quantitative difference between the two demand curves is small if the percentage of income spent on the commodity in question is small, as it generally is in actual applications, and approaches zero as that percentage approaches zero. Nonetheless, the difference in concept is highly important precisely because it does reflect a fundamental difference in approach.

The following discussion makes no explicit use of a demand curve. Yet it will be seen that the widely used analysis of the welfare effects of income and excise taxes, which it shows to be erroneous, is cut from the same cloth as the usual definition of the demand curve—both reflect the arithmetical approach to economic analysis. Of course, no approach makes error inevitable. An analyst may win through to correct results despite deficiencies in his approach and tools. Yet the fact that able and sophisticated analysts have been misled affords ample evidence that the defect is not unimportant.

The Alleged "Proof" of the Superiority of an Income Tax

Figure 3.1 summarizes an analysis that has frequently been offered as a "proof" that an income tax is superior to an excise tax yielding the same revenue.[2]

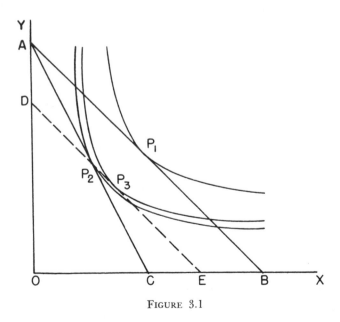

FIGURE 3.1

2. Most presentations of the "proof" derive from M. F. W. Joseph, "The Excess Burden of Indirect Taxation," *Review of Economic Studies,* 6 (June, 1939): 226–31; or

Consider a world of two goods, X and Y. Let the quantity of X be measured along the horizontal axis and that of Y along the vertical and draw the indifference curves of a consumer (a "representative" consumer [?]). Let AB represent the initial budget line, so P_1 is the initial equilibrium position. Let an excise tax of, say, 50 percent of the price inclusive of tax be placed on X (call this "Excise Tax A") and let it be entirely shifted to the consumer, so that the price of X to the consumer doubles. On the assumption (underlying the usual demand curve) that money income and other prices are to be held fixed in analyzing the effect of a change in one price, the budget line shifts to AC and the equilibrium position to P_2.

J. R. Hicks, *Value and Capital*, (Oxford, 1939), p. 41. T. Peacock and D. Berry, in "A Note on the Theory of Income Distribution," *Economica*, N. S., 18 (February, 1951): 83–90, which applies Joseph's analysis to a slightly different problem and hence is equally invalid, point out that Joseph was anticipated by Gino Borgatta in an article in the 1921 volume of the *Giornale degli economisti*. The "proof" is also repeated in George J. Stigler, *Theory of Price* (New York: Macmillan, 1946), pp. 81–82: Edward D. Allen and O. H. Brownlee, *Economics of Public Finance* (New York: Prentice-Hall, 1947), pp. 343–45; M. W. Reder, "Welfare Economics and Rationing," *Quarterly Journal of Economics*, 57 (November, 1942): 153–55 (the rest of Reder's article is characterized by the same fallacy as the "proof" he reproduces, attributing it to Hicks); Haskell Wald, "The Classical Indictment of Indirect Taxation," *Quarterly Journal of Economics*, 59 (August, 1945): 577–96, esp. 579–82; and A. Henderson, "The Case for Indirect Taxation," *Economic Journal*, 58 (December, 1948): 538–53, esp. 538–40. A logically equivalent argument is used to discuss the welfare effects of alternative forms of direct taxation by Kenneth E. Boulding, *Economic Analysis* (rev. ed; New York: Harper & Bros., 1948), pp. 773–75, and is repeated by Eli Schwartz and Donald A. Moore, who dispute Boulding's specific conclusions but do not question the validity of his argument, in "The Distorting Effects of Direct Taxation: A Re-evaluation," *American Economic Review*, 41 (March, 1951): 139–48.

The analysis of this problem by Joseph and Hicks is often considered identical with the earlier analysis of the same problem by Harold Hotelling in "The General Welfare in Relation to Problems of Taxation and of Railway and Utility Rates," *Econometrica*, 6 (July, 1938): 242–69, esp. 249–51. But this is a serious error, since Hotelling avoids the fallacy that mars the analyses listed in the preceding paragraph. An interchange between Hotelling and Ragnar Frisch on Hotelling's article, *Econometrica*, 7 (April, 1939): 45–60. deals rather obliquely with the point with which the present note is concerned. At bottom, the major difference between Frisch and Hotelling is that Frisch interprets Hotelling's proof as identical with that given by Joseph, although, of course, Joseph's proof is not referred to and had not appeared in print when Frisch wrote. Frisch fails to see the force of Hotelling's emphasis on the essential point of difference, namely, that Hotelling takes account of conditions of cost of production.

The "proof" is critically examined and correctly criticized by Earl R. Rolph and George F. Break, in "The Welfare Aspects of Excise Taxes," *Journal of Political Economy*, 57 (February, 1949): 46–55. Their analysis has much in common with that of the present chapter; they point out essentially the same defects in the "proof" and give an essentially correct analysis of the problem. A correct analysis of the problem is also given by I. M. D. Little, *A Critique of Welfare Economics* (Oxford, 1950), pp. 157–79. In an article, "Direct versus Indirect Taxes," *Economic Journal*, 59 (September, 1951): 577–84, which came to my attention only after the present chapter was in the hands of the printer, Little also points out the defects in the usual analysis. The chief difference between the present chapter and the relevant parts of the papers by Rolph and Break and by Little is that the present chapter is primarily concerned with the methodological issue involved in the analysis; the others with the substantive issue.

Suppose, now, that instead of the excise tax, an income tax had been imposed to yield the same revenue ("Income Tax A"). The budget line corresponding to this income tax is parallel to AB, since prices are assumed to be unaffected. Moreover, it must go through P_2 if the revenue from the income tax is to be equal to the revenue from the excise tax: under the excise tax, the individual spends his whole money income, which is taken to be the same whichever tax is imposed, on the bundle of goods indicated by P_2; this expenditure equals the tax payment plus the cost of P_2 at pretax prices. In consequence, if he pays the same amount in taxes under an income tax, he will be able to buy the bundle indicated by P_2 at the pretax prices with the rest of his income. The budget line under the income tax is therefore DE. But, with this budget line, the individual will not in fact buy the bundle indicated by P_2; he will instead buy the bundle indicated by P_3, which is on a higher indifference curve. It is therefore concluded that an income tax permits a consumer to attain a higher indifference curve than an excise tax yielding the same revenue,[3] that is, that

(1) Income Tax A is preferable to Excise Tax A.[4]

So far we have dealt with only a single individual. The *analysis* generally ends at this point, but the *conclusion* is immediately generalized to the community as a whole to yield the proposition that all members of the community would be better off (on higher indifference curves) if an excise tax were replaced by an income tax so levied that each member pays the same amount as an income tax that he formerly paid as an excise tax.

The Fallacy in the Alleged "Proof"

This "proof" contains two essential steps: first, the derivation of proposition 1 for an isolated individual; second, the generalization of this proposition to the community at large.

The analysis for an isolated individual is entirely valid. If Excise A or Income Tax A were imposed solely on one individual among many, they would have negligible indirect effects beyond those summarized in Figure

3. Total revenue from all taxes will necessarily be the same at P_2 and P_3 only if there are no differential excise taxes or subsidies in force at the initial position. If, for example, there is an excise tax on Y at the initial position, its yield will be less at P_3 than at P_2, and the preferability of the former may be interpreted as reflecting this smaller tax payment rather than the different form of the tax. The existence of a tax on Y at P_1 does not alter the argument in the text; it does change the meaning or interpretation of the conclusion.

4. The reader should perhaps be warned that the identification of "being on a higher indifference curve" with "is preferable to" is a far less innocent step than may appear on the surface. Indeed, the view expressed in an earlier footnote about the validity of the "new" welfare economics in general rests in considerable measure on the belief that this step cannot be justified within the utilitarian framework of that approach, though it can be within a different, and in my judgment preferable, philosophical framework. For a criticism of this step on somewhat different grounds see Little, *A Critique of Welfare Economics*, pp. 38–50. These considerations are not, however, relevant to the particular technical point made in this paper.

3.1, and that figure could serve as an adequate representation of the final position attained by the individual in question. Its arithmetic is impeccable, and arithmetic alone is relevant in this case.

The immediate generalization of the analysis to the community at large, on the other hand, is invalid. While Figure 3.1 is an adequate representation of the final position when taxes are imposed on one person alone, it is not adequate when taxes are imposed on all members of a community alike —as would indeed be painfully obvious except for the habitual patterns of thought engendered by the usual approach to demand curves. Consider, for example, the budget lines AB and AC in Figure 3.1. It is obvious directly, and without the use of indifference curves, that the alternatives available to the consumer when the budget line is AC are clearly inferior to those available when the budget line is AB. When it is AB, he can, if he wishes, have any of the alternatives available when it is AC *plus* all the bundles in the triangle ACB. Generalization of the analysis for an isolated individual to the community as a whole therefore supposes that the mere imposition of the excise tax reduces the range of alternatives open to every consumer in a way that is calculable by simple arithmetic. How can this be? The imposition of the excise tax per se does not change any of the technical production possibilities; it does not by itself lessen the physical resources available to the community. It may reduce the quantity of resources available to produce X and Y if the proceeds are used to produce goods under state direction which formerly were not produced (say goods Z). But, in that case, Figure 3.1 is not at all adequate, since an additional axis would be needed to represent goods Z. More important, the reduction in the alternatives open to the consumer would then depend on physical and technical possibilities, the kinds of resources needed for the goods produced by the state, and similar factors; the reduction cannot be computed by simple arithmetic from the knowledge summarized in Figure 3.1.

The above analysis says nothing about the destination of the proceeds of the excise tax; it would not be changed if the proceeds were impounded or used to give a per-unit subsidy on Y or an income subsidy to consumers. But in any of these cases the tax would not have reduced the range of alternatives technically available. If prices were temporarily rigid, the supply of money fixed except for the changes brought about by the tax, and the proceeds of the tax impounded, unemployment might of course occur in the short run (though there is then considerable ambiguity in the assumption that X and Y are the only goods in the world.) This would not, however, be a stable position; prices would tend to fall relative to money income, which would shift the line AC to the right. More important, if prices did not fall relative to money income, the most significant implication of either the excise tax or the income tax would be the same, namely, that either tended to produce unemployment and a reduction in the alternatives available to consumers. The difference between P_3 and a point at the original prices equivalent in utility to P_2 (the point of tangency between a budget line parallel to AB and the indifference curve through P_2) is small compared to the difference between either and P_1; indeed, the ratio of the former difference to the latter difference approaches zero as the excise tax (or equivalent income tax) approaches zero.[5] It follows that, if rigidity of prices and creation of unemployment are considered the major consequences, the conclusion would have to be that the income tax and excise tax have essentially identical effects on "welfare" and that any difference between their effects is of the "second order of smalls."

The analysis cannot be saved by this route. It is clearly intended to be a "long-run" analysis—comparative "statics," not dynamics—as is amply demonstrated by both the considerations just cited and the assumed complete shifting of the excise tax. We can therefore abstract from any short-run price rigidities and suppose complete adaptation to the new circumstances. But then it is clear that Figure 3.1 alone tells nothing about the final effects of either the income tax or the excise tax. For example, suppose the excise tax is used to give a per-unit subsidy on Y. The slope of the new budget line would then be known (and might be that shown by AC if the excise tax and subsidy were adjusted appropriately), but its position would not be; for its position would be determined not alone by the tastes of consumers and by arithmetic calculation but also by the technical possibilities open to the community.

A "Correct" Analysis

In order to bring the technical possibilities into the picture, let us suppose that we are dealing with a community of many identical individuals —identical in tastes and preferences and also in kind and quantity of resources owned by each individual. In this community, every individual will have the same income and consume the same bundle of goods, so we can represent the position of the community by the position of any one individual, as in Figure 3.2. Given the resources available to the community, there will be some set of combinations of X and Y that it is technically possible to produce. These can be represented by a production indifference curve. Since in our hypothetical community every individual will consume an aliquot share of each commodity, we can divide the coordinates of this production curve by the number of individuals and plot the result on any one individual's indifference map. GH on Figure 3.2 is such a production possibility curve. It shows the alternative combinations

5. The difference between P_1 and P_3 corresponds to the "income effect" as defined by Slutsky; between P_1 and the point at the original prices on the same indifference curve as P_2, to the "income effect" as defined by Hicks. As Mosak has shown, the difference between the two income effects approaches zero relative to the income effect itself as the price change approaches zero. See Jacob T. Mosak, "On the Interpretation of the Fundamental Equation of Value Theory," in Oscar Lange, Francis McIntyre, and Theodore S. Yntema (eds.), *Studies in Mathematical Economics and Econometrics* (Chicago: University of Chicago Press, 1942), pp. 69–74.

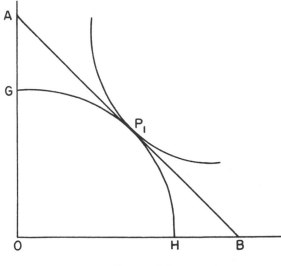

FIGURE 3.2

of X and Y that are technically available to each individual, given that every individual ends up with the same combination. It should be emphasized that Figure 3.2 is for an individual and therefore does not involve interpersonal comparisons; we are interested here in an "allocative," not a "distributive," problem and can abstract from the distributive problem by dealing with a society composed of identical individuals.

If the society were initially at a position of full competitive equilibrium, each individual would be at P_1. At this point, the rate of substitution in consumption (the slope of the consumption indifference curve) is equal to the rate of substitution in purchase on the market (the price ratio shown by the slope of the budget line), which, in turn, is equal to the rate of substitution in production (the slope of the production indifference curve). Technical possibilities are being fully exploited, as shown by the fact that P_1 is on the frontier of the alternatives technically capable of being produced (these obviously include not only those on GP_1H but also those between the production indifference curve and the origin).

How can we represent a proportional income tax on this diagram? If the proceeds are impounded or returned to individuals in the form of a per capita subsidy, the diagram obviously remains completely unchanged. For such an income tax and subsidy do not alter the relative prices of X and Y, the consumption indifference curves, or the production possibilities. They are a purely nominal matter on the present level of analysis. If the proceeds of the income tax are spent by the state to produce, say, Z, with resources formerly used to produce X or Y, the production possibilities are clearly changed. There will now be a new production indifference curve, showing the alternative combinations of X and Y capable of being produced, given the production of a specified amount of Z. But the change in the production indifference curve depends only on the amount of Z produced, not on how the funds are raised. If we suppose this amount of Z to be given and fixed, the new production indifference curve will be the same whether an income tax or an excise tax is imposed; hence, in investigating any difference between an income tax and an excise tax, we can, without loss of generality, suppose GP_1H to be the production indifference curve after the subtraction of resources to produce Z. Figure 3.2 can therefore represent the situation both before and after a proportional income tax for purposes of comparing such a tax with an excise tax.

What now of an excise tax? One condition is obvious. The position of equilibrium must be on the production indifference curve GH. Any position above the production indifference curve is technically impossible with the available resources; any position below it does not involve full use of available resources and is therefore unstable. Beyond this, the essential feature of an excise tax for our purposes is that it leads to a divergence between two prices—the price paid by the consumer and the price received by the producer—and, hence, between two price ratios that were formerly the same—the price ratio relevant to the consumer and the price ratio relevant to the producer. The terms on which the consumer can substitute one commodity for the other in purchase on the market, while keeping total expenditures the same, must be calculated from prices inclusive of tax; the terms on which the producer can substitute one commodity for the other in sale on the market, while keeping total receipts the same, must be calculated from the prices exclusive of tax. Equilibrium for consumers requires that the rate at which consumers can substitute in purchase be equal to the rate at which they are willing to substitute in consumption: that is, that the consumer budget line be tangent to a consumption indifference curve. Equilibrium for producers requires that the rate at which producers can substitute in sale be equal to the rate at which they can substitute in production: that is, that a constant-receipts line be tangent to the production indifference curve. A position of equilibrium satisfying these conditions is given by P_6 in Figure 3.3. The line IJ is the budget line as it appears to the consumer; the line KL, the constant-receipts line as it appears to producers. The two diverge because of Excise Tax A on X, which may be regarded as determining the angle between the two lines and which means that the extra amount of X consumers can purchase by giving up one unit of Y is less than the extra amount of X producers need to sell to recoup the loss from selling one fewer units of Y. At P_6, KL is tangent to the production indifference curve and IJ to a consumption indifference curve.

The ratio of the price of Y to the price of X when the excise tax is in effect (at P_6) cannot, as is assumed in drawing Figure 3.1, be calculated simply from the initial price ratio at P_1 and the rate of the tax. It depends also on production considerations. The less concave the production possibility curve, the larger the fraction of the tax that will be shifted to the

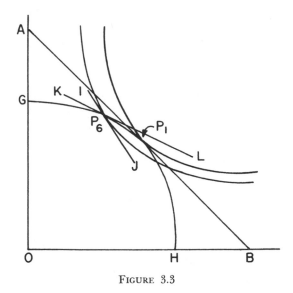

FIGURE 3.3

consumer and the smaller the fraction that will be shifted to the producer, and conversely. The whole of the tax will be shifted to the consumer, in the sense that the relative price of the two commodities exclusive of tax will be the same at P_6 as at P_1, only if the production possibility curve is identical with AB.

Given the shapes of the curves as in Figure 3.3, P_6 is necessarily inferior to P_1, in the sense that the individual is on a lower indifference curve. Given that the initial position is one of full competitive equilibrium with no taxes or subsidies, i.e., that it is P_1, Excise Tax A is inferior to Income Tax A.

Suppose, however, that the initial position had been P_6 instead of P_1, not because of governmental taxes or subsidies but because of some other deviation from fully competitive conditions, say because of monopolistic conditions in the production of X which produce the same position of equilibrium as Excise Tax A imposed under fully competitive conditions. Let an excise tax now be imposed on commodity Y of the same percentage as Excise Tax A, say 50 percent (call this Excise Tax B), and let us compare this with an income tax (Income Tax B) yielding the same revenue to the government.

The analysis summarized in the discussion of the alleged "proof" could be repeated for this excise tax and income tax and it would yield the same conclusion—that the income tax is preferable to the excise tax, since nothing is said in that analysis about the nature of the initial position, except possibly that it be a position in which there are no differential excise taxes or subsidies.[6]

6. This qualification is necessary if the two taxes compared are to have not only the same direct tax yield but also to *add* the same amount to the total tax yield.

Yet Figure 3.3 shows that this conclusion is wrong. Excise Tax B precisely offsets the effect of the assumed monopoly in the production of X; it eliminates the divergence produced by that monopoly between the price ratio relevant to consumers (the ratio of market prices inclusive of taxes) and that relevant to producers (the ratio of marginal revenues exclusive of taxes). The two ratios coincide and, in consequence, P_1 is the equilibrium position with Excise Tax B imposed on an initial position P_6. On the other hand, the imposition of Income Tax B leaves the divergence between the two ratios unchanged and leaves P_6 the equilibrium position. Hence Excise Tax B is preferable to Income Tax B, given that both are imposed when the initial position is P_6.

Conclusion

At this point the reader may well be tempted to regard the alleged proof as rehabilitated, to say that "of course" its validity depends on the assumption that the initial position is one of full competitive equilibrium and that, while the users of the "proof" have been careless in not stating this assumption explicitly, they have doubtless recognized its necessity. A re-examination of the "proof" will, however, show that no "assumption" about the nature of the initial position will render it a valid proof of the relevant economic proposition. The conclusion to which it is said to lead may be correct when the initial position is a position of full competitive equilibrium; but the argument does not demonstrate that it is correct or why it is correct. The alleged syllogism, "Socrates is a man, Socrates is X, therefore all men are X," happens to lead to a correct "conclusion" when X stands for "mortal," though not when X stand for "Greek." Nonetheless, the assumption that X stands for "mortal" will not render it a valid syllogism. The parallel is exact: the alleged proof that an income tax is superior to an excise tax is not a proof at all; no *step* in the alleged proof depends for its validity on the character of the initial position; hence, no "assumption" about the initial position can convert it into a valid proof, though the final statement in the "proof" may be correct for some conditions and not for others.[7]

The "correct" analysis shows that no general statement can be made about the relative effects on "welfare" of what we have been calling "income taxes" and "excise taxes." Everything depends on the initial conditions under which the taxes are imposed. But even this statement does not

7. Note the difference between this case for the community and the case for an isolated individual when the initial position already involves a special excise tax. In that case, though the analysis is no different, the meaning and interpretation of the conclusion is, as noted in preceding footnotes. But even for the individual, other deviations from competitive conditions at the initial position do not affect the validity or meaning of any step in the proof.

sufficiently indicate the limitations on the direct applicability of the results. What I, in common with the other writers on this problem, have called an *income tax* has little or no kinship with the taxes actually levied under that name. The latter are fundamental excise taxes more or less broad in scope. Even a straight proportional income tax on a broadly defined tax base does not fall equally on all goods and services produced with available resources; inevitably it leaves untouched goods and services not produced through the market: leisure, household activities, etc. It therefore makes the rate at which the consumer can substitute them for marketable goods and services different from the rate at which it is technically possible to substitute them. This effect is clearly greater if the income-tax base is more narrowly defined, an exemption is allowed, or the rates are progressive. The most that one can infer from the analysis is perhaps a presumption that, the broader the scope of the tax and the more equal its incidence, the less likely it is to falsify rates of substitution. But even this is at best a presumption to be tested in each case. Unfortunately, formal analysis can seldom if ever give easy answers to hard problems. Its role is quite different: to suggest the considerations relevant to an answer and to provide a useful means of organizing the analysis.

The "correct" analysis is clearly applicable to many problems other than the particular one to which it is here applied. Forces other than taxes may produce divergences between the rates of substitution whose equality is the essential condition of an "optimum" in the sense implicit in the above discussion. For example, as already noted, monopoly produces such a divergence, and it is this divergence that constitutes the fundamental argument, on strictly allocative grounds, against monopoly. Similarly, Marshall's argument for taxes on decreasing-return industries and subsidies to increasing-return industries, to the extent that it is valid, involves a divergence between the production indifference curve relevant to the producer and the production indifference curve relevant to society and hence a divergence between the rate at which a producer judges that he can substitute commodities in production and the rate at which producers as a whole can actually do so. In fact, our simple Figure 3.3 contains the essence of much of modern welfare economics.

To return to the initial theme, the approach to economics underlying the usual demand curve is the approach underlying the superficial analysis embodied in Figure 3.1; the approach underlying the alternative demand curve along which "real income" is held constant is the approach embodied in Figures 3.2 and 3.3; one who started with this approach would be heavily insulated against analyses such as that embodied in Figure 3.1. The great defect of the approach underlying the usual demand curve is that it emphasizes arithmetic considerations; the great virtue of the approach underlying the alternative demand curve is that it emphasizes economic considerations.

4

The Utility Analysis of Uncertainty

As long as economists took seriously the intuitive notion of diminishing marginal utility, it was impossible for them to rationalize observed behavior with respect to choices involving uncertainty by a simple extension of the theory of utility maximization. This can be seen immediately from the following example. Consider a gamble that involves a 50 percent chance of winning and a 50 percent chance of losing $100.00. The mathematical expectation of this gamble is zero. If the marginal utility of money is taken as diminishing, the moral expectation of this gamble, i.e., the expected change in utility as a result of accepting this gamble, is less than zero or negative, since the gain in utility from an extra $100.00 is less than the loss in utility from the loss of $100.00. Acceptance of the gamble implies a loss of utility; hence, Marshall and others concluded that gambling is "irrational." Activities such as gambling were supposed not to be explainable on the grounds of maximization of utility. If, however, we drop the assumption of diminishing marginal utility, it turns out that we can use the same hypothesis of utility maximization in the analysis of choices involving uncertainty as in the analysis of other choices.

Once uncertainty is introduced, the object of choice is no longer a bundle of goods of known composition but a set of exclusive alternatives, each with some specified probability. We can regard a sum of money—or an income—as representing each possibility (since the optimum allocation of the income among different goods has already been covered by the theory of choice under conditions of certainty). One object of choice would then be a probability distribution of income; for example, a probability

76

P_1 of receiving an income I_1, P_2 of receiving an income I_2, P_3 of receiving an income I_3, etc., the sum of the probabilities being unity. Another object of choice would be a different probability distribution. We can now take as our problem the construction of a theory to rationalize choice among such objects.

Maximizing Expected Utility

Let B stand for a generalized object of choice of this type, i.e., for a set or "bundle" of alternative incomes and associated probabilities. (If we want to contrast different sets, we shall use subscripts; i.e., B_1 will stand for one set, B_2 for another, etc.). We shall assume that the individual can rank these objects of choice and that these rankings obey the transitivity requirement, so that if he ranks B_1 above B_2 and B_2 above B_3, he will rank B_1 above B_3. Let the function G(B) describe this ranking, i.e., G(B) is a function that attaches a number to each object or bundle (each B), and these numbers have the property that the individual will choose a B with a higher number in preference to a B with a lower number, i.e., the numbers give a ranking of all bundles in order of his preference. In line with the language used in the theory of choices under conditions of certainty, G(B) can be described as giving the "utility" attached to various probability distributions of income.

Up to this point, the theory described is almost perfectly general and, accordingly, almost perfectly empty. It simply says that individuals rank alternatives and choose among those available to them the one they rank highest. Its only content is in the supposed consistency and transitivity of choices. The function G(B) we have introduced is simply a shorthand expression for the statement that individuals can be supposed to have a consistent and transitive ranking of possible objects of choice. We could, even in principle, determine an individual's G(B) only by observing his choice among all possible objects; if some object B had never been offered to him, we could never calculate its place in the ranking from other choices.

A special theory consists in specifying something about the form of G(B). One particular special theory that we shall consider is as follows: Let the object of choice B consist of a probability P_1 of income I_1, P_2 of income $I_2 \ldots$, P_k of income I_k. The special theory then is that G(B) can be written as

(1)
$$G(B) = \sum_{i=I}^{k} P_i \, F(I_i)$$

where F(I) is simply some function of I. Stated differently, this special theory consists of the hypothesis that there exists a function F(I) which has the property that G(B) calculated as in equation 1 yields a correct ranking of

TABLE 4.1

B			
I	*P*	*F(I)*	*P·F(I)*
100	1/4	10	2 1/2
200	1/2	20	10.0
300	1/4	25	6 1/4

possible objects of choice. To illustrate the meaning of the concept, suppose a particular B and F as in Table 4.1. The mathematical expectation of this bundle is 200, given by ΣPI. The G of this bundle is 18 3/4 given by ΣP · F(I).

It is important to emphasize the fact that the hypothesis $G(B) = \Sigma\ P \cdot F(I)$ is a very special one. For example, consider the following three bundles: B_1, B_2, and B_3, as in Table 4.2. In B_1, the individual has an even chance of

TABLE 4.2

B_1	B_2	B_3
1/2 (+50)	1/2 (+100)	1/4 (+100)
1/2 (−50)	1/2 (−100)	1/4 (+ 50)
		1/4 (− 50)
		1/4 (−100)

winning or losing $50.00. In B_2, the individual has an even chance of winning or losing $100.00. In B_3, the individual has a 25 percent chance of winning $100.00, a 25 percent chance of winning $50.00, a 25 percent chance of losing $50.00, and a 25 percent chance of losing $100.00. Suppose we know that the individual is indifferent with respect to accepting B_1 or B_2; i.e., $G(B_1)$ and $G(B_2)$ are identical. Under the special theory, this implies that $G(B_3)$ is equal to $G(B_1)$ and $G(B_2)$, i.e., that the individual is indifferent among B_1, B_2, and B_3.

In discussing our special theory further, we may start with the extreme case of choices among certain incomes. In this case, a bundle B consists of a single income, say I, with a probability of attaining it of unity, say $P_1 = 1$, and the probability of attaining any other income equal to zero. In this case, $G(B) = \Sigma P_i\ F(I_i) = F(I)$. This is the reason why F(I) is generally called the "utility" of certain incomes. We shall have occasion later to raise some questions about this usage, but for the moment we may accept it as a convenient manner of speaking. So long as we restrict ourselves to such choices, the most we could learn about F(I) would be the sign of its derivative, i.e., whether F increased or decreased with I. In consequence, as we saw in our earlier discussion of certainty, if we had one F(I) that rationalized such choices, any function of F with a positive first derivative would do so as well; i.e., if F(I) works, then any function f(F[I]) will do as well provided f′ > 0.

Now let us introduce double-valued alternatives. Consider an individual who is confronted by a set of incomes (a bundle, B) consisting of two incomes (I_1 and I_2) with probabilities P_1, P_2 ($P_1 + P_2 = 1$). The expected income $\bar{I} = P_1 I_1 + P_2 I_2$. The utility of this expected income is equal to F($\bar{I}$). $\tilde{U}$, the expected utility, is equal to $P_1 F(I_1) + P_2 F(I_2)$. If the curve relating the utility of income to income is concave from below, then the expected utility or $\tilde{U}$ is less than the utility of the expected income or F($\bar{I}$). Therefore, an individual offered $\bar{I}$ for certain would (if any special theory is correct) prefer this to a chance of obtaining I_1 or I_2. If the curve, however, is convex from below, then the expected utility or $\tilde{U}$ is greater than the utility of the expected income F($\bar{I}$). Therefore, an individual would prefer a gamble of I_1 or I_2 in preference to a certainty of $\bar{I}$. This is shown diagrammatically in Figure 4.1.

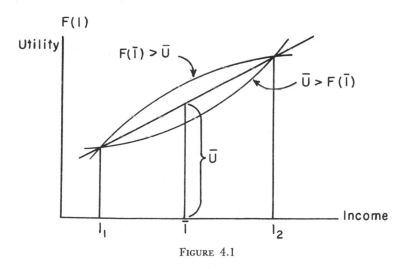

FIGURE 4.1

From choices such as we have just been considering, we shall show that if we accept the special hypothesis of G (B) = Σ PF(I), it is possible to derive an F(I) function that is arbitrary only with respect to scale and origin. Let us assume that if I = 0, then F(I) = 0; and if I = 1, then F(I) = 1. We now have eliminated indeterminancy with respect to scale and origin. Now we shall show how we may determine F(I) for I = 2. Assume the individual is offered \$1.00 for certain (call this bundle B_1) or a gamble of P_1 that he will receive nothing and a chance of $P_2 = 1 - P_1$ that he will receive \$2.00 (call this bundle B_2). Let us find a P_1 such that the individual is indifferent between these two choices. Suppose that this value of P_1 turned out to be 1/4. Since the individual is indifferent between these two bundles, G (B_1) = G(B_2). Since G = ΣPF(I), it follows that F(I) = P_1F(0) + P_2F(2). Since we have assumed that $F(0) = 0$ and $F(1) = 1$, it follows that $1 = 0 + P_2 F(2)$. From this it follows that $F(2) = \dfrac{1}{P_2}$; or since $P_2 = 3/4$, $F(2) = 4/3$. In a similar fashion, the utility of all other incomes can be calculated. We have been able to derive $F(2)$ uniquely because we have made arbitrary assumptions concerning scale and origin. More generally, we should say that if any $F(I)$ will rationalize choices, any function $aF(I) + b$ will do likewise, provided that $a > 0$, which brings out the indeterminacy with respect to scale and origin.

We have just seen that we can derive an $F(I)$, unique except for origin and unit of measure, from knowledge of the choices made by an individual among a *limited* set of bundles, each containing at most two possible incomes (in the example just given, the bundles B_1 and B_2 of that example plus other sets of two incomes, one of which is zero throughout). But once we know $F(I)$, it is clear that we know how the individual would rank any conceivable bundle, *if the special theory is valid,* since we can compute a $G(B)$ for any B. It follows that the special theory has very real content, i.e., is capable of being refuted.

We shall now try to draw an $F(I)$ function that would appear to be capable of accounting for most of the observed phenomena. We observe that people do not go around throwing money away and infer that people choose more income in preference to less. This implies that $F'(I) > 0$. We know that people buy insurance even though it is actuarially unfair. This implies that $F''(I) < 0$ for some incomes. On the other hand, we know that people, including those who buy insurance, gamble. This would be inconsistent if the gambles were identical with the risks they insure against, but they are not. Generally, the gambles they buy are like lotteries, which offer a small chance of a large prize. To rationalize these we may draw a curve as in Figure 4.2. In this figure, Region A is the region of insurance. The individual here prefers to take a certain small loss in his income in preference to the small chance of a large loss. This is because the utility of the expected income is greater than the expected utility. The existence of region B explains the phenomenon of gambling. Because of its existence, even people in region A may prefer the small chance of a large gain to the large chance of a small loss. The utility of the expected income is less than the expected utility. Zone C is necessary to account for the famous St. Petersburg paradox, which manifests itself also in the structure of prizes in lotteries. If it were not for the fact that the utility curve again becomes concave at some point, people should be willing to pay an infinite amount of money to play the game involved in the St. Petersburg paradox.[1] Like-

---

1. The St. Petersburg paradox refers to the following hypothetical game of chance. A (fair) coin is tossed repeatedly until a different side comes up for the first time. The player receives 2^R roubles where R is the length of the run (i.e., the number of heads that come up before the first tail, or the number of tails that come up before the first

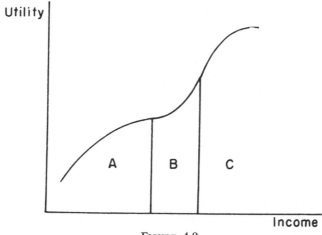

FIGURE 4.2

wise, we should expect lotteries to have one big prize instead of several if the utility curve did not again become concave at some point.

Perhaps a word should be said about the relationship of all this to the problem of measurable utility. If this hypothesis is correct, then we can construct an F (I) function, which is only indeterminate with respect to scale and origin. However, we need not regard F(I) as a utility function. Indeed, we earlier defined G(B) as the utility function. Now it is obvious that, even under our special theory, if one G(B) will rationalize choices, any function of G(B) will do so provided it does not change the order of the ranking; i.e., if you have one G(B) $= \Sigma P \cdot F(I)$, then any other function H[G (B)] = H[$\Sigma PF(I)$] will do so, providing H′ > 0.

Our special theory can be stated most generally as follows: There exists a set of functions aF(I) + b with a positive and b arbitrary, such that the set of functions H[G(B)] = H ($\Sigma P[aF(I) + b]$) with H′ > 0 yields a correct ordering of the individual's preference for alternative probability distribu-

---

head). The question is, how much would anyone pay for the privilege of playing the game?

It is easy to see that the actuarial value of the game is infinity, since each possibility has an actuarial value of 1, and there are an infinite number of possibilities.

Length of Run	Probability	Payment	Actuarial Value
1	1/2	2	1
2	$(1/2)^2$	2^2	1
R	$(1/2)^R$	2^R	1

The supposed paradox is that it is implausible that anyone would be willing to pay a very large sum, let alone an indefinite sum, for the privilege of playing the game.

Bernoulli coined the term *moral expectation* for the value that would be attached to such a game by contrast with its *mathematical expectation*.

tions of income, in the sense that if he is offered the choice between any two probability distributions (say B_1 and B_2) he will choose B_1 in preference to B_2, be indifferent between B_1 and B_2, or choose B_2 in preference to B_1 according as H $[G(B_1)] \gtrless$ H $[G (B_2)]$.

Obviously the original G(B) is the most convenient function to work with, but there is no necessity to do so. In consequence, there is no "absolute" sense in which utility can be said to be "measurable." Indeed, it is doubtful that in this sense the question whether utility is measurable is a meaningful question.

Evaluating Probabilities

The hypothetical experiment for deriving the function F(I) involves offering the subject gambles with specified probabilities. And the prediction of additional choices from that function requires being able to specify the probabilities attached to those choices. How can that be done?

The approach that fits best with our utility analysis is that of "personal probability" developed most fully by L. J. Savage, who was building on work by Bruno de Finetti.[2] This approach says that just as we can suppose that an individual acts as if he attached a definite utility—a generalized version of our F(I) function—to every possible event if it were to occur, so we can suppose that he acts as if he attached a definite probability to each such event. These "personal probabilities" are assumed to obey the usual laws of the mathematics of probability: e.g., the probabilities assigned to a set of mutually exclusive and exhaustive events (one of which must occur) add to unity; the joint probability assigned to two independent events (both occurring) is the product of the probabilities assigned to the individual events; and so on.

In principle, these personal probabilities can be identified by a series of hypothetical experiments like those that we introduced to derive F (I), except that the probability experiments are logically prior to the utility experiments, since the latter require the probabilities to be already known. These hypothetical probability experiments enable a personal scale of probabilities to be established for each individual, which can then be used to determine the probability he assigns to any event, however hypothetical.

Essentially, the idea of the experiments is to let the individual choose how he would like to be rewarded should a particular set of hypothetical events occur. For example, prior to tossing two coins, let the individual choose whether he would rather have one dollar if (A) both came up heads or (B) any other outcome (both tails, one heads, one tails). If, as you would

2. See L. J. Savage, *Foundations of Statistics* (New York: Wiley, 1954).

suspect, he chooses to receive the dollar if event B occurs, that means he regards B as having a probability greater than A, and since A and B are mutually exclusive and exhaustive events, greater than one-half. But of course there is nothing to guarantee that he will choose B. Perhaps he has examined the coins and discovered that both are trick coins with both sides heads. Note that utility valuation does not enter in. The reward is the same whether he chooses A or B. He is deciding on the eventuality under which he would rather receive the same addition to his utility. Note also that nothing is affected by any utility he attaches to the hypothetical, alternative events. He may have a special passion for seeing heads turn up rather than anything else, so he might get more utility from the event itself if A occurred than if B did. But his choice of the outcome on the basis of which he is to be rewarded does not affect what outcome occurs but only whether he receives the additional utility from the dollar reward if it does occur.

Experiment with such choices until you find one for which the subject is indifferent about the outcome that triggers a reward. For example, suppose (A) is a head on a single coin toss and (B) is a tail on that coin toss, and the subject turns out to be indifferent, half the time choosing A, half B. Then he assigns a probability of one-half to A, one-half to B, or one-half to a head on a single coin toss. In the language of probabilities, he regards the coin as a "fair" coin.

Having pinned down an event to which he assigns a probability of one-half, we can now determine whether he assesses any other event at more or less than one-half by making that event one of the alternative bases for triggering a reward. For example, would he rather have a specified reward five years from date if (A) a coin tossed on that date comes up heads or (B) Britain is still a parliamentary democracy. If he chooses B we know he assigns a probability greater than one-half to that possibility.

To get more exact estimates of personal probabilities, we have to construct a more refined comparison scale. For example, offer a reward on any one of four alternative results of tossing two coins: (A) two heads; (B) two tails; (C) head, tail; (D) tail, head. If the subject is indifferent to which outcome triggers the reward, we have a set of events to which he assigns a probability of one-fourth each, and we also have a joint test of the hypothesis that the usual laws of mathematical probability apply to his personal probabilities and that he regards the two tosses as independent.

In principle, experiments of this type would make it possible to get as fine a comparison probability scale for the individual as desired, and accordingly, to determine the probability he assigns to any hypothetical event to any desired degree of accuracy.

The combined hypothesis that each individual acts as if he assigned a personal probability and a utility value to any hypothetical event and chose among alternatives available to him in such a way as to maximize expected utility is now a hypothesis that in principle contains no unobservable elements.

The assertion that individuals act *as if* they assigned personal probabilities to all possible events is an hypothesis about behavior, not a description of individual psychology or an assertion that an individual will give a meaningful answer to a question about the probability he assigns to an event, such as the continuation of parliamentary democracy in Britain. If the event in question does not much affect his life or, even if it does, does not affect the part of his behavior subject to his control, there is no reason he should devote any effort to making up his mind about such a question, and he will doubtless give an offhand answer. On the other hand, if an important part of his behavior depends on whether parliamentary democracy continues in Britain (in terms of our hypothetical experiment, if the reward or loss triggered by that outcome is sizable), it will be worth his while to form a definite opinion.

The personal probability approach bypasses much of the dispute in the literature about "objective" and "subjective" probabilities. One way the personal probability approach can be linked with that distinction is to classify those sets of probabilities as "objective" for which personal probabilities of the group in question agree, and as "subjective" for which they disagree. An example especially relevant for economics is the distinction stressed by Frank Knight between "risk" and "uncertainty," "risk" in essence corresponding to so-called objective probabilities, "uncertainty" to subjective probabilities. This distinction largely loses its force if the personal probability approach is adopted.

5

The Relationships Between Supply Curves and Cost Curves

The Definition of a Supply Curve

Consider a two-dimensional graph in which the quantity of a commodity per unit time is measured along the horizontal axis and price per unit of the commodity is measured along the vertical axis (Figure 5.1). Each point on this graph denotes a combination of a price and a quantity. For a specific group of suppliers (which may as a special case consist of a single firm), a specific commodity, and given conditions of supply (to be defined more explicitly below), some of these points will be attainable in the sense that the suppliers would be willing to supply the indicated quantity at the indicated price, whereas others will be unattainable in the sense that the suppliers would not be willing to supply the indicated quantity at the indicated price. The supply curve of the specific group for the specific commodity is the boundary line between those points that are and those that are not attainable under the given conditions of supply.

For a full description, the supply curve must be accompanied by a specification of (a) the alternatives considered open to the suppliers and (b) which of the two areas into which the supply curve divides the space contains the attainable points.

As an example of the meaning of (a), the supply curve will be one thing if the suppliers are considered as having the alternative of supplying either the indicated quantity at the indicated price or nothing at all; it will be quite different if they are considered as having the alternative of supplying either the indicated quantity or any smaller quantity at the indicated

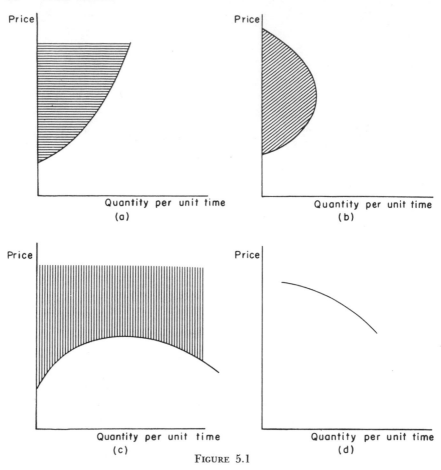

FIGURE 5.1

price. In general, we shall suppose the latter to be the alternative open to suppliers.

The relevance of (b) is exemplified in Figure 5.1, in which the shaded areas designate the attainable points. The supply curve in Figure 5.1 (a) can be described in either of two ways: as showing the maximum quantity that would be supplied at a specified price or as showing the minimum price at which a specified quantity would be supplied. The supply curve in Figure 5.1(b) can be described in only one of these ways: as showing the maximum quantity that would be supplied at a specified price. The supply curve in Figure 5.1(c) shows only the minimum price at which a specified quantity would be supplied. The negatively sloped portion of a supply curve like that in Figure 5.1(b) is frequently referred to as a "backward-bending" supply curve; a supply curve like that in Figure 5.1(c) is referred to as a "forward-falling" supply curve. The segment of a supply curve in Figure 5.1(d) is not completely defined; if points to the left of it are attainable, it is a "backward-bending" supply curve; if points above it are, it is a "forward-falling" supply curve.

There is some uncertainty as to how best to specify "given condition of supply," i.e., what *other things* it is generally appropriate to hold the same. However, this problem has little bearing on the issues to be discussed here, so we shall follow what seems to be current practice and include in the "other things" requiring explicit mention at least (1) technical knowledge —"the state of the arts;" (2) the prices of commodities closely related to this commodity in production (e.g., the price of wool for the supply curve of mutton, the price of industrial structures for the supply curve of residential housing); and (3) the supply curves of factors of production to the specific group of suppliers considered.

It should be noted that the "specific group" for which a supply curve is constructed need not include all suppliers of the "specific commodity" for which it is constructed. For example, the "specific group" could be "producers of wheat in Iowa"; the commodity could be wheat in general, whether produced in Iowa or elsewhere. As another example, the "specific group" could be an individual firm; the commodity, a product produced by many such firms which together comprise an industry.

Note that item 3 holds constant the supply curves of the factors of production *to the specific group*. Accordingly, its content may change as one proceeds from, say, a firm to an industry. To the firm, for example, the supply curves of some factors may be considered horizontal, so that item 3 is equivalent to holding their prices constant. To the industry, the supply curves of these same factors may not be horizontal, so item 3 is equivalent to permitting their prices to vary along the supply curve.

Note also that this definition of a supply curve holds for both short-run and long-run supply curves. The difference between short-run and long-run curves is in the precise content of item 3, i.e., the assumed shapes of supply curves of factors. The shorter the run, the larger the number of factors whose supply curves will be taken as vertical or nearly so.

The Formal Breakdown of the Output of an Industry into the Output of Individual Firms

In Figure 5.2, the curve SS represents the supply curve of all suppliers of commodity X for commodity X. It is an "industry" supply curve, showing the minimum price at which each quantity would be supplied. This curve is the one that is ordinarily of interest in the analysis of concrete problems. Further investigation into the supply curves or cost curves of individual firms is undertaken to learn something about why the shape of SS is what it is, rather than because of any special interest in the individual firm as such.

The curve SS has direct empirical meaning. For given conditions with respect to items 1, 2, and 3, there will in fact exist some minimum price at which a particular quantity of X will be supplied per unit time. The quantity OQ will be supplied at a minimum price QP; the quantity OQ′, at a minimum price Q′P′; and so on. Of course, the precise shape of SS will depend on the precise content of items 1 to 3, and, in particular, on the shape of the supply curves of factors of production to the industry. These factor supply curves will tend to depend on the period of time allowed for adjustment, so short-run and long-run supply curves can be considered as yielded by different specifications of item 3.

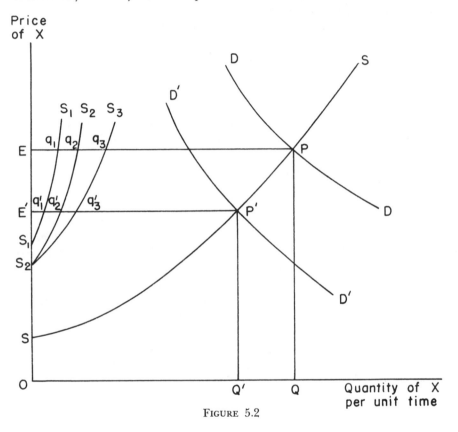

FIGURE 5.2

Now suppose the demand curve were DD, and market price PQ, output OQ. This output would in fact be supplied by a number of different firms, and one could mark off on the line EP = OQ the amount supplied by each firm. For example, Eq$_1$ might be supplied by firm 1, q$_1$q$_2$ by firm 2, q$_2$q$_3$ by firm 3, etc. If the demand curve were D′D′ instead of DD, the price would be P′Q′, the output OQ′, and one could similarly mark off on E′P′ the amount supplied by each firm—E′q$_1'$ by firm 1, q$_1'$q$_2'$ by firm 2, q$_2'$q$_3'$ by firm 3, etc. Suppose this were done for each price, and the points for each firm connected, as has been done on Figure 5.1 for firms 1, 2, and 3. S$_1$S$_1$ then shows the contribution that firm 1 would make to the total output at various prices, given that the entire industry expanded along SS. In general, however, it will not be a "supply curve of firm 1 for commodity X," as that term was defined previously. One reason is that as the industry expands, the prices of factors will change as required by the given supply curves to the industry. To the individual firm, this will typically involve a shift in the supply curves of factors to it, and hence a change in the conditions of supply. Another reason is that as the industry expands, technological conditions may change for the individual firm, though not for the industry, again involving a change in the conditions of supply. S_1S_1 might perhaps be called a *quasi-supply curve* of firm 1. Similarly, the horizontal difference between S_1S_1 and S_2S_2 shows the contribution of firm 2 to the industry's output at various prices.

This construction implicitly allows for changes in the number of firms at different prices for the product. At a price below that at which S_2S_3 cuts the vertical axis, no output at all is supplied by firms 1, 2, or 3; these firms would not "enter" the industry at such prices. At a higher price, firms 2 and 3 would "enter" the industry; at a still higher price—above that at which S_1S_1 cuts the vertical axis—firm 1 would enter. The actual expansion in supply shown by SS is in general a result of both expansion in the output of each firm separately and an increase in the number of firms.

At each point on the supply curve of the industry, say point P, there is implicit some set of quantities of factors of production used in producing the corresponding quantity of X. For example, let the factors of production be designated by A, B, C, etc. Then output OQ, offered for sale at price QP, is produced by using some quantities of A, B, C; say quantities a, b, c, etc. Output OQ′ is similarly produced by using, say, a′, b′, c′, etc. of the various factors. Given the supply curves of the factors of production to the industry, these quantities imply certain prices of the factors of production, say p_a, p_b, p_c, etc., for output OQ; p'_a, p'_b, p'_c, etc. for output OQ′. If the supply curves of all factors were horizontal, these prices would be the same for all outputs; otherwise, the prices will differ for different outputs, so to each point on SS (and hence on S_1S_1, S_2S_2, etc.) there is implicitly attached a set of prices of the factors of production.

Following Marshall (see *Principles*, p. 344), we could indicate the relation between the supply price of the product and the quantities and prices of the factors by subdividing the ordinates of SS (like PQ) just as we subdivided the abscissae (EP in Figure 5.2).

Figure 5.3 illustrates this point. To produce an output OQ under the given conditions, the quantity OA of A will be used. The number of units of OA per unit of product will be $\frac{OA}{OQ}$. Then $\frac{OA}{OQ} \cdot p_a$ is the price of the amount of A that is used per unit of product; this number is represented in Figure 5.3 by QP_1. Similarly, if OB is the quantity of B used to produce output OQ and p_b the price per unit of B, then $P_1P_2 = \dfrac{OB}{OQ} \cdot p_b$; and so the total supply price PQ can be subdivided into the supply prices of the factors of production used to produce OQ of X. Note that the scales for A, B, etc. at the bottom of Figure 5.3 are linked to the scale for X, and that equal horizontal distances on these scales in general will not refer to equal quantities. For example, suppose OQ is 4/3 of OQ′; it does not follow that OA is 4/3 of OA′, or OB 4/3 of OB′, since the combination of factors used to produce OQ need not be the same as that used to produce OQ′. If the supply of A is more elastic than the supply of B, it is likely that the amount of A used will increase by more than one-third and the amount of B by less than one-third, when the output of X is increased by one-third. Similarly, P_1Q and $P_1′ Q′$ will in general be prices for different sized units of A—they are prices for whatever amount of A is used per unit of product (of X), and for the reasons just cited, the amount of A per unit of product may be different at OQ than at OQ′.

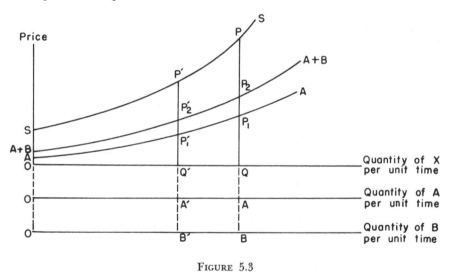

FIGURE 5.3

As we shall see later, if we are to explain the existence of many firms and admit the possibility of economic determinants of the size of firms, we shall need to assume the existence of one or more factors specific to the individual firm and not capable of being rented or hired by other firms. We shall use the term *entrepreneurial capacity* to describe the complex of such factors possessed by a firm. It is implicit in the construction of Figure 5.3 that the price of such factors is whatever is necessary to make the sum of segments like QP_1, P_1P_2, etc. exhaust QP. That is, if "total cost" is taken to include the return to such factors, our construction makes "total cost per unit of product" always equal to price.

The Formal Relation between the Supply Curve of the Individual Firm and its Contribution to the Industry's Output

Let us now turn our attention from the industry to the individual firm but waive, for the time being, the problem of defining either the *individual firm* or its *entrepreneurial capacity*. In Figure 5.4, curve S_1S_1, reproduced from Figure 5.2, shows the amount of X that firm 1 would provide at various prices of X, given the supply curves of the factors of production *to the industry* and given that the industry expands along its supply curve. As we have seen, at each point on S_1S_1 there is implicit some set of prices of the factors of production, say p_a, p_b, ... at point d; p'_a, p'_b, ..., at point d'.

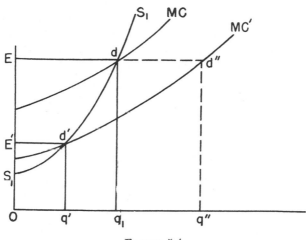

FIGURE 5.4

Suppose the price of X were OE', so that the individual firm is at point d' and is producing Oq'_1 of X. Under the conditions for which S_1S_1 is drawn, we know that if the price of X were OE, the individual firm would be at d instead of d'. The difference between d and d' can be viewed as a resultant of two kinds of forces: (1) the reaction of firm 1 to a higher price of X in light of technical and factor market conditions as the firm sees them when it is at d'; and (2) the reaction of firm 1 to the change in technical and factor market conditions as the firm sees them brought about by the reaction of all firms to the higher price of X.

To separate these two types of reactions, let us shift from the kind of quasi-supply curve given by S_1S_1 to a supply curve of firm 1 for X. That is, let us now suppose the conditions on the factor markets to firm 1 to be given and to be the same as at d' on S_1S_1. For simplicity let us suppose that firm 1 has no monopsonistic power over any factors whose amount it can vary, so that supply curves of such factors are horizontal at prices of p'_a, p'_b, . . . , the prices that implicitly correspond to d'.[1] Given these prices, there will be some optimum combination of factors for producing any given output, and some minimum marginal cost of producing any given output. If, for any given output, that marginal cost is less than the price, the firm has an incentive to expand output, and conversely. Accordingly, the marginal cost curve for the given prices of factors will be the firm's supply curve for X, given that the firm stays in business.

We know that at the specified prices for the factors of production and a price of OE' for the product, the firm produces Oq'_1. Accordingly, the marginal cost curve corresponding to p'_a, p'_b, . . . will pass through d'; it is represented on Figure 5.4 as MC'. This curve is drawn sloping upward because we are dealing with a competitive industry. If the curve sloped down, production at a rate at which price was equal to marginal cost would involve losses. The firm would either close down or expand to take advantage of lower marginal costs. Such "internal economies" would thus mean the absence of any limit to size. Accordingly, we assume "internal diseconomies." These can be rationalized in the long-run by the fixed entrepreneurial capacity of the firm and in the short-run by this and other factors whose amount cannot be varied.

EXTERNAL DISECONOMIES AFFECTING MARGINAL COST CURVES

If the price of X were taken as OE rather than OE' solely to firm 1, but as OE' for all other firms, curve MC' would tell the whole story. If the supply curves of factors to the industry were upward-sloping, firm 1 would tend to bid up a trifle the prices of factors of production by producing Oq''_1 rather than Oq'_1. This would affect all firms in the industry, firm 1 included, raising their cost curves a trifle and thereby leading each of the other firms to reduce output a trifle. These changes will be negligible to each individual firm if there are supposed to be many firms, but the aggregate effect on the employment of factors by all firms is of the same order of magnitude as the increased employment of factors by firm 1. In consequence, the increase in price of factors due to expansion by firm 1 is even less than might at first appear, being moderated by the release of resources by other firms, and the increase in output of the industry is less than $q'_1 q''_1$, the increase in output of firm 1. Firm 1 has imposed, as it were, "external pecuniary diseconomies" on all other firms in the industry and on itself, but to an amount that is negligible to each firm separately.

Now let us suppose the price of X to be OE rather than OE' for all firms in the industry. All firms now try, as it were, to proceed along their MC'

1. The qualification "over any factors whose amount it can vary" is included to permit the existence of "fixed factors," including in particular entrepreneurial capacity, and so to permit the same construction to cover short-run and long-run problems.

curves. If we retain the assumption of positively-sloped supply curves of factors to the industry, insofar as any firm succeeds in expanding output it imposes "external pecuniary diseconomies" on every other firm. (For some firms, proceeding along the MC' curve may mean producing instead of not producing, so we are implicitly allowing for the entry of new firms.) For the reasons just given, the "external pecuniary diseconomy" imposed by each firm alone on itself or any other firm is negligible; but the sum of a large number of negligible items need not be negligible. The cumulative effect of expansion by all firms is therefore to change the conditions faced by each firm in the factor market. This means that MC' is no longer the relevant marginal cost curve of firm 1 or the relevant supply curve of firm 1. The ultimate result will be to change (presumably, mostly to raise) the prices of factors from p_a', p_b', . . . to p_a, p_b, ... At these prices of factors, the marginal cost curve of firm 1 will be, let us say, MC. This must pass through d, since we know by construction of S_1S_1 that if factor prices are p_a, p_b, . . . and product price OE, firm 1 will produce Oq_1. The simultaneous attempt by all firms to move along their MC' curves, as it were, prevents any firm from doing so and forces all to move instead along curves like S_1S_1.

To put this point in another way, the attempt by each firm to expand output is equivalent to an increased demand for factors of production. But if factor supply curves to the industry slope positively, all firms together cannot get an increased quantity of factors of production at an unchanged price. Simultaneous movement along the MC' curve is therefore inconsistent with the assumed conditions of supply of factors of production.

We have now broken the total movement from d' to d into two parts: (1) the (hypothetical) movement from d' to d", which reflects the reaction of the individual firm to a rise in price of the product under unchanged conditions in the factor market as the firm sees them; and (2) the (hypothetical) movement from d" to d, which reflects the reaction of the individual firm to changed conditions in the factor market.

We have so far attributed the change in the firm's marginal cost curve entirely to external pecuniary diseconomies. It is possible that the simultaneous expansion of all firms in the industry might also impose external technical diseconomies; i.e., it might change the production function of the individual firm in such a way as to raise the cost curve. To give a trivial example that will illustrate what is involved, suppose firms in this industry were all in the same neighborhood; that an expansion of output by any firm involved an increased outpouring of smoke; and that this imposed extra cleaning costs on this and other firms. The extra cleaning costs would be neglible for each firm if any one firm expanded, but might be considerable if all firms did. In this case, without any change in the prices of factors of production, the marginal cost curve of the individual firm would shift upward as the industry expanded output.

It should be noted that the prices of or returns to any factors whose quantity the firm cannot vary, including what we have termed *entrepreneurial capacity,* do not explicitly enter into the above adjustment process; the only condition on them is that they not be negative in the aggregate.

In general, it may be expected that, as in Figure 5.4, external diseconomies will inhibit but not prevent expansion of output by the individual firm. However, this need not be the case for all ranges of prices for all firms. External diseconomies might be sufficient to eliminate any expansion in output, as in Figure 5.5(a), or indeed to produce a decline in output, as in Figure 5.5(b). Of course, the situations depicted in these figures could not be valid for the same range of prices for all firms in the industry, since that would contradict the positively sloping supply curve for the industry drawn in Figure 5.2. Put differently, it would be inconsistent with the expansion in the output of the industry that is required to produce the external diseconomies that raise the marginal cost curves. But there is no reason why some firms should not behave in the manner suggested by these figures. The change in factor prices and in technical conditions associated with the change in the price of the product from OE′ to OE need not be uniform for all factors or all firms. Factors whose supply is relatively inelastic will tend to rise more in price than factors whose supply is relatively elastic; and some firms may find their technical conditions affected more seriously than other firms. Firms whose entrepreneurial capacity happens to require relatively large use of factors that have risen much in price will find that their cost curves have risen relatively more than the cost curves of other firms and, in consequence, may curtail output or go out of business. The same is true for firms whose technical conditions have deteriorated the most.

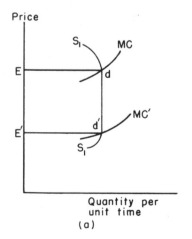

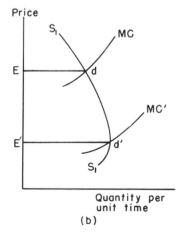

FIGURE 5.5

No external effects on marginal cost curves

We have so far been concentrating largely on those factors whose amount the individual firm is to be regarded as capable of varying for the problem at hand (call these the *variable factors*). Now it may be that the supply curves to the industry of these factors can be taken as horizontal. This may be so for precisely the same reasons as are adduced for regarding the supply curve of a factor to an individual firm as horizontal. That is, this industry may be only one of many using the factor; as this industry expands, it bids the price of the factor up a trifle; this affects, however, not only firms in this industry, but firms in all other industries using the factor as well. These changes are negligible to each individual firm in each industry but not in the aggregate. In short, this industry by its expansion imposes external diseconomies on itself and on other industries as well, and our preceding analysis of this case for firms in a single industry can be applied directly to the group of industries in question. For the industry as a whole, there is another reason why it might be appropriate to regard the supply curves of the variable factors to the industry as horizontal. It may be that the change in demand with which the entire analysis begins is to be regarded as associated with an opposite change in demand elsewhere: e.g., an increase in demand here is to be regarded as a shift of demand from elsewhere. In this case, the decline in demand elsewhere releases resources that are now available here. If the industry experiencing the decline in demand uses much the same resources as the industry experiencing the increase in demand, there is no reason why the latter industry need pay higher prices to get the use of the released resources.[2]

When, for either of these reasons, the supply curves of factors to the industry can be regarded as horizontal, expansion by an individual firm imposes no appreciable external pecuniary diseconomies on the other firms in the industry, taken as a group. If in addition, such expansion does not affect the technical conditions of other firms, there is no reason for the marginal cost curves to change. In this case, the firm's marginal cost curve will coincide with what we have been calling its quasi-supply curve, as in Figure 5.6, and the aggregate supply curve for the industry is then simply the sum of the marginal cost curves of the individual firms.

If the supply curves of all individual firms slope positively, as in Figure 5.6(a), then the aggregate supply curve will also slope positively. In this case, the return to the complex of factors we are treating as fixed to the individual firm will increase as the demand curve for the industry's product rises. This is indicated in Figure 5.6 by the difference between the triangle E′d′h and the triangle Edh (for firms that "enter" the industry in

2. This discussion raises problems about the meaning of the supply curve of a factor that we shall waive here.

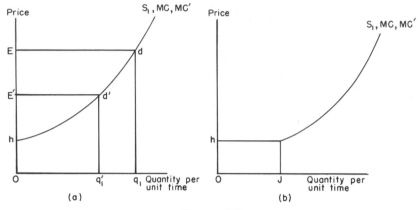

FIGURE 5.6

response to a rise in price from OE′ to OE, the return increases from zero to a positive amount). This increase in return can be regarded as arising from factors over which the individual firm has no control, namely (1) the rise in the demand for the product it produces and (2) the limited amounts of the product other firms are willing to supply at various prices. In consequence, one can regard this increase in return as "external" to the individual firm—as an external diseconomy not affecting marginal cost curves. From the point of view of the industry, one can regard the existence of a rising supply curve as reflecting the inelasticity of supply of entrepreneurial capacity and other factors, the amount of which the individual firm is not free to vary.

Over some range of output and for some firms, the marginal cost curves might, of course, be horizontal, as in Figure 5.6(b).[3] In this case, the firm would be willing to produce any amount not greater than OJ at a price of Oh, nothing at a price less than Oh. For the corresponding price, the supply curve for the industry will have a horizontal segment, albeit so short a one as to be negligible in terms of the units of quantity relevant to the industry. It might also be, of course, that many firms would have such a segment at precisely the same price, Oh. In that case, the supply curve for the industry would be horizontal at the price Oh up to the maximum quantity that such firms would provide at that price. This is the case of "constant costs" or perfectly elastic supply. It can be described as the case in which the supply curves of all factors, including those of which the maximum amount available to the firm is fixed, are perfectly elastic to the industry, or in which there are no "specialized factors." It is obviously most likely to be relevant in "the long run."

3. We are here neglecting discontinuities.

EXTERNAL ECONOMIES AFFECTING MARGINAL COST CURVES

The case of "external economies" is clearly the converse of the case of "external diseconomies" and hence can be dealt with briefly.

Expansion by the individual firm might confer external economies on other firms that tended to lower their cost curves: "external pecuniary economies" if the expansion in the purchases of factors lowered their prices; "external technical economies" if the expansion in the output of a firm somehow affected favorably the technical conditions faced by other firms. If these effects are more important than external diseconomies affecting marginal costs, we may say that there are "net external economies affecting marginal cost curves." The consequent decline in the marginal cost curves may be consistent with a positively sloped quasi-supply curve of the individual firm as in Figures 5.7(a) and (b); with a horizontal "quasi-

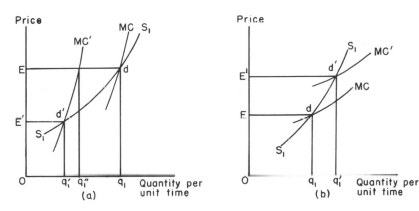

FIGURE 5.7

supply curve" as in Figure 5.8; or with a negatively sloped "quasi-supply curve" as in Figures 5.9(a) and (b).

Though in both Figures 5.7(a) and (b) the quasi-supply curves for the individual firm are positively sloped, the cases illustrated by these two figures are very different. Figure 5.7(a) implies a positively sloped supply curve for the industry, since the price associated with the increased demand (OE) is higher than the price associated with the initial demand (OE'). Every firm in the industry could be in the position illustrated by Figure 5.7(a). Figure 5.7(b), on the other hand, implies a negatively sloped supply curve for the industry, since the price associated with the increased demand (OE) is lower than the price associated with the initial demand (OE'). Firms in the position illustrated by Figure 5.7(b) must therefore be "exceptional," else whence comes the increased output that produces the economies lowering the cost curves?

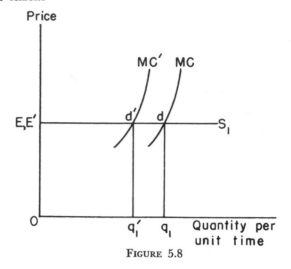

FIGURE 5.8

Figure 5.8 implies a horizontal supply curve for the industry. Figures 5.9(a) and (b), like Figure 5.7(b), assume a negatively sloped supply curve for the industry.

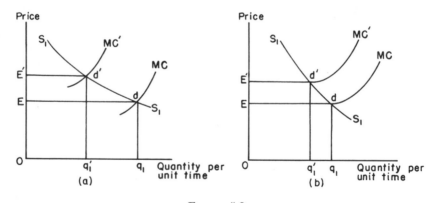

FIGURE 5.9

In Figures 5.7(a) and 5.8, the returns to the factors regarded as fixed to the individual firm increase, so one might say that the net external economies affecting marginal cost curves are more than offset, Figure 5.7(a), or exactly offset, Figure 5.8, by external diseconomies not affecting marginal cost curves. Figures 5.7(b) and 5.9(a) are consistent with either an increase, no change, or a decrease in the returns to the fixed factors, depending on the precise shapes of the curves; Figure 5.9(b) implies no change.

It should be noted that when there are net external economies or diseconomies affecting marginal cost curves, the quasi-supply curve of the individual firm for the product bears an especially intimate relation to the

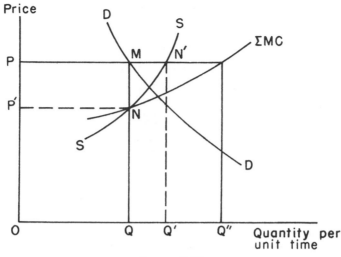

FIGURE 5.10

supply curve of the industry. The quasi-supply curve of the individual firm is valid only if the output is precisely that given by the industry supply curve. Figure 5.10 illustrates this point. Suppose the demand and supply curves for the industry are as shown in that figure, that the supply curve (SS) reflects external diseconomies affecting marginal cost curves, and that there is a legally imposed, and effectively enforced, *minimum* price of OP. At this price, OQ is the maximum quantity that can be sold. Suppose this quantity is sold, so that point M corresponds to the actual situation in the market. Suppliers would have been willing to provide this output at a price as low as OP', i.e., they would have been willing to operate at point N. Given that the industry is producing an output OQ, conditions in the factor market will be roughly the same as if suppliers were operating at point N: the quantities of various factor hired will be roughly the same, and in consequence their prices will be roughly the same.[4]

Accordingly, individual firms will be operating on the marginal cost curves and supply curves corresponding to point N, not on those corresponding to point N'. Suppose we add these marginal cost curves horizontally to get the curve designated as ΣMC on Figure 5.10. This curve now shows the sum of what individual firms "think" they would like to produce at various prices *given that the output of the industry is OQ*; it is, as it were, a "virtual" or "shadow" supply curve for the industry, the points on which, other than point N, could never be realized. Nonetheless, it has real

---

4. The qualification "roughly" is required because the distribution of the output among the individual firms may not be the same; it will depend on the arrangements whereby the quantity OQ is "rationed" among suppliers eager to produce a larger quantity.

significance, since it shows the pressure on the market at nonequilibrium prices. That is, from the market demand and supply curves, it would appear that maintenance of a minimum price of OP would require rationing production "quotas," as it were, aggregating OQ among producers desirous of producing OQ′, so that QQ′ measures the "excess supply" or "excess capacity" with which the "rationing authority" would have to contend. In fact, however, the "excess supply" with which the "rationing authority" would have to contend is not QQ′ but QQ″. This point is of more than academic interest. It explains why attempts to "rig" or "peg" prices frequently are subjected to considerably greater pressure than was anticipated, and why the abandonment of such attempts frequently produces less of a change in actual output than the pressure against them would lead one to expect. (One example is the allocation of crop quotas under one or another of our agricultural programs.)

Figure 5.11 illustrates the same point for the case in which external economies affecting marginal cost curves are sufficiently important to yield a negatively sloping supply curve to the industry. Let SS be this supply curve, DD the demand curve, and OP the minimum price legally enforced. Since at this price the amount demanded, as shown by the demand curve (OQ), is greater than the amount supplied, as shown by the supply curve (OQ′), it might appear that there is no problem of rationing the amount demanded among suppliers eager to produce a larger amount at the legal price. This is, however, false, as can be seen by supposing, tentatively, that only OQ′ is produced. In this case, the price would not be OP but OP″, since the eager demanders would bid up the price. But, if output of the industry is OQ′, the individual firms will be trying to adjust in the light of the marginal cost curves that correspond to the technical conditions and conditions on the factors markets associated with point N′ on SS. To each separately, this marginal cost curve rises, and so the sum of these marginal cost curves (ΣMC′) will rise. Accordingly, if the industry's output were OQ′ and market price were OP″, individual firms would try to produce more than OQ′. The sum of what they individually think they want to produce under these conditions would be P″R′ or RR′ in excess of the amount demanded—and ΣMC′ is the "virtual" or "shadow" supply curve. The attempts of individual firms to expand output to P″R′ would have two effects: the actual expansion in output would (1) lower price because of conditions of demand and (2) change the technical conditions and conditions on the factor market in such a fashion as to shift the marginal cost curves to the right. When price had fallen to the legal minimum, OP, output would be OQ. But at this output, technical conditions and conditions on the factor markets are those associated with point N on the supply curve, and the "shadow" supply curve would be ΣMC. Accordingly, individual firms "think" they would like to produce an output of OQ″, and there remains the problem of "rationing" an output of OQ among suppliers eager to produce OQ″. The market point would be M, on the de-

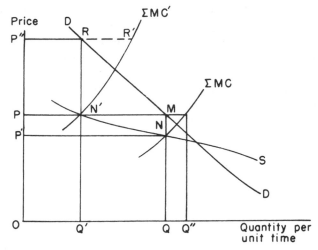

FIGURE 5.11

mand curve, and there would remain downward pressure on the minimum price.

This analysis illustrates how it is that whereas to each individual producer separately, his supply curve shows the *maximum* amount he would be willing to produce at the specified price, a negatively sloping curve for an industry produced by external economies shows the *minimum* quantity that would be supplied at each price.

This point is at once so important and so puzzling that it may be worth illustrating it for yet another case. In Figure 5.12, let OP be a legal maximum price. What will be the actual point achieved in the market so long as we suppose the supply curve to be sloped negatively everywhere? The answer is an output of zero, i.e., the point P. It is clear that no output

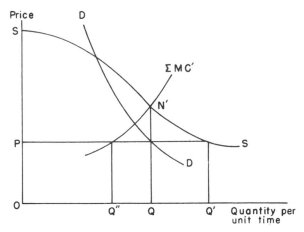

FIGURE 5.12

greater than OQ would be possible at the price OP since it could not be sold. But if, tentatively, OQ is supposed to be the output, the relevant marginal cost curves are those associated with point N' on SS, the sum of which is given by the curve labelled $\Sigma MC'$. But if suppliers were to try to adjust their output in the light of these marginal cost curves, they would try to produce OQ'' at a price of OP, or less than OQ. As they tried to do so, cost curves would rise and their desired output would fall. There is no end to this process short of an output of zero, so long as we insist on supposing the supply curve negatively inclined throughout. Of course, if, as might well happen, the supply curve had a positively sloping segment (as in Figure 5.13), the final solution would be at an output of OQ''.

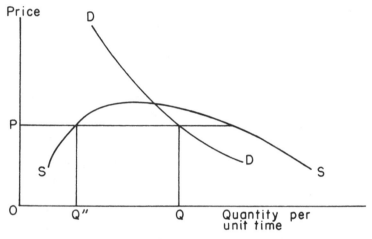

FIGURE 5.13

One way of combining this and the preceding example is to show on the figure not only the supply and demand curves but also the area of attainable points, as in Figure 5.14. The area indicated by vertical shading is attainable so far as conditions of supply alone are concerned; the area indicated by horizontal shading is attainable so far as conditions of demand alone are concerned; only points in the cross-hatched area (adc) are consistent with conditions of both supply and demand. The price corresponding to d (OP) is thus the lowest price consistent with this industry.[5]

5. It may be worth noting that this analysis in terms of "attainable areas" resolves in a satisfactory way the question of stable versus unstable equilibrium positions, which has been much discussed in the literature in terms of an alleged conflict between the "Walras" and "Marshall" conditions. It turns out that what determines the stability of equilibrium is not whether the market process is arbitrarily supposed to proceed alternatively by holding prices constant or quantities constant, but whether a negatively sloped supply curve is "backward bending" or "forward falling." If it is "backward bending," stability requires that the supply curve cut the demand curve from above; if it is "forward falling," from below, as in Figure 5.14.

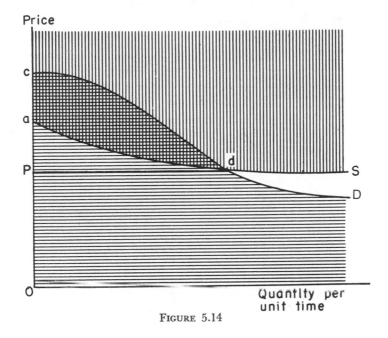

FIGURE 5.14

The Firm

So far we have taken the notion of a *firm* for granted. This notion is surrounded by difficulties, and a thoroughly satisfactory definition of a firm or a thoroughly satisfactory theory explaining the determinants of the number or structure of firms does not exist. Fortunately, many of these difficulties are not relevant for the present purpose, so we can beg the really troublesome questions. But somewhat more discussion of the meaning of the *firm* is desirable.

Let us think of all resources (factors of production) as owned by individuals. Let us suppose further that the individual can derive income from any resources that he owns in only one of two ways: (1) He can enter into a contractual arrangement with some other individual whereby the latter agrees to pay a fixed sum per unit for the use of that resource—i.e., he can "rent" the use of the resource to someone else. (2) He can use that resource alone or in cooperation with other "hired" resources to produce a product and receive his income as the difference between the amount he receives from the sale of products and the amount he pays the resources he "hires" —i.e., he can be a residual income recipient.[6] Each residual income re-

6. In fact, of course, resources are owned by legal entities such as "corporations" and not only by "natural" individuals; and incomes can be derived in a variety of ways involving any mixture of the two listed above. The price per unit of resource may be

Continued on page 104

cipient, together with the factors he hires to produce a product, then constitutes a firm, separated from other firms by the product produced and the nature of the contractual arrangements binding together the bundle of resources he "controls" either through ownership or through the contractual arrangements he has entered into with their owners.

In deciding how to use the resources he owns, each individual must be supposed to compare the expected returns (both pecuniary and nonpecuniary) from renting out his resources with the expected returns (again both pecuniary and nonpecuniary) from using them himself, and to select the method that yields the largest expected returns. It is here that the really troublesome questions we are begging arise. Why should the expected residual income differ from the expected contractual income? Why should it differ for some owners of resources in one direction and for others in the opposite direction? What factors are most important in explaining such differences?

For our purposes, it is enough to say that such differences between expected residual income and expected contractual income will arise, not only as temporary differences arising from market imperfections or momentary disequilibrium, but also as permanent differences consistent with "stable" equilibrium. We must suppose that expected residual income will exceed expected contractual income for some individuals and conversely for others, and that changes in factor and product prices will affect such differences and so lead to changes in the number of firms.

It seems both possible and desirable to suppose that "hired" resources (or their services) can be defined in physical terms in such a way that different units of what is called "a factor of production" can be regarded as perfect substitutes in production regardless of who owns them or of the quantity of that or other factors employed, whereas units of "different" resources cannot be regarded as uniformly perfect substitutes in production.

Our emphasis on the possible divergence between the expected residual income and expected contractual income of an owner of resources means that we cannot specify completely the resources owned by an individual simply by listing the number of units of each type of resource he owns, when the units are calculated as if the resources were all rented out to others. If this were a complete specification, it would deny the possibility of a permanent divergence between expected residual income and expected contractual income; it would be a matter of indifference whether the resources were "hired" or used by "firms" and we should be throwing

---

linked to a price index of the product produced or of products in general; there may be bonuses depending on gross or net receipts; two or many owners of resources may form a partnership and share residual income; and so on *ad infinitum*. But I believe that no essential generality is lost, while much is gained in simplicity of exposition, by restricting discussion to the "pure" types above.

out the feature we introduced to explain the existence and formation of "firms."

There is therefore implicit in the view we are adopting the notion that each individual can, as a formal matter, be regarded as owning two types of resources: (1) His resources viewed exclusively as "hired" resources—what his resources would be if he were not to form his own firm. These resources can be viewed in physical terms and can be combined with similar resources owned by others to give supply curves of all resources viewed solely in terms of their productivity if used as hired resources. If an individual does decide to be a residual income recipient, he must be viewed as hiring these resources from himself, and he must consider their market price as a cost identical in kind with the cost of other hired resources.[7] (2) A resource that reflects the difference between the productivity of his resources viewed solely as hired resources and their productivity when owned by his firm—we may call this *Mr. X's entrepreneurial capacity* or some similar term. This resource is specific to each individual; by definition, it has no value to any other firm. Whether it is used or not will depend on the price of the final product and the prices of hired resources or on the demand for the final product and the supply curve of hired resources, if the product and factor market are not competitive. For some sets of prices it will be supplied in its entirety; for other sets of prices, not at all. For this kind of factor, then, *given conditions of supply* means a statement of the economic characteristics of the firms—or of the "entrepreneurial capacities" of the founders of the firms—that would be formed under all possible sets of prices.

It should be emphasized that this distinction between the two types of resources is purely formal. Giving names to our ignorance may be useful; it does not dispel the ignorance. A really satisfactory theory would do more than say there must be something other than hired resources; it would say what the essential characteristics of the "something other" are.

Under our assumptions, the entrepreneurial capacity available to a firm is limited to that owned by the individual who decides to become a residual income recipient. Insofar as the "quantity" of entrepreneurial capacity can be compared between firms, it may differ from firm to firm. For any one firm, however, the quantity it owns sets a maximum to the quantity it can use. This introduces a limitation on a factor or an "indivisibility," sufficient to explain why there are limits to the size of individual firms. And it is, of course, precisely because we want to rationalize observed phe-

---

7. The resources he owns may, however, differ from others in that he may have to use all of his own resources in his own firm if he uses any (e.g., it may not be feasible for him to divide his labor power between his firm and other firms.) This difference need not, however, arise. It may be perfectly feasible for him to divide his resources in any fashion between his own firm and use as "hired" resources by other firms. We shall suppose this in general to be the case in order to avoid certain discontinuities that might otherwise occur.

nomena that suggest that the size of firms is not capricious or arbitrary or irrelevant that we have introduced this unknown something, which we have christened *entrepreneurial capacity*.

The Formal Economic Specification of "Entrepreneurial Capacity"

For simplicity, let us suppose that there are no nonpecuniary factors entering into an individual's decision whether to form his own firm or to rent out all the resources he owns.[8] For simplicity, also, let us suppose that the individual's entrepreneurial capacity, if used at all, will be used in the industry under discussion, so that we can beg the choice of what product to produce.[9]

The individual's entrepreneurial capacity can then be specified by a production function, showing the maximum quantity of product *he* is capable of producing under given conditions with given quantities of "hired" resources (including any he "hires" from himself). Thus if x_i represents the quantity of product produced by individual i, and a, b, c, . . . the quantities of various factors he uses, we can conceive of $x_i = f_i (a, b, c, . . .)$ as the production function attached to the individual. This production function will not in general be homogeneous of the first degree in a, b, c, . . . for all values of a, b, c, . . . since it does not contain all the variables that affect output but only those that the individual entrepreneur can control. In particular, entrepreneurial capacity is supposed to be not greater than the amount he owns, and there may be additional variables he cannot control (e.g., distance between cities for railroads, etc.). Indeed, if the production function were homogeneous of the first degree in a, b, c, . . . , this would imply that entrepreneurial capacity is not important in this instance and that there is no limit to the size of the firm.

It is conceivable that the production function could be identical for two individuals; i.e., that, say, $f_i (a,b,c, . . .) - f_j (a,b,c, . . .) = 0$ for all a, b, c, ... In this case these two individuals would have identical entrepreneurial capacity. If this were true for an indefinitely large number of individuals, it would be equivalent to a supply curve of entrepreneurial capacity that was perfectly elastic at a price, given our assumptions, of zero (since we have

8. This involves no essential loss of generality. Nonpecuniary returns can be handled by including a money equivalent in the costs the firm charges itself for the resources it owns or by regarding the firm as producing two products, the product marketed and the nonpecuniary advantages or disadvantages of entrepreneurship.

9. This too involves no essential loss of generality. For given conditions in other industries he might consider entering, the highest possible return to each individual from entering one of those industries will be a single number which can be included along with his other costs. This is precisely analogous to the effect on the supply curves of hired factors for this industry of alternative earning opportunities elsewhere and is one of the reasons for including item 2 in the list of "other things" above.

excluded nonpecuniary returns and use of entrepreneurial capacity in other industries). In equilibrium, the return to entrepreneurial capacity would be zero, yet so long as the production functions were not homogeneous of the first degree in a, b, c, . . . there would be a limit to the size of the firm. (Note that identity of production functions for different firms does not guarantee a horizontal supply curve for the industry; this requires in addition horizontal supply curves of a, b, c, ...)

If f_i (a,b,c, . . .) $>$ f_j(a,b,c, . . .) for all a, b, c, . . . , we can say unambiguously that individual i has greater entrepreneurial capacity than individual j. In general, however, there is no reason to expect such a relation to hold. For some sets of a, b, c, . . . , f_i will be greater than f_j; for some sets it will be less. If this is the case, there is no way of comparing unambiguously the entrepreneurial capacities of the two individuals.

External technical economies or diseconomies mean that one of the "given conditions" affecting the individual's production function is the output of the industry (or perhaps a collection of industries). This can be indicated formally by including the output of the industry, which we may designate by Q as a variable in the production function. The production function for individual i then becomes: $x_i = f_i(a, b, c, . . . , Q)$. There are external technical economies, no external technical economies or diseconomies, or external technical diseconomies for a particular set of values of a, b, c, . . . , Q, according as $\frac{\partial x_i}{\partial Q} \gtrless 0$.

The Economics of the Firm

UNAVOIDABLE ("FIXED") AND AVOIDABLE ("VARIABLE")
CONTRACTUAL COSTS, NONCONTRACTUAL COSTS ("PROFITS")

It is convenient to define *total costs* of a firm as equal to—or better, identical with—the firm's total receipts. Total costs then include all payments—which may be positive or negative, actual or imputed—to all factors of production, including the entrepreneurial capacity of the owner of the firm.

These total payments to factors of production can be divided, at least conceptually, into three parts:

(1) *Unavoidable contractual cost ("fixed" costs)*. There may be some minimum sum that the firm is committed to pay to factors of production no matter what it does and no matter how its actions turn out. Since this unavoidable contractual cost is not affected by the firm's actions and will have to be met no matter what the firm does, its magnitude cannot affect the firm's actions—"bygones are bygones," "sunk costs are sunk," etc. The costs under this heading are generally referred to as *fixed costs*. This term is convenient and we shall use it, though it may lead to confusion between

fixed costs and costs incurred on account of so-called fixed factors. As we shall see below, a so-called fixed factor may give rise to no fixed costs. Similarly, so-called variable factors may give rise to fixed costs.

(2) *Avoidable contractual costs ("variable" costs).* Another part of the firm's costs depend on what it does but not on how its actions turn out. The total payments to which the firm is committed once it has decided how much to produce and how to produce it we shall designate as *total contractual costs.* Under our assumptions, contractual costs include all payments to "hired factors" not owned by the firm plus imputed payments to factors owned by the firm equal to the amount that could be obtained for these factors by renting their use to other firms.[10] The excess of total contractual payments over the unavoidable costs we shall designate as *avoidable contractual costs.* The amount of such costs depends on the production decisions of the firm—decisions about how much to produce and how to produce that much—so such costs will play a crucial role in the firm's decisions. The costs under this heading are generally referred to as *variable costs.* This term is convenient and we shall use it, though it may lead to confusion between variable costs and costs incurred on account of so-called variable factors. As already noted, fixed factors may give rise to variable costs, and variable factors to fixed costs.

The distinction between fixed and variable costs will also depend on the range of choice considered open to the firm. For example, there may be some costs that can be avoided by going out of business but that cannot be avoided so long as the firm produces any output at all. Such costs will be variable costs if the range of choices includes the alternative of going out of business; otherwise they will be fixed costs.

(3) *Noncontractual costs ("profits").* Finally, there are payments whose amount depends on the actual receipts of the firm; these we shall call *noncontractual costs.* Their amount is equal to the difference between total receipts and total contractual costs and, under our assumptions, are received by the owner of the entrepreneurial capacity. These payments are generally designated as *profits.* This term is, however, somewhat misleading. The actual noncontractual costs can never be determined in advance. They can be known only after the event and may be affected by all sorts of random or accidental occurrences, mistakes on the part of the firm, and so on. It is therefore important to distinguish between actual noncontractual costs and expected noncontractual costs. The difference between actual and expected noncontractual costs constitutes *profits* or *pure profits*—an unanticipated residual arising from uncertainty. Expected noncontractual costs, on the other hand, are to be regarded as a *rent* or *quasi-rent* to entrepreneurial capacity. They are to be regarded as the motivating force be-

---

10. These factors owned by the firm are included in the supply curves of factors described below, along with identical factors owned by others.

hind the firm's decisions.[11] At any given output, the firm is regarded as seeking to minimize contractual costs in order to maximize noncontractual costs for that output; and it is regarded as choosing the output that yields the largest expected noncontractual costs.

Expected noncontractual costs may, of course, be negative. That is, expected total receipts may be less than total contractual costs. But, by definition, the firm need never accept negative, expected noncontractual costs that are larger in absolute value than fixed costs, since it can, at worst, decide to have zero variable costs and since its receipts cannot be negative. Accordingly, no set of production decisions can be regarded as optimum for the firm unless the algebraic sum of fixed costs and expected noncontractual costs is zero or greater. This is, of course, a necessary but not a sufficient condition for an optimum.

We can summarize by saying that the firm is to be regarded as seeking to maximize the difference between expected receipts and variable costs. Since, by definition, there is some production decision for which variable costs are zero, there will always be some decision for which this difference is not negative. The conditions determining expected receipts are to be analyzed in connection with the demand for the firm's output. The conditions determining variable costs are to be analyzed in terms of cost curves. It follows that in drawing cost curves we need consider solely variable costs.

SUPPLY CURVES OF FACTORS—THE LENGTH OF THE "RUN"

For simplicity, we may suppose that the supply curves of factors to the firm are either perfectly elastic everywhere, as in Figure 5.15(a), or perfectly elastic for one segment and perfectly inelastic thereafter, as in Figure 5.15(b).

Factors with supply curves like that in Figure 5.15(a) are ordinarily called *variable factors;* those with supply curves like that in Figure 5.15(b), *fixed factors.* These names are somewhat misleading. It may be perfectly feasible to vary the physical amount of a so-called fixed factor employed. The important point is that there is a maximum amount—OM in Figure 5.15(b)—that can be considered available for the set of adjustments in question. If the maximum reflects technical factors—for example, the fact that given kinds of machines have been built and must be used in that form for the adjustments in question—the horizontal segment of the supply curve will generally coincide with the horizontal axis. But even in this case, it may be possible to leave some of the machines idle and use the others. And even if this is impossible, because, let us say, there is a single machine, it may be possible to "vary" its use by using none of it at all. If

11. More precisely, expected utility corresponding to the probability distribution of noncontractual costs is what the firm is to be regarded as maximizing.

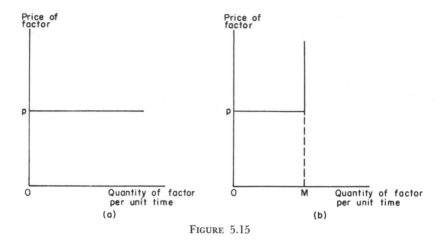

FIGURE 5.15

the maximum reflects contractual arrangements—say long-term contracts with a class of workers—the same technical possibilities are likely to be available. Whether, in that case, the horizontal segment coincides with the horizontal axis depends on the terms of the contracts; they may provide that the payment be higher if the factor is used than if it is not (e.g., an exclusive contract with a legal firm for legal services, involving an annual retainer plus a fee per unit of services rendered). Furthermore, for some problems, only the horizontal section of the supply curve in Figure 5.15(b) may be relevant, in which case the supply curve can be treated as if it were everywhere horizontal.

As already noted, costs incurred on account of fixed factors do not necessarily correspond with fixed costs, and costs incurred on account of variable factors do not necessarily correspond with variable costs. If the firm need pay nothing to the owner of a fixed factor if it uses none of it, all the payments for such a factor are to be included in variable costs. Or again, a fixed factor may be a factory building owned by the firm. If the firm were to give up completely the use of the building (which might require that it go out of business) it could sell the building, but otherwise it might be able to receive no return outside its own business from it. In this case, the annual or other time-unit equivalent of the sales price would be a variable cost incurred on account of the building. Similarly, the firm may be committed to paying a fixed sum to the owner of a variable factor whether or not it uses any of that factor. Such a sum would be included in fixed costs.

The distinction between fixed and variable costs will coincide with the distinction between fixed and variable factors if (1) total payments to every variable factor equal the ordinate of its supply curve times the associated quantity (Op times the quantity of the factor employed, in Figure 5.15(a)); (2) the horizontal sector of the supply curve of a fixed factor coincides with

the horizontal axis (Op = 0, in Figure 5.15(b)); (3) the contractual payment to a fixed factor is not changed by dispensing with its use entirely.

Our production functions do not include entrepreneurial capacity explicitly as a factor of production; it has, rather, been regarded as determining the form of the function. Yet we can assimilate it with other factors of
production by supposing its supply curve to each firm to be like that in
Figure 5.15(b), with OM equal to one unit, and the horizontal segment
coincident with the horizontal axis. But in proceeding in this way, we must
remember that the entrepreneurial capacity of each firm is a separate
factor of production, to be distinguished from the entrepreneurial capacity of every other firm.

As a formal matter, we shall distinguish among "runs" by the character
of the supply curves of the factors. In the shortest of short runs, all supply
curves will have an inelastic segment as in Figure 5.15(b): all factors are
fixed. In the longest of long runs, all supply curves will be as in Figure
5.15(a): all factors are variable. This longest of long runs, it should be
noted, implies that only the horizontal segment of the supply curve of entrepreneurial capacity is relevant and thus implies that there are an indefinitely large number of potential firms with identical production functions. Intermediate lengths of run involve some supply curves like that in
Figure 5.15(a), some like that in Figure 5.15(b). Of course, which factors
are to be placed in which category is to be determined by the problem in
hand.

CONDITIONS FOR A MINIMUM COST FOR A GIVEN OUTPUT

If a firm were to produce a specified output, there would be some combination of factors that would minimize the cost of producing that output.
As is well known, the conditions for minimizing the cost are given by the
equations

(1) $$\frac{\mathrm{MPP_a}}{\mathrm{MFC_a}} = \frac{\mathrm{MPP_b}}{\mathrm{MFC_b}} = \ldots$$
$$x_o = f_i (a, b, \ldots)$$

where $\mathrm{MPP_a}$ stands for the marginal physical product of factor A, i.e.,
$\mathrm{MPP_a} = \frac{\partial f_i}{\partial a}$, and similarly for $\mathrm{MPP_b} \ldots$; $\mathrm{MFC_a}$ stands for the marginal
factor cost of A, and similarly for $\mathrm{MFC_b} \ldots$; x_o is the specified output to
be produced; and $f_i (a, b, \ldots)$ is the firm's production function.

The conditions (1) are valid no matter what may be the shape of the
supply curves of factors of production, but for simplicity we shall continue
to restrict ourselves to supply curves of factors having the limiting forms
shown in Figures 5.15(a) and (b).

If the supply curve of a factor is taken to be perfectly elastic, like that in

Figure 5.15(a), marginal factor cost is equal to price (Op) so long as any of the factor is employed, and the price of the factor can be substituted for marginal factor cost in the relevant ratio in equations (1).[12]

If the supply curve is taken to be perfectly inelastic after some point, like that in Figure 5.15(b), the marginal factor cost is anything above Op for a quantity equal to OM, Op for a quantity between zero and OM.[13] In determining from equations (1) the optimum combination of factors to use in producing a given output, the ratio for such a factor (say factor D) can then be neglected in solving equations (1), provided that the solution obtained yields a common value of the ratios equal to or less than $\dfrac{MPP_d}{Op}$ (d = OM). The marginal factor cost can then be set equal to whatever number is required to make that ratio equal to the others, and a quantity OM of the factor used. If the common ratio is greater than $\dfrac{MPP_d}{Op}$ (d = OM), this is not the solution. MFC_d should then be replaced by Op in equations (1) and the new equations solved. This will involve the use of less than OM of factor D.[14] When Op is equal to zero, this second possibility will arise when the marginal physical product of OM of D is negative; the quantity of D employed will then be whatever quantity makes its marginal physical product equal to zero.

TOTAL, MARGINAL, AND AVERAGE VARIABLE COST CURVES

For each possible output, we may conceive of the firm deciding how to produce that output by solving equations (1). Corresponding to such a de-

12. The qualification "so long as any of the factor is employed" is required because there may be no single factor cost at a zero quantity. Two main cases can be distinguished: (1) The usual case, in which, as the quantity of the factor purchased approaches zero, the payment to the factor approaches the payment when none of the factor is employed. In this case, marginal factor cost at zero can be taken as given by the part of the vertical axis below p in Figure 5.15(a), i.e., as being between zero and Op. (2) The case in which, as the quantity of the factor purchased approaches zero, the payment to the factor does not approach the payment when none of the factor is employed—e.g., electricity may be purchased under terms involving a fixed fee per month plus a fixed fee per kilowatt hour; the payment thus approaches the fixed fee per month as the quantity purchased approaches zero, whereas the payment would be zero if electricity were eliminated entirely. In this case, marginal factor cost at zero can be taken as given by the part of the vertical axis above p in Figure 5.15(a), i.e., as being between Op and infinity.

13. The preceding footnote applies at zero.

14. This statement glides over a number of complications. (1) If the fixity of the factor is technical, it may not be possible to use less than OM of D. In this case, the marginal physical product of D will be indeterminate at OM and the solution must be either zero or OM of D. (2) There may be multiple solutions of equations (1), one with quantities of each of the factors greater than zero, the others with a zero quantity of one or more of the factors whose conditions of supply correspond to case 2 of the preceding two footnotes. The one of these solutions that would then be chosen is that involving the lowest total cost.

cision there is some total variable cost—a sum equal to the difference between contractual costs at that output and the minimum contractual costs
corresponding to any decision by the firm. We can plot total variable cost
as a function of output. This curve may take any of a wide variety of
shapes depending on the precise conditions of supply of factors of production and the precise form of the firm's production function. A number of
the possibilities are depicted in Figures 5.16(a) and (b) to bring out the
factors responsible for the shape of the total variable cost curve.

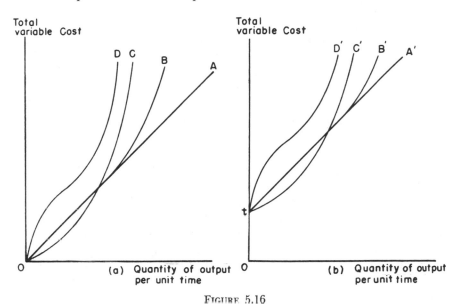

FIGURE 5.16

In Figure 5.16(a), all of the curves have the property that they pass
through the origin; i.e., total variable costs approach zero as output approaches zero. This means that there are no costs that can be avoided only
by going out of business. Curve A shows cost increasing at a constant rate
—twice the output involves twice the cost, etc. This is the curve that might
be expected if all hired factors were variable and the firm's production
function was homogeneous of the first degree so that entrepreneurial capacity was unimportant.

Curve B is identical with A at first but then shows costs increasing more
rapidly than output. This could arise from the existence of one or more
fixed factors, including entrepreneurial capacity, and the absence of any
indivisibilities. For low outputs, the optimum combination of factors
would require less than the maximum amount of the fixed factors, that is,
the firm would be operating on the horizontal sectors of all factor supply
curves. Increased output would be obtained by increasing the use of all

factors proportionately. This would be impossible once the maximum available amount of the fixed factor was required, at which point B departs from A.

Curve C involves essentially the same conditions as B except that the limitations imposed by fixed factors or by factors outside the control of the firm are operative to some extent from the beginning. Curve D shows costs increasing initially less than in proportion to output. This could arise from indivisibilities in any of the factors employed or in factors outside the control of the firm.

Figure 5.16(b) reproduces essentially the same four cases with the modification that total variable costs do not approach zero as output approaches zero. In all four cases, there are costs Ot that could be avoided by going out of business entirely but that cannot be avoided so long as the firm remains in business—all the cost curves should be interpreted as including the segment of the vertical axis between O and t. These costs may consist of such items as the interest sacrificed on the scrap value of the plant, fixed payments to factors under contracts that are terminable if the firm goes out of business, annual license fees, etc.

For each output, we can ask how much total variable cost changes per unit change in output, for small changes in output. This is, of course, given by the slope of the total variable cost curve and is designated as *marginal cost*.[15] It is clear that marginal cost, so defined, will be the same for curves A and A′, B and B′, C and C′, and D and D′, and the four resulting marginal cost curves are drawn in Figure 5.17. The identity of the marginal cost curves for the total cost curves of Figs. 5.16(a) and (b) conceals, however, a not unessential detail. For the curves in Figure 5.16(a), total variable cost is equal to the area under the corresponding marginal cost curve;

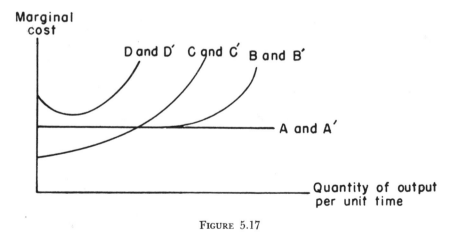

FIGURE 5.17

15. Marginal cost is equal to the reciprocal of the common value of the ratios in equations (1).

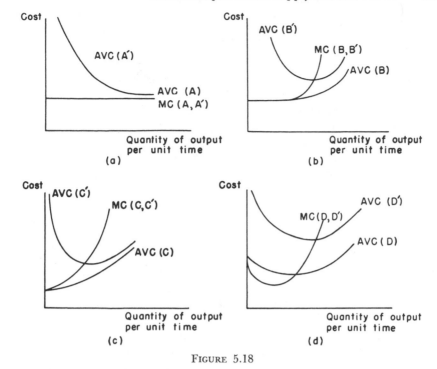

FIGURE 5.18

for the curves in Figure 5.16(b), total variable cost exceeds by Ot the area under the corresponding marginal cost curve.

This difference can be brought out by drawing the average variable cost curve, a curve showing the variable costs per unit of output at each output. Figures 5.18(a) to (d) shows the relation between the average variable cost curves and the marginal cost curves. If total variable costs approach zero as output approaches zero, the average variable cost approaches marginal cost as output approaches zero; otherwise average variable costs approach infinity as output approaches zero. In all cases, of course, average variable costs fall if they exceed marginal costs and rise otherwise.

These average variable cost curves are themselves to be regarded as rather special kinds of marginal cost curves—they show the change in cost per unit of output occasioned by producing the given output rather than none at all, whereas the usual marginal cost curves show the change in cost per unit of output occasioned by producing a little more or a little less.

THE FIRM'S OUTPUT DECISIONS

The cost curves in Figure 5.18 provide the basis for answering a number of different questions about the firm's decisions. Though in general we have been dealing with competitive conditions on the product market, we may here be more general and include monopolistic conditions as well.

(1) *Optimum output for a given demand curve*

The demand curve for the product of the individual firm shows the maximum quantity the firm can sell at various prices under given conditions of demand. The curve marginal to the demand curve shows the marginal revenue: that is, the rate at which total receipts change per unit change in output in consequence of selling a little more or less. The prices on the demand curve itself show the average revenue from the corresponding sales. Like the average variable cost curve, the average revenue curve can also be regarded as a rather special kind of marginal curve: it shows the change in total receipts per unit of product occasioned by selling the given output rather than none at all.

Let us now ask what the optimum output for the firm is under given conditions of cost and demand. This question can in turn be subdivided into two questions: (1) Should the firm produce anything at all? (2) Given that it is going to produce something, what is the optimum amount to produce?

The answer to the first question is given by a comparison of the average revenue (i.e., demand) curve and the average variable cost curve; these are the appropriate marginal curves for this purpose. If the average revenue curve is everywhere below the average variable cost curve, the firm will add more to its costs by producing something than it will add to its receipts, and it will therefore be better off to produce nothing. If the average revenue curve is above the average variable cost curve at one or more points, it will be preferable to produce at one of these points rather than not to produce at all.

Given that the firm is to produce something, the optimum amount to produce is given by a comparison of the marginal revenue and marginal cost curves. If for any output, marginal revenue is greater than marginal cost, more will be added to total receipts than to total costs by producing a little more; hence it pays to produce a little more. Conversely, if marginal revenue is less than marginal cost, less will be subtracted from total receipts than from total costs by producing a little less; hence it pays to produce a little less. The optimum output is therefore that at which marginal revenue equals marginal cost.[16]

If we neglect the possibility that the firm produces nothing, equations (1) can be extended to include the firm's output decision and to describe the general equilibrium of the firm by eliminating the restriction to a particular output and adding the requirement that marginal cost equals marginal revenue. They then become:

16. Note that this output will necessarily be one of those for which average revenue exceeds average variable costs and that this condition is already implicit in those stated above, as can be seen from the geometry of the relation between the average and marginal curves.

$$\frac{\text{MPP}_a}{\text{MFC}_a} = \frac{\text{MPP}_b}{\text{MFC}_b} = \ldots = \frac{1}{\text{MC}} = \frac{1}{\text{MR}}$$

$$x = f_i\,(a, b, \ldots)$$

where MC is marginal cost and MR marginal revenue.

For a given demand curve and given conditions of cost, the optimum output is clearly a number. To get a function relating the optimum output to the demand curve it would be necessary to describe the demand curve by some list of parameters and then express the optimum output as a function of these parameters. For example, if one could restrict oneself to straight-line demand curves, the optimum output, for given cost conditions, could be expressed as a function of the height and slope of the demand curve.

A particularly important special case in which it is possible to describe the demand curve by a single parameter is that of competition, in which the demand curve for the firm's product is taken to be a horizontal line. This demand curve is then completely described by its height, which is the market price of the product. The function relating optimum output to the demand curve can then be described as relating optimum output to price.

In this special case, the average revenue curve and the marginal revenue curve become identical and equal to price. The firm will produce nothing unless price is above minimum average variable costs; if price is above this level, it will produce an output that will make price equal to marginal cost. The locus of optimum outputs for various prices is summarized in Figure 5.19 for the cost curves for case **D′** in Figure 5.18(d). At a price be-

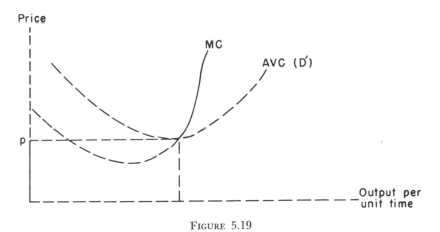

FIGURE 5.19

low Op, the optimum output is zero, so the solid part of the y axis is the locus of optimum outputs; at a price above Op, the solid part of the marginal cost curve is the locus of optimum output. At Op, there is a discontinuity; the horizontal dashed line connects two alternative points, but no point on it is an optimum. This discontinuity is not present in cases A, B, and C of the preceding section. In case A (and A') of the preceding section, the optimum output is infinite for any price above the (constant) marginal cost, which is the reason why this case is incompatible with competition.

(2) The firm's supply curve

It will be recalled that a supply curve of a particular group for a particular commodity was defined as "the boundary line between those points that are and those that are not attainable under the given conditions of supply" and that points were defined as attainable if "the suppliers would be willing to supply the indicated quantity at the indicated price." One further point must be made explicit before we can use our cost curves to draw a supply curve as so defined: In asking whether the suppliers would be willing to supply the indicated quantity at the indicated price, what alternatives do we suppose him to have? There are two main possibilities: (1) We might suppose him to have only the alternative of shutting down—we might consider him faced with an all-or-nothing proposition. (2) We might suppose him to have the alternative of supplying the indicated amount or any smaller amount.

In the first case—the all-or-nothing case—the average variable cost curve clearly is the boundary line between attainable and unattainable points. The firm would prefer any point above the average variable cost curve to the alternative of producing nothing and would prefer to produce nothing rather than to accept a point below the average variable cost curve.

The second case—in which the alternatives include supplying less than the indicated amount—is much the more useful of the two and is the one generally intended when supply curves are drawn. In this case, the boundary line between the attainable and unattainable points is slightly more complicated. For any output, the minimum supply price is the ordinate of either the average variable cost curve or the marginal cost curve, whichever is higher; the supply curve is then the locus of these minimum supply prices. This construction is illustrated in Figure 5.20 for case D'. The solid lines are the supply curve; the shaded area (plus the vertical axis) the points that are attainable. Points to the right of the minimum variable costs and between the marginal cost and average variable cost curves, which are attainable on an all-or-nothing basis, are now ruled out because the costs avoidable by a slight reduction of output are now above the revenue yielded by that amount of output and it will be in the firm's interest to produce less. In general, one can think of the marginal cost curve and the average variable cost curve as both showing marginal costs appropriate to different kinds of changes in output—the marginal cost curve to small increases or decreases in output, the average variable cost curve to the cessation of output. If both kinds of changes are open to the firm, the one involving the larger marginal cost is clearly the one that should dominate, and hence it is the higher of the two curves that is relevant. In cases A, B, and C of the preceding section, the average variable cost curve is nowhere above the marginal cost curve, so the supply curve can be said to be identical with the marginal cost curve, and also with the locus of optimum outputs at various prices; but this identification is clearly not valid in general.

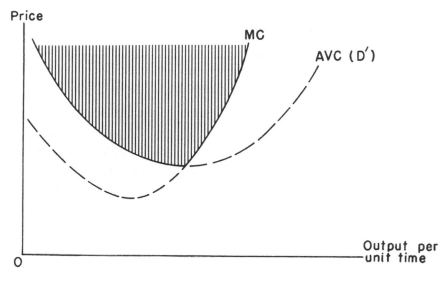

FIGURE 5.20

For most purposes the segment of the supply curve given by the marginal cost curve will be relevant, since firms prefer points on this curve to attainable points involving the same price but a smaller output. But this may not always be so. For example, suppose that there are no external economies or diseconomies (so that we can suppose the firm's supply curve to be independent of the industry's output), that there are a large number of potential firms with a supply curve identical with that in Figure 5.20, that the government fixes a minimum price above the minimum point on the average variable cost curve and assigns equal output quotas to any firm that requests one, always keeping the total of the quotas equal to the amount demanded at the fixed price. The equilibrium position will in this case be on the average variable cost segment of the supply curve, since firms will enter until the quota is reduced to that amount. This idealized model also applies to many private cartel arrangements.

The Relations between Supply Curves for Different "Runs"

So far we have been dealing with a single "run," that is a single set of supply curves of factors of production. It is clear, however, that the supply curves for different runs must be related to one another. It will simplify our description of this relation to neglect some of the complications introduced in the preceding section, and in particular, those which arise from falling average variable costs. Accordingly, we shall return to the simpler case considered earlier in which discontinuities are neglected, so that the firm's supply curve for any "run" can be taken to be its marginal cost curve for the corresponding "run."

THE INDIVIDUAL FIRM

Let us consider, first, the longest of long runs for any individual firm. In this case, the supply curves of all the hired factors will be horizontal if we restrict ourselves to the extreme forms of the supply curves of factors depicted in Figures 5.15(a) and (b), or positively sloping but nowhere perpendicular to the quantity axis if we consider the general case.

But what of the entrepreneurial capacity of the firm? This is defined, it will be recalled, by "the production function of the firm," so that if the longest of long runs is to involve different conditions of supply of entrepreneurial capacity, it would mean that the production function of the firm must be taken to be different in the longest of long runs than in other runs.[17] In particular, the most reasonable interpretation of an infinitely elastic supply of entrepreneurial capacity to the individual firm seems to be that the production function becomes homogeneous of the first degree with respect to all hired factors, so that multiplying the quantity of all of them by a constant would multiply output by the same constant.[18] But then there is nothing on the supply side that sets a limit to the size of firms; either monopoly will result, or the division of the output among firms is arbitrary and capricious, or the meaning of a firm disappears. This interpretation of the longest of long runs makes our theory useless for one of the central problems in which we are interested: the determination of the number and size of firms. Accordingly it seems an inappropriate construction for our purposes.

Instead, we shall suppose that the production function is the same for all runs. That is, we are interpreting entrepreneurial capacity as reflecting the performance of a function, the need for which remains no matter

17. It might seem that an alternative meaning would be that a different segment of the production function is relevant in the longest of long runs than in shorter runs. But this is not acceptable, since, as we shall see, to every long-run situation there corresponds an identical short-run situation.

18. The qualifications "to the individual firm" and "with respect to all hired factors" are intended to permit the above statement to be consistent with external technical economies or diseconomies. If we could conceive of a production function to the industry, it need not be homogeneous of the first degree, even though the production function of each individual firm could be treated as homogeneous of the first degree. The difference would reflect the existence of nonhired, nonentrepreneurial factors fixed in amount to the industry (e.g., the size of the world, the constant of gravity, etc.), all of which might be irrelevant to the individual firm.

how complete the adjustments to new circumstances, and for which hired factors are an imperfect substitute, no matter how complete the reorganization of hired factors.[19]

For this longest of long runs, the optimum combination of factors to produce any output, say x_0, will be obtained by solving equations (1) which may be repeated here:

$$(1) \qquad \frac{\text{MPP}_a}{\text{MFC}_a} = \frac{\text{MPP}_b}{\text{MFC}_b} = \frac{\text{MPP}_c}{\text{MFC}_c} = \cdots = \frac{1}{\text{MC}}$$

$$x_0 = f_i\,(a, b, \ldots)$$

The marginal factor costs will be computed from the long-run supply curves of factors. If these are horizontal, marginal factor costs will be equal to price of the factors; otherwise, marginal factor costs will be functions of the quantity of the factors used. Suppose the optimum combination of the factors is given by $(a_0, b_0, c_0, \ldots)$. This means that with this combination of factors an output x_0 will be produced, and that the ratios in (1) will all be equal. The common value of these ratios will be the number of units of output added per extra dollar spent on factors of production; that is, it will be the reciprocal of the long-run marginal cost. Suppose now we consider any short run defined by fixing the quantities of some factors at the values appropriate to this particular long run—say we fix a at a_0, that is, make the supply curve of A vertical at $a = a_0$, but let all the other factors be variable. We can then essentially eliminate the first ratio in equations (1), set $a = a_0$ in the production function, and solve for the values of the other factors. It is obvious that the solution will be $(b_0, c_0, \ldots)$, i.e., the same as before. Our long-run solution tells us that these values, together with $a = a_0$, will yield an output of x_0 and make the ratios in (1) all equal to one another.

Thus, corresponding to any long run, there exists a whole set of short runs for which marginal cost is equal to long-run marginal cost. Indeed, this is an obvious condition for an optimum long-run combination of factors: costs for a given output can be at a minimum only if any conceivable way of adding a unit to output will add as much to costs as, and no more than, any other conceivable way. But in particular, holding some factors constant in amount and changing the quantities of other factors is one conceivable way of adding a unit to output. Hence, through every point on a long-run marginal cost curve, there will pass a set of short-run marginal cost curves. We may call these the short-run marginal cost curves corresponding to x_0.

Consider now what happens as we pass from output x_0 to a larger output, say $x_0 + \Delta x$. Corresponding to this new output there will be a new

19. For example, the "function" may be the willingness to accept risk; and the world corresponding to full equilibrium, a world in which risk still remains for the individual unit.

optimum long-run combination, say $(a_o + \Delta a_o, b_o + \Delta b_o, c_o + \Delta c_o, \ldots)$, and a new long-run marginal cost, say LRMC. The increase in costs is the product of Δx and LRMC. This increase in cost by definition cannot be greater than the increase in cost from any other way of adding Δx to output; otherwise the new combination would not be an optimum. In particular, the increase in cost cannot be greater than ways of adding Δx to output that involve *not* changing the amount of one or more of the factors of production. It follows that at outputs greater than x_o, long-run marginal cost must be less than or equal to the short-run marginal cost shown by any marginal cost curve corresponding to output x_o. Conversely, if output is reduced, the long-run technique of doing so must subtract at least as much from costs as any short-run technique of doing so. It follows that at outputs less than x_o, long-run marginal cost must be greater than or equal to the short-run marginal cost shown by any marginal cost curve corresponding to output x_o.

This same argument applies to any pair of runs which differ in that the "shorter" run holds constant all factors held constant in the "longer" run and some more besides. For example, if we think of a particular ordering of the "runs," so that, say, the next to longest run involves holding $a = a_o$, the next one, $a = a_o$, $b = b_o$, and so on, with the shortest holding all factors constant, the set of marginal cost curves corresponding to x_o would grow progressively steeper as we proceeded from longer to shorter runs.

This situation is depicted in Figure 5.21 which shows two sets of marginal cost curves, one corresponding to x_o, one to x_1. The numbers 0, 1, 2, 3 attached to the short-run marginal cost curves typify successively longer runs, 0 being the shortest of short runs. As more and more scope for adapta-

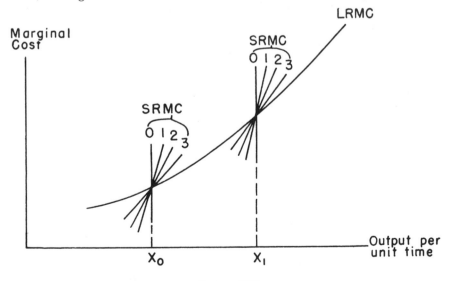

FIGURE 5.21

tion is allowed the firm, the marginal cost curves become progressively flatter. Of course there are a large number of possible orderings of "runs," and indeed one can conceive of an indefinite number of runs, so that one would have a continuum of curves filling entirely the space between the curve labeled 0 and the long-run marginal cost curve. The particular problem will have to determine both the ordering of runs and the number of runs it is worth considering explicitly.

THE INDUSTRY

If there were no external economies or diseconomies, the supply curve of the industry for any run would simply be the sum of the marginal cost curves for the corresponding run, and nothing further would need to be said. Through each point on the industry long-run supply curve, there passes a bundle of short-run supply curves, growing progressively flatter as the length of the run increases.

The introduction of external economies or diseconomies causes the industry supply curve to diverge from the sum of the marginal cost curves. The only complication this introduces in connection with the present problem is that the degree of divergence may differ for different runs. The external effects are likely to be connected with particular factors. For runs for which these are held constant, there may be no external effects; for longer runs there may be external effects. This does not however disturb the conclusion that the longer the run, the flatter the supply curve.

Returns to Entrepreneurial Capacity: Rents and Quasi-Rents

COMPETITIVE EQUILIBRIUM

Returns to the various factors of production obviously depend on the conditions of demand in the industry as well as of supply. These determine the actual amounts of various hired factors employed and hence, through the supply curves of the factors, their price per unit; they determine the number of firms in the industry and their output, and hence the difference between expected receipts and expected contractual costs. The hired factors raise no particular difficulty, but it may be worth discussing in somewhat more detail the returns to what we have called entrepreneurial capacity.

Figure 5.22 illustrates some of the possibilities corresponding to a single equilibrium position. The final panel depicts the situation of an industry with a positively sloped supply curve; the other panels, the situations of four different firms. The letters after the designations of the firm refer to the cases described above. Total variable costs for firms 1 and 2 approach zero as output approaches zero, as is shown by the fact that marginal cost and average variable cost are identical for an output of zero. Firm 1 has constant marginal costs until limited entrepreneurial capacity—or another fixed factor—causes costs to rise. As drawn, price happens to be equal to minimum average variable costs, so expected receipts are exactly equal to expected variable costs, leaving no return for entrepreneurial capacity and to cover fixed costs. If a decline in demand occurred and did not lower the cost conditions for firm 1 (through external effects), the firm would cease operations. Firm 2 has marginal costs that at first decline and then rise, reflecting the operation of some technical indivisibility. The shaded area represents the amount available as a return for entrepreneurial capacity and to cover fixed costs. In this case, the shaded area is also given by the area between the marginal cost curve and the horizontal price line, since the area under the marginal cost curve equals total variable costs. Firm 3 is like firm 2, except that total variable costs do not approach zero as output approaches zero, so that the shaded area, which is the amount available as a return for entrepreneurial capacity and to cover fixed costs, is less than the area between the marginal cost curve and the price line. Firm 4 is like firm 3, except that its variable costs are so high that there is nothing left as a return for entrepreneurial capacity and to cover fixed costs.

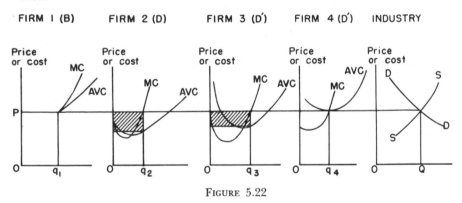

FIGURE 5.22

The situation exemplified in Figure 5.22 might perfectly well be a long-run equilibrium position in which there are no fixed costs. The fact that firms 2 and 3 receive a return for entrepreneurial capacity, shown by the shaded areas, is no threat to the stability of the equilibrium so long as there are no potential firms that have an incentive and are in a position to take the return away; that is, so long as there are no firms not now producing this product that have minimum average variable costs below OP.

For a long-run equilibrium position, the shaded areas can be described as a "rent" to the "scarce" entrepreneurial capacity possessed by firms 2 and 3. In estimating the capital value or "wealth" of the owners of firms 2 and 3, this "rent" would be capitalized, since it is a permanent return. Frequently, this rent is included in "total costs" and hypothetical average

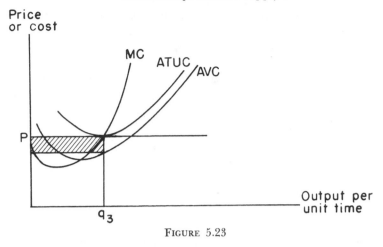

FIGURE 5.23

costs are computed for other outputs on the assumption that the "rent" would be the same at other outputs, yielding an average total unit cost curve like that drawn in Figure 5.23 for firm 3. But it should be noted that this curve has an entirely different meaning and role than the other curves: it is a result or consequence of the final equilibrium, not a determinant of it, and no point on it other than that at q_8 has any importance, whether or not there are external economies or diseconomies. For example, suppose there are no external economies or diseconomies, and suppose the demand curve for the industry rises. The marginal and average variable cost curves for the firm would be unaffected and would determine the firm's output. But the shaded area would then increase and the ATUC curve would have to be redrawn. This is the reason no use has been made up of this curve up to this point; it is more misleading than it is helpful.

If the situation depicted in Figure 5.22 is not a long-run equilibrium position but a particular short-run position, the shaded areas will include not only the return to entrepreneurial capacity but also the return to other fixed factors in excess of any payments to them included in variable costs. If demand remains unchanged, the passage to a longer run will mean a change in the cost curves and the industry's supply curve, and this will mean an increase or decrease in the size of the shaded areas. In this case, the shaded areas can be described as including "quasi-rents" to the fixed factors: "rents" because like the rents to entrepreneurial capacity they are, for the particular run in question, "price determined" rather than price determining; "quasi-" because unlike the rents to entrepreneurial capacity, they are only temporarily price determined.

Returns to entrepreneurial capacity will be zero in the long run for all firms only if all firms are in the position of firms 1 or 4 of Figure 5.22. The condition for this is that there be a sufficiently large number of firms having identical minimum average variable costs. No other conditions need be imposed. The shape of the cost curves may vary in any other respects, so long as minimum average variable costs are identical. If, in addition, the supply curves of all hired factors to the industry are horizontal and there are no external or internal technical economies, the industry supply curve will be horizontal. This can be described as a case in which the industry uses no specialized factors. Note, however, that the marginal cost curves of individual firms need not be horizontal, so that the number and size of firms is still determinate.

MONOPOLY

If a firm is regarded as a monopoly, that is, as facing a negatively sloping demand curve for its product, the concept of a supply curve is of little help in explaining its behavior. The function that is then relevant is one relating its optimum output to the shape and form of its demand curve. The preceding discussion of return to entrepreneurial capacity is, however, entirely valid.

Figure 5.24 depicts the situation for a monopoly, and for simplicity, we may suppose it to depict a long-run equilibrium situation in which there are no fixed costs. The shaded area again represents the return to entrepreneurial capacity. Again, the fact that this is a long-run equilibrium means that the positive return to entrepreneurial capacity is no threat to the equilibrium. Apparently there is no potential firm capable of taking it away that has an incentive to do so. The shaded area can again be described as a "rent" to the scarce entrepreneurial capacity.

Again, in estimating the capital value or "wealth" of the owner of the

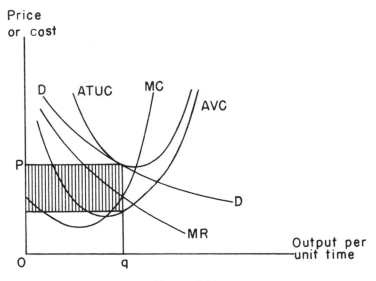

FIGURE 5.24

firm, the "rent" shown by the shaded area would be capitalized, since it is a permanent return. And again, a hypothetical average total unit cost curve could be computed on the assumption that the "rent" would be the same at other outputs, yielding a curve like the ATUC curve drawn in Figure 5.24. But again this curve has an entirely different meaning and role than the other cost curves: it is a result of or consequence of the final equilibrium, not a determinant of it, and no point on it other than that at q has any importance. Indeed, the demand curve itself has a better right than the curve labelled ATUC to be regarded as an average total unit cost curve, since if the firm through error produced an output other than Oq, the actual total unit cost would be given by the ordinate of the demand curve at the corresponding output.

In particular, the inference frequently drawn from a figure like Figure 5.24, that a monopoly tends to operate at less than the technically most efficient scale, is obviously invalid. The hypothetical ATUC curve has nothing to say about technical efficiency; it merely is a translation of the convention that total costs equal total receipts. Let demand conditions change yet technical conditions not change, and the marginal and average variable cost curves will be unchanged, but the ATUC curve will have to be redrawn so as to be tangent to the new demand curve at the new optimum output. In this respect, competitive and monopolistic firms are the same. Both seek to minimize total variable costs at any given output; both seek to maximize the return to their entrepreneurial capacity; both may re-receive a positive return to their entrepreneurial capacity at long-run equilibrium; this "rent" must be capitalized for both in computing the total wealth of the owner of the firm. For both, the "scale" of plant is "optimum" if for that plant and that output short-run marginal cost (for every possible "short-run") equals long-run marginal cost.

A Mathematical Summary

We may summarize the analysis, and at the same time provide a check on its completeness, by setting forth the conditions that jointly determine the supply curve of a competitive industry in the form of a system of simultaneous equations. For simplicity, we shall suppose that supply curves of factors to individual firms are either infinitely elastic (variable factors) or completely inelastic (fixed factors), and that no costs would be avoided by dispensing with the use of one or more fixed factors short of going completely out of business.

THE INDIVIDUAL FIRM

Each potential firm is described by a production function

(2) $$x_j = f_j (a_{1j}, a_{2j} \ldots a_{mj}, x)$$

where x_j is the output of the j-th firm, $A_1, A_2, \ldots, A_m$ are the various factors of production, a_{ij} the amount of A_i employed by the j-th firm, and x the output of the industry. Let us suppose $A_1, \ldots, A_k$ to be variable factors, $A_{k+1}, \ldots, A_m$ fixed factors, p_{ai} (i = 1, \ldots, k), the price per unit of a variable factor A_i, $\bar{a}_{ij}$ (i = k + 1, \ldots, m), the amount of a fixed factor A_i available to the j-th firm, and p_x the price of the product. Then the optimum output and combination of factors for the firm, given that it is going to produce something, is obtained by solving a system of equations consisting of equation (2) and the following equations:

$$(3) \qquad p_x \frac{\partial f_j}{\partial a_{ij}} = p_{ai} \qquad (i = 1, \ldots k)$$

$$(4) \qquad a_{ij} = \bar{a}_{ij} \qquad (i = k + 1, \ldots, m)$$

All told, the system of equations (2), (3), and (4) contains m + 1 equations, which can be solved for the m + 1 variables x_j, a_{ij} (i = 1, \ldots, m), as functions of p_x, p_{ai} (i = 1, \ldots, k), $\bar{a}_{ij}$ (i = k + 1, \ldots, m), and x.

If, now, for any particular set of values of p_x, p_{ai}, and x, the solutions of equations (2), (3) and (4), satisfy the inequality

$$x_j p_x \geq \sum_{i=1}^{k} a_{ij} p_{ai} + c_j$$

where c_j are costs that the firm can avoid by going out of business but not otherwise and that are assumed for simplicity to be independent of p_{ai}, then the solutions of equations (2), (3) and (4) are the equilibrium values for the firm for the corresponding values of p_x, p_{ai}, and x (i = 1, \ldots, k).

If, however, the solutions of equations (2), (3), and (4) satisfy the inequality,

$$x_j p_x < \sum_{i=1}^{k} a_{ij} p_{ai} + c_j,$$

the equilibrium values are given by

$$(2)' \quad x_j = 0 \qquad (i = 1, \ldots, k)$$
$$(3)' \quad a_{ij} = 0 \qquad (i = k + 1, \ldots, m).$$
$$(4) \quad a_{ij} = \bar{a}_{ij}$$

THE DEMAND AND SUPPLY OF FACTORS

If there are n potential firms, the total amount of each factor demanded is given by

$$(5) \qquad a_i = \sum_{j=1}^{n} a_{ij} \qquad (i = 1, \ldots, m).$$

The supply of the variable factors to the industry can be described by

(6) $a_i = g_i (p_{a1}, p_{a2}, \ldots, p_{ak})$ $(i = 1, \ldots k)$

where g_i may also depend on prices of other products and the like, variables that are taken as fixed to the industry. No supply equations for the fixed factors need be included, since, by virtue of equations (4), they would be identical with equations (5) for $i = k + 1, \ldots, m$.

THE SUPPLY OF THE PRODUCT

Finally, the total supply of the product is given by

(7)
$$x = \sum_{j=1}^{n} x_j .$$

THE NUMBER OF VARIABLES AND EQUATIONS

We may now count the number of variables and equations to check for completeness.

The variables are as follows:

Variables

Name	Symbol	Number
Output of the industry	x	1
Output of each firm	$x_j (j = 1, \ldots, n)$	n
Total quantity of each factor	$a_i (i = 1, \ldots, m)$	m
Quantity of each factor employed by each firm	$a_{ij}(i = 1, \ldots, m)$ $(j = 1, \ldots, n)$	mn
Price of the product	p_x	1
Price of the variable factors	$p_{ai} (i - 1, \ldots, k)$	k
Total number of variables		$2 + k + n + m + mn$

The equations are as follows:

Equations	Number
(2), (3), (4), or (2)′, (3)′, (4)	$n(m + 1)$
(5)	m
(6)	k
(7)	1
Total number of equations	$1 + k + n + m + mn$

There is one more variable than equations. We can therefore eliminate all variables except, say, x and p_x, and be left with one equation. If we solve the resulting equation for x to yield, say

(8) $x = S(p_x)$,

this equation is the supply curve of the industry.

6

The Law of Variable Proportions and a Firm's Cost Curves

We have just gone through in a formal way the various types of supply conditions that may obtain. We have seen that the supply conditions depend on the cost curves of the individual firm. We now turn to the firm, to examine the conditions underlying its cost curves. Our interest here is, of course, not in the firm per se but rather in a fuller understanding of the factors determining the supply conditions in an industry. We must remember that a supply curve is a meaningful concept only for a competitive industry. Otherwise, price alone does not describe completely the conditions of demand facing the individual firm. We must also remember that in going from cost curves to supply curves we have to be on the lookout for the possible existence of external economies or diseconomies—economies or diseconomies external to the firm but internal to the industry and hence affecting the supply curve of that industry.

The Law of Variable Proportions

We may regard the firm as an intermediary between factor markets, wherein it buys resources, and product markets, wherein it sells products. For the firm, the demand conditions for the product it produces are summarized in the demand (or average revenue) curve for its product. The supply conditions on factor markets are summarized in the supply curves of factors of production to the firm. The technological conditions governing the firm are summarized in the production function, which shows the (maximum) quantity of product it can produce for given quantities of each of the various factors of production it uses.

130

One of the properties assigned to this production function is generally described as "the Law of Diminishing Returns." This terminology is closely connected with the explanation of the so-called law in terms of fixed and variable factors of production. At bottom, however, the issue in question has little or no relation to this distinction between fixed and variable factors; it is rather concerned with the effect of varying the proportions in which different factors are employed, and all factors enter in completely symmetrical fashion. Accordingly, it will perhaps avoid misunderstanding to call it "the Law of Variable Proportions."

A hypothetical production function designed to illustrate this law is given in tabular form in Table 6.1 and in graphic form in Figure 6.1. For this example, let us suppose that only two factors of production, say A and B, are used to produce the product. Column 1 gives selected values of the number of units of B per unit of A, i.e., of the ratio in which the factors

TABLE 6.1

$\frac{B}{A}$	$\frac{A}{B}$	$\frac{X}{A}$	$\frac{X}{B}$	$\Delta\left(\frac{X}{A}\right)$	$\Delta\left(\frac{B}{A}\right)$	$\frac{\Delta\frac{X}{A}}{\Delta\frac{B}{A}}=\frac{\partial x}{\partial B}$	$\Delta\left(\frac{X}{B}\right)$	$\Delta\left(\frac{A}{B}\right)$	$\frac{\Delta\frac{X}{B}}{\Delta\frac{A}{B}}=\frac{\partial x}{\partial A}$
(1)	(2)	(3)	(4)	(5)	(6)	(7)	(8)	(9)	(10)
0	∞	0	Ind.						
				1	1/16	16	Ind.	−∞	0
1/16	16	1	16						
				3	1/16	48	16	−8	−2
1/8	8	4	32						
				5	1/8	40	4	−4	−1
1/4	4	9	36						
				9	1/4	36	0	−2	0
1/2	2	18	36						
				7	1/2	14	−11	−1	11
1	1	25	25						
				11	1	11	−7	−1/2	14
2	1/2	36	18						
				0	2	0	−9	−1/4	36
4	1/4	36	9						
				−4	4	−1	−5	−1/8	40
8	1/8	32	4						
				−16	8	−2	−3	−1/16	48
16	1/16	16	1						
				Ind.	∞	0	−1	−1/16	16
∞	0	Ind.	0						

NOTE: Ind. stands for indeterminate.

Verbal descriptions of column headings:

(1) No. of units of B per unit of A
(2) No. of units of A per unit of B
(3) Product per unit of A
(4) Product per unit of B
(5) Change in product per unit of A

(6) Change in no. of units of B per unit of A
(7) Marginal product of B
(8) Change in product per unit of B
(9) Change in no. of units of A per unit of B
(10) Marginal product of A

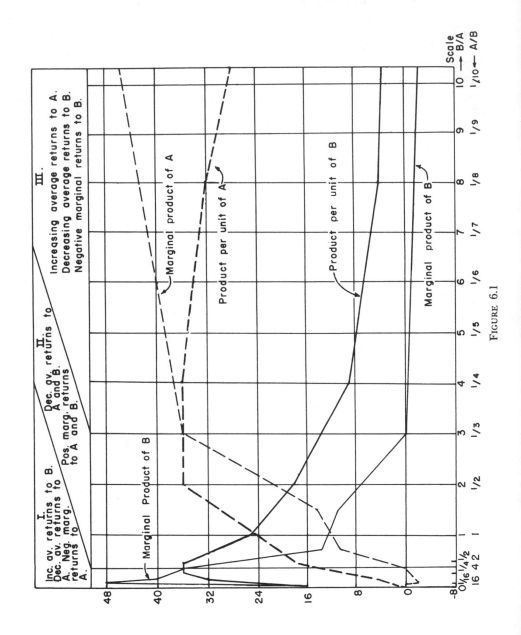

FIGURE 6.1

are supposed combined. Let us skip column 2 for the moment. Column 3 shows the number of units of output per unit of A for each ratio of B to A. For example, it says that if one-sixteenth as many units of B as of A are used, then one unit of product will be produced for each unit of A employed; if equal number of units of B and of A are used, then 25 units of product will be produced for each unit of A employed.

Now the mere possibility of making statements of this kind already says a great deal about the character of the production function. For it might be, say, that one unit of B and one unit of A would produce twenty-five units of product, but two units of B and two units of A would produce either more or less than fifty units. In that case, the knowledge that equal numbers of units of A and B were employed would not be enough to determine the output per unit of A; in addition, one would have to know the absolute number of units. Output per unit of A will be a function solely of the ratio of the factors of production if and only if the production function has the property that multiplying the quantities of all factors by a constant will multiply output by the same constant—e.g., that doubling quantities of all factors will double the output. Functions having this property are by definition homogeneous functions of the first degree, and our illustrative table is drawn for such a function.

We shall discuss the meaning and significance of this property later. For the moment, it will suffice to say that we want ultimately to distinguish between two sets of considerations affecting the costs of an individual firm: the proportions in which it combines factors and the scale on which it operates. The law of variable proportions deals with the first set, and we can best abstract from the influence of scale by provisionally supposing it to have no influence; this is precisely what is involved in supposing the firm's production function to be homogeneous of the first degree in A and B, and A and B to be the only two factors of production involved. We shall see, further, that the influence of scale can itself be viewed as the result of the operation of the law of variable proportions, so we are making a less special assumption than might at first be supposed.

Given that the production function is homogeneous of the first degree and that only two factors are involved, a pair of columns like 1 and 3 describes it completely if the entries are sufficiently numerous. For consider the general question: how much X can be produced if there are a_1 units of A and b_1 units of B? The answer can be obtained by computing $\frac{b_1}{a_1}$ entering it in column 1, finding the corresponding entry in column 3, and multiplying the result by a_1. This is what we mean by saying that in this case everything depends only on the proportions in which the different factors are combined. It follows that all the rest of Table 6.1 can be obtained from columns 1 and 3, and examination of the column headings will confirm this: column 2 is simply the reciprocal of 1; column 4 is equal to column 3 divided by column 1 or multiplied by column 2; and so on.

One reason for entering both columns 1 and 2 is to enable us to translate this table readily into terms of variable and fixed factors. Suppose the firm must use one unit of A, but can use varying amounts of B. Then column 3—or product per unit of A—is "total" product; column 4—or product per unit of B—is "average product" of the "variable" factor; and column 7—marginal product of B—is "marginal product" of the "variable" factor. Similarly, if the firm must use one unit of B but can use varying amounts of A, we can take column 2 to show the amount of A used. We shall then, of course, want to read the table from the bottom up, since this will correspond to increasing amounts of the "variable" factor. Column 4—or product per unit of B—is then the "total product," column 3 —product per unit of A—the average product of the "variable factor"; and column 10—marginal product of A—the "marginal" product of the variable factor.

Let us now turn to the numerical values in the table and the graph. This particular example is set up so as to illustrate most of the cases that are arithmetically possible within the framework of a two-variable homogeneous production function of the first degree. Not all cases are arithmetically possible; for example, average product cannot increase as the relevant variable increases and at the same time be greater than the corresponding marginal product. In checking for this kind of internal consistency in the figure, it should be kept in mind that A *decreases* relative to B as one goes from left to right, and, hence, in interpreting the A curves they should be read "backwards," as it were.

The terms *increasing returns* and *diminishing returns* are sometimes used to refer to marginal returns and sometimes to average returns, so it will be best to indicate explicitly which is intended. Furthermore, they always refer to the behavior of returns as the quantity of the corresponding factor increases. Marginal returns to B increase at first, thereafter diminish, and ultimately become negative. Average returns to B increase over a longer range (until a ratio of 1/4 of a unit of B per unit of A if we stick only to the designated points and avoid interpolation), are the same at a ratio of B to A of 1/2 as at 1/4, and then diminish. A behaves, of course, in the same way, as we shall see most readily if we read from the bottom of the table up, or from the right of the graph to the left. Marginal returns to A increases to somewhere between 1/16 and 1/8 of a unit of A per unit of B, then decline, and ultimately become negative. Average returns increase to 1/4 of a unit of A per unit of B, are the same at 1/2 as at 1/4, and then diminish.[1]

_____

1. The first and last entries in the table deserve a word of explanation. The product per unit of A is set at 0 for B/A = 0; this implies that B is an "essential" factor in the sense that no output is possible without some B. Since column 4 is column 3 divided by

The table and graph supposedly summarize the technological conditions governing the production of the product in question. That is, they are designed to answer the technological question: given specified amounts of the two factors of production, what is the maximum amount of product that can be produced? Let us now see how we would use this information; in the process, we can also test whether all the arithmetically possible cases they contain are economically or technologically relevant.

Suppose, for example, that we have 8 units of A and 64 units of B. The table shows an output of 32 per unit of A when the ratio of B to A is 8 to 1, which would mean a total output of 256. But is this really the best we can do? Further examination of the table suggests that it is not. If it costs nothing to "throw" B away—*not* to "use" it—we can get an output of 36 per unit of A, or 288 in all, simply by using only 16 or 32 of our units of B, that is, either 2 or 4 units of B per unit of A. If the table had more entries, perhaps some number between 2 and 4 would be even better. Obviously, the situation is the same for any larger number of units of B per unit of A, so no matter how plentiful B is, it will not be sensible to use more than 4 units of B per unit of A. Similarly, suppose we had the same 8 units of A but only 1 unit of B. The entry under a ratio of B to A of 1/8 shows an output of 4 per unit of A or 32 in all. But again this is not really the best we can do. Suppose we were to "throw" away, i.e., not use, 4 of the units of A. We should then be operating with a ratio of B to A of 1/4, for which the output per unit of A is 9; multiplied by the 4 units of A being used, total output is 36. In consequence, no matter how "scarce" B is, it is not sensible to use less than 1/4 of a unit of B per unit of A—or stated in reverse, no matter how plentiful A is, it is not sensible to use more than 4 units of A per unit of B. Suppose now that the ratio of B to A is between 1/4 and 4, say 8 units of A and 8 units of B, or a ratio of 1, does anything similar occur? Clearly it does not. By using all of the A and all of the B, output per unit of A is 25, total output is 200. By using less of the A, say only 4 units, output per unit of A can be raised to 36, but since only 4 units are used, total output is reduced to 144; similarly, by using less of the B, say only 4 units, output per unit of B can be raised to 36, but only at the expense of reducing total output to 144.

These examples show that the three regions marked off in Figure 6.1 according to the behavior of average returns have very different meanings and significance. In the first region, average returns to B are increasing and average returns to A are diminishing; in the second region, average returns to both A and B are diminishing. The third region is the counterpart of the first—average returns are increasing to one factor, in this case A, and

---

column 1, the corresponding product per unit of B is 0/0, hence indeterminate. It is possible that some product could be produced by use of A alone. In this case, the first entry in column 3 would be finite, and in column 4 ∞. Similar remarks apply to the last entry.

diminishing to the other. Now our examples show that the first and third regions are ones to be shunned. Put differently, the figures entered in our table for these regions, while *arithmetically* possible under our assumptions, are technologically inconsistent with those entered elsewhere. The table purports to show the *maximum* output technologically possible for different combinations of factors. But it does not do so, for, as we have seen, when the ratio of B to A is 8 to 1, there is a way of using the factors that will produce an output of 36 per unit of A and hence of 4 1/2 per unit of B, whereas the table shows an output of only 32 and 4 respectively. In other words, on technological grounds alone, the table is wrong, given the assumptions that the production function is homogeneous of the first degree and that A and B are perfectly divisible (this point is discussed below).

For $B/A = 1/16$, the entry in column 3 should be $2\frac{1}{4}$, in column 4, 36;
for $B/A = 1/8$, the entry in column 3 should be $4\frac{1}{2}$, in column 4, 36;
for $B/A = 8$, the entry in column 3 should be 36, in column 4, $4\frac{1}{2}$;
for $B/A = 16$, the entry in column 3 should be 36, in column 4, $2\frac{1}{4}$.

This then is the law of variable proportions relevant for economics: insofar as possible, production will take place by the use of such a combination of factors that the average returns to each separately will diminish (or at most remain constant) with an increase in the amount of that factor used relative to the amounts of other factors. And this "law" is not a fact of nature, in the sense that nothing else is possible, or that it is demonstrated by repeated physical experiments; it is a maxim of rational conduct.

It may seem somewhat paradoxical that "increasing returns," which sound like something good, should be something to be avoided. This appearance of paradox may be reduced by noting that in both the table and the figure, the region of increasing average returns to one factor coincides with negative marginal returns to the other factor. This is no accident; it is a necessary consequence of the fact that the production function is homogeneous of the first degree, as can readily be demonstrated. Suppose that 1 unit of A plus B_1 units of B produce X_1 units of product and that this is a region of increasing average returns to A. Then 2 units of A plus B_1 units of B will produce more than $2X_1$ units of product, say $2X_1 + \Delta X$ where $\Delta X > 0$. But because of homogeneity of first degree, 2 units of A plus $2B_1$, units of B will produce only $2X_1$ units of product. Hence the additional units of B have diminished output, so B must have a negative marginal product. The common saying, "There's no use going further because you've already reached the point of diminishing return," is highly misleading. The point not to be exceeded is the point of vanishing (marginal) returns; the prudent man will seek to exceed the point of diminishing (average) returns.[2]

2. Note that the equivalence between increasing average returns to one factor and negative marginal returns to the other is valid only for a homogeneous function of the

Can entries like those in the first and third regions of Table 6.1 and Figure 6.1 ever be relevant? There are two sets of circumstances under which they can. The first is trivial and involves only a verbal exception: Suppose that "using" a factor is paid for, i.e., involves a negative cost, as, for example, when it involves using laborers who are learning a trade and are willing to pay for it. It may then be worth going into the region of increasing return to the other factor and negative return to this one. But in that case, the firm is really producing two products, the output entered in the table and education, and the table is not a complete summary of production conditions. Another example of the same case is where it costs something to "throw away" a factor, but again this must mean that there are other factors of production or other products involved.

The more important case is suggested by the qualification *insofar as possible* in the statement above of the law of variable proportions. It may not be possible for a firm to get into the region of diminishing returns for either of two reasons: because the quantities of relevant factors of production are outside of its control or because of indivisibilities. Let us postpone the first reason for the time being and consider only the second. Suppose factor A is land, plus labor, etc., in fixed ratios to the amount of land; factor B, services of a tractor in cultivating it; and the product is, say, wheat. Suppose, further, that tractors come in two sizes, one of which, size II, can be regarded as "twice" as much tractor as the other, or size I. For a given amount of Factor A, it may well be that *total* output is less with one tractor of size II than with one tractor of size I, because the smaller tractor does enough work per unit of time to cultivate the given area with the given other factors, while the only additional effect of the bigger tractor is to trample down more of the wheat. This means that with the bigger tractor, we are in the region of negative marginal returns to tractors and increasing average returns to land. Yet if only the bigger tractor is available it may be better to use it than to use no tractor at all. In this case, it is not physically possible to throw "half" the tractor away, though it would be desirable to do so. Note that this effect does not come from owning the tractor rather than renting it; the same effect arises if a tractor can be rented by the hour, say, but the only tractor that can be rented is one of size II. Using this tractor half the time may not be equivalent to using a tractor of size I all the time. The number of "tractor days" of service that can be used may be perfectly continuous, yet indivisibility may be present.

---

first degree. Suppose the production function is homogeneous but not of the first degree and contains only two variables. If the degree of the function is less than one, then increasing returns to one factor implies negative marginal returns to the other, but the converse does not hold: negative marginal returns to one factor are consistent with diminishing average returns to the other. If the degree of the function is greater than one, negative marginal returns to one factor imply increasing average returns to the other, but the converse does not hold: increasing average returns to one factor are consistent with positive marginal returns to the other.

Note also that the indivisibility of one factor means increasing average returns to the *other* factor, not to the first.

In the particular example, the indivisibility could presumably be removed on the market by selling the larger tractor and buying a small one. But it is clear that this may not be possible, since there will be some minimum size or scale of tractor made. Ultimately, most such indivisibility traces to the indivisibility of the human agent (the absence of the "half-size man" to drive or make the "half-size tractor").

Translation of the Law of Variable Proportions into Cost Curves

Let us now turn to the determination of cost curves from a production function like that summarized in Table 6.1. Suppose, first, that there are no indivisibilities and that the firm is perfectly free to hire any number of units of either of the factors of production. There is now no definite number of units of each factor of production available. Instead, the firm is limited by the price (or under monopsony, the supply curve) of the factors of production. Assume competition in the factor market, and suppose the price of B is zero. This is analogous to an unlimited amount of B being available, and obviously the optimum combination of B to A will be between two and four units of B per unit of A. This will mean an output of thirty-six per unit of A or a cost of $\frac{P_a}{36}$ per unit of product, where P_a is the price per unit of A. Clearly, under the given assumptions, this cost is independent of output, so the cost curves will be horizontal, as in Figure 6.2.

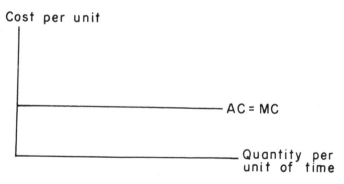

FIGURE 6.2

Similarly if P_a were zero, but P_b (the price per unit of B) were not, the cost would be $\frac{P_b}{36}$ and two to four units of A would be used per unit of B. Suppose, now, that neither price is zero. We know from our earlier analysis that the optimum combination will be given by $\dfrac{\text{MPP}_a}{\text{P}_a} = \dfrac{\text{MPP}_b}{\text{P}_b}$. For example, suppose $\text{P}_a = \$1.40$, $\text{P}_b = \$1.10$; then the optimum combination would be between one and two units of B per unit of A. For one unit of A to one unit of B, the cost per unit of product would be 10¢; for two units of B per unit of A, 10¢; for four units of B per unit of A, 16 1/9¢. Again the marginal and average cost curves would coincide as in Figure 6.2.

The analysis until now has shown that if all factors were perfectly divisible and obtainable by the firm at a constant supply price, then the optimum combination of A/B would be the same for all levels of output. The marginal and average cost curves would then be coincident and their height would be determined by factor prices.

This case is not, however, the only relevant one, or even the most significant. In the first place, horizontal cost curves would imply either monopoly (if the height of the cost curve were lower for one firm than for others) or complete indeterminancy of the size of firms (if several or many firms had curves of the same height). In the second place, it is not useful in analyzing different "runs," which are distinguished precisely by the different possibilities of changing the amounts of various factors. What this case does bring out is that for homogeneous production functions of the first degree, rising cost curves, hence limitations on the size of firms, must be sought in limitations on the firm in the possibility of varying the amounts of some factor or other.

Suppose that the supply of A is fixed to the firm at one unit—either temporarily for a short-run problem or permanently. The firm can then vary its output only by varying the amount of B employed. Its cost conditions can then be derived directly from Table 6.1, together with 1) the price of B and (2) knowledge whether the unit of A is divisible or not. Table 6.2 and Figure 6.3 give the results when the price of a unit of B is $1.10.

Whether or not A is indivisible makes a difference only for small amounts of B, for clearly B is taken to be divisible; when large amounts of B are supposed employed, there is clearly nothing to prevent some of the B from not being used. For smaller amounts of B, when A is indivisible, the figures in the original Table 6.1 are relevant; when A is divisible, the revised figures take account of the possibility of not using some A, i.e., of not letting the ratio of B to A in use fall below $\frac{1}{4}$.

The marginal costs can be calculated in either of two ways: by dividing the increment in column 4 by the corresponding increment in column 2 or 3, or by dividing the price of a unit of B by its marginal product as shown in column 7 of Table 6.1, for A indivisible—or in an appropriately revised column, for A divisible.

When B/A is between 1 and 2, we have the combination that turns out

TABLE 6.2

(1)	(2)	(3)	(4)	(5)	(6)	(7)	(8)
No. of	Output		Total	Marginal cost		Average variable cost	
units of B employed	A indivisible	A divisible	variable cost (1) × $1.10	A indivisible	A divisible	A indivisible	A divisible
0	0	0	0			Ind.	.03 1/18
				$.06 7/8	$.03 1/18		
1/16	1	2 1/4	$0.06 7/8			.06 7/8	.03 1/18
				.02 7/24	.03 1/18		
1/8	4	4 1/2	0.13 6/8			.03 7/16	.03 1/18
				.02 3/4	.03 1/18		
1/4	9		0.27 4/8			.03 1/18	
				.03 1/18			
1/2	18		0.55			.03 1/18	
				.07 6/7			
1	25		1.10			.04 2/5	
				.10			
2	36		2.20			.06 1/9	
				∞			
4	36		4.40			.12 2/9	
				∞			
8	36		8.80			.24 4/9	
				∞			
16	36		17.60			.48 8/9	
				∞			
∞	36		∞			∞	

to be optimum in our earlier example of both factors variable when $P_a =$ $1.40 and $P_b =$ $1.10. Since the price of B is assumed the same in this example, the marginal cost, for that combination of factors, is, of course, the same as before, 10¢ per unit.

The dashed lines in Figure 6.3 are for A indivisible. The indivisibility produces a decline both in average variable costs and marginal costs, the counterpart of increasing average returns to B and negative marginal product to A. That it is no advantage for marginal costs to decline, or even for it to be lower for a segment than the marginal cost when A is divisible, is clear from the higher average variable cost during this interval when A is indivisible than when it is divisible.

For A divisible, the marginal cost and average variable cost are horizontal (and therefore coincide) initially. This is because the limitation on A is irrelevant for this interval; this is essentially our earlier case, when A was a free good, because in this interval it is not worth while employing all of A. To put this in other terms, the supply curve for A is taken to be as in Figure 6.4. For low outputs, the horizontal segment of the supply curve of A is relevant.

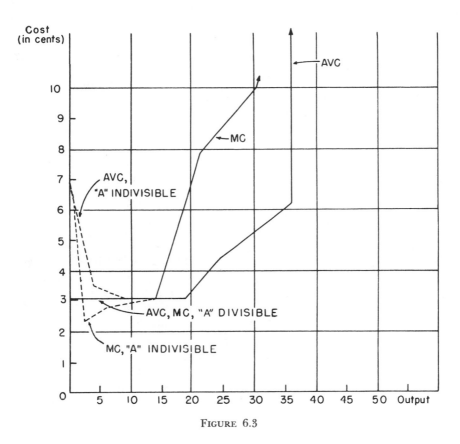

FIGURE 6.3

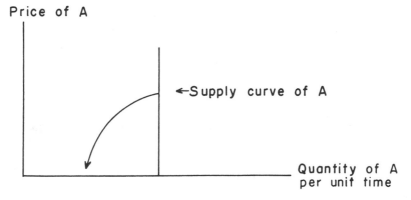

FIGURE 6.4

Homogeneous First-Degree Production Functions: The Problem of Scale

The examples just discussed indicate that the use of a production function that is homogeneous of the first degree is compatible with almost any kind of cost conditions—with declining average variable costs if there are indivisibilities, with rising average variable costs if there are limitations on the quantity of one factor employed. Indeed, it begins to look as if a homogeneous production function of the first degree can be viewed not as an empirically special kind of function but as a manner of speaking about all functions, as a framework of reference, or tautology.

This is one way of viewing it, and an extremely useful way of doing so. From this point of view, the concept of a homogeneous function of the first degree can be considered equivalent, on the one hand, to the concept of a controlled experiment, and on the other, to the concept that the units chosen for measuring quantities are irrelevant (the principle of relativity). Fundamental to science is the conception that if an experiment is repeated under identical conditions, it will give identical results. But is not doubling the quantity of each of the factors equivalent to repeating an experiment? If the initial bundle of factors yielded X units of output, must not an identical bundle under the same conditions yield X also? Hence, must not the two bundles together yield 2X? Or if the two bundles together yield 2X, while it is said that one bundle alone yields less than X, must not that mean that the conditions were not the same and the experiment was not really the same experiment? If the one-bundle experiment were a precise replica of the two-bundle experiment in all details, except uniformly on half the scale, must it not yield X? Or to turn to the other argument—from dimensions—can anything be considered changed if we look at objects through telescopes or microscopes? If we change units from rates of flow per week to rates of flow per month?

If we think of homogeneity of the first degree as a truism, it cannot, of course, be contradicted. Yet certain obvious examples seem to contradict it, such as the parable of the fly, which, it is said, if it were reproduced accurately on a larger scale would be unable to support its own weight. The answer is, of course, that there must be some "relevant" factor of production that has not been increased in scale along with the fly's dimensions—in this case, presumably the air pressure and the force of gravity. In the same vein is Pareto's answer to someone who said that doubling the subway system of Paris would not yield twice the return (or perhaps involve twice the cost). For homogeneity of the first degree to be relevant, he said, there would have to be two Parises.

The usefulness of this tautology depends on the value of the classification it suggests of the things that may affect cost conditions. It leads to a classification into (1) those that operate through explicit changes in the proportions among the factors of production, the chief of which are prices (or conditions of supply) of factors of production; (2) those that operate through limiting the quantities of some factors of production available to the firm—these account for rising cost curves and include the existence of conditions affecting cost (size of cities, amount of coal in the ground, constant of gravity, etc.) outside the control of the individual firm, limitations imposed by contractual arrangements, and those largely anonymous conditions concealed in the notion of "entrepreneurial capacity;" and (3) those that produce indivisibilities—these account for the possibility of decreasing cost curves and in most cases can be ultimately traced back to the indivisibility of the human agent, as is suggested by the fact that the gains from division of labor and specialization of function are all included under this heading.

Conceiving of the underlying production function as homogeneous of the first degree does not imply that the production function *as viewed by the firm* is homogeneous of the first degree. The firm is only concerned with those factors of production, or other conditions affecting costs, over which it has control. In consequence, the production function to the firm can be regarded as a cross-section of the underlying production function—that is, as obtained from the underlying production function by giving to the variables over which it has no control the constant values which they have for the problem in question. Indeed, it is precisely this step that enables us to conceive of rising long-run cost curves for individual firms and hence to rationalize the existence of limits to the size of firms. This is what was meant earlier by the remark that the "scale" of firms can itself be regarded as rationalized by the law of variable proportions.

Statistical Cost Curve Studies and Output Flexibility

A considerable number of empirical studies of cost curves of individual firms have been made within the past two decades. These have been mainly concerned with estimating short-run curves. Most of them suggest that short-run marginal cost curves are horizontal over the usual range of output, whereas the preceding analysis would rather suggest rising marginal cost because of the existence of limits to the amounts of some factors of production, even in the long run and certainly in the short run. In an excellent discussion of these studies and some of their implications, Hans Apel points out that the statistical evidence for this conclusion is quite limited and not particularly representative.[3] In particular, much of the evidence is for periods in which output was relatively low, so there might

3. "Marginal Cost Controversy and Its Implications," *American Economic Review* (December 1948): 870–85.

have been "unused capacity:" i.e., in terms of our preceding analysis, there might have been periods in which it was possible to keep the ratio of factors fixed when output was increased despite the limited quantities of some factors, because it had previously been rational not to use part of the latter factors.

But it is not at all clear that the results can be entirely explained in this way. In any event, consideration of these statistical results led George Stigler to suggest a force, hitherto neglected, that might make horizontal short-run marginal cost curves a deliberate objective of maximizing behavior.[4] This force is the desire to obtain flexibility. When a plant is built, it is not expected that precisely a single output will be produced year in and year out. It is known that there will be fluctuations in demand and in desired output. The problem, in other words, is not to minimize the cost of a given output steadily and regularly to be produced but to minimize the cost of a probability distribution of outputs, indicating the fraction of time each output will be produced. The relevant variable to measure along the horizontal axis is not "the" output but the "average" output, taking full account of variations from that output. For example, consider the average variable cost curves shown in Figure 6.5. Method of production A is a rigid method, which is highly efficient for a particular output but not for any other. The A curve shows the average cost if precisely the output indicated on the horizontal axis is produced day after day. The A′ curve shows the average cost if the horizontal axis is regarded as the average output over time and actual output is regarded as fluctuating from day to day about this average in some given fashion.[5] The two curves B and B′ have the corresponding meanings for a "flexible" method of production. For the figures as drawn, it is clear that the better method of production for a given unchanged output is A; for a distribution of outputs varying from day to day around x_1, B.

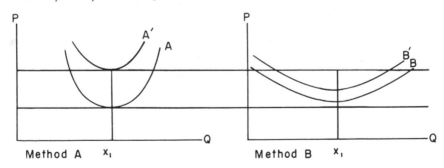

FIGURE 6.5

4. "Production and Distribution in the Short Run," *Journal of Political Economy* (June 1939): 312–22.

5. Note that A′ need not be above A everywhere as in this graph. In general, A′ will be above A, the same as A, or below A at any point according as A is concave upward, linear, or concave downward, for the relevant region about this point.

Comment on Statistical Cost Curves*

I have great sympathy with Caleb Smith's conclusion that the right questions have not been asked of the data on the costs of firms of different sizes. My quarrel with him is that he does not go far enough. I believe that cross-section, contemporaneous accounting data for different firms or plants give little if any information on so-called economies of scale. Smith implies that difficulty arises because the observed phenomena do not correspond directly with the theoretical constructs because there is no single, homogeneous product, and so on. I believe that the basic difficulty is both simpler and more fundamental; that the pure theory itself gives no reason to expect that cross-section data will yield the relevant cost curves. Some of the bases for this view are suggested by Smith in his discussion, but he stops short of carrying them to their logical conclusion.

NO SPECIALIZED FACTORS OF PRODUCTION

Let us consider first the simplest theoretical case, when all factors of production are unspecialized so there are numerous possible firms, all potentially alike. This is the model that implicitly or explicitly underlies most textbook discussions of cost curves. For present purposes, we may beg the really troublesome point about this case—why there is any limit to the size of the firm—and simply assume that there is some resource (entrepreneurial ability) of which each firm can have only one unit, that these units are all identical, and that the number in existence (though not the number in use) is indefinitely large, so all receive a return of zero.

In this case, the (minimum) average cost at which a particular firm can produce each alternative hypothetical output is clearly defined, independently of the price of the product, since it depends on the prices that the resources can command in alternative uses. The average cost curve is the same for all firms and independent of the output of the industry, so the long-run supply curve is horizontal and hence determines the price of the product.[6] In the absence of mistakes or changes in conditions, all firms would be identical in size and would operate at the same output and the same average cost. The number of firms would be determined by condi-

---

Pages 146–51 are reprinted from my "Comment" on Caleb A. Smith's "Survey of the Empirical Evidence on Economies of Scale," in *Business Concentration and Price Policy* (Princeton University Press, for the National Bureau of Economics Research, 1955), pp. 230–38, by permission of the publisher; copyright 1955 by Princeton University Press.

6. This neglects some minor qualifications, of which two may deserve explicit mention: first, the irrelevance of the output of the industry depends somewhat on the precise assumptions about the source of any increased demand; second, strictly speaking, the supply curve may have tiny waves in it attributable to the finite number of firms. On the first point, see Richard Brumberg, *"Ceteris Paribus* for Supply Curves," *Economic Journal* (June 1953): 462–63.

tions of demand. In this model, the "optimum" size firm has an unambiguous meaning.

Suppose this model is regarded as applying to a particular industry. Differences among firms in size (however measured) are then to be interpreted as the result of either mistakes or changes in circumstances that have altered the appropriate size of the firm. If "mistakes" are about as likely to be on one side as the other of the "optimum" size, the mean or modal size firm in the industry can be regarded as the "optimum"; but there is no necessity for mistakes to be symmetrically distributed, and in any event this approach assumes the answer that cross-section studies seek.

What more, if anything, can contemporaneous accounting data add? Can we use them to compute the average cost curve that was initially supposed to exist? Or even to determine the size of the firm with minimum average cost? I think not. Consider a firm that made a "mistake" and is in consequence, let us say, too large. This means that the average cost per unit of output that would currently have to be incurred to produce the firm's present output by reproducing the firm would be higher than the price of the product. It does not mean that the current accounting cost is higher than the price of the product—even if there have been no changes in conditions since the firm was established, so that original cost corresponds to reproduction cost. If the firm has changed hands since it was established, the price paid for the "good will" of the firm will have taken full account of the mistake; the original investors will have taken a capital loss, and the new owners will have a level of cost equal to price. If the firm has not changed hands, accounting costs may well have been similarly affected by write-downs and the like. In any event, cost as computed by the statistician will clearly be affected if capital cost is computed by imputing a market return to the equity in the firm as valued by the capital market. In short, differences among contemporaneous recorded costs tell nothing about the *ex ante* costs of outputs of different sizes but only about the efficiency of the capital market in revaluing assets.

In the case just cited, data on historical cost would be relevant. However, their relevance depends critically on the possibility of neglecting both technological and monetary changes in conditions affecting costs since the firms were established. A more tempting possibility is to estimate reproduction costs. This involves essentially departing from contemporaneous accounting data and using engineering data instead, in which case there seems little reason to stick to the particular plants or firms that happen to exist as a result of historical accidents.

Under the assumed conditions, the unduly large firms would be converting themselves into smaller ones, the unduly small firms into larger ones, so that all would be converging on "the" single optimum size. Changes over time in the distribution of firms by size might in this way give some indication of the "optimum" size of the firm.

SPECIALIZED FACTORS OF PRODUCTION

The existence of specialized factors of production introduces an additional reason why firms should differ in size. Even if output is homogeneous, there is no longer, even in theory, a single "optimum" or "equilibrium" size. The appropriate size of firm to produce, say, copper, may be different for two different mines, and both can exist simultaneously because it is impossible to duplicate either one precisely—this is the economic meaning of "specialized" factors. Or, to take another example, Jones's special forte may be organization of production efficiently on a large scale; Robinson's, the maintenance of good personal relations with customers; the firm that gives appropriate scope to Jones's special ability may be larger than the firm that gives appropriate scope to Robinson's. It follows that in any "industry," however defined, in which the resources used cannot be regarded as unspecialized, there will tend to be firms of different sizes. One could speak of an "optimum distribution of firms by size," perhaps, but not of an "optimum" size of firm. The existing distribution reflects both "mistakes" and intended differences designed to take advantage of the particular specialized resources under the control of different firms.

The existence of specialized resources not only complicates the definition of *optimum size;* even more important, it makes it impossible to define the average cost of a particular firm for different hypothetical outputs independently of conditions of demand. The returns to the specialized factors are now "rents," at least in part, and, in consequence, do not determine the price, but are determined by it. Take the copper mine of the preceding paragraph: its cost curve cannot be computed without knowlededge of the royalty or rent that must be paid to the owners of the mine, if the firm does not itself own it, or imputed as royalty or rent, if the firm does. But the royalty is clearly dependent on the price at which copper sells on the market and is determined in such a way as to make average cost tend to equal price.

The point at issue may perhaps be put in a different way. The long-run conditions of equilibrium for a competitive firm are stated in the textbooks as "price equals marginal cost equals average cost." But with specialized resources, "price equals marginal cost" has a fundamentally different meaning and significance from "price equals average cost." The first statement is a goal of the firm itself; the firm seeks to equate marginal cost with price, since this is equivalent to maximizing its return. The second statement is not, in any meaningful sense, a goal of the firm; indeed, its avoidance could with more justification be said to be its goal, at least in the meaning it would be likely to attach to average cost. The equality of price to average cost is a result of equilibrium, not a determinant of it; it is forced on the firm by the operation of the capital market or the market determining rents for specialized resources.

Consider a situation in which a group of competitive firms are all appropriately adjusted to existing conditions, in which there is no tendency for firms to change their output, for new firms to enter, or for old firms to leave—in short, a situation of long-run equilibrium. For each firm separately, marginal cost (long-run and short-run) is equal to price—otherwise, the firms would be seeking to change their outputs. Suppose that, for one or more firms, total payments to hired factors of production fall short of total revenue—that average cost in this sense is less than price. If these firms could be reproduced by assembling similar collections of hired factors, there would be an incentive to do so. The fact that there is no tendency for new firms to enter means that they cannot be reproduced, implying that the firms own some specialized factors. For any one firm, the difference between total receipts and total payments to hired factors is the rent attributable to these specialized factors; the capitalized value of this rent is the amount that, in a perfect capital market, would be paid for the firm. If the firm is sold for this sum, the rent would show up on the books as "interest" or "dividends." If it is not sold, a corresponding amount would be imputed as a return to the "good-will" or capital value of the firm. The equality between price and average cost, in any sense in which it is more than a truism, thus reflects competition on the capital market and has no relation to the state of competition in product or factor markets.

For simplicity, the preceding discussion is in terms of a competitive industry. Clearly, the same analysis applies to a monopolistic firm with only minor changes in wording. The firm seeks to equate marginal cost and marginal revenue. The capital market values the firm so as to make average cost tend to equal price. Indeed, one of the specialized factors that receives rent may be whatever gives the firm its monopolistic power, be it a patent or the personality of its owner.

It follows from this analysis that cross-section accounting data on costs tell nothing about "economies of scale" in any meaningful sense. If firms differ in size because they use different specialized resources, their average costs will all tend to be equal, provided they are properly computed so as to include rents. Whether actually computed costs are or are not equal can only tell us something about the state of the capital market or of the accounting profession. If firms differ in size partly because of mistakes, the comments on the preceding simpler model apply; historical cost data might be relevant, but it is dubious that current accounting cost data are. And how do we know whether the differences in size are mistakes or not?

THE DEFINITION OF COST

The preceding discussion shares with most such discussions the defect of evading a precise definition of the relation between total costs and total receipts. Looking forward, one can conceive of defining the total cost of producing various outputs as equal to the highest aggregate that the resources required could receive in alternative pursuits. Total cost so estimated need not be identical with anticipated total revenue; hence *ex ante* total cost, so defined, need not equal total revenue. But after the event, how is one to classify payments not regarded as cost? Does some part of receipts go to someone in a capacity other than as owner of a factor of production?

All in all, the best procedure seems to me to be to define total cost as identical with total receipts—to make these the totals of two sides of a double-entry account. One can then distinguish between different kinds of costs, the chief distinction in pure theory being between costs that depend on what the firm does but not on how its actions turn out (contractual costs) and the rest of its costs or receipts (noncontractual costs). The former represent the cost of factors of production viewed solely as "hired" resources capable of being rented out to other firms; the latter represent payment for whatever it is that makes identical collections of resources different when employed by different firms—a factor of production that we may formally designate *entrepreneurial capacity,* recognizing that this term gives a name to our ignorance rather than dispelling it.

Actual noncontractual costs can obviously never be known in advance, since they will be affected by all sorts of accidents, mistakes, and the like. It is therefore important to distinguish further between expected and actual noncontractual costs. Expected noncontractual costs are a "rent" or "quasi-rent" for entrepreneurial capacity. They are to be regarded as the motivating force behind the firm's decisions, for it is this and this alone that the firm can seek to maximize. The difference between expected and actual noncontractual costs is "profits" or "pure profits"—an unanticipated residual arising from uncertainty.

Definitions of total costs that do not require them to equal total receipts generally equate them either with contractual costs alone or with expected costs, contractual and noncontractual, and so regard all or some payments to the entrepreneurial capacity of the firm as noncost payments. The difficulty is, as I hope the preceding discussion makes clear, that there are no simple institutional lines or accounting categories that correspond to these distinctions.

Smith mentions the possibility of relating cost per dollar of output to size. Presumably one reason why this procedure has not been followed is that it brings the problems we have been discussing sharply to the surface and in consequence makes it clear that nothing is to be learned in this way. If costs *ex post* are defined to equal receipts *ex post,* cost per dollar of output is necessarily one dollar, regardless of size. Any other result must imply that some costs are disregarded, or some receipts regarded as noncost receipts. Generally, the costs disregarded are capital costs—frequently called *profits.* The study then simply shows how capital costs vary with size, which may, as Smith points out, merely reflect systematic differences in factor combinations according to size. One could, with equal validity, study wage costs or electricity costs per unit of output as a function of size.

The use of physical units of output avoids so obvious an objection; clearly it does not avoid the basic difficulty and, as Smith points out, it introduces problems of its own. The heterogeneity of output means that any changes in average cost with scale may merely measure changes in the "quality" of what is taken to be a unit of output. Insofar as size itself is measured by actual output, or an index related to it, a much more serious bias is introduced tending toward an apparent decline of costs as size increases. This can most easily be brought out by an extreme example. Suppose a firm produces a product the demand for which has a known two-year cycle, so that it plans to produce 100 units in year one, 200 in year two, 100 in year three, etc. Suppose, also, that the best way to do this is by an arrangement that involves identical outlays for hired factors in each year (no "variable" costs). If outlays are regarded as total costs, as they would be in studies of the kind under discussion, average cost per unit will obviously be twice as large when output is 100 as when it is 200. If, instead of years one and two, we substitute firms one and two, a cross-section study would show sharply declining average costs. When firms are classified by actual output, essentially this kind of bias arises. The firms with the largest output are unlikely to be producing at an unusually low level; on the average, they are clearly likely to be producing at an unusually high level, and conversely for those that have the lowest output.[7]

SIZE DISTRIBUTION OF FIRMS

It may well be that a more promising source of information than cross-section accounting data would be the temporal behavior of the distribution of firms by size. If, over time, the distribution tends to be relatively stable, one might conclude that this is the "equilibrium" distribution and defines not the optimum scale of firm but the optimum distribution. If the distribution tends to become increasingly concentrated, one might conclude that the extremes represented mistakes, the point of concentration the "optimum" scale, and similarly with other changes. Whether, in fact, such deductions would be justified depends on how reasonable it is to suppose that the optimum scale or distribution has itself remained unchanged and that the emergence of new mistakes has been less important than the correction of old ones. None of this can be taken for granted; it would have to be established by study of the empirical circumstances of the particular industry, which is why the preceding statements are so liberally strewn with "mights."[8]

7. This is the general "regression fallacy" that is so widespread in the interpretation of economic data.

8. Note added to this edition: The approach suggested in this paragraph has since been developed by George J. Stigler under the term *the survivor principle* and applied empirically in his article, "The Economies of Scale," *Journal of Law and Economics,*

THE RELEVANT QUESTION

I share very strongly Smith's judgment that one of the main reasons why the evidence accumulated in numerous studies by able people is so disappointing is that insufficient attention has been paid to why we want information on so-called economies of scale; foolish questions deserve foolish answers. If we ask what size firm has minimum costs, and define *minimum costs* in a sense in which it is in a firm's own interest to achieve it, surely the obvious answer is: firms of existing size. We can hardly expect to get better answers to this question than a host of firms, each of which has much more intimate knowledge about its activities than we as outside observers can have and each of which has a much stronger and immediate incentive to find the right answer: much of the preceding discussion is really only a roundabout way of making this simple point.

But surely studies of this kind are not really directed at determining whether existing firms make mistakes in pursuing their own interests. Their purposes are quite different. They are, I believe, designed to predict the effect on the distribution of firms by size of one or another change in the circumstances determining their interests. The particular question may well suggest relevant criteria for distinguishing one kind of cost from another and in this way enable cross-section accounting data to provide useful information. For example, Smith discusses studies supposedly showing that assembly and distribution costs rise with the size of plant, whereas manufacturing costs decline. This finding might be decidedly relevant to predicting the effect of a decline in transportation costs on the distribution of firms by size. Or, again, the fact that some firms may use different combinations of factors from others may be due to identifiable differences, geographical or otherwise, in the prices of what in some sense are similar factors. The combinations of factors employed by different firms may then be relevant information in predicting the effect of changes in factor prices. This is the implicit rationale of some of the studies of production functions.

In many cases, the changes in circumstances that are in question are less specific. What would be the effect, for example, of repealing the Sherman antitrust laws on the distribution of firms by size? Of eliminating patents, or changing the patent laws? Of altering the tax laws? As Smith says, there must be much evidence available that is relevant to answering such questions. Unfortunately, as he recognizes, the generalizations assembled by him at the conclusion of his paper do not make much of a contribution; in the main, they simply confirm either the absence of obvious discrepancies between the existing size of firms and the size that is in their own interests or the effectiveness of the capital market in writing off mistakes.

vol. 1 (October 1958), reprinted in George J. Stigler, *The Organization of Industry* (Homewood, Ill.: Richard D. Irwin, 1968), pp. 71–94.

Addendum to Chapter 6

At this point in my course, I generally discuss special problems in the economics of the individual firm, using as a springboard specific problems that had earlier been assigned to the class as "take-home" examinations, such as those given in Part I of Appendix B, pages 329–44. An exhaustive treatment would cover the contents of a course on industrial organization; hence I typically cover only one or two problems in detail, and for the same reason, I refrain from explicit discussion here. The introductions to the problems generally give a brief indication of the relevant theory, which the student is to develop and apply to the particular case outlined. The general topics have included diversification, tie-in sales, internal pricing, price discrimination, and cartels. More expanded developments of many of these topics can be found in the literature, especially in articles by George J. Stigler, who, with Aaron Director, was the original source from whom many of the problems came.

The reader specially interested in one or more of these topics is referred especially to the collection of Stigler's articles in *The Organization of Industry* and to the bibliographical references included therein.

The reader is urged, however, first to try working out the problems on his own before he turns to the published expositions.

7

Derived Demand

The distinction generally made between the theory of the pricing of final products and the theory of the pricing of factors of production is something of a carryover from the early division of economics into two parts, "value" and "distribution." The theory of value concerned itself with the prices of final products, and the theory of distribution concerned itself with the prices of factors of production, primarily as a guide to understanding the division of the total product among major social classes (hence the designation, "distribution"). The theory of general equilibrium merged these two inquiries as parts of one pricing problem involving the simultaneous determination of both sets of prices. At the same time, Marshall's emphasis on supply and demand as an "engine of analysis" rather than on the substantive thing analyzed made it clear that the same analytical apparatus is applicable to the pricing of final products and of factors; in both cases the problem can be expressed in terms of demand and supply and the crucial question is what determines the shapes of these curves.

It is here that the pricing of final products and of factors of production differs. The demand for final products reflects directly the "utility" attached to them; the demand for factors of production does so indirectly, being derived from the demand for the final products. The link between the demand for the final product and the demand for factors is closest when the amount of the factor required is rigidly and technically linked to the amount of the product. Therefore, before proceeding to a general analysis of the demand for productive services, we will find it helpful to consider this special case, which Marshall deals with under the heading, "the theory of joint demand."

The theory of joint demand begins with the notion that the demand for the final product is, in some sense, a joint demand for all the inputs. This notion becomes more than a trite truism if we assume fixed proportions, that the product can be made only by one unique proportion of A/B. From a descriptive viewpoint, such a state of affairs is hardly typical. However, analytically it is a useful abstraction for many problems, especially those of a short-run character. Keeping in mind this assumption of fixed proportions, we shall now proceed with the construction of a derived demand curve. Let us assume that 1 handle + 2 blades = 1 knife.

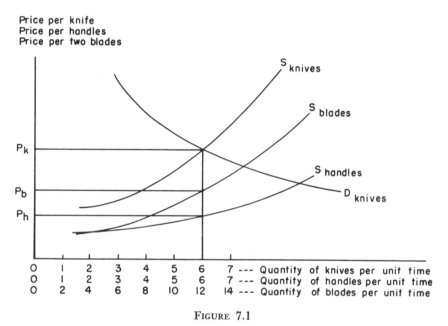

FIGURE 7.1

Figure 7.1 gives the demand for knives and the supply of blades and handles separately. Note that the scales must be drawn appropriately if the curves are to be comparable: for blades and handles, the unit must be the quantity required for one knife. For this reason the quantity scale shows for each number of knives the same number of handles but twice that number of blades. Similarly, the price scale shows price per knife and per handle but the price per two blades. With these scales, and given fixed proportions, it is obvious that the supply price of a knife for any given quantity of knives is equal to the supply price of a handle for the same quantity of handles plus the supply price of two blades for twice that quantity of blades. These supply prices are the minimum prices at which the handle and blades required for a knife will be forthcoming. Hence, if we suppose the cost of assembling to be negligible, their sum is the minimum price at which the corresponding quantity of knives will be forthcoming. The curve labeled the supply of knives is therefore the vertical sum of the two other supply curves. Its intersection with the demand curve for knives gives the equilibrium price of knives, and the supply prices for the corresponding quantity of handles and blades give the equilibrium prices of handles and blades.

How can we construct a demand curve for one of the jointly demanded items separately? The maximum price per knife that can be obtained for any given quantity of knives is given by the demand curve for knives. The maximum price per two blades for that quantity of blades will clearly be this maximum price for knives minus the minimum price per handle that needs to be paid for the corresponding quantity of handles, and, for fixed supply conditions of handles, the latter is given by the supply curve of handles. It follows that the derived demand price per two blades is given by the vertical difference between the demand curve for knives and the supply curve of handles, as in Figure 7.2.

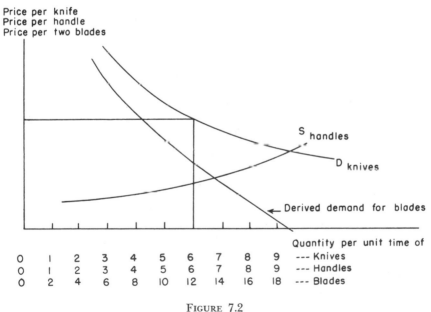

Price per knife
Price per handle
Price per two blades

S handles

D knives

Derived demand for blades

Quantity per unit time of

0	1	2	3	4	5	6	7	8	9	--- Knives
0	1	2	3	4	5	6	7	8	9	--- Handles
0	2	4	6	8	10	12	14	16	18	--- Blades

FIGURE 7.2

The reason we want such a curve is, of course, to trace the influence of changes in supply conditions of blades. The intersection of the supply curve for blades with this derived demand curve for blades will give the equilibrium price of blades, for given supply conditions of handles and demand conditions for knives.

In similar fashion, a derived demand curve for handles could be constructed as in Figure 7.3. Note, however, that the two derived demand curves cannot be regarded as simultaneously valid except at the original equilibrium point, for each assumes the price of the other component to be on its supply curve. A movement along the derived demand curve for handles implies that the price of blades is being determined by a movement along the supply curve of blades, not along the derived demand curve of blades. Only at the equilibrium position is the demand price for each component equal to its supply price; hence only at this point are the two derived demand curves consistent.

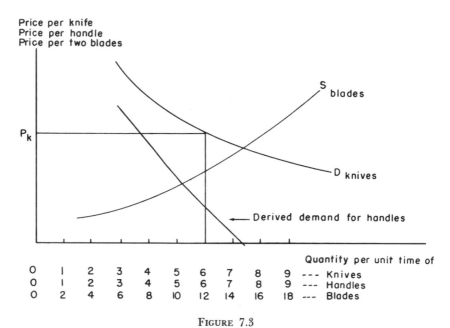

Price per knife
Price per handle
Price per two blades

S blades

P_k

D knives

Derived demand for handles

Quantity per unit time of

O	1	2	3	4	5	6	7	8	9	---	Knives
O	1	2	3	4	5	6	7	8	9	---	Handles
O	2	4	6	8	10	12	14	16	18	---	Blades

FIGURE 7.3

The same analysis can be carried through for joint supply as in Figure 7.4(a) and (b). The supply price of the quantity of hides yielded by a steer for any quantity of hides is the supply price of a steer for the corresponding quantity of hides minus the demand price of the amount of beef in a steer for the corresponding quantity of beef.

Manipulation of these curves readily yields the familiar propositions that an increase in the supply (i.e., reduction in the supply price for each quantity) of one of a pair of jointly demanded items will tend to raise the price of the other item, and that an increase in the demand for one of a pair of jointly supplied items will tend to reduce the price of the other.

As in all problems of demand, the elasticity of the derived demand curve is a very important property. What factors determine the elasticity of a derived demand curve?

Marshall (Book V, chap. 6) gives four principles governing the elasticity

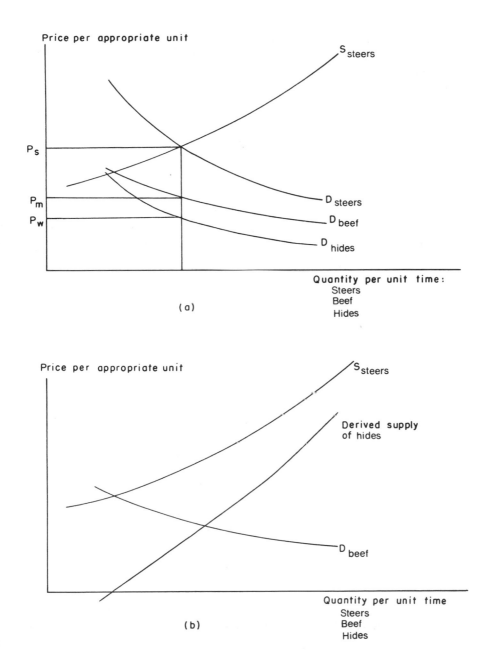

FIGURE 7.4

of the derived demand curve. The derived demand for any factor used in fixed proportions with other factors will be more inelastic: (1) the more essential the factor in question—this condition is guaranteed in extreme fashion by the assumption of fixed proportions and its inclusion is implicitly a generalization to cases in which proportions are not rigidly fixed; (2) the more inelastic is the demand curve for the final product; (3) the smaller the fraction of total cost that goes to the factor in question; and (4) the more inelastic the supply curve of the other factors.

The three final conditions may be demonstrated geometrically, as in Figures 7.5, 7.6, and 7.7.

The dashed alternative demand curve for knives in Figure 7.5 (condition 2) is more inelastic at the equilibrium price than the original, and it is

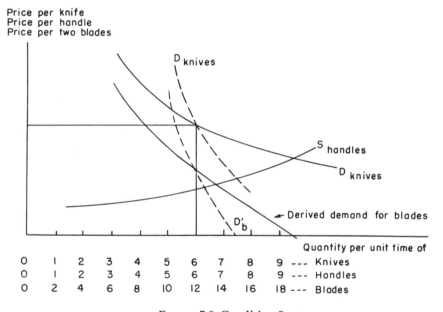

FIGURE 7.5 Condition 2

obvious that so is the dashed alternative derived demand curve for blades.

The dashed alternative supply curves for handles in Figure 7.6 (condition 3) shows double the original supply price for each quantity. In consequence, the demand price for blades at the former equilibrium is less than before. Assume that an appropriately shifted supply curve for blades left the equilibrium quantity of knives unchanged; then the price of blades would be a smaller fraction of total price. It is obvious that the dashed alternative derived demand curve is more inelastic than the original for two reasons: (a) it is steeper so $\frac{dq}{dp}$ is smaller in absolute value; (b) the price of blades is less, so $\frac{p}{q}$, by which $\frac{dq}{dp}$ is multiplied to get elasticity, is smaller.

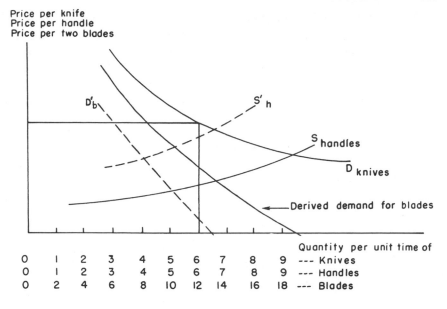

FIGURE 7.6 Condition 3

The dashed alternative supply curve of handles in Figure 7.7 (condition 4) is more inelastic than the original and so is the dashed alternative derived demand curve for blades.

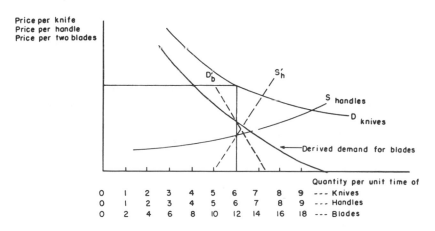

FIGURE 7.7 Condition 4

This analysis will be most useful in those cases in which changes in proportions of factors are of least importance for the problem at hand. This is particularly likely to be the case in problems involving short-run adjustment. The longer the time allowed for adjustment the greater is likely to be the error involved in neglecting changes in proportions.

The usefulness of the analysis can be illustrated by applying it to the problem of interpreting the effectiveness of unions in altering wages and the circumstances on which this effectiveness depends. This is a good illustration, partly because short-run considerations bulk large in union behavior.[1]

The power of unions, as of any other monopoly, is ultimately limited by the elasticity of the demand curve for the monopolized services. Unions have significant potential power only if this demand curve is fairly inelastic at what would otherwise be the competitive price. Even then, of course, they must also be able to control either the supply of workers or the wage rate employers will offer workers.

Demand for Labor*

The theory of joint demand developed by Marshall is in some ways the most useful tool of orthodox economic theory for understanding the circumstances under which the demand curve will be inelastic. It will be recalled that Marshall emphasized that the demand for one of a number of jointly demanded items is the more inelastic: (1) the more essential the given item is in the production of the final product, (2) the more inelastic the demand for the final product, (3) the smaller the fraction of total cost accounted for by the item in question, and (4) the more inelastic the supply of cooperating factors.[2] The most significant of these items for the analysis of unions are the essentiality of the factor and the percentage of total costs accounted for by the factor. Now, a factor is likely to be far more essential in the short run than in the long run. Let a union be organized and let it suddenly raise the wage rate. Employment of the type of labor in question is likely to shrink far less at first than it will over the longer run, when it is possible to make fuller adjustment to the change in wage rate. This adjustment will take the form of substitution of other factors for this one, both directly in the production of each product, and indirectly in consumption as the increased price of the products of unionized labor leads consumers to resort to alternative means of satisfying their wants.

* The following discussion of unions is reprinted from my essay, "The Significance of Labor Unions for Economic Policy," in D. McC. Wright (Ed.), *The Impact of the Union* (Harcourt Brace, 1951), pp. 207–15, by permission of Mr. Wright; copyright 1951 by Harcourt, Brace & Company, Inc.

1. As this is being revised in the year 1975, the demand for petroleum provides another excellent, topical, illustration. Note the near identity with the situation of successful craft unions analyzed below: petroleum is far more essential (closer to fixed proportions) in the short run than in the long run. In many uses, the cost of petroleum is a small part of total costs. Hence the short-run demand curve facing the OPEC cartel was extremely inelastic.

2. Alfred Marshall, *Principles of Economics,* 8th ed. (New York: Macmillan, 1920), pp. 385–86.

This simple point is, at one and the same time, important in understanding how unions can have substantial power and how their power is sharply limited in the course of time.

The importance of the percentage of total cost accounted for by the factor leads one to predict that a union may be expected to be strongest and most potent when it is composed of a class of workers whose wages make up only a small part of the total cost of the product they produce—a condition satisfied, along with essentiality, by highly skilled workers. This is the reason why economic theorists have always been inclined to predict that craft unions would tend to be the most potent. This implication of the joint-demand analysis seems to have been confirmed by experience. While industrial unions have by no means been impotent, craft unions have in general been in a stronger economic position and have maintained it for longer periods.

Simple though they are, these implications of the joint-demand analysis have considerable value in interpreting experience, primarily because other economic changes frequently conceal from "casual" observation the action of the forces isolated in the theoretical analysis. This point can be exemplified by a brief examination of three major apparent exceptions to the generalization that industrial unions are likely to be less potent than craft unions. In each case, it will be found that other economic changes tended to make the strength of the unions appear greater than it actually was.

(1) The United Mine Workers' Union appeared highly successful from shortly before 1900 to about 1920. This period coincided with a long upward movement in general prices and wages, so at least part, and perhaps most, of the apparent success of the union can be attributed to its receiving credit for wage increases that would have occurred anyway. Scanty evidence suggests that wages in soft coal may have risen somewhat more than wages in general during this period, so that all of the wage rise may not be attributable to general inflation. The difference may be evidence that the union had some effect on wage rates, or may reflect the operation of still other forces affecting the supply of and demand for labor in coal mining, such as changes in levels of education, in the composition of the stream of immigrants, etc. It would take a far more detailed examination of the evidence than we can afford here even to form an intelligent judgment about the relative importance of the various forces.

From 1920 to 1933, the general price level was stable or falling, coal was increasingly being replaced by oil, and the United Mine Workers' Union practically went to pieces. It was unable to prevent the underlying economic forces from working themselves out. Yet at least events of the earlier part of this period are a tribute to the short-run strength of the union: the union was clearly responsible for keeping coal wage rates from declining for some time in the face of the sharp drop in wages and prices generally after 1920. This illustrates the implication of the joint-demand analysis that the strategic position of unions will be stronger in the short than in the long run. It also illustrates a not atypical train of events. Attendant favorable circumstances enable a union to gain strength in the number and adhesion of its members by appearing to accomplish more than its basic economic power would permit; the attendant favorable circumstances without which the union might never have survived disappear, but the historical process is not completely reversible: the union for a time at least remains strong and capable of preventing the readjustment that would otherwise take place, though sooner or later it is likely to weaken and die if other favorable circumstances do not come along.

This train of events may be repeating itself in coal. Since 1933, prices and wages in general have again been rising fairly steadily, at a particularly rapid pace, of course, during and after the war, and the union has reestablished itself. Once again, the union seems to be showing real strength less in the wage rises it has attained than in its prevention of a subsequent readjustment.

(2) The garment workers' unions—the International Ladies Garment Workers' Union and the Amalgamated Clothing Workers—achieved their initial successes in the decade prior to 1920, reaching a peak along with the postwar inflation in 1920. Again, the unions may have made the wage rise somewhat greater than it would have been otherwise, but clearly a large and probably the major part of the wage rise for which the unions received credit would have come anyway. Though these unions declined in membership and importance during the 1920s and early 1930s, they fared better than the United Mine Workers' Union, in my view largely or wholly because of an attendant favorable circumstance. These unions were in an industry that had been largely supplied by immigrants from Eastern and Southern Europe. Union or no union, the stringent restrictions on immigration imposed after World War I were bound to reduce the supply of workers and thus to strengthen their economic position. The next spurt in union strength came during the period of generally rising prices and wages following 1933. Thus these unions too have flourished only when underlying economic conditions were generally inflationary.

(3) The more recent large industrial unions—the auto and steel unions in particular—have been operating throughout their lives in a generally inflationary environment. The strength that this has permitted them to gain will be demonstrated in a somewhat paradoxical way: we shall argue later that they were responsible for preventing the wages of their members from rising after World War II as much as they would have in the absence of the union. I doubt that these unions had much effect on wages prior to 1945. The recent (i.e., recent in 1951), much-publicized agreement between the United Automobile Workers and the General Motors Corpo-

ration seems to me almost a public announcement of union weakness.[3]

An interesting and instructive example of the tendency, suggested by joint-demand analysis, for the strategic position of unions to appear stronger in the short run than in the long run is provided by the medical profession. In economic essentials, the medical profession is analogous to a craft union. It consists of a highly skilled group of workers, closely organized, and in an especially strategic position to keep the supply of workers down through control over state licensure and, as a consequence, over admission to medical schools. True, the medical profession differs from the usual craft union in that the return to the worker (medical fees) accounts for a considerably larger fraction of the total cost of the final product. However, even this difference can easily be overstated; costs of hospitals, medications, and the like are by no means negligible. Moreover, this difference is typically supposed to be counter-balanced by inelasticity in the demand for medical care.

There is little doubt that the medical profession has exercised its powers on various occasions to limit entry to the profession fairly drastically: over a considerable period about one out of every three persons who are known to have tried to enter American medical schools has been unable to gain admission, and it is clear that the number of persons seeking entry is considerably less than it would be if it were not for the known difficulty of entry. Further, serious impediments have been placed in the path of potential entrants trained outside the country. Yet, restriction of entry has succeeded in raising average incomes in medicine only by something like 15 to 20 percent.[4] Chiropractors, osteopaths, faith healers, and the like have turned out to be important substitutes, and the increase in their numbers has been one of the most important effects of the restriction of entry into medicine proper, an impressive example of the possibilities of substitution in the long run. The short-run effects of restriction are more noticeable than the means whereby the strength of the union is undermined in the long run, which as noted below, is one of the chief factors that leads to an exaggeration of the effect of unions.

3. The agreement calls for a steady annual increase in the basic rate, plus cost-of-living adjustments. In considerable part, these changes are costless to the company, since, as experience in the automobile industry before unionization and in other industries amply documents, they are the kind of wage changes that come anyway, though they are perhaps larger in magnitude. They represent a clear case of a union seeking to gain credit for what would happen anyway. Assuring itself such credit in so public and dramatic a fashion may be extremely clever union tactics; the need for using such tactics is significant evidence of basic weakness. The length of the agreement is of major value to the company, which is assured thereby of uninterrupted control of its affairs. I doubt that a really strong union would have granted such terms.

4. For evidence on the use of restrictive practices and on their effect on income see Milton Friedman and Simon Kuznets, *Income from Independent Professional Practice* (National Bureau of Economic Research, 1945), pp. 8–20, 118–137.

Supply of Labor and Control over Wage Rates

Another line along which orthodox economic analysis has some interesting implications is the role of so-called restrictive practices. It is clear that if a union can reduce the supply of persons available for jobs, it will thereby tend to raise the wage rate. Indeed, this will be the only way of raising the wage rate if the union cannot exercise any direct control over the wage rate itself. For example, in a field like medicine, there is no significant way of exercising direct control over fees charged or over annual incomes of physicians. The only effective control is over the number of physicians. In consequence, medicine is a clear example of the kind of situation that is usually envisaged in which the wage rate or its equivalent is raised by deliberate control over entry into the occupation.

This line of reasoning has led to the view that, in general, unions may be regarded as exercising control over the wage rate primarily by controlling the supply of workers and that, in consequence, the so-called restrictive practices—high union initiation fees, discriminatory provisions for entrance into unions, seniority rules, etc.—have the economic function of reducing the supply of entrants so as to raise wage rates. This is an erroneous conception of the function of these restrictive practices. They clearly cannot serve this function without a closed or preferential shop, which already implies control over employers derived from sources other than control over entrance into unions. To see the function of these practices and the associated closed shop, let us suppose that the wage rate can be fixed above its competitive level by direct means, for example, by legal enactment of a minimum wage rate. This will necessarily mean that fewer jobs will be available than otherwise and fewer jobs than persons seeking jobs. This excess supply of labor must be disposed of somehow—the jobs must be rationed among the seekers for jobs. And this is the important economic function the so-called restrictive practices play. They are a means of rationing the limited number of jobs among eager applicants. Since the opportunity to work at a wage rate above the competitive level has considerable economic value, it is understandable that the restrictive practices are important and the source of much dispute.

The question remains how the wage rate can be controlled directly by means other than legal enactment of a minimum wage rate. To do this, unions must be able to exercise control over employers—they must be able to prevent existing employers from undercutting the union wage rate, as well as the entry of new employers who would do so. They must somehow be able to force all employers to offer the union wage rate and no less. The devices whereby this is done are numerous and can hardly be fully enumerated here. However, one feature of the various devices whereby wage rates are directly enforced or entry into an occupation limited is essential for our purposes, namely, the extent to which they depend on political assistance. Perhaps the extreme example is again medicine, in which practice of the profession is restricted to those licensed by the state and licensure in turn is in general placed in the hands of the profession itself. State licensure applies in similar fashion to dentists, lawyers, plumbers, beauticians, barbers, morticians, and a host of other occupations too numerous to list. Wherever there is licensure, it is almost invariably in the hands of the existing members of the occupation, who almost as invariably seek to use it to limit entry. Of course, in many cases, these techniques are largely ineffective, either because it is not feasible to restrict drastically the number of licenses granted, or because it is possible to evade the licensure provisions. But they do exemplify how political power can be used to control entry directly. Only slightly removed from this kind of licensure provision, and in many ways far more effective, is local political support through building codes, health regulations, health ordinances, and the like, all of which serve numerous craft unions as a means of preventing nonunion workers from engaging in their fields through substitution or elimination of materials or techniques, and of preventing potential employers from undercutting the union wage rate. It is no accident that strong unions are found in railways, along with federal regulation. Again, union actions involving actual or potential physical violence or coercion, such as mass picketing and the like, could hardly take place were it not for the unspoken acquiescence of the authorities. Thus, whether directly in the form of specific laws giving power to union groups or indirectly in the form of the atmosphere and attitude of law enforcement, direct control over union wage rates is closely connected to the degree of political assistance unions can command.

Here again, there is a very close parallel between labor unions on the one hand and industrial monopolies on the other. In both cases, widespread monopolies are likely to be temporary and susceptible of dissolution unless they can call to their aid the political power of the state.

8

The Theory of Distribution with Fixed Proportions

The joint demand analysis superficially seems to explain the determination of the price of each of two factors of production that must be combined in rigidly fixed proportions to produce a product, but it does so only by taking as given the supply curves of each of the two factors of production. Now these supply curves in turn depend on conditions in markets for other products; they reflect the quantities of factors that would be available for this use rather than some other, and hence depend indirectly on derived demand conditions in other markets. The question arises whether the joint demand analysis can be generalized from the partial analysis so far considered to a more general one. What explains the prices of factors of production if every product satisfies the conditions of the joint demand analysis, i.e., every product is produced under conditions of fixed proportions? ("Constant coefficients of production" is another way of describing this case.)

Let us first suppose that the proportions in which the factors are combined is the same in all industries: that, say, it takes one unit of A plus one unit of B to produce one unit of X or one unit of Y, etc. In this case, any two "commodities" are perfect substitutes in production: that is, the indifference curve (or transformation curve) showing the various combinations of, say, X and Y that can be produced with any given quantities of A and B will be a straight line as in Figure 8.1 for 100 units of A and 100 units of B.

Clearly, X and Y must sell for the same price in a free market, and similarly for the other commodities, no matter what quantities of them are pro-

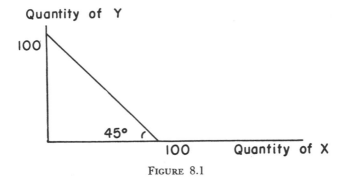

FIGURE 8.1

duced. The relative demands for them will determine the quantities produced but will have no effect on their price. The fact that there are different commodities, therefore, is unimportant on the side of demand for factors of production. Since their relative prices are always rigidly fixed, it is as if there were only one commodity, say Z. This simple case illustrates an important general point, namely, that substitution in production is an alternative to substitution in consumption and vice versa.

Let us now construct a derived demand curve for factor B along the lines of our joint demand analysis. To do so, we need the demand curve for Z and the supply curve of A. How shall we draw the demand curve for Z, the single commodity in the community? Our analysis is concerned with relative prices, not absolute prices, since we have introduced no "money" into the economy, so this question involves deciding on the "numeraire" in terms of which to express prices. Since our fundamental problem is the division of the total output among the cooperating factors, and since, thanks to fixed relative prices among final products (which justifies our treating them all as a single product), there is no problem how to measure output, it seems convenient to express the prices of factors of production in terms of the final product; i.e., to take Z as a numeraire. But then the price of Z in terms of itself as numeraire is clearly unity by definition, no matter how much or little Z there is. But this means that (by definition) the demand curve for Z is a horizontal line at a price of unity, as in Figure 8.2.

What of the supply curve of A? There is presumably some maximum flow of A that can be made available to the production of this commodity, say 100 per unit time. If we stick rigorously to the assumption that Z is the only final product, there is nothing else that these services can be used for, and hence they will be available for this use at any price, i.e., the supply curve of A will be perfectly inelastic for any positive price, and perfectly elastic at a price of zero. It is drawn as OFG in Figure 8.2. (The elasticity of the supply curve of factors to the market as a whole reflects the existence of nonmarket uses of productive services, here ruled out by definition.)

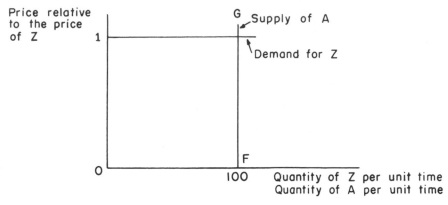

FIGURE 8.2

By our preceding analysis, the demand for B is given by the vertical difference between the demand curve for Z and the supply curve of A, which yields a demand curve for B as in Figure 8.3. Note that this demand curve is nearly identical with the value of the marginal product curve for B. Given 100 units of A, the marginal product of B is unity so long as the quantity of B is less than 100, 0 thereafter. To get the equilibrium price of B, we need to know the supply curve of B. As in the case of A, it will be perfectly inelastic at any positive price, so it can be described by a single number. Suppose the number of units of B available per unit time is less than 100. The supply curve of B (S_B in Figure 8.3) will then intersect the demand curve for B at P_1 or at a price of 1, so the equilibrium price will be equal to unity for B, which means, of course, 0 for A (as can be shown directly by carrying through the same analysis for it). If the supply of B is greater than 100 ($S'B$ in the above diagram), the supply curve intersects the demand curve at P_2, implying a price of 0 for B and of unity for A.

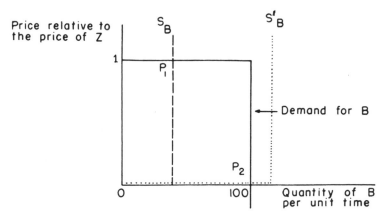

FIGURE 8.3

These two cases are relatively simple and straightforward. If one or the other of the factors is so plentiful relative to the other that not all of it can be used, then in the absence of combination (implicitly ruled out in drawing our supply curves) it will be a "free" good. But what if the quantity of B available is precisely the same as that of A, i.e., 100 in the example? The supply and demand curves will then be as in Figure 8.4. Clearly any price

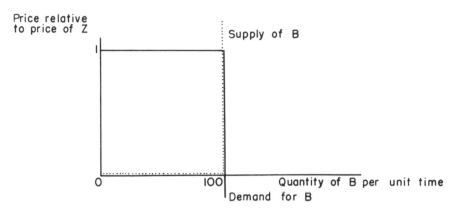

FIGURE 8.4

of B not greater than 1 or less than 0 is consistent with equilibrium. Given the price of B, say P_B, the price of A will clearly be $P_A = 1 - P_B$, since the total amount to be divided between 1A and 1B is one unit of Z, the amount they produce.

This solution is understandable: we have no way of determining the separate contributions of A and B to the total product, hence no way on grounds of their marginal contributions of determining their separate economic value. Only a bundle of an A plus a B is an economically meaningful unit. The product of such a unit is 1, so $P_A + P_B = 1$. Any values of P_A and P_B such that they add up to unity will do. There are an infinite number of values that are compatible with this type of equilibrium. Economic forces as such do not dictate a unique pair of values for P_A and P_B. They merely set up limits, i.e., that $P_A + P_B = 1$. The actual values of P_A and P_B depend on other factors. If no "noneconomic" considerations are relevant, it is irrelevant how the total of unity is divided between a partnership of an A and a B, for only the combined unit is significant, just as it is of little significance what part of a man's wages is to be attributed to his right hand and what to his left. The problem of the division of the product between A and B is significant only if there are noneconomic considerations that make the distinction of an A from a B significant. In this case, these noneconomic considerations will completely determine the division; we will have the relative returns determined by "pure bargaining," as it were.

We have introduced pure bargaining to explain the division of the product between A and B only when their supply curves coincide. But, it may be asked, may we not also have to introduce it when the supply curves do not coincide, because the implicit assumption that there is no coalition among the A's or among the B's will be invalid? If, say, the quantity of A available per unit time is 150, but of B only 100, cannot the owners of A (call them A's) secure a return above 0 by forming a coalition? Suppose, for a moment, they do, agreeing to divide equally among themselves any amount they get, and suppose for the moment that they succeed in getting 9/10 of the product for themselves, so each of the 100 units of B (who do not, we suppose, form a coalition) gets 1/10 of a unit of Z, while the coalition of 150 units of A gets 90 units of Z.

Is this a stable position? Clearly not, so far as economic considerations are concerned. Each A separately is receiving 6/10 of a unit of Z, each B, 1/10 of a unit of Z. Clearly there is an incentive for an A and a B to get together outside the coalition. To each A separately, it appears that if he leaves the coalition while the others stay, he can bribe a B to depart from the coalition and still have something more left for himself, since the total product of the A and B partnership outside the coalition will be 3/10 of a unit greater than the sum of their returns so long as the coalition is unbroken. This means that the coalition of the A's is unstable, and that economic forces will be perpetually tending to disrupt even if it once is established.

So far, we have considered a world in which the proportions of factors of production are not only fixed in each industry but also the same in all industries. Let us now suppose that while fixed in each industry separately, they are not the same in all industries. As the simplest case, we may suppose two sets of industries. Call the (composite) product of one set X, the other Y, and assume that it takes one unit of A plus one unit of B to produce one unit of X, and one unit of A plus two units of B to produce one unit of Y. These production conditions will yield a production possibility curve like that in Figure 8.5 for 100 units of A and 150 units of B.

Except at P_1, not all units of A or of B are used. Between Y_1 and P_1, some units of A are unemployed, between P_1 and X_1, some units of B. Clearly in either of these sectors, we are back in our earlier problem. Between Y_1 and P_1, the price of A will be zero, the rate of substitution of X for Y will be fixed by the number of units of B required and will be two units of X for one unit of Y, so the price of Y will be twice the price of X. Between P_1 and X_1, the price of B will be zero, the rate of substitution of X for Y will be fixed by the number of units of A required and will be one unit of X for one unit of Y, so the price of X will equal the price of Y. Whether the final equilibrium will be in one of these sectors will depend on conditions of demand. If we suppose Figure 8.5 to be for one individual (in a society, say, of identical individuals), we can superimpose on it the

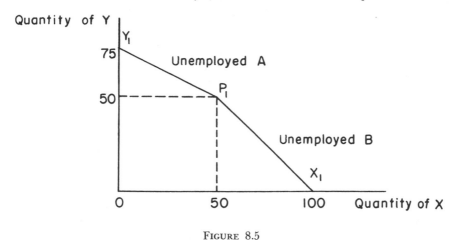

FIGURE 8.5

consumption indifference curves of the individual, which yields the three possibilities summarized in Figure 8.6.

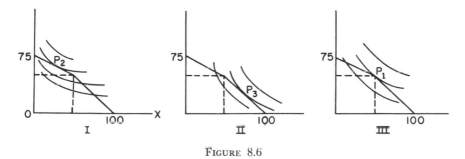

FIGURE 8.6

In (I), the point of equilibrium involves the unemployment of some A, hence a price of zero for A; in (II), the unemployment of some B, hence a price of zero for B. These are essentially the same as our earlier case. In (I), it is as if we had one commodity, the quantity of which was obtained by treating two units of X as equal to one unit of Y; in (II), as if we had one commodity, the quantity of which was obtained by treating one unit of X as equal to one unit of Y. In either of these cases, demand, as it were, determines only the relative quantities of X and Y, and production conditions determine relative prices.

The interesting case is (III). Here production conditions determine relative quantities and demand conditions relative price. The price of Y is somewhere between the price of X and twice the price of X, the exact point depending on what price ratio will induce the public to consume the same amount of X as of Y. Suppose that it took a price of Y that was 1.6 times the price of X to induce the public to consume the same amount of X as of Y. Let p_x, p_y, p_a, p_b, be the price of X, Y, A, and B respectively. It would then follow that:

(1) $$p_a + p_b = p_x$$

(2) $$p_a + 2p_b = 1.6p_x$$

or, substracting equation (1) from equation (2),

$$p_b = .6p_x$$

which, from equation (1), means

$$p_a = .4p_x.$$

These prices are equal to the marginal product of A and B respectively at the margin. If a unit of A is added, it can be employed by producing one fewer units of Y, which will release one unit of A and two units of B, and two additional units of X, which will require the two units of A and two units of B available. The marginal product of A is therefore two units of X minus one unit of Y, or in value terms, $2p_x - p_y = .4p_x$. Similarly, the marginal product of B is one unit of Y minus one unit of X, or, in value terms, $p_y - p_x = .6p_x$.

More generally, we can derive the marginal product of each factor and the value of the marginal product for different amounts of it, i.e., we can derive marginal productivity curves, which in this case will also be demand curves for the factor. Consider, first, the marginal product of A, given that there are 150 units of B. If we think of adding units of A to the 150 units of B, we have a choice when we use the first unit of A whether to combine it with 2 B to produce one unit of Y or with 1 B to produce one unit of X, or partly one and partly the other. Since, under these conditions, the rate at which Y can be substituted for X is one to one (since B is superabundant), the price of X and of Y would have to be the same if both are to be produced. By our convention of taking the price of X as the numeraire, the price of both will be equal to 1 and so will total income. Now at these prices and this income, conditions of demand ("utility functions") will determine how the first unit of A will be divided between production of X and of Y. At one extreme, consumers might prefer only Y, at the other, only X. In either of these extreme cases, the price of only one of the products will be defined, but even when this is the price of Y, it will be simplest, and valid, to regard it as equal to 1. More generally, the consumers will distribute their unit income among both products, so both will be produced. In all three cases, however, the marginal product of A is unity at the outset.

Let us continue to add units of A. For a time, it is clear, everything is the same as when the first unit is applied to the 150 units of B. B is superabundant, so X and Y are equal in price, the value of the marginal product of a unit of A is unity, the physical product being divided between X and Y in proportions dictated by demand. How many units of A must be added before a point is reached at which B is no longer superabundant, hence no longer a free good? Clearly this depends on conditions of demand. If at a price of unity for both, X is in much greater demand than Y, so the bulk of each increment to total output is composed of X, then B will not become a "limitational" factor until close to 150 units of A have been added to the 150 units of B available. At the other extreme, if at a price of unity for both, Y is in much greater demand than X, so the bulk of each increment to total output is composed of Y, then B will become a "limitational" factor when slightly more than 75 units of A have been added to the 150 units of B available.

To be concrete, let us suppose that demand conditions are summarized by

(3) $$\frac{x}{y} = \frac{5}{8} \frac{p_y}{p_x}$$

This "demand curve" implies that the ratio of Y to X depends only on the price ratio of the two products and not on the absolute level of income.[1] If $p_y = p_x$, the ratio of X to Y is 5/8, which means that in the initial phase, as units of A are added, 5/13 of each unit is used to produce 5/13 of a unit of X; 8/13 of each unit to produce 8/13 of a unit of Y. So long as this continues, the amount of B required is given by

(4) $$b = \frac{5}{13} a + \frac{16}{13} a = \frac{21}{13} a$$

where a is the amount of A employed, b the amount of B required. This can continue so long as the amount of B required is less than 150, i.e., until

(5) $$\frac{21}{13} a = 150$$

or

(6) $$a = 92 \, 6/7,$$

at which point 35 5/7 units of X and 57 1/7 units of Y are being produced.

Once this point has been reached, further units of A can no longer be employed in this fashion. An extra unit of A can be employed only by producing one unit fewer of Y, and using the unit of A and 2 units of B thereby released together with the additional unit of A to produce two units of X. In physical terms, then, the marginal product of A becomes two units of X minus one unit of Y. At the prices of X and Y prevailing when this point is reached, namely $p_y = p_x = 1$, the value of the marginal product

1. The set of utility functions that will yield this demand curve is given by $U = F(xy^{\frac{8}{5}})$, where $F' > 0$.

is $2p_x - p_y$ or unity as before. But as additional units of A are added, the prices of Y and X cannot remain the same, for the quantity of Y is declining relative to the quantity of X, so the price of Y must rise relative to the price of X in order to induce consumers to buy Y and X in the proportions in which they are being made available, which means that the value of the marginal product of A declines. Additional units of A will be used to produce two additional units of X and one fewer units of Y so long as the value of this combination is positive, i.e., so long as the price of one unit of Y is less than the price of two units of X. When p_y becomes equal to $2p_x$, the value of the marginal product of A is zero, and additional units of A will not be used at all.

In our special case, when a $\geq$ 92 6/7, the amount of X produced will be equal to

$$(7) \qquad x = 2(a - 92\ 6/7) + 35\ 5/7 = 2a - 150;$$

$$(8) \qquad y = -(a - 92\ 6/7) + 57\ 1/7 = 150 - a.^2$$

Inserting equations (7) and (8) into equation (3), the price of Y will be

$$(9) \qquad p_y = p_x \frac{8}{5} \frac{(2a - 150)}{(150 - a)},$$

so that

(10) Value of marginal product $= 2p_x - p_y$

$$= p_x \left(2 - \frac{8}{5} \frac{2a - 150}{150 - a} \right) = p_x \left(\frac{2700 - 26a}{5(150 - a)} \right)$$

This will be equal to zero when $a = \dfrac{2700}{26} = 103\ \dfrac{11}{13}$.

The resulting value of marginal product curve is given in Figure 8.7. The value of the marginal product is unity when the quantity of A is 92 6/7 or less, declines at an increasing rate from 92 6/7 to 103 11/13, and is 0 thereafter. If the amount of A available is 100, as earlier assumed, the price of A is .4, as shown by the intersection of the supply curve and the value of marginal product curve. This curve is of course valid only if b is equal to 150.

By exactly the same procedure, the value of marginal product of B can be derived, and you will find it a useful exercise to go through the arithmetic of deriving it.

The indeterminacy that arose when the proportions were both fixed and the same in different industries is entirely eliminated by the existence of

2. These equations can be checked most readily by noting that they refer to the interval in which all units of A and of B are used. The amount of A used is given by $x + y = a$; the amount of B by $x + 2y = 150$, in the case in question. Solving these two equations gives (7) and (8) directly.

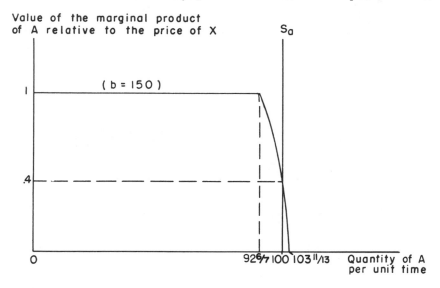

FIGURE 8.7

two alternative proportions in which the factors can be combined, as can be seen from the preceding figure. If the quantity of A is less than 92 6/7, its price is unity (the price of B is zero); if the quantity of A is greater than 103 11/13, its price is 0 (the price of B is unity); if the quantity of A is between 92 6/7 and 103 11/13, its price is given by $\dfrac{2700 - 26a}{5(150 - a)}$, or the ordinate of the curve plotted in Figure 8.7. There no longer remains any scope for a "pure bargaining" theory of wages.

9

The Theory of Marginal Productivity and the Demand for Factors of Production

The case just considered—of fixed proportions among the factors of production in each industry separately—is a special case of the general theory of marginal productivity. In that special case, an increase in the supply and consequent reduction in price of a particular factor increases the quantity of the factor demanded solely through substitution in consumption: the lowered price of this factor makes the products in whose production it is relatively important cheaper relative to other products, and this leads consumers to substitute them for the other products. More generally, substitution will also take place in production. For each product separately, producers will have an incentive to substitute the relatively cheaper factor for others, and in general it is possible to do so, at least to some extent.

The "theory of marginal productivity" is sometimes described as the "theory of distribution." This statement is misleading. The theory of marginal productivity at most analyzes the factors affecting the demand for a factor of production. The price of the factor depends also on conditions of supply. The tendency to speak of a "marginal productivity theory of distribution" arises because in many problems and contexts it is useful to think of the supply of factors of production as given quantities, as perfectly inelastic. This is particularly relevant if the problem concerns both market and nonmarket uses of factors of production. In such cases, there is a sense in which supply conditions determine only the quantity of the factors, while demand conditions (summarized in the phrase *marginal productivity*) determine price. But note that even in this case a change in supply—in the fixed amount of a factor—will change the price of the factor, unless demand is perfectly elastic. So it will be better in all cases to regard the theory of marginal productivity as a theory solely of the demand for factors of production. A complete theory requires a theory of both the demand for and the supply of factors of production.

In the main, the marginal productivity theory is a way of organizing the considerations that are relevant to the demand for a factor of production. It has some, but not very much, substantive content. This is reflected in our ability to speak of an abstract factor of production—factors A or B, etc.—without having to specify it any further. To say that wages are equal to the value of the marginal product, for example, says relatively little in and of itself. Its function is rather to suggest what to look for in further analysis. The value of the marginal product is not a single number determined by forces outside the control of individuals or society; it is rather a schedule or function of many variables. It will depend on the quality and quantity of workers, the quantity of capital they have to work with, the quality of the management organizing their activities, the institutional structure of the markets in which they are hired and the product sold, etc. In concrete applications, the basic substantive issue is likely to be what determines the marginal productivity and how the changes under consideration will affect it.

The analysis of the demand for factors of production is closely related to the analysis of the supply of products, and, indeed, is really only another way of looking at or organizing the same material. In analyzing the supply curve of a product, we are interested in tracing the effect of changes in the demand for it under given conditions on the factor markets. In consequence, we direct attention to the output of the firm or industry and take for granted the changes in the quantity of the various factors of production employed and in their prices as demand for the product and with it output of the product change. In distribution theory, our interest centers in the factor markets, and so we concentrate attention on a different facet of the same adjustment by the firm. To put it differently, the statement that a firm seeks to equate marginal factor cost to marginal value product is another way of saying that it seeks to equate marginal revenue to marginal cost rather than an additional condition on the equilibrium of the firm.

As in the theory of supply of products, there are several different levels of analysis, and the demand curve will change as we shift our point of view from the reactions of the firm to the reactions of an industry. And in this case, there is also a third level that is significant, the economy as a whole, since many different industries may employ what for any particular problem it is useful to regard as a single factor of production.

The demand curve for a factor of production by a particular group of demanders (which may as a special case be a single firm) shows the maximum quantity of the factor that will be purchased by the group per unit of time at each price of the factor, for given conditions. As in previous problems, there is some uncertainty how it is best to specify the "given conditions." They clearly include (1) technical knowledge—the "state of the arts" or the production functions of actual and potential firms; and (2) the conditions of demand for the final producst. The uncertainty attaches primarily to the handling of other factors of production. One procedure is to take as given (3) the supply curves of other factors of production to the group of demanders considered. The problem with item 3 is that at least for the economy as a whole, constant supply curves for other factors may mean an increase in the total resources of the community as we move along the demand curve for this factor in response to an increase in its supply. The alternative is to take the "total resources" of the community, appropriately defined, as fixed, and thus to regard changes in the supply of this factor as changes in its supply relative to other factors but not in the total resources of the community. We shall for the most part beg this question, since most of our discussion wold be unaffected by its resolution.

It should be noted that the precise meaning of items 2 and 3 as stated above depends on the particular group of demanders considered. To a firm selling its product on a competitive market, item 2 is equivalent to holding the price of the product constant; to an industry producing a single product, it is equivalent to holding the demand function for the product constant. To a firm, item 3 is equivalent to holding constant the *price* of factors that it buys on competitive markets, and the *supply curves* of other factors. In particular, it is equivalent to holding constant the amount of "fixed" factors. To an industry, item 3 may still be equivalent to holding constant the price of some factors, namely those of which the industry as a whole buys only a small part of the total, so that the supply curve of the factor to the industry is effectively horizontal. To the economy as a whole, especially if this is regarded as including the nonmarket as well as the market sector, item 3 may be equivalent to holding the quantities of other factors constant (though this obviously depends critically on how the uncertainty about item 3 is resolved).

Note also that the difference between short- and long-run demand curves is in the precise content of items 2 and 3.

Finally, the list of "other things" is not exhaustive for all problems. For many problems, for example, it will be desirable to give special consideration to closely related factors of production.

The Individual Firm

In analyzing the demand for factors of production by the individual firm, we may again start with the fundamental equations defining its equilibrium position:

(1)
$$\frac{1}{MR} = \frac{MPP_a}{MFC_a} = \frac{MPP_b}{MFC_b} = \frac{MPP_c}{MFC_c} = \cdots = \frac{1}{MC}$$

(2)
$$x = f(a, b, c, \ldots)$$

If there is competition on the product market, MR will, of course, be equal to the price of the product or p_x; if a factor is purchased on a competitive market, its marginal factor cost will, of course, be equal to its price. For the time being, we may suppose that any factors are either purchased competitively, so that we can replace their marginal factor costs by their prices, or are "fixed" to the firm, so that we can regard the quantity (or maximum quantity) available as given. The shorter the run, the larger the number of factors the available quantity of which are to be regarded as given, and conversely. Indeed, as we saw in the discussion of supply, this is essentially the definition of length of run.

From a purely formal point of view, the demand curve for a factor of production by an individual firm can be derived immediately and directly from equations 1 and 2. Let the firm be selling on a competitive market, let factors A, B, ... be purchased competitively, and A′, B′, ... be the factors whose quantities are fixed to the firm for the run considered. Then the demand curve for, say, factor A, will be given by

(3)
$$a = h(p_a; p_x; p_b, \ldots; \bar{a}', \bar{b}', \ldots),$$

where $\bar{a}'$, $\bar{b}'$, ... stand for the fixed quantities of these factors available to the firm. Now this equation is simply a rearrangement of equations 1 and 2. For any given set of values of the independent variables in equation 3, equations 1 and 2 can be solved to give the quantities of the various factors employed and the quantity of product produced. This can therefore be done for every set, and the quantity of A employed can be expressed as a function of these variables, as in equation 3.

If the product market is not competitive, p_x in equation 3 is replaced by the demand curve for X; if the factor market for B is not competitive, p_b is replaced by the supply curve of B to the firm, etc.

We shall, however, gain insight if we proceed more slowly and less formally to this final result. It is helpful to rewrite equation 1 in the following form:

(4)
$$MR \cdot MPP_a = MFC_a,$$
$$MR \cdot MPP_b = MFC_b,$$
$$\cdots\cdots\cdots\cdots\cdots\cdots$$

If we have competition on both factor and product markets, these reduce to

(5)
$$p_x \cdot MPP_a = p_a,$$
$$p_x \cdot MPP_b = p_b,$$
$$\cdots\cdots\cdots\cdots\cdots,$$

or the familiar equations that marginal value product of a factor equal its marginal factor cost, in the general case, or value of the marginal product of a factor equal the price of the factor, in the competitive case.

Consider the first of equations 5. This shows a relation between the price of A and its quantity: for each price of A, it shows the quantity of A that would have a marginal product whose value would be equal to that price of A. It is tempting to interpret this as the demand curve of the firm for A, and, indeed, the demand curve for A is often loosely described as given by the value of marginal product curve for A. But this is strictly correct only in one special case: that in which the firm is not free to vary the quantity of any factor other than A, i.e., all other factors are "fixed." In that case, the only adjustment the firm can make to a change in the price of A is to change the quantity of A employed; all equations other than the first in 5 become irrelevant and are replaced by equations of the form: $b' = \bar{b}'$. The firm will move along the marginal product curve for A until the value of the marginal product is equal to the new price of A and this curve will be its demand curve.

Suppose, however, that not all other factors are fixed, that, for example, B can be varied and is purchased competitively. Hypothetically, suppose the price of A to fall and the firm to make its first adjustment along the marginal product curve for A, so that it increases the employment of A until the marginal product falls enough to satisfy the first of the equations 5. The remaining equations are now no longer satisfied, despite the fact that they initially were and that the quantity of other factors is, by assumption, the same as initially. The reason, of course, is that the marginal product of the other factors depends on the amount of A employed. Some other factors will be close substitutes for A; the marginal product of these will be reduced by the increased employment of A. Other factors will tend to have their marginal product increased by increased employment of A, since in effect there is less of them per unit of A. In general, we may expect the latter effect to dominate, as should be clear from our earlier discussion of the law of variable proportions. The firm will therefore want to change the amount of other factors employed, reducing the employment of those whose marginal product is now less than initially and increasing the employment of the others. But these adjustments will in turn change the marginal productivity of A, tending to increase it for each quantity of A; both the reduction in quantity of competitive factors and the increase in quantity of others operate in general in this direction. The final position will be one at which the equations 5 are satisfied. At this final position, the price of A is equal to the value of its marginal product, yet this point is not on the initial value of marginal product curve. The essential point is that the marginal product curve is drawn for fixed quantities of other factors; the demand curve, in our special case, for fixed prices of variable factors.

Figure 9.1 summarizes the situation. The solid lines are value of mar-

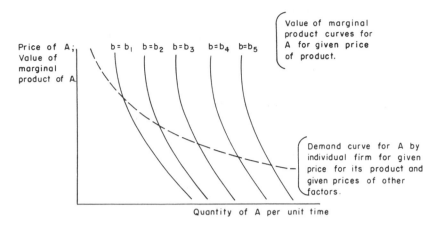

Figure 9.1

ginal product curves for different amount of B (used here to stand for all other factors). The dashed line is a demand curve for A by the individual firm. Since competition is assumed on both product and factor markets, the price of the final product and of other variable factors of production is the same at all points on it. But, as seen, the quantity of B is not; it varies in such a way as to keep equations 5 satisfied. Accordingly, the demand curve cuts through the value of marginal product curves, in general going through successively higher curves as the price of A falls.

If demand for the product is not competitive, given demand conditions imply different prices as the output varies. Marginal value product diverges from value of marginal product and is the quantity relevant to the individual firm. With this change in nomenclature, Figure 9.1 can summarize the situation, except that there is no longer any presumption that the quantities of other factors in general will increase as the price of A falls or that the demand curve will pass through marginal value product curves for successively higher quantities of b. The reason is that while an increase in the quantity of A employed in response to a decline in its price would in general raise the marginal physical product of given quantities of the other factors, it will also mean an increase in output, a decline in the price of the product, and perhaps also a decline in marginal revenue. This may offset or more than offset the rise in the marginal physical product of the other factors and so lead to a decline in the quantity of those employed. We shall meet an analogous effect again when we combine competitive firms and examine the demand curve of an industry.

If the market for factor A is not competitive, so that the firm is a monopsonistic purchaser of A, how much the firm would employ at various prices is no longer a meaningful or relevant question, since the firm affects the price by its action and determines the price and quantity simultaneously.

The corresponding question is then the reaction of the firm to changes in the supply of the factor, and these changes cannot be summarized by the single parameter, price of the factor, as they can when the market for A is competitive. What would otherwise be the "demand curve" for factor A still retains significance. It shows the quantity that would be purchased at various marginal factor costs. However, in so interpreting it, it must be kept in mind that a single supply curve will in general have different marginal factor costs for different quantities supplied, and that many different supply curves can have the same marginal factor cost for the same quantity supplied. (This case is discussed more fully in the following pages.)

In the above analysis we have taken as our (hypothetical) first approximation the change in quantity of A with fixed quantities of other factors. This, of course, implies that even in the first reaction, the firm changes its output. There is then an additional change in output when the quantities of other factors are adjusted and the quantity of this one readjusted. Another way of breaking down the reaction of the firm is to take as the first approximation the change in the purchase of A that would occur if the firm kept its output the same. This is, as it were, the pure substitution in production effect. If the price of A falls and output is kept constant, A will be substituted for other factors, implying in general a movement from the initial marginal productivity curve for A to a lower one. At this point, all the equalities in equation 1 except the first are satisfied: the firm is producing this output in the optimum manner, given the new price of A. The reduction in the price of A has, however, increased the common value of the ratios of marginal physical products to marginal factor costs; it has increased the number of units of output attainable by spending an additional dollar, that is, it has reduced marginal cost. Marginal cost is therefore now lower than marginal revenue, which means that output is less than the optimum. An expansion effect is therefore added to the substitution effect. In expanding, the firm will employ more of all factors, in general. This increase in employment of A adds to the increase due to the substitution effect. For other factors, it offsets the initial decrease. As before—since the final position is the same—the final position will tend to involve the employment of more of the other factors in general but may involve the employment of less of close substitutes for A.

Figure 9.2 shows the three curves we have been talking about. P is the initial point of equilibrium, and so all three pass through it. The steepest (at P) shows the amount of A that the firm would purchase if it kept output constant; the next steepest shows the amount of A it would purchase at given product prices if it kept the amount of other factors employed constant; the flattest shows the amount of A it would purchase at given product price and given prices for other factors.

You will find it instructive to check and prove statements made about the order of these curves; to show that monopoly on the product market

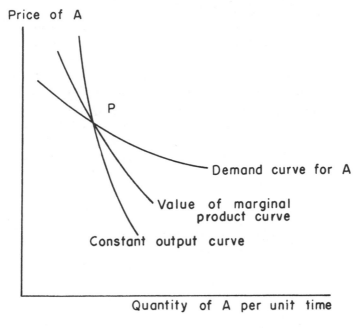

Price of A

P

Demand curve for A

Value of marginal
product curve

Constant output curve

Quantity of A per unit time

FIGURE 9.2

can change the order of these curves; and to translate the above in terms of production indifference curves.

The Competitive Industry

In reacting to conditions on the product and factor markets as they see them, individual firms obviously change those conditions: they impose external effects on themselves and other firms in their own industry, and the combined reactions of all firms in a single industry impose external effects on other industries.

Let us first confine our attention to a single industry. In response to a decline in the price of A, each individual firm seeks to move along its demand curve for A, which will involve expanding its output. But all individual firms obviously cannot do so without changing the conditions for which those demand curves are drawn. For one thing, the increased output by all firms will lower the price of the product, and this will shift the demand curve for A of each individual firm downward, since each of these is drawn for a fixed price of the product. This would be the only external effect to be considered at this stage if the industry uses no specialized (variable) factors, i.e., if it employs only a small part of the total available supply of all other (variable) factors, so that their supply curves to the industry can be taken as essentially horizontal. The final increase in the amount of

A purchased by all firms in response to a reduction in the price of A (to this industry alone) will be less than that shown by the sum of the demand curves for the individual firms in the industry, as shown in Figure 9.3. The flattest curve through P is the sum of the demand curves for A of the individual firms in the industry; the next steepest curve is the demand curve for A of the industry as a whole. Through each point of the demand curve of the industry there passes such a sum of demand curves of the individual firms, showing the sum of the amounts the individual firms would want to employ if the price of the product were not altered as a consequence of their increased production. The more elastic the demand for the product of the industry, the less will tend to be the divergence between these two curves.

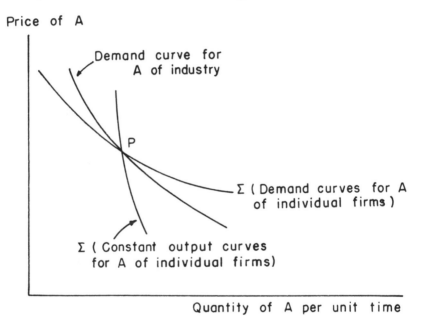

FIGURE 9.3

The changes in the price of the product will affect not only the amount of A employed but also the amount of all other factors. As noted earlier, with a constant price for the product, there is a presumption that the demand for other factors will on the average rise with a decline in the price of A. There is no longer any such presumption, once account is taken of the effect of the expansion of output on the price of the product. This can be readily seen by taking the extreme example in which demand for the product is perfectly inelastic. In this case, the price of the product will fall to whatever extent is necessary to keep total output unchanged, and the demand curve for A of the industry will be approximately the same (in this special case of given other factor prices to the industry) as the sum of the constant output curves for the individual firms drawn earlier. The qualification "approximately the same" is necessary because all firms in the industry need not have the same production functions, and the decline in the price of A may affect different firms differently. In consequence, the unchanged total output of the industry may conceal decreases in output by some firms, balanced by increases by other firms. But as we saw before, these curves imply the substitution of A for all other factors as a group (though not for every single one, since there may be some highly complementary with A), and so reduced employment of other factors on the average. As this example implies, the demand curve for A of the industry will, as shown on the figure, tend to be between the sum of the constant output curves and the sum of the demand curves of the individual firms, its exact position depending on the elasticity of the demand for the product.

If the industry uses some specialized resources, a further effect will be produced on the prices of these resources. The remarks in the preceding paragraph show that we cannot specify the direction of effect on the average. The demand for specialized resources that are highly competitive with A will tend to fall with a reduction of the price of A under almost any circumstances, and so their prices will tend to fall. Taken by itself, the reduction of the price of highly competitive factors reduces the incentive to substitute A for them, but also reduces marginal cost and so increases the incentive to expand output. There is perhaps a presumption that the combined effect is likely to be a smaller increase in the employment of A than if the price of these highly competitive factors had remained unchanged. The demand for specialized resources that are highly complementary with A will tend to rise with a reduction in the price of A under almost any circumstances, and so their prices will tend to rise. This tends clearly to make for a smaller increase in the employment of A than if the price of these highly complementary factors had remained unchanged, both by reducing the advantage in substituting A for other factors and by raising marginal cost. The demand for the remaining resources may move in either direction. The more elastic the demand for the product, the more likely is the demand for, and price of, these other resources to rise, in which case the aggregate effect of the changes in prices of specialized resources will be to make for a smaller increase in the employment of A than if all resource prices other than that of A had remained unchanged. On the other hand, the more inelastic the demand for the product, the more likely is the demand for, and price of, these other resources to fall, and they may fall enough to lead to a greater increase in the employment of A than if all resource prices other than that of A had remained unchanged.

In addition to these external pecuniary effects of the changed pattern of production stimulated by the fall in the price of A, there may, of course, also be external technical effects of the kinds considered in the discussion of supply curves. These may operate in either direction on the employment of A.

So long as we restrict ourselves to the effects of the reactions within a single industry to the decline in the price of A, the net result will be an increased purchase of A and an increased output of the product. The effects external to the individual firm but internal to the industry may make these increases smaller or larger than they would have been without the external effects, but they cannot—aside perhaps from pathological special cases—convert them into decreases. It is precisely the increase in output that makes the price of the product decline and so makes expansion seem less attractive to the individual firm than it would at the initial price; and the prices of other resources cannot on the average rise except as a result of a generally increased demand for them, which also means an increase in output. But while this is true for the industry as a whole, it need not be true for every single firm. The different firms may be using different techniques of production and combinations of factors. Some, for example, may be using techniques that involve particularly heavy use of a factor that rises in price as a result of external effects, and for such firms this rise in price may be enough to produce a decline in output. Some may be specially affected by external technical effects, and so on.

The Economy as a Whole

Much of the preceding discussion applies equally in passing from each industry considered separately to the economy as a whole. Each industry in reacting to the change in the price of A imposes external effects on itself and other industries.

Resources highly competitive with A will obviously tend to fall in price, and resources highly complementary to A to rise in price, almost no matter how (i.e., relative to what) their price is measured and what their conditions of supply are. There is little to add to our previous discussion about such resources. What, however, about all resources other than A, in general? Obviously, the fall in price of A *is* a rise in the price of other resources relative to A, and hence relative to the average price of all resources, and we are talking throughout only about relative prices. The effect on the average price of all resources (including A) relative to the average price of final goods and services depends to some extent on our initial assumptions about the source of the increase in the supply of A that produces the decline in its price (i.e., about the meaning of given conditions of supply of resources). If the increase in supply of A is taken to be solely an increase in relative supply compensated by a decrease in the supply of all other factors sufficient to keep total resources available unchanged in an appropriate sense, then in that same sense aggregate output will be unchanged, and hence the average price of all resources will remain unchanged relative to the average price of goods and services. This, however, means that the average price of resources other than A rises relative to the average price of final goods and services. If the increase in supply of A is supposed to be a net addition to the total resources of the community, with the supply of other resources unchanged, then it obviously permits a greater aggregate output. It is not clear what effect this will have on the average price of all resources relative to the price of final goods and services; it is clear, however, that the average price of all resources other than A will rise relative to the average price of final goods and services, as in the preceding case.[1] The important thing throughout is to recognize that we cannot speak about changes in "price" for the economy as a whole without defining the base relative to which price is measured.

As just noted, according to at least one possible interpretation of "given conditions of supply of factors of production," total output must in one sense remain the same despite the reduction in the relative price of A. Yet we saw in the preceding section that, if we took account only of the reactions within a single industry, the decline in the price of A would lead to an increase in output in each industry separately. Obviously there must be some external effects that reverse this result for some or many industries. External effects via the prices of particular resources highly competitive with or complementary to A may do so. More generally, however, the external effect that is important in this connection is on the relative prices of final goods and services and the associated substitution in consumption— the effect that we saw working in pure form in the case of fixed proportions. In the preceding section, we took account of the changes in resource prices that each industry produced by its own reactions. But these changes impose external effects on other industries. As we saw in the previous paragraph, a decline in the price of A means that the price of other resources in general rises relative to the price of A and also relative to the average price of all resources and to the average price of final goods and services. For products produced predominantly with these other factors, this rise in their price will more than offset the fall in the price of A. The cost of producing such products will therefore rise and their supply curves shift to the left. This occurs for these industries as a result not of their own reactions to the reduced price of A but because of external effects imposed on them by the reactions of other industries. The output of such industries will tend to decline, though their employment of A may not, for, like other industries, they have an incentive to substitute A for other factors. But the decline in output may be enough to produce also a decline in employment of A. Thus, while the demand curve for A by every industry separately is negatively sloped, a curve showing the amount of A finally employed by an industry at various prices (account being taken of all internal and external

---

1. Here as elsewhere in this section we are begging index number problems involved in measuring "average" price. These are of the same kind as those considered in the section on consumer demand.

effects) need not be negatively sloped. A particular industry may employ less A at a lower price for A. Of course, such cases will, for the usual reasons, be exceptions.

Essentially, these same comments apply if the increased supply of A is taken to be a net addition to the total resources of the community. In this case, total output can increase so it is not impossible for every industry to increase output. In general, however, if the output of those products produced with relatively little A does not decrease, it will tend to increase less than the output of products produced with relatively much A. This is about the only change in our exposition required.

If the increase in the supply of A is taken to be a net addition to the total resources of the community, and if we suppose the supply curves of other factors to be perfectly inelastic, competition to reign throughout, and external technical effects to be absent, then the demand curve for A for the economy as a whole is a value of marginal product curve for the economy as a whole. (You will find it instructive to see why each of these qualifications is necessary.) But it is not the sum of the value of marginal product curves for each firm separately. The curves for the individual firms not only are for given prices of products, they are also for given quantities of other resources employed by each firm separately. The curve for the economy, on the other hand, takes account of shifts of resources between firms and industries—it is for given quantities of other resources to the economy as a whole. It shows the value of the addition to the total product attainable by adding one unit of A to an unchanged quantity of all other resources, when the allocation of all resources between firms and industries is rearranged in the optimum fashion. The rearrangements that are possible depend, of course, on the assumed conditions and in particular on the adjustment time permitted, so they will be more extensive in the long than in the short run. For any run, the marginal product curve for the economy will tend to be more elastic than the sum of the marginal product curves for the firms, because some rearrangement is possible. And the longer the run, the more elastic the marginal product curve will be, because the wider will be the range of possible rearrangements.

Whichever assumption is made about the source of the increased supply of A, the demand curve for A for the economy as a whole will tend to be between the sum of the demand curves for A of all individual firms and the sum of the constant output curves for A of individual firms, so Figure 9.3 applies for the economy as a whole as well as for an individual industry.

Summary for Competitive Factor Markets

The demand curve for a factor of production for the economy as a whole reflects the effect of substitution in both production and consumption. If prices of products and other factors were unchanged, an increase in the supply of a factor and consequent decline in price would give each firm an incentive to substitute that factor for other factors in producing its initial output and to expand its output. The attempt by many firms to make these adjustments will, however, raise the prices of other factors relative to product prices. This will raise costs of products produced with relatively little of the now cheaper factor relative to the costs of products produced with relatively much of the now cheaper factor, leading to corresponding changes in the supply of these products and thereby in their prices. This adds substitution in consumption between industries to substitution in production within firms and industries. These general effects will be complicated by special effects arising through special relations between factors in production and products in consumption. Factors that are close substitutes to the now cheaper factor in production will tend to fall relatively in price; factors that are highly complementary will tend to rise in price, with further secondary effects on prices of products in the production of which these factors are specially important. Similarly, products that are close substitutes in consumption for the products produced with relatively much of the now cheaper factor will tend to fall in price and products that are close complements to rise in price, and so on.

For each firm in the economy separately, equilibrium requires that marginal factor cost of the quantity of a factor employed be equal to the marginal value product of that quantity of the factor. For a competitive factor market, this means that at each point on the economy's demand curve for a factor, the price of the factor is equal to the marginal value product of the factor to each firm in the economy separately. This is the central proposition in the marginal productivity theory of the demand for factors of production. But as we have seen, it is a much more complex proposition than may at first appear. Different points on the demand curve involve not only different amounts of the factor in question but extensive readjustments in the organization and use of other factors, the scope of the adjustments depending on the length of run considered. The individual firm seeks equality between marginal value product and price of the factor. It achieves this equality by changing methods of production and output, and so marginal value product, not by changing the price of the factor, over which it has no direct control.

Monopsony

It may be worth considering in somewhat more detail the case in which the factor market is not competitive. Let us suppose that there is perfect competition among the sellers of a particular factor service, so that a supply curve for the factor is meaningful, but that a particular firm is the sole purchaser of the factor service in question: the case of monopsony. As noted above, in this case the question of how much the firm would

employ at various prices is no longer a meaningful question, since the firm
determines the price and quantity simultaneously.

This case is depicted in Figure 9.4. The curve VV (labelled the *hypothetical demand curve*) is precisely what the demand curve for this factor
would be if the firm were a competitive purchaser of the factor and is to be
derived precisely as the demand curve for a factor was derived above. As
will be seen from that derivation, it shows, for each quantity of A, the
(maximum) amount that the firm can add to its revenue per unit increase
in the amount of A employed. If the quantities of all other factors available to the firm were fixed, it would be a marginal value product curve for
A. If the quantities of all other factors available to the firm are not fixed,
the firm will vary the amount of these other factors employed as it uses
more or less A in such a way as to keep their marginal value products equal
to their marginal factor costs, so the curve VV is no longer a marginal value
product curve, since the quantities of other factors are not the same for
all points on it.

Curve SS is the supply curve of the factor A to the firm. It shows the
maximum amount of the factor the firm could purchase at various prices.
The ordinate of any point on SS is therefore the average cost per unit of A
to the firm if it buys the amount given by the abscissa of that point. The
ordinate of the curve marginal to SS (curve MM) gives, therefore, the
amount that the firm would add to its costs per unit increase in the amount
of A employed, or the marginal factor cost for various amounts of A. It obviously pays the firm to hire more A so long as the amount it thereby adds
to its receipts (the ordinate of VV) exceeds the amount it adds to its costs
(the ordinate of MM). The intersection of these two curves therefore gives

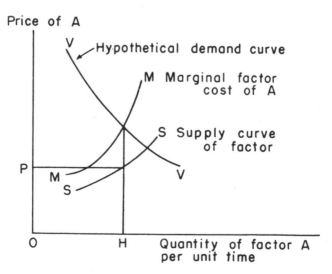

FIGURE 9.4

the optimum amount of A to employ, in this example, OH. The price paid per unit is then the ordinate of the supply curve at H, or OP.

Note that many different prices of the factor are consistent with the same VV curve and the same amount of A employed, since different supply curves can have the same marginal factor costs at a particular quantity of the factor. One example is depicted in Figure 9.5.

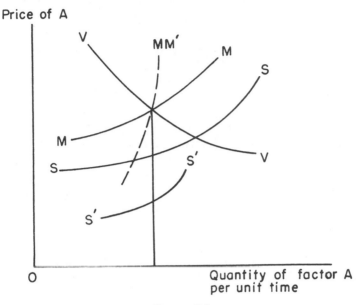

FIGURE 9.5

The factor market may fail to be competitive not because the firm is the sole purchaser of the factor but because there is a single seller. This case is essentially the same as monopoly in the sale of a product. The seller of the factor services is faced by a negatively sloped demand curve, and he will seek to equate marginal revenue with whatever he may regard as his marginal cost.

If a monopsonistic purchaser of a factor faces a monopolistic seller, we have a case of bilateral monopoly. The maximum return for the two monopolists together is given by the intersection of the marginal cost curve of the monopolistic seller and the VV curve of the preceding figures for the monopsonist buyer; this is the amount of the factor that would be used if the two monopolies combined. If the bargaining between the two monopolists does not lead to the use of this amount of the factor, the position is unstable, in the sense that there is a further gain that could be gotten by merging: that is, either monopolist can afford to offer the other a larger sum to buy his monopoly position than the value of that monopoly position to the latter, so there is a further deal by which both can gain. This argument suggests that there is a uniquely determined quantity under such a bilateral monopoly, at least if merger is not ruled out by some non-economic obstacle; but it does not provide any means of determining how the monopoly returns will be divided between the two monopolists, and in this respect the solution must be regarded as largely indeterminate.

One interesting special application of this monopsony analysis has been to demonstrate the possibility that the imposition of a legal minimum wage higher than the prevailing wage can raise the amount of labor employed. This is illustrated in Figure 9.6. The solid curves apply in the absence of the minimum wage, so OA is the equilibrium amount of labor employed at a wage of OW_1. Suppose a legal minimum wage of OW_2 is imposed and effectively enforced. The supply curve to the firm is no longer SS, but now becomes $OW_2 CS$, since at a wage below OW_2 the firm cannot hire any labor. The marginal factor cost is then no longer MM but OW_2CDM, which intersects the VV curve at E. Therefore the equilibrium employment is OB, larger than previously, despite a rise in the wage rate

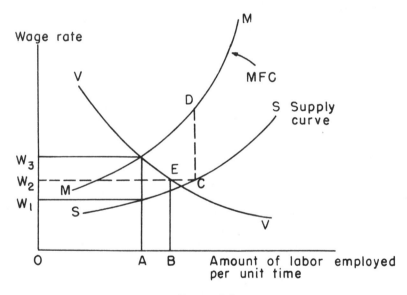

FIGURE 9.6

from OW_1 to OW_2. In order for this effect to occur, it is obvious that the minimum wage must be between W_1 and W_3. If it is above W_3, it will have the usual effect of diminishing employment.[2]

2. An instructive example of the subtleties embodied in such an apparently simple analysis and of how easy it is to go wrong is provided by a series of comments in the *American Economist*, which were triggered by Frank Falero, Jr.'s criticism of this analysis, "A Note on Monopsony, Minimum Wages, and Employment," *American Economist*, 10 (Fall 1966): 39–42. There have since been six further items: Richard C.

It is perhaps worth noting explicitly that this case is little more than a theoretical curiosum and cannot be regarded as of any great practical importance. This is partly because significant degrees of monopsony are particularly unlikely to occur for factors of the kind affected by minimum wage rates, partly because even in such cases there is no presumption the minimum wage rate will fall in the interval analogous to OW_1 to OW_3.

Yates and Benjamin J. Taylor, "A Note on Monopsony, Minimum Wages, and Employment: Comment," ibid., 11 (Fall 1967): 56–61; Frank Falero, Jr., "A Note on Monopsony, Minimum Wages, and Employment: A Reply," ibid., 12 (Spring 1968): 52; William P. Gramm and Robert B. Ekelund, Jr., "Monopsony, Minimum Wages, and Employment: A Reconsideration," ibid.: pp. 52–54; Ralph Gray and John E. Morrill, "A Note on Monopsony, Minimum Wages, and Employment: Extended," ibid.: pp. 55–64; William P. Gramm and Robert B. Ekelund, Jr., "Monopsony in a Muddle," ibid.: 12 (Fall 1968): 79–80; and Houston H. Stokes, "Monopsony, Minimum Wages, and Employment: A Further Comment," ibid.: 14 (Fall 1970): 79–81. For a comprehensive correct analysis, it is necessary to combine the final three items.

10

Marginal Productivity Analysis: Some General Issues

As we have seen, marginal productivity analysis does not provide a complete theory of the pricing of factors of production. It summarizes the forces underlying the demand for factors of production, but the price of factors depends also on the conditions under which they are supplied. To complete the theory, we shall have to analyze the forces underlying the supply curves of factors of production. Before turning to that task, however, it will be well to consider some general issues that have arisen in connection with the marginal productivity theory, issues that are connected primarily with the central proposition that has been used in analyzing the demand for factors of production—that factors tend to receive their marginal value product—rather than with the conditions of supply.

The Exhaustion of the Product

One question that arose almost from the outset of marginal productivity theory is whether there is any assurance that payment in accordance with marginal product will exhaust the total product. May it not be that if each factor is paid according to its marginal product, the sum of all the payments to factors will either exceed or fall short of the total amount available to be paid? In this case, what happens to the difference?

Wicksteed gave what was, for a time, the most widely accepted answer to this question. He pointed out that if the production function was homogeneous of the first degree, then Euler's theorem demonstrated that payment in accordance with marginal productivity would exhaust the total

194

product. Let a, b, . . . be the quantities of the factors of production and x = f (a, b, . . .) be the production function. Now f(a, b, . . .) is a homogeneous function of the t-th degree if

(1) $$f(\lambda a, \lambda b, \ldots) = \lambda^t f(a, b, \ldots).$$

Euler's theorem asserts that for a homogeneous function of degree t:

(2) $$\frac{\partial f}{\partial a} \cdot a + \frac{\partial f}{\partial b} \cdot b + \ldots = tf(a, b, \ldots) = tx$$

If t is unity, this becomes

(3) $$\frac{\partial f}{\partial a} \cdot a + \frac{\partial f}{\partial b} \cdot b + \ldots = x.$$

The partial derivatives are precisely the marginal physical products of the various factors of production, and they are multiplied by the amount of the corresponding factors. Hence, each term on the left-hand side is the total payment to a factor in physical terms (if each factor gets its physical marginal product) and their sum is precisely equal to the total quantity of product available. This equality is not altered by multiplying through by the price of the product, which is in effect what happens under perfect competition.

But this solution is, in a sense, too good. If the production function for the individual firm is everywhere homogeneous of the first degree, then payment in accordance with marginal product will exhaust the total product regardless of the proportions in which the factors are combined, and returns to the factors will be independent of the scale of the firm. Furthermore, if there is any monopoly, then payment in accordance with marginal value product will not exhaust the total product. Finally, while we have seen earlier that it is reasonable to regard production functions as homogeneous of the first degree from a sufficiently broad point of view, it does not follow from this way of looking at them that they are homogeneous of the first degree everywhere from the viewpoint of the individual firm. It is, as it were, an empirical accident if they are, and it seems rather unsatisfactory to base a fundamental proposition of economics on an empirical fact, the determination of which is not even in the realm of economics but in the realm of technology.

A more satisfactory solution is to argue that exhaustion of the product, far from being a necessary resultant of particular technical facts, is a condition of equilibrium. Consider a particular position: if one resource owner pays all other resource owners their marginal product, he has left over more than the marginal product of the resource he owns. Then all other owners of such resources have an incentive to do what he is doing and in the process to eliminate the difference. Conversely, if the residual is less than the marginal product of his resource, he has an incentive to cease being a residual income recipient, end his present activity, and rent out the use of his resource for its marginal product. The result is that, under competition, the individual firm will tend to operate at an output and with a combination of resources at which its production function is homogeneous of the first degree.

The Role of Marginal Productivity in Positive and Normative Analysis

In discussing marginal productivity analysis, it seems desirable to depart from our general principle of avoiding normative issues. The reason is that confusion between positive and normative issues is perhaps the basic source of misunderstanding of marginal productivity analysis and the fundamental reason for the continual controversy about the theory.

Perhaps the simplest form this confusion takes is in the argument that if marginal productivity analysis is valid, it makes the wage rate (or rate of return to any other resource) inevitable, determined by the "laws of nature," and not susceptible to change by human action, and this is such objectionable a result that the analysis cannot be accepted. Of course, even if this inference were correct, it would not be valid grounds for rejecting the analysis. We may bemoan the fact that the world is round and that there is nothing we can do about it, yet this is hardly grounds for rejecting it as a fact. But as is clear from the preceding analysis, the inference is not correct. Indeed, the marginal productivity analysis is a means of analyzing the ways in which the wage rate in, say, a particular occupation can be changed by human action. It can be raised by any action that will raise the marginal productivity of the number of employees hired. This can be accomplished by reducing the number hired, by raising the efficiency of the workers, by increasing the efficiency of the management, by increasing the amount of capital with which they work, etc.

A more sophisticated form of the confusion is the set of objections to marginal productivity analysis frequently made in undergraduate textbooks—particularly in labor economics—to the effect that the theory "assumes" perfect mobility of resources, perfect knowledge of available alternatives, perfect competition, etc. Aside from the general problem raised by such statements about "assumptions," it is clear that in this particular case they are entirely beside the point if marginal productivity is viewed as a tool of positive analysis, as a means of understanding the forces underlying the demand for factors of production and hence of understanding why the prices of resources are what they are. Suppose labor of a particular kind is completely immobile between the North and the South. This means that labor of this kind in the North is, in effect, a different resource from labor of this kind in the South. These are two different resources, each having its own supply curve. The prices of these two resources will be determined by the intersection of their respective supply and demand curves. The demand curve for northern labor will depend on its value productivity, which, of course, will depend on the price of southern labor, and conversely, just as the demand for labor may depend on, say, the price of land. If a unit of northern labor is a perfect substitute in production for a unit of southern labor (i.e., many activities can be carried out equally well and at equal cost either in the North or the South), demand conditions will dictate the same price for the two; if they are not perfect substitutes, their prices will differ; and so on. Hence, marginal productivity analysis is useful to determine the effects of immobility. Similarly, ignorance, like immobility, will affect conditions of supply of factors of production. And we have seen how readily the analysis can cover monopolistic conditions.

The reason these "assumptions" are introduced is because they are relevant in judging the normative implications of payment in accordance with marginal product. Suppose ignorance of opportunities in other furniture factories keeps laborers in one group of factories from seeking jobs in another group in which a higher wage rate is being paid, so that essentially the same type of labor gets a higher wage rate in one group of factories than in another, although in each group separately each laborer gets the value of his marginal product. Clearly, the removal of the ignorance will add to the total product. The worker who shifts from the lower-paid to the higher-paid job will add more to product in his new employment than he will subtract from product by giving up his old employment.

As this example illustrates, the normative function of payment in accordance with marginal product is to achieve efficiency in the allocation of resources. Payment to the worker of his marginal product gives him an incentive to seek employment where his marginal product is the highest. Suppose wage rates in the two groups of furniture factories were equal despite the difference in marginal product; the workers would then have no incentive to shift where their marginal product is higher. Similarly, payment in accordance with marginal product gives the buyer of resources an incentive to use the resources best adapted to his purpose. For example, suppose there are two types of laborers, A and B. Suppose A and B are perfect substitutes in activity 1, while B has higher productivity in activity 2 than A. If payment is in accord with marginal productivity, B will get a higher wage rate than A because of his higher productivity in activity 2 (if the amount of B is sufficiently limited so that all can be employed in equilibrium in activity 2). Employers in activity 1 have an incentive to hire A instead of B, since to get B they would have to pay his marginal product in activity 2. On the other hand, suppose the wages of A and B are arbitrarily made the same, which means that they cannot be in accord with marginal productivity. Then employers in activity 2 still have an incentive to get hold of B instead of A, but employers in activity 1 have no incentive to hire A instead of B. And, of course, in all these cases the "incentive" itself depends on the employer's being paid in accordance with *his* marginal product, for his productivity consists precisely in choosing the resources best adapted to his purpose, and if his reward does not depend on how well he performs this task, where does he find an incentive to do it well?

More generally, payment in accordance with marginal product can be seen to be a means of making the rate of substitution of final products in purchase on the market equal to the rate at which it is technically possible to substitute final products in production. This can be seen most readily by eliminating all intermediaries. Suppose the marginal product of an hour's labor, with other resources given, is either one bushel of corn or one bushel of wheat. The technical rate of substitution is then one for one. Unless corn and wheat sell at equal prices, the apparent rate of substitution is not one to one, and the alternatives actually open to the consumer are falsified. So far this only requires that rates of return be proportional to marginal product. But unless the rate of return is equal to marginal product, the rates of substitution between market and nonmarket goods will be falsified. Suppose that in the above case the price of the hour of labor is one-half bushel of wheat. To the laborer it appears that he can get an hour of leisure by sacrificing a half-bushel of wheat, yet in fact the community sacrifices a whole bushel of wheat.

A full analysis of these normative issues would involve a much more extended discussion, particularly of the problems raised by unappropriable benefits and unborne costs ("neighborhood effects," divergence between private and social product). But perhaps enough has been said to indicate why problems of ignorance, immobility, and degree of competition bulk large in analyzing the normative implications of payment in accordance with marginal product. Perhaps, also, enough has been said to indicate that the function of securing an "appropriate" allocation of resources is performed by the setting of *rates per unit of resource,* not of total incomes to identifiable individuals, which depends not only on such rates but also on the amount of resources owned by individuals.

The Ethics of Distribution

The normative issue about which there has been most controversy has not, however, been the role of marginal productivity in achieving allocative efficiency; it has rather been whether it also produces distributive justice. The marginal productivity theory has been taken as a defense of the justice of the existing distribution of income. Given a reasonable approximation to competitive conditions, it is argued, marginal productivity theory shows that each man gets what he produces. Clearly, a man de-

serves what he produces. Consequently, it is said, the existing distribution
of income is just.

One objection that can be made to this argument is that private product
—in accordance with which an individual is paid—may diverge from social product. For example, the producers of burglar's jimmys are being
paid their marginal (private) product. But this objection is hardly fundamental; it attacks what is essentially a minor premise in the argument, for
it merely argues that in some cases the market measure of product is not
an appropriate measure. It does not deny that, if product is appropriately
measured, individuals should get their product.

The basic postulate on which the argument rests is the ethical proposition that an individual deserves what is produced by the resources he
owns. Aside from the acceptability of this proposition, it must be recognized that it is widely and unthinkingly accepted. It is essential for the
stability of a society that there be a set of beliefs that are unthinkingly accepted by the bulk of the society, beliefs that are taken for granted and not
questioned. In my judgment, this proposition is or has been one of those
beliefs in our society, and the fact that it is so is part of the reason why
society has accepted the market system and its associated methods of reward. The function of payment in accordance with marginal product may
"really" be to achieve allocative efficiency. Yet payment is permitted to
perform this function only because it is widely, if perhaps mistakenly, believed that it produces distributive justice.

A striking indication of how deeply this ethical proposition is embedded
in the values of our society is its implicit acceptance by the most extreme
opponents of our system. One of Karl Marx's chief criticisms of the capitalist system is his theory of exploitation of labor. Labor, he says, is exploited because labor produces the whole product but gets only part of it.
Even if there were some meaningful sense in which labor produces the
whole product, why is the result "bad" or a sign of "exploitation?" It is
"bad" only if labor "ought" to get what it produces—which is the fundamental ethical proposition stated above. If the Ruskinian slogan, "From
each according to his ability, to each according to his need," is accepted
(again waiving all questions of defining the terms *ability* and *need*), the
entire Marxian argument disappears. To establish "exploitation," one
would then have to show not that labor gets less than it produces in some
sense but rather that it gets less than it "needs."

Of course, even if one accepts the basic ethical proposition, the Marxian
theory of exploitation is logically fallacious. Clearly, some part of current
product is attributable to nonhuman capital. The Marxian answer is that
nonhuman capital is the product of past labor—"embodied" labor, as it
were. But if this were so (and I do not mean to imply that it is), the
Marxian slogan would have to be rephrased: "Present and past labor produce the whole product, but present labor gets only part of the product."

At most, this implies not that present labor is exploited but that "past labor" is, and a new ethical proposition would have to be introduced to argue that present labor should get what present and past labor produce.

The purpose of considering this Marxian doctrine is not, of course, to give a complete analysis of it, but only to show that this criticism of the capitalist system is itself based on acceptance of the capitalist ethic.

If one examines in more detail the proposition that an individual deserves what is produced by the resources he owns (his labor power and his nonhuman capital), I believe that it can neither be wholly accepted nor wholly rejected. For two individuals in comparable circumstances and with equal opportunities, the proposition is entirely reasonable, because payment through the market covers only part of the use of resources, and payment in accordance with marketable product is required to achieve equality of total return. But for two individuals with unequal opportunities, the principle seems much less reasonable. One man is born blind, another with his sight; is it "just" that the former receive less than the latter because his productivity is smaller? The difficulty is that it is hard to see any other principle to apply. The fundamental "injustice" is the original distribution of resources—the fact that one man was born blind and the other not. It is clear that in such cases we do not, in fact, apply the principle of payment in accordance with product.

It is sometimes thought that the principle applies more fully to payment for the use of human resources than to payment for the use of nonhuman resources: that an individual "deserves" what he produces by his own labor or by the capital he himself produces, but not what is produced by the capital he has inherited. As the preceding example suggests, this distinction is largely false and irrelevant. If a man deserves what he produces by his labor, this means he is entitled to consume his product as he wishes, provided that he does not interfere with others. If he may use it in riotous living but may not give it to his son, is he getting what his labor produces? Mr. Jones inherits wealth from his father; Mr. Smith inherits rare and highly paid physical or mental ability. Alternatively, Mr. Jones uses the proceeds of his labor to give his son a technical education, which will enhance his son's earning power; Mr. Smith uses the proceeds of his labor to buy a business for his son, which will enhance his son's earning power by the same amount. Wherein is the difference?

This is a superficial and incomplete discussion of complicated and subtle issues. Its purpose is not to present any complete or satisfactory analysis but rather to show that the marginal productivity analysis of the determination of rates of return to resources does not have any unique ethical implications. Acceptance of this analysis in no way commits one to acceptance of the existing distribution of income as the right or the appropriate distribution—or, for that matter, to its rejection.

11

The Supply of Factors of Production

The Factors of Production

Our discussion of demand for factors of production was in highly abstract terms; we did not consider the specific character of the factors of production or give them names. The reason is that on the demand side, there seems no empirical classification of factors that has such special importance as to deserve being singled out; the classification that is useful will vary from problem to problem. On the demand side, the chief consideration in classifying factors is substitution in production. A single factor consists of units that are regarded as perfect substitutes in production; different factors consist of units that are not perfect substitutes. For some problems, it will be desirable to separate out many different factors of production; for others, only a few.

It has traditionally been supposed that conditions of supply give a more substantial and empirically significant basis for distinguishing among factors of production in specific terms. The classical economists distinguished three main factors of production: land, capital, and labor. Land they regarded as a permanent, nonreproducible resource fixed in amount, the supply of which was therefore perfectly inelastic to the economy as a whole. Capital they regarded as a reproducible resource, the amount of which could be altered through deliberate productive action, so its supply was not perfectly inelastic. Indeed, in the main, they tended to regard it as highly elastic. Labor, like capital, they regarded as reproducible and expansible, and, indeed, as supplied to the economy in the long-run at constant cost, yet to be distinguished from capital because of its dual status as a productive resource and an ultimate consumer.

This particular tripartite division was doubtless a consequence of the particular social problems that were important at the time the classical theory was developed and the social structure in which the industrial revolution occurred in England. There may still be some problems for which it is important to distinguish land from other resources, but for most problems it hardly seems important to do so. In most contexts now important, land, in any economically relevant sense, is indistinguishable from other forms of capital. The productive power of the soil can be produced at a cost by drainage, fertilization, and the like and is clearly not permanent. Land rent, even in the customary meaning of the term, has become a much smaller fraction of total income in advanced countries in the course of time.

From a broad viewpoint, there is much to be said for regarding all sources of productive power as capital. Much of the productive power of what we call *labor* is clearly the product of deliberate investment and is produced in the same sense as machinery or buildings. Human productive power is substitutable for nonhuman productive power and can be produced in place of the latter at a cost. Indeed, one of the striking features of capitalist development is the tendency for a larger and larger fraction of total investment to take the form of human capital. What is designated as *property* income is in general a smaller fraction of total income the more advanced the society, despite the much greater absolute amount of physical capital. It is a smaller fraction in the United States, for example, than in Burma or India, probably also than in France or Great Britain, and probably also in the United States today than a hundred years ago.

Even though we recognize that all sources of productive services can be regarded as capital, our social and political institutions make it desirable to recognize that there is an important distinction for many problems between two broad categories of capital—human and nonhuman capital. We can explore the significance of this distinction by examining Marshall's discussion of the special "peculiarities" of labor, which in his view justify distinguishing it from other factors. He lists five peculiarities:

1. "The worker sells his work but retains capital in himself."
2. "The seller of labor must deliver it himself."
3. "Labor is perishable."
4. "The sellers of it are often at a disadvantage in bargaining."
5. A "great length of time [is] required for providing additional supplies of specialized ability."

As Marshall recognizes, the first two of these peculiarities stand on a rather different footing than the others. Labor is perishable in the sense that the depreciation of the source of labor services (the human being) depends primarily on time rather than on rate of use, so if today's labor services are not used they cannot very readily be stored, and there is not a correspondingly larger amount available tomorrow. But this is equally true of much nonhuman capital; of the services of a bridge or a road or a machine that deteriorates primarily with time, or, economically speaking, of an automobile, whose physical characteristics can be preserved but whose economic value cannot because of obsolescence.

Again, the bargaining disadvantage is by no means always on the side of labor, as Marshall points out and as experience has amply demonstrated since. Insofar as there is any systematic difference on this score, it would seem to be an indirect effect of item 1. Since nonhuman capital can be bought and sold, it is easier to borrow on such capital than it is to borrow on prospective earning power, and it is possible to get funds by selling some of it, whereas this is not possible with human capital. More generally, a "bargaining" problem of any kind arises only when the market is not competitive, and indeed, strictly speaking, only when it is competitive on neither the selling nor the buying side. But then the bargaining advantage depends on which party is the monopolist, or if both are, on their relative monopoly power, and it is hard to see that this depends intimately on whether the resource in question is or is not labor.

Again, item 5 is, at most, a question of degree. A great length of time is required for other kinds of capital: the Suez and Panama Canals and the investments involved in the early stages of the radio, aviation, and television industries come readily to mind.

Items 1 and 2 are on a different footing, since they derive from the basic institutional character of our society. These peculiarities would disappear only in a slave society, and there only for the slaves. The fact that human capital sources cannot in our society be bought or sold means, as was noted above, that human capital generally does not provide as good a reserve against emergencies as nonhuman capital. In consequence, the larger the fraction of any given total income that comes from human capital, the greater, in general, the desire to save.

The qualification "generally" is required because these statements hold only if there is considerable security to person and property. For groups that are, or feel themselves to be, in constant danger of having their property expropriated or of being expelled from their place of residence, human capital will be a far better reserve than nonhuman capital. Recent examples are the refugees from Nazism before World War II, from Cuba in the 1960s, and from Viet Nam in 1975. Persons with generally valued human skills—physicians, for example—had a far better reserve for that emergency than persons with extensive property holdings. As an older example, the superiority of human capital in such circumstances is a major factor explaining the emphasis that Jews put on education during their long exile.

A second effect of the inability to buy or sell human capital is to reduce the scope of market forces in investment in human capital. The individual who invests in a machine can own the machine and so be sure that he gets the return from his investment. The individual who invests in another individual cannot get this kind of assurance. Individuals have incentives to invest in themselves or their progeny that they do not have to invest in machines. Hence, there may readily be either underinvestment or overinvestment in human capital relative to nonhuman capital.

Finally, the inability to buy and sell human capital sources is the basic reason for Marshall's second peculiarity: it is only for this reason that the seller of labor must deliver it himself. But this means that nonpecuniary considerations become relevant to the use of human capital in a way that they generally do not for nonhuman capital. The owner of land, for example, has no reason to be concerned whether the land is used in a way that is "pleasant" or "unpleasant" or the owner of a horse whether the horse is used in work that is "enjoyable" or not "enjoyable," provided both types of work involve the same effect on the land's or the horse's subsequent productivity. The owner of labor-power, on the other hand, does have reason to be concerned. He is required, as it were, to make a tie-in contract: his sale of labor-power is tied-in with the "purchase" of the conditions of work, the pleasantness of the task, etc.

These special considerations applying to human capital affect its supply in ways that deserve further consideration, so we shall turn to a consideration of the supply of labor in general in the short and long run, and then of the supply of labor in different occupations. Similar consideration is not required for the other factors.

The Supply of Labor as a Whole

Labor is, of course, not homogeneous: an hour of labor of a ditch-digger is not equal to an hour of labor of an airplane pilot. Yet, as always, we can think of constructing a supply curve for labor in general by taking for granted some structure of wage rates and adopting some convention for adding together different kinds of labor. For example, we may define our assumed structure of wage rates in terms of fixed ratios of wages and then convert actual hours of labor into "equivalent" hours by using these ratios. If we suppose the wage rate of the pilot to be fixed at ten times the wage rate of the ditch-digger, we can regard one hour of the pilot's labor as equivalent to ten ditch-digger hours. In this way, we can conceive of the total number of equivalent hours of labor supplied as a function of some index number of the structure of wage rates, say the rate for the ditch-digger, recognizing that at each such rate, the total supply consists, in fact, of so many hours of the ditch-digger's labor, so much of the pilot's labor, etc. And, as always, in following this procedure, we are not supposing that the structure of relative wage rates is in fact determined outside the economic system or is independent of the level of wage rates; we are simply dividing up our problems and consider them one by one.

It seems desirable to distinguish between two kinds of supply curves of labor in general: the supply of labor for a given population of given capacities—the short-run supply of labor—and the supply of labor without such restrictions—the long-run supply of labor. The second clearly involves a "theory" of population.

THE SHORT-RUN SUPPLY OF LABOR

Our given conditions obviously mean that the short-run supply of labor for *all* purposes is perfectly inelastic: twenty-four hours times the number of people is the available daily supply of labor if we neglect the corrections for different qualities of labor. But clearly, the problem that we are interested in is the supply of labor, not for all purposes, but for use through the market. So the problem we are concerned with is essentially the factors that determine the fraction of the total labor power that is offered for sale on the market.

In our modern society, this fraction is relatively small, so there is considerable room for variation in it. Something less than half the total population is classified as "in the labor force," and these individuals devote only a minor part of their total time to market activities—perhaps one-fourth. Moreover, the fraction has undoubtedly varied considerably over time and from country to country.

Perhaps the most widely accepted hypothesis about the short-run supply curve of labor is that it is backward bending above some wage rate, as in Figure 11.1. Each point on this curve is to be interpreted as showing the *maximum* quantity offered at the given price, which is why the negatively sloped segment is said to be "backward bending" rather than "forward-falling." A variety of empirical evidence points to this conclusion. In the first place, as the real wage rate has increased secularly over long periods of time in advanced countries, the average number of hours a week has tended to decline, and the fraction of children in the labor market to decrease. The fraction of women has not behaved so systematically but has probably increased. Yet all in all, if such observations over a long period of time were regarded as being on the supply curve, they would produce a backward-bending segment. Additional evidence is furnished by experience in underdeveloped countries, where it seems to be common experience that beyond a fairly low level, an increase in wage rate per hour will reduce the number of hours worked. The natives act as if they wanted a certain sum of money almost regardless of how long they have to work for it; if they can get that sum in fewer hours, they will work fewer hours.

The theoretical explanation offered for the backward-bending segment of the supply curve is that a rise in the real wage rate arising from an in-

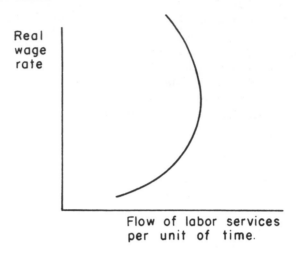

Real
wage
rate

Flow of labor services
per unit of time.

FIGURE 11.1

creased demand for labor has two effects. (1) It makes leisure more expensive, since the cost of an hour of leisure is the wage that could be earned in that hour. This is the substitution effect and by itself would tend to raise the number of hours worked. (2) If the individual were to work the same number of hours, the rise in the real wage rate increases his real income, which would lead him to want to purchase more of various kinds of goods, including leisure. This is the income effect, and by itself would tend to reduce the number of hours worked unless leisure is an inferior good. The argument, then, is that beyond some point the income effect dominates the substitution effect. It shows up in people working fewer hours, in the withdrawal of supplementary workers (children, etc.) from the labor force, etc. This way of putting it also makes it clear that much depends on the value attached to goods purchased with money through the market relative to goods that can be acquired through nonmarket activity. In a primitive society, the initial low wage rate at which the income effect becomes dominant reflects a lack of familiarity with market goods and a limited range of tastes. As tastes develop and knowledge spreads, the point at which the income effect dominates tends to rise.

An objection sometimes raised to an analysis like the above is that individuals cannot determine for themselves the number of hours they work; this is an institutional datum that the individual must take or leave. This objection is almost entirely specious. In the first place, we have seen that much of the adjustment may take the form of the fraction of the people in the labor force. In the second place, even at any given time, a particular individual has some leeway. He can work overtime or not, take off more or less time during the year, choose the kind of occupation or employer that offers the number of hours of work he wants, etc. But none of these is the basic fallacy. The important point is that the individual is like the perfect competitor: to each individual separately, the number of hours of work per week may be fixed, yet the level at which it is fixed is the result of the choices of the individuals as a group. If, at any moment, this level of hours is larger, on the average, than people prefer at the given wage rate, this means that any employer who makes them shorter and who adjusts them to the workers' preferences will make employment with him more attractive than employment with others. Hence he can attract the better people or attract people at a lower wage rate. Employers thus have an incentive to adjust working conditions and hours to the preferences of the workers. (In our earlier terminology, because of the tie-in character of the transaction, employers are sellers of conditions of work as well as buyers of labor.) Competition in this way does permit individuals, in effect, to determine for themselves the number of hours they work.

Although the supply curve under discussion is a short-run curve, in the sense that it holds the population constant, we have been talking in terms of the effect of alternative levels of real wage rates, each of which is regarded as permanent, i.e., is expected to continue. Clearly, the reaction to a temporary higher wage rate which reverts to a lower level will tend to be very different than the reaction to a higher wage rate expected to be permanent. The temporary higher wage rate would seem more likely to bring forth an increased quantity of labor from a fixed population than a permanently higher one, since there would be strong temptation to take advantage of the opportunity while it lasts and to buy the leisure later.

An interesting case in point is the experience in the United States during World War II, when both the fraction of the population in the labor force and the average number of hours worked per week were substantially higher than during the prewar period. At first glance, it seems that this increase cannot reflect a response to a higher real wage rate expected to be temporary: money wages rose sharply but so did prices, both openly and indirectly through deterioration in the quality of products, so that average money wages per unit of time divided by an index of prices of consumer goods corrected for quality deterioration may not have risen at all and may even have fallen. Some economists have rationalized this apparent conflict between a constant real wage and an increased quantity of labor supplied by introducing the notion of a *money illusion,* namely that suppliers of labor react to nominal money wage rates, not to real wage rates, and that they would behave differently if, say, all nominal prices and wages were doubled.

It is not, however, necessary to introduce a *deus ex machina,* such as a money illusion, to explain this phenomenon. It can readily be rationalized for two reasons on the grounds that the apparent failure of real wages to rise is itself an illusion. First, many additional persons who entered the labor market would not have been hired previously at the prevailing real wage rate; the real wage rate they could get increased even though average wage rates did not. Indeed, it is possible for the real wage rate to have increased in the relevant sense for every individual separately, yet for the average to have remained unchanged.[1] Second, people may very well have thought that the rise in prices of consumer goods during the war was temporary and that after the war prices would return to their prewar level. Any part of their wages saved should be deflated by the expected postwar price level, not the wartime price level. But if this were done, it would be seen that real wages, as evaluated by their recipients, were higher than would be indicated by deflating by current prices alone. This second force is especially important, if, as has been argued, part of the increase in labor supplied is to take advantage of a temporary opportunity. This would mean that laborers would have planned to save an abnormally large part of any increase in income, which would make the expected future price level particularly important. This interpretation is indirectly supported by a number of facts, in particular by the abnormally high fraction of income saved during the war period and the extent to which such savings were accumulated in the form of assets fixed in nominal value (government bonds, cash, etc.) rather than equity securities or real goods. Of course, the expectations about the future price level were, in the event, disappointed, but a mistaken prediction of the future is very different from an illusion about the present.

The Long-Run Supply of Labor

If we turn to the problem of the long-run supply of labor, we must analyze the effect of the real wage rate on the size of the population and the qualities and skills it possesses. We need, that is, a theory of population and a theory of investment in the human agent. It is clear that these two are related: additional labor power can be produced either by increasing the number of laborers or by investing more capital in each laborer. For simplicity, we shall phrase the following discussion in terms of the size of the population, though much of it also applies to investment in the human agent.

To begin with, the theory of population was regarded as an essential ele-

1. To illustrate this possibility, suppose there is no variation possible in the number of hours worked by a laborer; the wage rate at which labor of type A can initially get employment is $1 an hour; labor of type B, $.50 an hour; there are fifty laborers of type A and fifty of type B; the laborers of type A are willing to work at $1 an hour; laborers of type B are unwilling to work at $.50 an hour. Initially, then, only labor of type A will be working and the average wage rate will be $1 an hour. Let the (real) wage rate offered for labor of type A go up to $1.25 an hour and for labor of type B to $.75 an hour. Suppose that at these wage rates, laborers of both types are willing to work and that both work the same number of hours. The average wage rate will still be $1 an hour, yet the wage rate that is relevant to the supply of labor has risen for every worker separately.

ment of economic theory, and the Malthusian theory of population was a cornerstone of classical economic theory. In its crudest form, the Malthusian doctrine was that labor is a form of capital which, like other capital, can be produced at a cost; that it is produced under conditions of constant cost, the level of this constant cost being the minimum standard of living consistent with preservation. If the wage provides a standard of living above this level, marriages will tend to occur earlier, the birth rate to rise, the death rate to fall, and the population tend to increase, and conversely. In this form, the theory leads to a perfectly elastic, long-run supply curve of labor, as in Figure 11.2, where OW is the wage rate that provides the minimum standard of living.

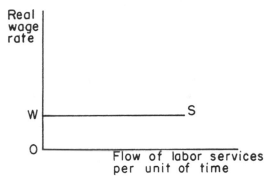

FIGURE 11.2

Even in this crude form, the theory is consistent with much observed evidence, some available to Malthus and more experienced since his time. Some extreme examples are furnished by the Phillipines and Puerto Rico. The large amount of capital invested in the Phillipines by the United States over the period of a half-century was accompanied by an approximate tripling of the population with little or no change in the average standard of living. Similarly, a major effect of increased U.S. assistance to Puerto Rico, especially since 1933, has been a very rapid rise in population. Numerous other examples could be cited.

At the same time, if OW is interpreted as essentially a technologically determined datum, the experience of most countries in the Western world contradicts the crude Malthusian theory. In such countries, the real wage has risen dramatically in the past century and a half. True, population has also risen, but by nothing like the extent that would have been required to wipe out the gain in average real income.

This apparent contradiction of the Malthusian theory led to its rejection by economists and, indeed, essentially to the exclusion of population theory from economics. Population, it was said, depends primarily on a host of noneconomic considerations that are not within our competence or

field of interest. For our purposes, we shall take population for granted
and leave the explanation of population change to demographers, soci-
ologists, and the like. More recently, economists have renewed their interest in population theory and have again become concerned with reinte-
grating the theory of population with economic theory—a development
that is to be encouraged.

One way of working toward a theory of population that is consistent
with experience in the Western world and at the same time is coherent
with economic theory as a whole is to re-examine the Malthusian theory
and interpret it in a more sophisticated fashion. Instead of taking the
essence of the Malthusian theory to be the existence of a technologically
determined cost of production of human beings, we can regard its essence
as being the notion that the production of human beings is to be regarded
as if it were a deliberative economic choice determined by the balancing
of returns and costs. From this point of view, children are to be regarded
in a dual role: they are a consumption good, a way of spending one's income to acquire satisfaction, an alternative to purchasing automobiles or
domestic service or other goods; and they are a capital good produced by
economic activity, an alternative to producing machines or houses or the
like.

Viewed as a consumption good, the amount produced will be determined by the relative cost of children versus other consumer goods, the income available for all uses, and the tastes and preferences of the individuals in question. Noneconomic forces enter the picture primarily in determining these tastes and preferences. Viewed as a capital good, the
amount produced will be determined by the returns that this capital good
is expected to earn relative to other capital goods and the relative costs of
producing this and alternative capital goods. A major difference between
this and other capital goods is the possibility of appropriating the returns
by the individual who makes the initial capital investment. The fact that
children are, in this sense, a joint product means that the two sets of considerations need to be combined: the returns from the children as capital
goods may be taken as reducing their costs as consumer goods. Were it not
for this factor, it is pretty clear that gross underinvestment in human capital would be almost inevitable in a free society.

From this broader point of view, OW in Figure 11.2 is not to be regarded
as a technologically determined datum but as a rather complex resultant
of the factors just discussed—a phenomenon that was already emphasized
in Malthus's time in the description of OW as a "conventional" minimum,
with emphasis on the possibility of raising it by altering people's tastes and
values.

Along these lines, the failure of population to increase in the Western
world as fast as crude Malthusian theory suggested may have reflected
simply a rise in the costs of children relative to the return from them and

need not even have involved a change of tastes. A number of factors that presumably operated in this direction come to mind. (1) The cost of raising children is clearly greater in the city than in rural areas, and economic development in the Western world involved extensive shifts to cities. (2) Returns from children as capital goods are also lower in the city than in the country, because they are in general less valuable at early ages, and, moreover, the mores in the city are such that they are likely to cease contributing the returns from their productive use to the family at an earlier age. (3) The loosening family ties that came as a concomitant of industrialization made the children less valuable as a means of providing unemployment and old-age security. (4) With growing real income, the aspect of children as consumer's goods became more important than as factors of production—that is, the services yielded by children as a consumer's good are a superior good. But this meant sending children to school longer and keeping them out of the labor market longer, which reduced the positive return to parents from children, increased the cost involved, and made children more expensive relative to other consumer goods. This list is not intended to be exhaustive but rather to be suggestive. Clearly some counterbalancing items need to be included as well.

The modified Malthusian doctrine may be consistent not only with historical developments in the Western world but also with many currently observed phenomena. For example, the higher birthrate in the country than in the city is clearly consistent with the considerations cited above. Indeed, from this point of view, the long-time tendency for a net migration from the country to the city in the United States can be interpreted very differently than is generally the case. It is usually interpreted as reflecting a disequilibrium position in the process of correction, but with so much friction that the corrective process proceeds slowly or "too slowly," so the return to the farmer is on the average below its long-run equilibrium value relative to the return to the city dweller. The alternative interpretation suggested by the above analysis is that rural areas have had a comparative advantage in the production of human capital as well as of food; that people in rural areas are involved, as it were, in two industries that are pursued jointly—the production of food and human capital—and that they engage in net exports of both to the city. On this interpretation, the net flow of population from country to city is no evidence of disequilibrium but of equilibrium, and part of the returns to rural families are the returns they get either in pecuniary or nonpecuniary form from their children.

Another observed phenomenon that may fit this analysis is the strong tendency for the number of children produced per family to be smaller in "higher" socioeconomic classes than in "lower" socioeconomic classes (smaller among professional and business people, for example, than among unskilled workers). Yet it is not clear whether there is a tendency within socioeconomic classes for the number of children to be lower the higher the income. Items 3 and 4 above indicate one way in which these phenomena can be explained. Because of different kinds of taste and opportunities, the relative costs of children are different in different socioeconomic classes. Perhaps the major factor is that in the higher classes, the child is likely to stay in school longer and, of great importance, to get a kind of education that must be privately paid for, whereas in the lower classes, education is more likely to be publicly paid for or earned by the child himself. Thus children are more expensive relative to other consumer goods the higher the socioeconomic class. But these factors may not operate within socio-economic classes, so it would not be surprising to find that the higher the income within such a class, the larger the number of children.

Again, indirect evidence for such an interpretation is provided by the relation between the birthrate and general economic conditions and by the effects of special subsidies provided by state action for children. Both Hitler and Mussolini introduced such subsidies, and various family allowance schemes, for example, the current French scheme, involve such a subsidy. There seems some evidence that such schemes have in fact had a significant effect on the rate of population growth.

This analysis can by no means be regarded as well established or even well defined. But it does seem one of the more promising directions in which an economic theory of population is capable of being developed.[2]

2. Much work has been done along these lines since this section was first written.

12

Wage Determination and Unemployment

One topic that rests uneasily between price theory and monetary theory is the relationship of the preceding analysis of wage determination to the fluctuations that occur in the aggregate level of employment and unemployment. If wages are determined by the interaction of demand and supply, how can there be "involuntary" unemployment? Why do wages not move to clear the market?

One answer is the economist's catch all excuse for all failures to provide a satisfactory explanation of observed phenomena: imperfections in the market, in this case in the form of "rigid" or "inflexible" wages. In its simplest form, as in Figure 12.1, the assertion is that, while a wage rate W_O would clear the market with E_O units of labor employed, there is some imperfection that prevents the wage rate from falling below W_U, at which wage rate $W_U U$ units of labor are employed; UB unemployed, of which UA is the excess of the "full" employment level over the actual level, and AB the additional units available for employment at a wage of W_U rather than W_O.

This formulation is not an answer but simply a restatement of the problem. Why are wages inflexible at W_U? There are obviously some special cases for which an answer is readily forthcoming, such as a legal minimum wage, in which case $W_U BS$ is the effective supply curve, replacing SS, and the solution is at the intersection of the (effective) supply and demand curves. But clearly this answer is not general.

Keynes gave a more sophisticated answer in his *General Theory* by arguing that Figure 12.1 is an incomplete summary of the forces determining

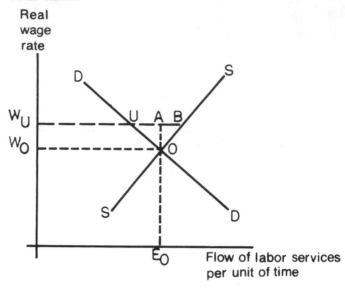

Real
wage
rate

W_U

W_O

D

U A B

S

O

S'

D

E_O

Flow of labor services
per unit of time

FIGURE 12.1

the real wage rate because it omits a different set of considerations, namely, those having to do with equating the amount some people want to save with the amount other people want to invest at an interest rate consistent with monetary conditions. This is not the place to examine his argument, which belongs in monetary theory rather than price theory. (See chapter 17, however, for an analysis of one phase of it.) Its significance for our purposes is that, according to Keynes, the real wage rate consistent with these saving-investment monetary conditions might be different from the real wage rate consistent with "full" employment, say, W_U instead of W_O. In such a case, Keynes argued, a decline in "real" wage rates would add to employment, but such a decline could not be achieved by a decline in "money" or "nominal" wage rates, since such a decline would be matched by an exactly parallel decline in "money" or "nominal" prices. Workers, he argued, were therefore wise to resist declines in nominal wage rates. His argument is a different reason for regarding the "effective" supply curve as W_UBS, not SS, so the wage rate is at the intersection of the (effective) supply and demand curves.

This answer too is unsatisfactory. In the first place, as we shall see in greater detail below, it shifts back and forth in a loose way between "nominal" and "real" wages. In the second place, and more fundamentally, as long as the economy is at point U, the owners of an amount of labor services equal to UB have an incentive to offer their labor services at a slightly lower real wage than W_U. How is this force contained? How is employment of W_UU rationed among suppliers willing to offer W_UB? "Custom," or trade union rigidity and the like may be plausible as factors delaying the adjustment, but treating them as factors enforcing a long-run, stable equilibrium position at less than "full" employment again begs the real issue.

Two related developments over the past several decades have resulted from the search for satisfactory answers. One is the so-called Phillips curve, linking unemployment and inflation; the other is the analysis of the role of specific human capital and "search" costs in producing temporary wage rigidity.

The Phillips Curve*

The discussion of the Phillips curve started with truth in 1926, proceeded through error some thirty years later, and by now has returned back to 1926 and to the original truth. That is about fifty years for a complete circuit. You can see how technological development has speeded up the process of both producing and dissipating ignorance.

Fisher and Phillips

I choose the year 1926 not at random but because in that year Irving Fisher published an article under the title "A Statistical Relation between Unemployment and Price Changes."[1]

THE FISHER APPROACH

Fisher's article dealt with precisely the same empirical phenomenon that Professor A. W. Phillips analysed in his celebrated article in *Economica* some 32 years later.[2] Both were impressed with the empirical observation that inflation tended to be associated with low levels of unemployment and deflation with high levels. One amusing item in Fisher's article from a very different point of view is that he starts out by saying that he has been so deeply interested in this subject that "during the last three years in particular I have had at least one computer in my office almost constantly at work on this project."[3] Of course what he meant was a human being operating a calculating machine.

---

* This section is reprinted with two additions (the discussion of Figure 12.6 and the final section on "A Positively Sloping Phillips Curve?") from my paper, *Unemployment versus Inflation: An Evaluation of the Phillips Curve*, IEA Occasional Paper 44 (London: Institute of Economic Affairs, 1975). The paper was originally given as a lecture in London in September, 1974. The figures have been renumbered and the footnotes differently designated to conform to the rest of the book.

1. Irving Fisher, *International Labour Review*, June 1926, pp. 785–92. It was reprinted in the *Journal of Political Economy* (March/April, 1973): 496–502.

2. A. W. Phillips, "The Relation between Unemployment and the Rate of Change of Money Wage Rates in the United Kingdom, 1861–1957," *Economica* (November 1958): 283–99.

3. Fisher, op. cit., p. 786.

There was, however, a crucial difference between Fisher's analysis and Phillips's, between the truth of 1926 and the error of 1958, which had to do with the direction of causation. Fisher took *the rate of change of prices* to be the independent variable that set the process going. In his words,

> When the dollar is losing value, or in other words when the price level is rising, a business man finds his receipts rising as fast, on the average, as this general rise of prices, but not his expenses, because his expenses consist, to a large extent, of things which are contractually fixed. . . . Employment is then stimulated—for a time at least.[4]

To elaborate his analysis and express it in more modern terms, let anything occur that produces a higher level of spending—or, more precisely, a higher rate of increase in spending than was anticipated. Producers would at first interpret the faster rate of increase in spending as an increase in real demand for their product. The producers of shoes, hats, or coats would discover that apparently there was an increase in the amount of goods they could sell at pre-existing prices. No one of them would know at first whether the change was affecting him in particular or whether it was general. In the first instance, each producer would be tempted to expand output, as Fisher states, and also to allow prices to rise. But at first much or most of the unanticipated increase in nominal demand (i.e., demand expressed in dollars) would be absorbed by increases (or faster increases) in employment and output rather than by increases (or faster increases) in prices. Conversely, for whatever reason, let the rate of spending slow down, or rise less rapidly than was anticipated, and each individual producer would in the first instance interpret the slowdown at least partly as reflecting something peculiar to him. The result would be partly a slowdown in output and a rise in unemployment and partly a slowdown in prices.

Fisher was describing a *dynamic* process arising out of fluctuations in the rate of spending about some average trend or norm. He went out of his way to emphasise the importance of distinguishing between "high and low prices on the one hand and the rise and fall of prices on the other."[5] He put it that way because he was writing at a time when a stable level of prices was taken to be the norm. Were he writing today, he would emphasize the distinction between the rate of inflation and changes in the rate of inflation. (And perhaps some future writer will have to emphasise the difference between the second and the third derivatives!) The important distinction—and it is quite clear that this is what Fisher had in mind—is between *anticipated* and *unanticipated* changes.

THE PHILLIPS APPROACH

Professor Phillips's approach was from exactly the opposite direction. He took the level of *employment* to be the independent variable that set

4. Ibid., p. 787.
5. Ibid., p. 788.

the process going. He treated the rate of change of wages as the dependent variable. His argument was a very simple analysis—I hesitate to say simple-minded, but so it has proved—in terms of *static* supply and demand conditions. He said:

> When the demand for a commodity or service is high relatively to the supply of it, we expect the price to rise, the rate of rise being greater the greater the excess demand. . . . It seems plausible that this principle should operate as one of the factors determining the rate of change of money wage rates, which are the price of labor services.[6]

Phillips's approach is based on the usual *(static)* supply and demand curves as illustrated in Figure 12.2. At the point of intersection, O, the market is in equilibrium at the wage rate W_O, with the amount of labor employed E_O equal to the amount of labor demanded. Unemployment is zero—which is to say, as measured, equal to "frictional" or "transitional" unemployment, or to use the terminology I adopted some years ago from Wicksell, at its "natural" rate. At this point, says Phillips, there is no up-

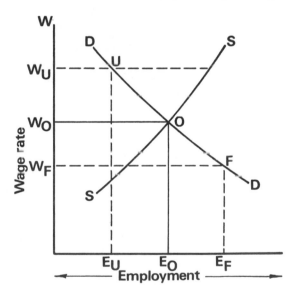

FIGURE 12.2

ward pressure on wages. Consider instead the point F, where the quantity of labor demanded is higher than the quantity supplied. There is over-employment, wages at W_F are below the equilibrium level, and there will be upward pressure on them. At point U, there is unemployment, W_U is above the equilibrium wage rate and there is downward pressure. The larger the discrepancy between the quantity of labor demanded and the

6. Phillips, op. cit., p. 283.

quantity supplied, the stronger the pressure and hence the more rapidly wages will rise or fall.

Phillips translated this analysis into an observable relation by plotting the level of unemployment on one axis and the rate of change of wages over time on the other, as in Figure 12.3. Point E_0 corresponds to point O

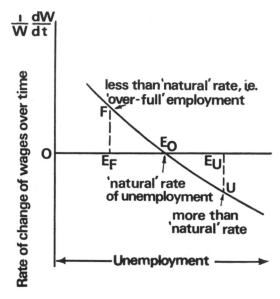

FIGURE 12.3

in Figure 12.2. Unemployment is at its "natural" rate so wages are stable (or in a growing economy, rising at a rate equal to the rate of productivity growth). Point F corresponds to "overfull" employment, so wages are rising; point U to unemployment, so wages are falling.

Fisher talked about price changes, Phillips about wage changes, but I believe that for our purpose that is not an important distinction. Both Fisher and Phillips took it for granted that wages are a major component of total cost and that prices and wages would tend to move together. So both of them tended to go very readily from rates of wage change to rates of price change, and I shall do so as well.

THE FALLACY IN PHILLIPS

Phillips's analysis seems very persuasive and obvious, yet it is utterly fallacious. It is fallacious because no economic theorist has ever asserted that the demand and supply of labor are functions of the *nominal* wage rate (i.e., wage rate expressed in dollars). Every economic theorist from Adam Smith to the present would have told you that the vertical axis in Figure 12.2 should refer not to the *nominal* wage rate but to the *real* wage rate.

But once you label the vertical axis $\frac{W}{P}$ as in Figure 12.4, the graph has nothing to say about what is going to happen to *nominal* wages or prices. There is not even any *prima facie* presumption that it has anything to say. For example, consider point O in Figure 12.4. At that level of employment, there is neither upward nor downward pressure on the real wage. But that real wage can remain constant with W and P separately *constant,* or with W and P each *rising* at the rate of 10 percent a year, or *falling* at the rate of 10 percent a year, or doing anything else, provided both change at the *same* rate.

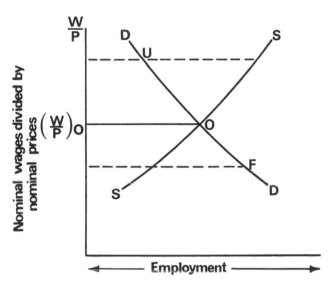

Figure 12.4

The Keynesian Confusion Between Nominal and Real Wages

How did a sophisticated mind like Phillips's—and he was certainly a highly sophisticated and subtle economist—come to confuse nominal wages with real wages? He was led to do so by the general intellectual climate that had been engendered by the Keynesian revolution. From this point of view, the essential element of the Keynesian revolution was the assumption that prices are highly rigid relative to output, so that a change in demand of the kind considered by Fisher would be reflected almost entirely in *output* and very little in prices. The price level could be regarded as an institutional datum. The simple way to interpret Phillips is that he was therefore assuming the change in nominal wages to be equal to the change in real wages.

But that is not really what he was saying. What he was saying was slightly more sophisticated. It was that changes in *anticipated* nominal wages were equal to changes in *anticipated* real wages. There were two components of the Keynesian system that were essential to its construction: first, the notion that prices are rigid in the sense that people in planning their behavior do not allow for the possibility that the price level might change, and hence regard a change in nominal wages or nominal prices as a change in real wages and real prices; second, that real wages *ex post* could be altered by *unanticipated* inflation. Indeed, the whole Keynesian argument for the possibility of a full employment policy arose out of the supposition that it was possible to get workers (at least in the 1930s when Keynes wrote *The General Theory*) to accept lower real wages produced by inflation that they would not have accepted in the direct form of a reduction in nominal wages.[7]

These two components imply a sharp distinction between *anticipated* nominal and real wages and *actual* nominal and real wages. In the Keynesian climate of the time, it was natural for Phillips to take this distinction for granted and to regard anticipated nominal and real wages as moving together.

I do not criticize Phillips for doing this. Science is possible only because at any one time there is a body of conventions or views or ideas that are taken for granted and on which scientists build. If each individual writer were to go back and question all the premises that underlie what he is doing, nobody would ever get anywhere. I believe that some of the people who have followed in his footsteps deserve much more criticism than he does for not noting the importance of this theoretical point once it was pointed out to them.

At any rate, it was this general intellectual climate that led Phillips to think in terms of nominal rather than real wages. The intellectual climate was also important in another direction. The Keynesian system, as everybody knows, is incomplete. It lacks an equation. A major reason for the prompt and rapid acceptance of the Phillips curve approach was the widespread belief that it provided the missing equation that connected the real system with the monetary system. In my opinion, this belief is false. What is needed to complete the Keynesian system is an equation that determines the equilibrium price level. But the Phillips curve deals with the relation between a rate of change of prices or wages and the level of unemployment. It does not determine an equilibrium price level. At any rate, the

---

7. J. M. Keynes, *The General Theory of Employment, Interest, and Money* (Macmillan, 1936): "Whilst workers will usually resist a reduction of money-wages, it is not their practice to withdraw their labor whenever there is a rise in the price of wage-goods" (p. 9). ". . . The workers, though unconsciously, are instinctively more reasonable economists than the classical school. . . . They resist reductions of money-wages . . . whereas they do not resist reductions of real wages' (p. 14). ". . . Since no trade union would dream of striking on every occasion of a rise in the cost of living, they do not raise the obstacle to any increase in aggregate employment attributed to them by the classical school" (p. 15).

Phillips curve was widely accepted and was seized on immediately for policy purposes.[8] It is still widely used for this purpose as supposedly describing a "trade-off" from a policy point of view, between inflation and unemployment.

It was said that what the Phillips curve means is that we are faced with a choice. If we choose a low level of inflation, say stable prices, we shall have to reconcile ourselves to a high level of unemployment. If we choose a low level of unemployment, we shall have to reconcile ourselves to a high rate of inflation.

Reaction Against the Keynesian System

Three developments came along in this historical account to change attitudes and to raise some questions.

One was the general theoretical reaction against the Keynesian system which brought out into the open the fallacy in the original Phillips curve approach of identifying nominal and real wages.

The second development was the failure of the Phillips curve relation to hold for other bodies of data. Fisher had found it to hold for the United States for the period before 1925; Phillips had found it to hold for Britain for a long period. But, lo and behold, when people tried it for any other place they never obtained good results. Nobody was able to construct a decent empirical Phillips curve for other circumstances. I may be exaggerating a bit—no doubt there are other successful cases; but certainly a large number of attempts were unsuccessful.

The third and most recent development is the emergence of "stagflation," which rendered somewhat ludicrous the confident statements that many economists had made about "trade-offs," based on empirically fitted Phillips curves.

SHORT- AND LONG-RUN PHILLIPS CURVES

The empirical failures and the theoretical reaction produced an attempt to rescue the Phillips curve approach by distinguishing a short-run from a long-run Phillips curve. Because both potential employers and potential employees envisage an implicit or explicit employment contract covering a fairly long period, both must guess in advance what real wage will correspond to a given nominal wage. Both therefore must form anticipations about the future price level. The real wage rate that is plotted on the verti-

8. For example, Albert Rees, "The Phillips Curve as a Menu for Policy Choices," *Economica*, August 1970, pp. 227–38, explicitly considers the objections to a stable Phillips curve outlined below, yet concludes that there remains a trade-off that should be exploited. He writes: "The strongest policy conclusion I can draw from the expectations literature is that the policy makers should not attempt to operate at a single point on the Phillips curve. . . . Rather, they should permit fluctuations in unemployment within a band" (p. 238).

cal axis of the demand and supply curve diagram is thus not the *current* real wage but the *anticipated* real wage. If we suppose that anticipations about the price level are slow to change, while the nominal wage can change rapidly and is known with little time-lag, we can, for *short* periods, revert essentially to Phillips's original formulation, except that the equilibrium position is no longer a constant nominal wage, but a nominal wage changing at the same rate as the anticipated rate of change in prices (plus, for a growing economy, the anticipated rate of change in productivity). Changes in demand and supply will then show up first in a changed rate of change of nominal wages, which will mean also in anticipated real wages. Current prices may adjust as rapidly as or more rapidly than wages, so real wages *actually* received may move in the opposite direction from nominal wages, but *anticipated* real wages will move in the same direction.

One way to put this in terms of the Phillips curve is to plot on the vertical axis not the change in nominal wages but that change minus the anticipated rate of change in prices, as in Figure 12.5, where $\left(\dfrac{1}{P}\dfrac{dP}{dt}\right)^*$, standing for the anticipated rate of change in prices, is subtracted from $\dfrac{1}{W}\dfrac{dW}{dt}$. This curve now tells a story much more like Fisher's original story

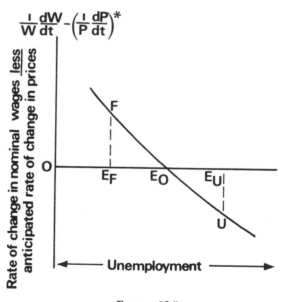

FIGURE 12.5

than Phillips's. Suppose, to start with, the economy is at point E_0, with both prices and wages stable (abstracting from growth). Suppose something, say, a monetary expansion, starts nominal aggregate demand growing, which in turn produces a rise in prices and wages at the rate of, say,

2 percent per year. Workers will initially interpret this as a rise in their real wage—because they still anticipate constant prices—and so will be willing to offer more labor (move up their supply curve), i.e., employment grows and unemployment falls. Employers may have the same anticipations as workers about the general price level, but they are more directly concerned about the price of the products they are producing and far better informed about that. They will initially interpret a rise in the demand for and price of their product as a rise in its relative price and as implying a fall in the real wage rate they must pay measured in terms of their product. They will therefore be willing to hire more labor (move down their demand curve). The combined result is a movement, say, to point F, which corresponds with "overfull" employment, with nominal wages rising at 2 percent per year.

But, as time passes, both employers and employees come to recognise that prices *in general* are rising. As Abraham Lincoln said, you can fool all of the people some of the time, you can fool some of the people all of the time, but you can't fool all of the people all of the time. As a result, they raise their estimate of the anticipated rate of inflation, which reduces the rate of rise of anticipated real wages and leads you to slide down the curve back ultimately to the point E_0. There is thus a *short-run* "trade-off" between inflation and unemployment, but *no long-run* "trade-off."

Figure 12.6 expresses this same analysis in a way that brings out more

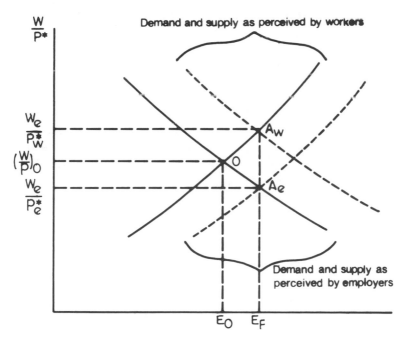

FIGURE 12.6

explicitly the difference between the considerations relevant to employers and employees. As in earlier figures, E_0 is the equilibrium employment, and $\left(\dfrac{W}{P}\right)_0$ is the equilibrium real wage rate. For simplicity, assume an initial equilibrium position with constant price level. Now let something produce a widespread increase in nominal demand which leads employers to seek to hire more employees. How will this be perceived by workers? To them, the real wage that matters is their nominal wage divided by a price index of the goods and services they buy. As yet they have no reason to suppose a change in the price level, hence they have no reason to change their supply function. It will remain the solid supply curve on Figure 12.6, if we interpret P* as the price level *perceived* or *anticipated* by workers. To them, it will appear as if the demand for labor has shifted to the right, to the dashed demand curve. At each nominal wage rate (also real wage rate as perceived by them), employers are seeking to hire more workers. The new equilibrium will be A_w, involving a higher nominal and perceived wage rate, or its equivalent, and a higher level of employment.[9]

From the point of view of the employer, the situation is quite different. The real wage that matters to him is not its command over goods and services in general, but the relation between the nominal wage and the price of the good he is producing—that is, the price that enters into equation (5) of chapter 9. If we express his demand for labor in terms of the nominal wage divided by this price, his demand for labor is unchanged, and so is the aggregate demand curve for labor for the economy, if P* is taken to be not the perceived price level for the economy as a whole but the average of prices as perceived by individual producers. The demand curve remains the solid demand curve in Figure 12.6. However, the supply curve, in terms of this perceived price level, is different. Employers faced with an increased nominal demand for their products will count on being able to get a higher price or the equivalent.[10] The same nominal wage means a lower real wage in terms of that higher price of his product. For employers as a whole, it will appear as if the supply curve has shifted to the right to the dashed supply curve in Figure 12.6. The new equilibrium will be A_e, involving a lower perceived real wage rate, though a higher nominal wage rate, and a higher level of employment.

It is no accident that A_e and A_w correspond to the same level of employment. The righthand shift of the supply curve from the point of view of the employers is simply another way of describing the righthand shift of

9. The "equivalent" may be more overtime work, or more regular work, or nonmonetary perquisites, rather than a change in quoted wage rates.

10. The "equivalent" may be lower sales costs, fewer special concessions or discounts, etc. Hence, the quoted price, which enters into published index numbers, may not change yet the relevant price may.

the demand curve from the point of view of the workers. The two must give the same answer.

As Figure 12.6 is drawn, it appears as if $\frac{W}{P_w^*}$, the real wage as perceived by the workers, exceeds the initial real wage, $\left(\frac{W}{P}\right)_0$ by just about as much as $\frac{W}{P_e^*}$, the real wage as perceived by the employers, falls short of the initial real wage, and hence, for our example, as if the rise in the average of perceived prices (roughly, the rise in the actual price level)[11] is about twice the rise in nominal wages.[12] But this result is simply an accident of the particular graph, reflecting the similar elasticity (in absolute value) of the demand and supply curves. The average of perceived prices must rise by more than nominal wages, else the real wage as perceived by employers would not decline, but the amount of the excess depends on the elasticities of the demand and supply curves. At one extreme, if the supply curve were perfectly elastic, nominal wages would not rise at all; at the other, if the demand curve were perfectly elastic, nominal wages would rise just as much as the average of perceived prices. Between these extremes, the more elastic the supply curve and the more inelastic the demand curve, the smaller the ratio of the rise in nominal wages to the rise in prices. As for employment, the more elastic the two curves, the greater the expansion of employment.

The situation depicted in Figure 12.6 corresponding to employment E_F is temporary. Two sets of forces tend to change it. First, employees come to recognize that prices in general have risen, which leads them, as it were, to slide back down their supply curve from A_w to O. Employers, who initially have treated other nominal prices (or supply curves of factors in nominal terms) as given, come to recognize that they have risen, which leads them to reduce their demand for labor (on the average) at given ratios of nominal wage rates to the price of their own product. They are led, as it were, to slide back up the demand curve from A_e to O. The dashed demand and supply curves move to the left, and again in a linked way. The rise in prices as perceived by workers comes to approach the rise in prices as perceived by employers and both to approach the rise in nominal wages.

By incorporating price anticipations into the Phillips curve as I have

---

11. *Roughly* is used because of the qualifications in the preceding footnote.

12. To illustrate, suppose $\left(\frac{W}{P}\right)_0 = 1$, $\frac{W}{P_w^*} = 1.10$, $\frac{W}{P_e^*} = .9$. Since we have assumed that $P_w^* = P_0$, $W = 1.1\,P_0$, hence $P_e^* = \frac{1.1}{.9}\,P_0 = 1.22\,P_0$. That is, the average of perceived prices has risen by roughly twice as much as the average nominal wage paid.

just done, I have implicitly begged one of the main issues in the recent controversy about the Phillips curve. Thanks to recent experience of 'stagflation' plus theoretical analysis, everyone now admits that the apparent short-run Phillips curve is misleading and seriously overstates the *long-run trade-off*, but many are not willing to accept the view that the *long-run trade-off is zero*.

We can examine this issue by using a different way of incorporating price anticipations into the Phillips curve. Figure 12.7 keeps the rate of

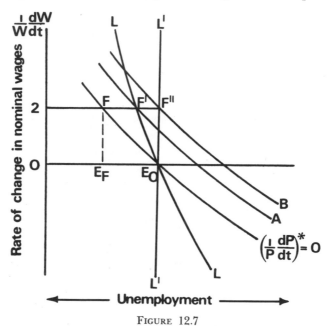

FIGURE 12.7

change of nominal wages on the vertical axis but contains a series of different curves, one for each anticipated rate of growth of wages. To put it algebraically, instead of writing the Phillips curve relation as

$$(1) \qquad \frac{1}{W}\frac{dW}{dt} - \left(\frac{1}{P}\frac{dP}{dt}\right)^* = f(U),$$

where U is unemployment, we can write it in more general form as

$$(2) \qquad \frac{1}{W}\frac{dW}{dt} = f\left[U, \left(\frac{1}{P}\frac{dP}{dt}\right)^*\right].$$

Now suppose something occurs to put the economy at point F at which wages are rising at 2 percent a year and unemployment is less than the natural rate. Then, as people adjust their expectations of inflation, the short-run Phillips curve will shift upwards and the final resting place would be on that short-run Phillips curve at which the anticipated rate of inflation equals the current rate. The issue now becomes whether that Phillips curve is like A, so that the long-run curve is negatively sloping, like LL, in which case an anticipated rate of inflation of 2 percent will still reduce the level of unemployment, though not by as much as an unanticipated rate of 2 percent, or whether it is like B, so that the long-run curve is *vertical,* that is, unemployment is the *same* at a 2 percent anticipated rate of inflation as at a zero percent anticipated rate.

No Long-Run Money Illusion

In my presidential address to the American Economic Association in 1967, I argued that the long-run Phillips curve was vertical, largely on the grounds I have already sketched here: in effect, the absence of any long-run money illusion.[13] At about the same time, Professor E. S. Phelps, now of Columbia University, offered the same hypothesis, on different though related grounds.[14] This hypothesis has come to be called the *accelerationist* hypothesis or the *natural rate* hypothesis. It has been called *accelerationist* because a policy of trying to hold unemployment below the horizontal intercept of the long-run vertical Phillips curve must lead to an *accelerated* inflation.

Suppose, beginning at point E_0 on Figure 12.7, when nobody anticipated any inflation, it is decided to aim at a lower unemployment level, say E_F. This can be done initially by producing an inflation of 2 percent, as shown by moving along the Phillips curve corresponding to anticipations of no inflation. But, as we have seen, the economy will not stay at F because people's anticipations will shift, and if the rate of inflation were kept at 2 percent, the economy would be driven back to the level of unemployment it started with. The only way unemployment can be kept below the natural rate is by an *ever-accelerating* inflation, which always keeps current inflation ahead of anticipated inflation. Any resemblance between that analysis and what has been happening in Britain is not coincidental: what recent British governments have tried to do is to keep unemployment below the natural rate, and to do so they have had to accelerate inflation—from 3.9 percent in 1964 to 16.0 percent in 1974, according to official statistics.[15]

MISUNDERSTANDINGS ABOUT THE "NATURAL RATE" OF UNEMPLOYMENT

The hypothesis came to be termed the *natural rate* hypothesis because of the emphasis on the natural rate of unemployment. The term

13. "The Role of Monetary Policy," *American Economic Review* (March 1968): 1–17.

14. "Money Wage Dynamics and Labour Market Equilibrium," in E. S. Phelps (Ed.), *Microeconomic Foundations of Employment and Inflation Theory* (New York: Norton, 1970).

15. United Kingdom General Index of Retail Prices, *Department of Employment Gazette.*

the *natural rate* has been misunderstood. It does not refer to some *irreducible minimum* of unemployment. It refers rather to that rate of employment which is consistent with the *existing real conditions* in the labor market. It can be lowered by removing obstacles in the labor market, by reducing friction. It can be raised by introducing additional obstacles. The purpose of the concept is to separate the monetary from the nonmonetary aspects of the employment situation—precisely the same purpose that Wicksell had in using the word *natural* in connection with the rate of interest.

In the past few years, a large number of statistical studies have investigated the question whether the long-run Phillips curve is or is not vertical. That dispute is still in train.

Most of the statistical tests were undertaken by rewriting equation 2 in the form:

(3)
$$\frac{1}{W}\frac{dW}{dt} = a + b\left(\frac{1}{P}\frac{dP}{dt}\right)^* + f(U)$$

or

$$\frac{1}{P}\frac{dP}{dt} = a + b\left(\frac{1}{P}\frac{dP}{dt}\right)^* + f(U),$$

where the left-hand side was either the rate of change of wages or the rate of change of prices. The question then asked was the value of b.[16] The original Phillips curve essentially assumed b = 0; the acceleration hypothesis set b equal to 1. The authors of the various tests I am referring to used observed data, mostly time-series data, to estimate the numerical value of b.[17] Almost every such test has come out with a numerical value of b less than 1, implying that there is a long-run "trade-off."[18] However, there are a number of difficulties with these tests, some on a rather superficial level, others on a much more fundamental level.

16. This is the coefficient of the anticipated rate of inflation, that is, the percentage point change in the current rate of change in wages or in prices that would result from a one percentage point change in the anticipated rate of inflation.

17. I might note as an aside that one much noticed attempt along these lines was contained in lectures given in Britain by Robert Solow a few years ago (*Price Expectations and the Behaviour of the Price Level,* Manchester University Press, 1969). Unfortunately, his test has a fatal flaw that renders it irrelevant to the current issue. In order to allow for costs as well as demand, he included on the right-hand side of an equation like equation 3 the rate of change of wages, and, on the left-hand side, the rate of change of prices. In such an equation, there is no reason to expect b to be unity even on the strictest acceleration hypothesis, because the equation is then an equation to determine what happens to the margin between prices and wages. Let the anticipated rate of inflation rise by one percentage point, but the rate of change of wages be held constant, and any resulting rise in prices raises the excess of prices over costs and so stimulates output. Hence, in Solow's equation, the strict acceleration hypothesis would imply that b was less than 1.

18. A succinct summary of these studies is in S. J. Turnovsky, "On the Role of Inflationary Expectations in a Short-Run Macro-Economic Model," *Economic Journal* (June 1974): 317–37, especially pp. 326–27.

One obvious statistical problem is that the statistically fitted curves have not been the same for different periods of fit and have produced very unreliable extrapolations for periods subsequent to the period of fit. So it looks very much as if the statistical results are really measuring a *short-term* relationship despite the objective. The key problem here is that, in order to make the statistical test, it is necessary to have some measure of the anticipated rate of inflation. Hence, every such test is a joint test of the accelerationist hypothesis and a particular hypothesis about the formation of anticipations.

The Adaptive Expectations Hypothesis

Most of these statistical tests embody the so-called adaptive expectations hypothesis, which has worked well in many problems. It states that anticipations are revised on the basis of the difference between the current rate of inflation and the anticipated rate. If the anticipated rate was, say, 5 percent but the current rate 10 percent, the anticipated rate will be revised upward by some fraction of the difference between 10 and 5. As is well known, this implies that the anticipated rate of inflation is an exponentially weighted average of past rates of inflation, the weights declining as one goes back in time.

Even on their own terms, then, these results are capable of two different interpretations. One is that the long-run Phillips curve is not vertical but has a negative slope. The other is that this has not been a satisfactory method of evaluating people's expectations for this purpose.

A somewhat more subtle statistical problem with these equations is that, if the accelerationist hypothesis is correct, the results are either estimates of a short-run curve or are statistically unstable. Suppose the true value of b is unity. Then when current inflation equals anticipated inflation, which is the definition of a long-run curve, we have

$$(4) \qquad\qquad f(U) = -a.$$

This is the vertical long-run Phillips curve with the value of U that satisfies it being the natural rate of unemployment. Any other values of U reflect either short-term equilibrium positions or a stochastic component in the natural rate. But the estimation process used, with $\frac{1}{P}\frac{dP}{dt}$ on the left-hand side, treats different observed rates of unemployment as if they were exogenous, as if they could persist indefinitely. There is simply no way of deriving equation 4 from such an approach. In effect, the implicit assumption that unemployment can take different values begs the whole question raised by the accelerationist hypothesis. On a statistical level, this approach requires putting U, or a function of U, on the left-hand side, not $\frac{1}{P}\frac{dP}{dt}$.

Rational Expectations

A still more fundamental criticism has recently been made by a number of economists in the United States. This criticism has its origin in an important article by John Muth on rational expectations. The rational expectations approach has been applied to the problem in recent articles by Robert Lucas of Carnegie-Mellon (now of Chicago), Thomas Sargent of the University of Minnesota, and a number of others.[19]

This criticism is that you cannot take seriously the notion that people form anticipations on the basis of a weighted average of past experience with fixed weights—or any other scheme that is inconsistent with the way inflation is really being generated. For example, let us suppose that the current course of the price level is the one drawn on panel A of Figure 12.8, that inflation is accelerating. With a fixed exponential weighting pat-

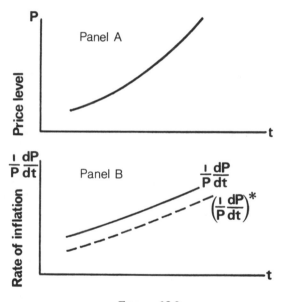

FIGURE 12.8

19. John Muth, "Rational Expectations and the Theory of Price Movements." *Econometrica* (July 1961): 315–35; Robert E. Lucas, "Econometric Testing of the Natural Rate Hypothesis," in Otto Eckstein (Ed.), *The Econometrics of Price Determination Conference* (Washington, D.C.: Board of Governors of the Federal Reserve System and Social Science Research Council, 1972); Robert Lucas, "Econometric Policy Evaluation: A Critique," Carnegie-Mellon University Working Paper, 1973: Robert Lucas, "Some International Evidence on Output-Inflation Tradeoffs," *American Economic Review* (June 1973): 326–34; Thomas J. Sargent, "Rational Expectations, the Real Rate of Interest, and the 'Natural' Rate of Unemployment," in *Brookings Papers on Economic Activity*, vol. 2 (1973): 429–72; and Thomas J. Sargent and Neil Wallace, " 'Rational' Expectations, the Optimal Money Instrument and the Optimal Money Supply Rule," *Journal of Political Economy* (April 1974).

tern (with weights summing to unity), the anticipated rate of inflation will always be lagging behind, as in Panel B. But people who are forming anticipations are not fools—or at least some of them are not. They are not going to *persist* in being wrong. And more generally they are not going to base their anticipations solely on the past history of prices. Is there anybody whose anticipation of inflation next year will be independent of the result of the coming British elections? That is not reported in the past record of prices. Will it be independent of policies announced by the parties that come into power, and so on? Therefore, said Muth, we should assume that people form their anticipations on the basis of a correct economic theory: not that they are right in each individual case but that over any long period they will *on the average* be right. Sometimes this will lead to the formation of anticipations on the basis of adaptive expectations, but by no means always.

If you apply that idea to the present problem, it turns out that if the true world is one in which people form expectations on a rational basis so that on the average they are right, then assuming that they form expectations by averaging the past with fixed weights will yield a value of b in equation 3 less than unity, even though the true value is unity.

Consider a world in which there is a vertical long-run Phililps curve and in which people form their expectations rationally, so that on the average, over a long period, their expectations are equal to what happens. In such a world, the statistician comes along and estimates equation 3 on the assumption that people form their anticipations by averaging past experience with fixed weights. What will he find? It turns out that he will find that b is less than 1. Of course, this possibility does not prove that the statistical tests incorporating adaptive expectations are wrong but only provides an alternative interpretation of their results.

In a series of very interesting and important papers, Lucas and Sargent have explored the implication of the rational expectations hypothesis and have tried to derive empirical tests of the slope of the long-run Phillips curve without the possibly misleading assumption of adaptive expectations.[20]

Their empirical tests use a different kind of information. For example, one implication of a rational expectations hypothesis is that, in a country in which prices have fluctuated a great deal, expectations will respond to changes in the current rate of inflation much more rapidly than in a country in which prices have been relatively stable. It follows that the observed short-run Phillips curve will be steeper in the first country than in the second. Comparisons among countries in this way, as well as other tests, seem so far entirely consistent with what any reasonable man must surely expect: which is that, *since you can't fool all the people all the time, the true long-run Phillips curve is vertical.*

20. See footnote 19.

Implications for Theory and Policy

The evidence is by no means all in. Some of the articles I have referred to are not yet published, and some have been published only in the past few years. So we certainly cannot regard the matter as settled. Even so, it is worth noting how far-reaching are the implications of this view not only for the Phillips curve problem but also for policy.

One very strong and very important implication for policy is that, if you treat people as forming expectations on a rational basis, no fixed rule of monetary or fiscal policy will enable you to achieve anything other than the natural rate of unemployment. And you can see why. Because—to go back to my initial Phillips curve analysis—the only way in which you ever get a reduction of unemployment is through *unanticipated* inflation.

If the government follows any fixed rule whatsoever, *so long as the people know it,* they will be able to take it into account. And consequently you cannot achieve an unemployment target other than the natural rate by any fixed rule. The only way you can do so is by continually being cleverer than all the people, by continually making up *new* rules and using them for a while until people catch up on them. Then you must invent a new set of rules. That is not a very promising possibility.

This analysis provides a different sort of intellectual background for a view that some of us have held for a long time: that it is a better approach to policy to say that you are going to cooperate with the people and inform them of what you are doing, so giving them a basis for their judgments, rather than trying to fool them. What the Sargent-Lucas argument and analysis really suggests is that you are fooling yourself if you think that you can fool them.

That is about where the present state of the argument is. I might summarise by saying that there is essentially no economist any longer who believes in the naive Phillips curve of the kind originally proposed. The argument has shifted now to a second level, where everybody agrees that the long-run Phillips curve is steeper than the short-run Phillips curve. The only argument is whether it is vertical or not quite so vertical. And here the evidence is not quite all in. But there is a line of approach in analysis and reasoning that enables you to interpret, so far as I know, all the existing evidence consistently on the hypothesis of a long-run vertical Phillips curve.

A Positively Sloping Phillips Curve?

The preceding analysis explains why full-employment policies have in fact been associated with accelerating inflation, but it does not explain another feature of recent experience, namely, the tendency for average rates of unemployment to be higher along with average rates of inflation, i.e., for a strictly empirical long-run or longer-run Phillips curve to be positively sloped rather than either negatively sloped or vertical.

The reason for this feature is that the preceding analysis is implicitly for situations of "open" inflation. It allows for the possibility that slow adjustment of anticipations to experience, long-term contracts, government interventions into specific markets, and other elements of "friction" or "rigidity" may prevent prompt adjustment of prices to changed circumstances and may make the "natural" unemployment rate higher than is attainable. But it does not allow for the possibility that these "frictions" or "rigidities" will themselves be a function of the rate of inflation.

In practice, under current political conditions, inflations are not likely to be permitted to be "open" in this sense. The authorities will be driven to trying to repress inflation by extending the scope of governmental interventions into particular industries through "jawboning," or formal price or wage controls for particular industries, or general price or wage controls, euphemistically referred to as "incomes policies," or other similar measures. And the higher the rate of inflation (actual or potential), the more such measures are likely to interfere with the operation of the price system.

Under some circumstances, such as wartime, suppressed inflation is likely to lead to overemployment. This arises partly because patriotic feelings make the enforcement of price control more effective than it can ordinarily be, partly because the expectation that the situation is temporary leads an apparently reduced current real wage rate to be perceived as an increased real wage rate by employees (see pages 207–208 in chapter 11), and partly because of a changed composition of demand, with a much larger fraction coming from a single purchaser, the government.

Under ordinary peacetime circumstances, however, the increased intervention at higher rates of inflation is likely to mean an increase in the natural rate of unemployment, because it makes the labor market less efficient. The result is a positively sloped, statistical Phillips curve for observations averaged over a period of years.

Cyclical Unemployment

The preceding analysis of the Phillips curve rests implicitly on certain elements that only recently have been given explicit attention in economic theory: in particular, imperfect information, the costs of acquiring information, and the role of human capital in determining the form of labor contracts. The pioneering work in these areas was done by George Stigler in his 1961 article, "The Economics of Information," and by Gary Becker in his 1964 book, *Human Capital.*

Imperfect information underlies the differences between real wages as perceived by employers and employees. For both groups, it is difficult and costly to find out what is likely to happen to prices in general. For workers, it is costly to find out what alternative employment opportunities are, yet their incentive to do so is great, so they are likely to be better informed about available nominal wages than about the price level in general. For employers, it is both most important and least costly to find out what is happening to the demand for their own product, hence they are likely to be better informed about the prices of their own product and of resources they use than about the price level in general.

The costs of acquiring information also play a decisive role in determining the length of time that it takes for adjustment in response to unanticipated changes in aggregate demand. One strand of work in this area in recent years has been emphasis on "search costs" in the labor market.

It takes time and effort for a worker to find out what alternative employments are available. It is difficult for him to hunt for a new job while employed. Hence, a worker who is unemployed, whether because he has just entered the labor market or because he has left or lost a job, may be unwilling to take the first job offered him. The cost of doing so is to reduce his probability of finding a "better" job. He will take the first job offered only if the wage offered is high enough to compensate for this cost. That, in turn, depends on his anticipations about the labor market. On this interpretation, unemployment as commonly understood is not simply waste and idleness; it rather corresponds to "time between jobs," or to the production activity of searching for the best use of resources.

Let there be an unanticipated increase in aggregate demand of the kind assumed to start out our Phillips curve analysis. Employers will try to hire more workers. Workers searching for jobs will more readily find offers that on the basis of their unchanged anticipations are attractive enough to compensate them for giving up the search. The average time between jobs (or between entering the labor force and a job) will decline and with it recorded unemployment.[21] As the more favorable employment situation becomes more widely known, job-seekers will revise their anticipations about opportunities, become more choosy, and recorded unemployment will rise toward its "natural" level. This is another way to interpret the movement in Figure 12.6 from point O to point A_w and back again.

Conversely, let there be an unanticipated decline in aggregate demand,

___

21. Note that recorded unemployment is an extremely tricky concept. It records the number of people who at a point in time report themselves as seeking work. This number can change without any change at all in the number who are unemployed at some time or other during a specified period. To take a highly simplified example, suppose it took everyone precisely two weeks (ten working days) to find a job; that every working day 400,000 persons start to look for a job, and the same number are employed. The number of unemployed on any particular day would then be 4,000,000—the number who started to look for a job on the prior ten working days. Now let the numbers looking for a job and finding one each day be the same, but the time it takes to find a job double to four weeks. The number recorded as unemployed will then double, without a single additional identifiable individual having become unemployed at any time.

In practice, the cyclical rises and falls in the percentage unemployed reflect both fluctuations in time between jobs and the number unemployed during a specified period.

so that employers are willing to hire fewer workers at each real wage rate as perceived by them. Workers searching for jobs will find fewer offers that on the basis of their unchanged anticipations are attractive enough to compensate them for giving up the search. The average time between jobs will lengthen and so will recorded unemployment. As the less attractive employment situation becomes more widely known, job-seekers will revise their anticipations about opportunities, become less choosy, and recorded unemployment will decline toward its natural level.

This brief sketch is in no way inconsistent with the existence of a supply curve of labor of the usual kind, if we recall that that curve shows the *minimum* wage at which a given amount of labor is available, or the *maxi- -mum* amount of labor available at a given wage. But the sketch is incomplete, because for simplicity it concentrates entirely on job-seekers. Employers seeking workers have costs of search, too. The terms they offer depend on what they believe the market situation to be. Their demand price is the maximum price they are willing to pay. However, the extension to employers is rather straightforward.

The more important and interesting question is why the phenomena described, which are so prominent in the labor market, appear largely absent in such markets as the security and commodity markets. In these markets, unanticipated shifts in demand are reflected rapidly and fully in prices. "Search" behavior doubtless occurs, but it proceeds so rapidly and efficiently that it does not prevent almost instantaneous adjustment of prices. The counterpart in the labor market would be continuous and substantial changes in wage rates paid to employed workers, negligible unemployment as currently measured, and little or no fluctuation in unemployment.

The chief explanation of this difference that has been offered, primarily in the work that has been done on human capital, centers on the first two "peculiarities" of labor listed by Marshall: "The worker sells his work but retains capital in himself." "The seller of labor must deliver it himself." One effect is that labor tends to be less homogeneous than the kinds of securities or commodities traded on organized markets. True, one bushel of wheat may differ from another, but wheat is fairly readily graded into standard quality classes; the purchaser of wheat can buy it by grade, he does not have to examine each bushel separately to see whether it meets his needs. That is, search costs are small. The employer of labor for most tasks is generally in a different position. When he is not—as in casual day labor—markets can and do develop in which the price changes from day to day and in which conditions approximating commodity markets develop.

A more important effect is that the productivity of a worker depends not only on his personal characteristics but his training and experience, on his human capital. Insofar as this human capital is "general," that is, its value is independent of the particular use, it raises no additional problem. But insofar as it is "specific," that is, more valuable to a particular employer than to others, it does. And much human capital is specific: that is, many workers are more valuable to their current employers, because of the experience and training they have received which is especially relevant to his business, than they would be to others.

Consider a particularly simple, if extreme, case. Here is a worker whose "general" marginal productivity without special experience or training is $5 an hour to a number of potential employers. After a year's experience with a particular employer, his "specific" marginal productivity will be $7 an hour, but if he were then to leave that employer for another, his initial marginal productivity would revert to $5 an hour. In advance, there is competition. After a year, if wages are set daily, say, there is a bilateral monopoly position. The obvious solution is an advance agreement for a more or less fixed period at a wage between $5 and $7. Competition between employers will drive the wage to a level such that the excess of the wage over marginal productivity during the training period just balances the excess of marginal productivity over the wage after the training period.

Specific human capital, which, on the one hand, is inseparable from the employee, and, on the other, is more valuable to a particular employer than to others, therefore makes for relatively long-term contracts with respect to wage rates. This feature, in turn, enhances the importance of anticipations, necessarily imperfect, about the future and makes it worth devoting considerable effort and time, on the part of workers and employers, to search activities.

This analysis explains search and long-term contracts but does not explain the form of those contracts, especially the alleged fact that they tend to commit the employer to the wage he pays but not to the amount of work he provides. This is another form of the initial question of why adjustments to unanticipated changes in aggregate demand take the form of changes in employment rather than wages. Most graphically, for reductions in demand, why layoffs?

One answer is that the alleged fact is at best dubious. Many contracts—and here the college professor on tenure can speak with a loud voice—do guarantee employment as well as wage rates. But this is not a wholly satisfactory answer and a number of alternative explanations are currently being proposed and explored.

Granted this analysis, is it adequate to explain not only the fluctuations in employment and unemployment during the relatively mild recessions of the postwar period, but also the massive unemployment of the great depression when, at the trough in 1932 and 1933, the unemployed numbered more than a fifth of the labor force? The answer is not entirely clear. On the one hand, there were a series of sharp, unanticipated declines in aggregate demand, so that recurrent and ever bigger readjustments in anticipations were required. This is suggested by the successively more rapid rates of decline in the quantity of money, which finally produced a cut of one-third in the total quantity of money between 1929 and 1933. On the other hand, in the most nearly comparable earlier episode, 1873–79, while nominal income fell about as much as from 1929–33, nominal wages and prices fell much more, employment fell much less, and unemployment was apparently much less serious. Clearly, in the intervening half-century, wages and prices had become much more rigid. We do not have a satisfactory reconciliation of the two episodes, but obvious candidates for explanations include: the growing complexity of production processes, rendering specific human capital more important; the declining importance of agriculture; the growth in government intervention into economic activity; the growth of trade unions; and the suspension of unlimited immigration, which in the 1870s could take up the slack as it could not in the 1930s.

A much more troublesome contradiction until just recently has been the supposed continuation of massive unemployment during the years from 1933–39, when there was a massive expansion in nominal aggregate demand. According to the generally accepted estimates, unemployment reached 25 percent in 1933, then fell to 14 percent in 1937, rose to 19 percent in 1938, and only fell below 14 percent after the United States began an active rearmament program prior to getting into World War II. No satisfactory explanation in terms of "search" theory or "human capital" has been offered.

And a good thing! Because it now turns out that these generally accepted estimates grossly overstated unemployment during the 1930s in terms of the currently accepted definition of unemployment. As unemployed, they included persons who were employed by federal, state, and local governments in "emergency" or "work-relief" programs (though the amounts paid them were included in the national income estimates as "wages" paid rather than as transfer payments). According to estimates by Michael Darby, the level of unemployment, calculated on current definitions, reached a peak of 23 percent in 1933 and then fell to 9.2 percent in 1937, when the fall was interrupted by the recession of 1937–38, which raised the percentage to 12.5 percent in 1938.[22] These are annual averages, so the reduction in unemployment between the trough of the Great Contraction in March 1933 and the subsequent peak just over four years later in May 1937 must have been even more dramatic. There is little evidence there of any significant failure of the labor market to respond to changes in aggregate demand.[23]

22. Michael R. Darby, "Three-and-a-half Million U.S. Employees have been Mislaid; or, An Explanation of Unemployment, 1934–1941," *Journal of Political Economy,* 84 (February 1976).

23. The increase in output from 1933 to 1937 was larger than in any prior four-year period for which we have data.

13

Wages in Different Occupations

In discussing the supply curve of labor in general, we have taken for granted the structure of wage rates for labor of different kinds—relative wages in different occupations. This structure of wages is itself determined by the relative demand for and supply of labor of different kinds. The reason we have been putting it aside and are able to analyze it separately is because the major forces determining the supply curves of labor in particular occupations can be regarded as largely, though of course not entirely, independent of those determining the total supply of labor.

At any given time, there will exist some structure of relative wage rates (or average earnings) in different occupations. It is useful to regard this structure as the result of three kinds of forces or phenomena producing differentials between wage rates in different occupations:

1. Factors other than wage rates that affect the attractiveness of different occupations to individuals in a position to choose among them: Even if there were perfect competition, perfect and costless mobility, and all members of the population had identical abilities, money wage rates in different occupations would by no means be equal. Some occupations are less attractive than others and will therefore have to offer a higher wage than others if they are to attract people to them. Given differences in tastes, the precise set of differentials that will arise in this way depends not only on the characteristics of the occupations but also on the conditions of demand. If the demand for an occupation is relatively small, it may be possible to staff it entirely with people who regard it as more attractive than other occupations, in which case the wage rate would, on this score alone, be relatively low. If, on the other hand, the demand is relatively large, it can be met only by attracting people into the occupation who regard other occupations as more attractive, in which case the wage rate would have to be relatively high. Differentials in wage rates that arise from this set of forces may be termed *equalizing differences.*

2. *Factors that produce noncompeting groups:* For a variety of reasons, not all people are in a position to choose freely—not even once during their lifetime—among occupations. The existence of such barriers to the staffing of particular occupations produces a series of partly sheltered, though not entirely unrelated, markets and inhibits the operation of the forces discussed above. Differences in natural ability can be classified under this heading, although they could perhaps also be classified under the preceding one. Differentials in wage rates arising from this set of forces may be termed *differences arising from noncompeting groups.*

3. *Incomplete adjustment to changes in demand or supply:* The immediate effect on wage rates of any change in the demand for or supply of labor of various kinds may be very different from its ultimate effect. This is a market in which it may take a long time for the ultimate effect to be felt—for the immediate effect to produce reactions that will lead to a new equilibrium. At any time, therefore, some part of the differences in wage rates may be regarded as attributable to incompleteness of adjustment. Of course, what comes under this heading depends on one's viewpoint and on the conditions that are being held constant for the purpose in hand, since by *adjustment* we mean adjustment to some given set of conditions. If this given set of conditions defines market demand and supply curves, the existing position involves full adjustment to them, and nothing comes under this heading. The longer the run, which means the narrower and more ultimate the set of conditions taken as given, the more comes under this heading. Differentials in wage rates arising from incompleteness of adjustment may be termed *transitional differences.*

EQUALIZING DIFFERENCES IN WAGE RATES

To simplify the discussion of the supply of labor in different occupations, let us concentrate on two particular occupations, say A and B. We can then summarize the conditions of supply for these occupations as in Figure 13.1. The vertical axis shows the wage rate in A relative to the wage rate in B, both being expressed in some common and convenient form, say per hour. The horizontal axis shows the number of man-hours supplied in A relative to the number in B. The curve then shows the maximum relative number of man-hours that would be supplied at various relative wage rates.

This method of summarizing supply conditions is not, of course, perfectly general and implies something about the conditions of supply. For it might be that the relative number of man-hours supplied depends not only

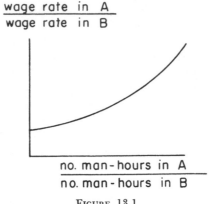

FIGURE 13.1

on the relative wage rate but also on the absolute wage rates—for example, that the relative supply would be different at wage rates of $3 in A and $1.50 in B than at wage rates of $6 in A and $3 in B. However, this kind of effect is not something we are going to be able to say much about, and its neglect is more than compensated for by the convenience of the above mode of summarizing supply conditions. Of course, the supply curve is only valid for given "other" conditions, in particular, for given alternative employment opportunities.

If all individuals had identical tastes and abilities, they would, given the same information, evaluate identically the relative merits of different occupations. The result would be that a supply curve like that in Figure 13.1 would be horizontal: there would be some relative wage rate that would be regarded by all as making the two occupations equally attractive. At any higher relative wage rate, all would go into A; at any lower relative wage rate, all would go into B. Differences in tastes, abilities, or information about the two occupations will lead to differences among individuals in the relative wage rates regarded as making the two occupations equally attractive and will introduce a slope into the curve, as in Figure 13.1.

We can organize our discussion most conveniently by classifying the factors affecting the supply curve into three categories: (1) those that determine the relative pecuniary attractiveness of the two occupations, (2) the variability of income in the two occupations, and (3) nonpecuniary differences among the occupations. A major reason for this particular breakdown is that the factors in the first category affect all individuals (at least, all of equal ability) alike and so should affect mainly the height of the supply curve; they are almost the only factors that would have to be taken into account in a "slave" society, and their counterparts are relevant in drawing the supply curve of the services of nonhuman capital for one use or another. The second and third categories introduce the factors that become important because of the peculiarities attached to human capital.

1. Factors capable of actuarial evaluation: Consider a slave owner deciding whether to specialize and train his slaves to pursue occupation A or occupation B. This decision may not, of course, be irrevocable; an individual trained for A may be able at a later date to shift to B, but generally only at considerable cost. In making his decision, the slave owner would want to know much more than the wage rate per hour in the two occupations. A, for example, might be seasonal, B not seasonal, which might make the expected number of hours of work per year lower in A than in B. A might be more affected by cyclical movements than B, so the expected number of years of work would be lower in A than in B. A might be an occupation requiring great physical strength, so that the number of years during which an individual could be employed in A might be lower than in B, which might be a sedentary occupation. A might require a longer period of training.

The effect of all such factors can be summarized in the expected net returns from each occupation for any given wage rate and for each age of the worker, as in Figure 13.2. The net return for any occupation and year depends, of course, on precisely what are regarded as occupational expenses and so deducted from gross returns. A literal slave owner would regard the cost of feeding, housing, and clothing the slaves as an occupational expense; he would be interested only in the excess of earnings over this sum. Thanks to the dual nature of human beings in our society—as factors of production and as ultimate consumers for the satisfaction of whose wants production is carried on—it is impossible or nearly impossible to distinguish the part of a man's consumption that is to be regarded as an occupational expense (required to maintain him as a productive resource) from final consumption.[1] Perhaps the best procedure is to deduct only those occupational expenses that are clearly special to a particular occupation and to regard the minimum expenses beyond this that are necessary to maintain the human being as a factor of production as the same in all occupations. This treatment accounts for the initial segment of zero net returns in Figure 13.2, which is intended to display the features of a "typical" pattern of lifetime returns. The subsequent segment of negative returns refers to the period of training, when special outlays—for tuition fees, books, equipment, etc.—are likely to exceed any positive returns. Thereafter, in general, net returns rise to a peak and subsequently decline. In addition to the more obvious occupational expenses, it is clear that income taxes should also be deducted in computing net returns.

Since the figures plotted are *expected* net returns, they conceal wide dif-

1. One of the ways of rationalizing the personal exemption and credit for dependents under the income tax is as an allowance for occupational expenses of this kind. Similarly, the pressure for an "earned income credit" derives from the recognition that all expenses are deducted in computing taxable income from nonhuman capital, but not in computing taxable income from human capital.

ferences among the returns to different individuals and are affected by the likelihood of unemployment. Similarly, the declining segment in part reflects not only a possible decline in the productivity of the active worker with age, but also the smaller probability that an individual will be actively earning income as he grows older because of voluntary retirement, retirement or idleness forced by ill health, or death. Note also that the vertical axis shows the returns if occupation A is *chosen* and not from the practice of occupation A. It therefore includes earnings from other occupations that may be followed instead of A by people who choose A initially. The reason is that one factor affecting the attractiveness of different occupations is precisely the relative value that training for an occupaion has in carrying on other occupations.

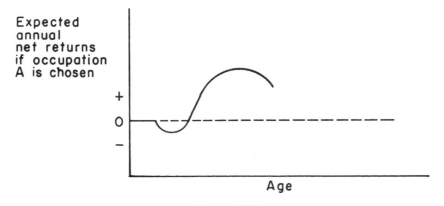

FIGURE 13.2

While the shape of the curve in Figure 13.2 is reasonably typical, it will of course differ from occupation to occupation in detail. The amount of capital investment varies widely and with it the age at which expected earnings become positive. The peakedness of the curve and the age at which the peak is reached likewise vary widely.

The simple average level of lifetime earnings is not, of course, adequate to summarize the attractiveness of a particular lifetime earnings pattern, even to the impersonal slave owner; in a world in which the interest rate is not zero, the timing of the returns matters also. For example, suppose the lifetime earnings patterns for A and B are as in Figure 13.3 and that both have the same average level. A is then clearly the more attractive financially, since the excess earnings in A in early years could be invested at interest and so yield a sum not available in B. To take account of this effect, we can co   .te the present capital value of the expected net returns in each occu   .ion. Let E_1 E_2, . . . be the expected annual returns in years 1, 2, . . . and r be the interest rate. Then $V = \dfrac{E_1}{1+r} + \dfrac{E_2}{(1+r)^2} + \ldots$ is the capital value in year zero of the stream of expected returns.

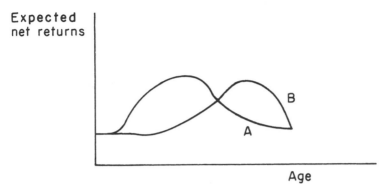

FIGURE 13.3

It will be recalled that the lifetime earning curves and so the capital values were computed for particular wage rates. To summarize the effect of the category of factors now under consideration, we can ask what relative wage rate would make the capital values in the two occupations equal. Suppose this were a wage rate 1.4 times as high in A as in B. We could then say that at this rate the two occupations would be equally attractive financially or actuarially, and that if actuarial attractiveness were the only consideration, the supply curve would be a horizontal line at a relative wage rate of 1.4, as in Figure 13.4.

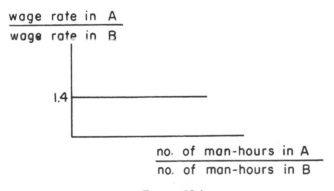

FIGURE 13.4

We have already listed many of the factors that will affect the relative wage rate that will make two occupations equally attractive financially: seasonal and cyclical variability of employment, length of training, direct cost of training, direct occupational expenses subsequent to training, tax structure, length of working life in an occupation, temporal pattern of earnings over the course of a working lifetime, etc. There are doubtless many others that might be important for one or another particular occupation, so that a complete statement is impossible. A self-contained analytical apparatus for taking such factors into account is both possible and desirable; a self-contained and complete list of the empirical factors to be taken into account is not.

2. *Variability of returns:* As already noted, the average net returns that enter into the capital values defined above conceal differences of return from individual to individual. These differences are of little importance to the slave owner—at least if we assume him to own enough slaves—since they will tend to cancel out and so he can concentrate on the expected return. To the individual in our society choosing an occupation, they cannot so easily be put to one side. He will want to know not only the present capital value of expected returns but also the distribution of returns—or more compactly, the probability distribution of present capital values. Occupations A and B, for example, may be equally attractive financially, yet A may be an occupation like, say movie acting, offering a small chance of a very high reward together with a large chance of a small reward, while B may be an occupation like typing, offering reasonable certainty of a particular return with no great chance of wide departures in either direction.

The effect of this variability depends, of course, on the tastes of individuals with respect to risk or uncertainty. If we accept the expected utility theory of choice, the wage rates that render two occupations equally attractive to an individual are those that equate the expected utility from them rather than the expected money return or capital value.

If all people had the same tastes with respect to uncertainty, the effect of different variability of returns would be to raise or lower the height of a supply curve like the horizontal one in Figure 13.4 for A and B at a relative wage rate of 1.4 for A. If, for example, A offered a small chance of a large return while B offered only moderate variability, and if people in general preferred the former kind of uncertainty to the latter, the effect of variability would be to reduce the height of the curve from 1.4 to a lower number, say 1.3, the difference measuring, as it were, the price people are willing to pay to get the kind of uncertainty they like. For example, it is probably true that more people prefer the kind of variability ascribed above to movie acting to the kind ascribed to typing, and in consequence it is my guess that the average return to movie actors—account being taken of failures as well as of successes—is less than the average return to typists.

Of course, people do not all have the same tastes. Some prefer the kind of variability just attributed to A, some the kind attributed to B. The former will be attracted to A at a wage rate below 1.4, the latter only at a higher wage rate, so the supply curve will be given a positive slope as in Figure 13.5. If OA exceeds unity, it would be reasonable to say that on balance people prefer the kind of variability offered by A, and conversely.

3. *Nonpecuniary advantages:* In addition to the factors affecting the money returns from different occupations, there are many other factors that affect their attractiveness to any given individual—the kind of work

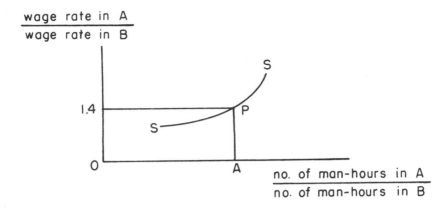

FIGURE 13.5

involved, the location at which it is carried on, the social prestige attached to it, and so on. Like variability of income, some such factors may be evaluated pretty much alike by most people; in this case, their effect is to shift the supply curve upward or downward. Insofar as people differ in their evaluation of nonpecuniary advantages and disadvantages, the effect is to impart a slope to the supply curve. Perhaps the extreme case of difference is if some prefer occupation A over B and others B over A, no matter what the relative pecuniary returns. In this case, the supply curve will be perfectly inelastic.

If there were no differences in tastes or abilities and an essentially perfect market, all supply curves would be perfectly elastic and relative wage rates would be determined completely by conditions of supply; conditions of demand would determine only the number in each occupation. In this case, all differences in return would be equalizing, and equalizing to all individuals. That is, the structure of wage rates would be such that each individual would be indifferent to which occupation he pursued; there would then be no "rents." At the other extreme, at which individuals are swayed exclusively by nonpecuniary considerations and there are wide differences in tastes, supply curves would be completely inelastic and relative wage rates would be determined by conditions of demand. All wages would, as it were, be price-determined instead of price-determining and so would be "rents."

In the more general case, in which there are differences in tastes and abilities but they do not completely determine the choice of occupations, supply curves will be positively sloped. In this case, differences in return will be equalizing *only at the margin*. Some individuals will be receiving a rent in the sense that they would be willing to pursue their occupation at a lower total return, though even these individuals too will be on the margin in the sense that they regard the additional return from working a little longer or harder as just compensating for the additional costs involved in doing so. That is, there is an extensive margin and an intensive one. An increase in demand will tend to push the extensive margin outward by attracting more individuals into the occupation. Its effect on the intensive margin is less certain for the reasons discussed above in connection with the backward bending, short-run supply curve of labor in general.

4. *The effect of income taxes:* The effect of income taxes seems worth singling out for special attention: first, because income taxes have so greatly increased in importance in recent years; second, because there is such general misunderstanding of their role and such widespread belief that they cannot be "shifted"; and third, because they are omitted from the list of factors discussed explicitly by Friedman and Kuznets (see Reading Assignments, page 327).

As already noted, the relevant figure for the individual to compare in judging the relative attractiveness of two occupations is return after taxes, not return before taxes. It has frequently been argued that income taxes do not affect this choice because a larger income before taxes means also a larger income after taxes, and hence if one occupation is more attractive than the other before taxes, it will be more attractive after taxes. Unfortunately, this is not true, partly because the base of the tax is not the same as the figure that is relevant in considering net pecuniary return and partly because the tax base cannot take account of nonpecuniary factors.

Consider first a straight proportional income tax with no exemptions. Even this tax will affect the relative returns in different occupations. The most obvious reason will be if the tax base does not permit the deduction of all expenses regarded as occupational expenses in choosing between occupations, and these differ from occupation to occupation. But even if the tax base is the same in this sense as the return relevant to the choice among occupations, it is almost sure to differ in other senses. For example, let one occupation yield a return that varies from year to year for any given individual and is sometimes negative, whereas another yields the same income during each year of work. Unless the tax provides for a subsidy (a negative payment) when net income is negative, the tax burden will be heavier on the first occupation than on the second, so that at a relative wage rate that would make the present capital value of the two occupations equal before taxes, the capital value will be smaller in the first occupation after allowance for taxes. This particular effect is by no means a curiosity; it arises especially between occupations that require training and those that do not, since in the former the return is, as we saw earlier, likely to be negative during earlier years. In these cases, the neglect of negative incomes is the same as not permitting the expenses of training to be deducted in computing taxable income.

The effects so far considered could in principle be eliminated by proper definition of the base. But this is hardly possible if two occupations differ in nonpecuniary attractiveness, so that a higher monetary return is required in one than in the other to make them equally attractive. In this case, it would take a higher relative return with the tax than without it to make the two occupations equally attractive. In effect, the nonpecuniary advantages of the lower-paid occupation are not subject to the tax, so that one way to avoid the tax is to engage in occupations with large nonpecuniary advantages.

The introduction of an exemption and of graduated rates has additional effects. An occupation in which an individual's income fluctuates from year to year will tend to be more heavily taxed for a given present value before tax than one in which it is constant from year to year. Here again, changes in the tax law to provide "averaging" of income might eliminate this effect, but no changes can very well eliminate a comparable effect when the variability is between people. Suppose that occupations A and B promise in advance the same average income before tax, but in A income varies more from individual to individual than in B. Then with a graduated tax schedule, average income after tax will be lower in A than in B. The graduated tax accentuates the effect of the nonpecuniary advantages mentioned above, for with such a tax, the ratio of incomes after tax will be lower than before tax.

It follows that the existence of an income tax does affect the choice of occupations and so the allocation of resources among different uses. Indeed, if all differences in income were equalizing, in the sense that supply curves of the kind we have been drawing were horizontal, an income tax would have no redistributive effects at all, no matter how steeply graduated. Relative wages after tax would be the same with a steeply graduated tax as with a flat tax. The reason is that people would leave occupations especially affected by the steeply graduated tax (occupations that are highly paid to compensate for extreme nonpecuniary disadvantages, or that offer highly variable returns, etc.) and enter those less affected by it, until this pattern of relative wage rates was attained. The same relative wage rates after tax would, of course, mean higher wage rates before tax in the occupations affected by the steeply graduated tax, and this would curtail the quantity demanded to match the reduced quantity supplied.

More generally, differences in taste will produce a positively sloping supply curve, so that the form of tax will affect the relative wage rates. The reduction in numbers employed in the occupation especially affected by the steeply graduated tax would be produced by the exodus (or more realistically the failure to enter) of those who had the least attachment to these occupations on nonpecuniary grounds. The final result would be a lower relative wage after tax than with a flat tax, though, of course, a higher relative wage before tax.

It is clear that this analysis of the income tax parallels the usual analysis of excise taxes. And indeed, it seems likely that corresponding to any given income tax, there is, in principle, some set of excise taxes on final services that would have precisely the same allocative and distributive effects.

DIFFERENCES ARISING FROM NONCOMPETING GROUPS

In order for differences in return to be predominantly equalizing—that is, produced by the factors discussed in the preceding section—it is clearly necessary that many individuals be in a position to choose freely among the occupations in question. To a very large extent this is the case, and, accordingly, many existing differences in wage rates can be regarded as equalizing differences. But there is considerable evidence that not all differences in return can be so regarded. In particular, differences in return between such broad classes of occupations as professional and nonprofessional seem considerably larger than can be explained in terms of differences in costs, nonpecuniary advantages or disadvantages, and the like.

The additional factor that enters in such cases is a barrier of some kind or other to entry into the better-paid occupations. Only some individuals are free to choose these occupations; they constitute, in Cairnes's happy term, a *noncompeting group*. Many different causes may give rise to barriers to entry and so to the establishment of noncompeting groups, and it may be desirable to list some of the more important.

1. Deliberate restrictions on entry: Immigration restrictions, for example, make American workers a noncompeting group relative to workers in other countries. Within the country, the requirement of a license to practice an occupation—as in medicine, law, and the like—may be a means of deliberately restricting entry. The granting of licenses is generally placed in the hands of people currently in the occupation, and they have an understandable incentive to restrict entry. Again, trade union power to force an employer to pay no less than an agreed-upon wage is a means of restricting entry into the occupation.

Restrictions of this kind are extremely numerous in detail and have been growing in recent decades. But, however vexatious, I would judge that except perhaps for the immigration restrictions, they have not been of major empirical importance; almost surely they have not been as important as some of the other barriers to be mentioned.

2. Geographic immobility: This is often cited as a cause of differences in return, particularly for alleged differences between North and South and country and city. It seems doubtful, however, that, except for particular and isolated cases, it is of any major importance in the United States. Census figures show quite extraordinary movements of people. During the 1940s, for example, the movement within the United States quite dwarfed in magnitude the forced movements of population in Europe, both those forced by the Nazis and those forced by the Soviets. And it must be recalled that it is not necessary for everyone to move. Mobility at the margin is enough.

3. Differences in ability: It is somewhat arbitrary whether to regard differences in ability as creating noncompeting groups or to combine them with differences in taste and regard them as giving rise to equalizing differences. It is clear that they will produce greater differences in returns between individuals than are required to compensate for differences in costs incurred and the like; in effect, one individual is more units of labor power than another, more human capital. The effect on wage rates in identifiable occupations arises because different occupations tend to be staffed with— or to require—different average levels of ability. Of course, there is no objective standard of "higher" and "lower" abilities that will be respected by the market: whether a particular type of ability will be highly remunerated depends entirely on whether the demand for it is high relative to the supply available.

Some examples may perhaps show why it is difficult to distinguish differences in "ability," in the economically relevant sense, from differences in "taste," and why it is tempting to include them with the factors giving rise to equalizing differences. Is the relatively high compensation of a deep-sea diver to be regarded as a reward for being willing to work under water and in dangerous circumstances or for the nonpecuniary disadvantages of the trade? What of the stunt artist? The physician? Obviously there is a large area where "ability" and "tastes" merge.

4. Socioeconomic stratification of the society: In many countries it is still true and in most countries it was true not so long ago that perhaps the major source of internal barriers to entry was posed by the stratification of the population into social classes. In general, the learned professions and certain other occupations have been freely open only to members of the upper classes, and so on down the line. Of course, stratification was never complete— there was always some possibility of upward mobility—but the hindrances in the path of such mobility sufficed to maintain wide differentials in rate of return.

This kind of strictly social stratification has never been as important in this country as in most others, and it has clearly been decreasing greatly over time, in large measure because of the wide availability of schooling. Its decreasing importance is clearly revealed in the behavior of relative wages in clerical and manual professions. Literacy was at one time sufficiently rare to give rise to a noncompeting group; it clearly is no longer the case. In consequence, there has been a long-term downward trend in the ratio of earnings in clerical pursuits to earnings in manual pursuits. From being considerably higher paid, clerical pursuits are probably now, in general, lower paid. On a higher level, the same phenomenon is repeating itself in the ratio of the salary of college teachers to the salary of high school teachers: this ratio has been declining steadily over time.

The difficulty or impossibility of having a good capital market for investment in human capital is a major reason why social and economic position can affect the alternatives open to a young man in choosing his career. The possibility of getting expensive training depends on the ability of a parent or benefactor to finance it, or the willingness and capacity of the young man to "work his way through," and even then, on the ability of the young man's family to do without the earnings he might otherwise get during his training. These factors remain important for certain careers and doubtless are one of the most important sources of differences in earnings attributable to noncompeting groups.

5. *Color* might have been included under the preceding heading, but it seems better to separate it out for special treatment. Clearly, blacks have not been in the same position as whites to choose among occupations. They have not had the same possibility of getting training and schooling, partly because of the lessened availability of public facilities, partly because of discrimination in private institutions. But the effect of color is much more complicated than this. Because of the prejudices of both customers and fellow workers, being a black involves having a lower economic productivity in some occupations, and so color has the same effect on earnings as a difference in ability. As a result, the stratification of the population by color has clearly been one of the most potent forces producing nonequalizing differences in return in the United States.

TRANSITIONAL DIFFERENCES IN RETURN

This heading requires very little discussion. Clearly the supply of labor of a particular kind is likely to be much less elastic in the short run than in the long run, so any change in demand is likely to have much sharper effects initially than ultimately. Perhaps the only point that needs fuller illustration is the point made at the outset—that what we call a *transitional difference* depends on our point of view. Consider the changes in the ratio of clerical to manual earnings noted above. The excess of clerical earnings a century or so ago could have been regarded as transitional from a sufficiently broad point of view, since high clerical earnings were leading (along with other factors) to the provision of schooling and to increased prestige of white-collar work. These, in the course of several generations, would reduce or erase the excess. Yet it is clear that for many problems this is a much broader point of view than is desirable.

14

Relation Between the Functional and Personal Distribution of Income

The preceding chapters deal with the prices of productive services. These prices, in conjunction with the quantities of productive services, determine what is called the *functional* distribution of income or output, that is, distribution according to the productive function performed by resources. From many points of view, however, there is more interest attached to what is called the *personal distribution of income,* that is, the distribution among identifiable income units, such as individuals or families or households.

Initial and Final Personal Distribution

The initial market distribution among income units is determined not only by the prices of productive services but also by the distribution of ownership of sources of productive services among income units: each unit gets an amount equal to the number of units of productive services it furnishes on the market multiplied by the price per unit of each productive service.

This initial market distribution is altered by redistribution via governmental taxes and subsidies of a wide variety of kinds, so that the final distribution of income available for consumption or savings can be very different from the initial distribution ground out by the market.

The distinction between the initial and final distribution is extremely important, yet also complex and ambiguous. Consider a piece of land that is supposedly "owned" by Mr. X, who rents its services to Mr. Y, and pays a "property tax," which happens to be equal to half the rent he receives. He can be viewed as receiving the whole rent in the initial distribution and then paying half of that in the course of the government-imposed redistribution. Alternatively and more satisfactorily for this simple case, the government can be viewed as a "silent partner" owning a half-share in the land, with Mr. X owning the other half-share and operating as the active partner. Clearly, the sum Mr. X or anyone else would pay to buy the land is the capitalized value of the part he receives, not of the total rent. He may write the check that goes to the government, but there is no economically meaningful sense in which he "pays" the tax unless he happened to be the owner of the land when a wholly unanticipated tax was levied on it, in which case he experienced an initial capital loss—a wealth tax.

This case is particularly simple, but the essential point applies to the whole range of redistribution. The U.S. federal government can be viewed as a "silent partner" owning 48 percent of every corporation of more than moderate size, since that fraction of the pretax income is collected as the corporation income tax of corporations. Similarly, who owns the human resources corresponding to personal income taxes on earnings? The individual who initially receives the earnings (or more accurately, is credited with the earnings, since withholding of taxes at source short-circuits the process)? The federal or state or local government? Or is the individual to be regarded rather as receiving the whole of the income but then paying part of it to purchase governmental services—as, for example, the driver who pays gasoline taxes that are required to be used for highway maintenance and construction?

Aside from ambiguities of definition, important substantive issues enter into the distinction between the initial and final distribution, as we have seen in preceding chapters. The existence of taxes (or partial government ownership of resources) changes the incentives to the active partner controlling their use. Taxes thereby alter the supply of resources of various kinds for various uses as well as altering more indirectly the demand for them and the prices per unit of resources. (One more sophisticated aspect of this possible effect is considered in the next chapter.)

This is not the place to deal exhaustively with these issues, which have traditionally been treated in courses on public finance under the heading of "shifting and incidence of taxation." It is enough here simply to stress the difference in this respect between the arithmetic and the economics of the comparison frequently made between the "before tax and subsidy" distribution of income and the "after tax and subsidy" distribution.[1] In

1. See, for example, *Economic Report of the President* (February 1974) chapter 5, especially tables 35 and 49, pp. 143 and 178.

the absence of the taxes and subsidies, the "initial" distribution would be very different than in their presence.

Aside from the question of redistribution, one of the most widespread fallacies in this area is the belief that one can go readily from the functional to the personal distribution. Wages and salaries, it is believed, are the income of the "poor"; interest, dividends, rents, and earnings of individual businesses, are the income of the "rich"; hence anything that raises wage rates relative to other factor returns will tend to render incomes less diverse, and conversely. Fortunately or unfortunately, this conclusion is false for two rather different reasons. First, it begs the whole question of the precise meaning of a personal distribution and the diversity associated with it. What is true for a personal distribution defined in one way is not true for a personal distribution defined in another. Second, it oversimplifies greatly the connection between types of income and the economic position of people.

Meaning of Personal Distribution

My own conclusion, which is based on many attempts to trace the effects of a change in the prices of productive services on the personal distribution of income by size, is that it is almost impossible to do so with any confidence. Statements that such and such a measure will diminish or enhance diversity or inequality should be taken with a grain of salt. I shall sketch the basis for this conclusion by first discussing in this section some of the key issues involved in defining the personal distribution, then in the next section sketching a few of the broader facts about types of income, and then considering two specific examples.

There are three basic issues that must be resolved in constructing a personal distribution of income by size: (1) the income unit, (2) the definition of income, and (3) the time unit for which income is to be measured. For each issue, the choice depends critically on the purpose of the distribution. Is it to promote an understanding of labor markets? Of resources available for capital formation? Of disparities in command over productive resources? Of disparities in levels of living?

1. Income unit: Should the income unit be the person? If so, all persons? All persons over fourteen (or some other conventional age)? All persons in the labor force? Or these plus other persons with some income from sources other than earnings?

Alternatively, should the income unit be the family? If so, how defined? By blood relationship only? By blood relationship and common dwelling unit? By blood relationship and "pooling" income? Or should the income unit be the "household," including unrelated persons who may be sharing a dwelling unit?

Questions of this kind are not easily resolvable by either abstract analysis or empirical evidence yet have a major effect on results. For example, consider the difference between a distribution of income among persons over fourteen years of age and a distribution among families of two or more persons. Do you want to show how bad poverty is? Stress that more than 40 percent of the people in the United States over fourteen years of age had money incomes less than $2,000 a year in 1973. Do you want to show how little poverty there is? Stress that fewer than 3 percent of families of two or more had money incomes less than $2,000 a year in 1973.[2]

For most purposes connected with judgment of level of living, the "family" is the more relevant unit, but that concept itself requires further consideration. A la Gertrude Stein, shall we say that a family is a family is a family whether it consists of one person living alone, of a husband-wife couple with two children, of a husband-wife and four children, or of some other combination?[3]

For families with different numbers of children, much depends on the point of view. If the point of view is that of the parents, and if the parents are regarded as choosing the number of children by comparison with alternative ways of spending their income, there is no reason to distinguish among families of different sizes. Families with the same income but different numbers of children are to be regarded as at the same economic level, differing simply because some parents prefer to use their income to acquire children, others to acquire cars or boats or hi-fi sets.[4]

From the point of view of the children, regarded as ultimate human beings and not simply as sources of consumption services to parents, and from the point of view of parents unable and unwilling to choose the number of children, the situation is very different. Of two families with the same income but with different numbers of children, the child in the small family will have more resources available to finance his personal consumption than the child in the large family.

This is by no means a minor issue. Indeed, historically perhaps *the* major source of relative economic deprivation has been large families. Every social survey of the past century or of this one documents that observation graphically. Two workers with the same wage could have very different levels of living if one had few children, the other many. Indeed, I conjecture that the one thing that has done more than anything else in the Western world in this century to reduce relative deprivation and misery has been the widening spread of knowledge about and techniques for birth

2. For a useful survey of facts about the distribution of annual money income in the U.S., see U.S. Bureau of the Census, *Current Population Reports, Consumer Income,* Series P–60.

3. The U.S. Bureau of the Census defines the term *family* as "a group of two or more persons related by blood, marriage, or adoption and residing together," so in their terminology there are no one-person families.

4. I am waiving the possibility considered below—that the measurement of income may be biased by number of children because of the omission of nonmoney income.

control and the resulting sharp reduction in the number of families with many children.

For the "unrelated individual" (the euphemism used in official Census Reports to refer to persons who are not living with any relatives) versus the family of two or more, the same income cannot from any point of view be regarded as corresponding to the same level of living (except, I suppose, for the family consisting of a single adult plus children resulting from deliberate choice).

There is a large literature on alternative ways of allowing for the size of family in combining distributions of income for families of different sizes and compositions. One obvious device is to express incomes per capita, but that has always seemed unsatisfactory, partly because of deficiencies in the definition of income, partly because of presumed differences in the "requirements" of different persons. Two may not be able to live as cheaply as one, but surely, it is said, they can live more cheaply than twice one— that is, it takes less than twice the income for two persons living together to achieve in some sense the same level of living (i.e., the same level of utility) as each separately can achieve.[5]

It seems even clearer that children should not be counted as equivalent to adults, or infants equivalent to young children. Accordingly, most attempts to allow for the size and composition of families have consisted of establishing scales of equivalence, specifying, for example, that if a male aged eighteen to forty-five is treated as one unit, then a female of the same age is eight-tenths of a unit; a child zero to two years is three-tenths of a unit; etc. Two of the most famous scales of this kind were called *Ammain* and *Fammain scales*—for "Adult Male Maintenance" and "Food Adult Male Maintenance," the first for consumption in general, the second for food.

The search for such equivalents has been connected partly with the development of compact methods of analyzing data on family budgets and partly with the perennial quest for some way to define objectively *minimum standards of living*, or *poverty levels*.[6] Fortunately, or unfortunately, there is no way to do so. The levels of living regarded as *poverty* are al-

---

5. This sentence, which sounds so reasonable, is full of ambiguity, and you will find it a useful exercise, in which you will almost surely fail, to try to state the idea it embodies in a rigorous manner. Does the conclusion arise from omitting "nonmoney" income so that it would be false for a correct definition of income? Or is it simply a truism reflecting "revealed preference"—the couple would not live together unless, by doing so, utility rose as perceived by both parties? Or does it reflect economies of scale in household production? If so, what prevents similar economies from being attained by "unrelated individuals"? How compare the level of utility for two together with the levels of utility attained by each separately? Can that be done if it involves one person being "better" off, the other "worse" off? And so on.

6. See Milton Friedman, "A Method of Comparing Incomes of Families Differing in Composition," *Studies in Income and Wealth*, 15 (New York: National Bureau of Economic Research, 1952): 9–20.

ways judged by any society relative to the general level of living. In the early work for sixteenth- or seventeenth-century France, the "minimum adequate level of living" was defined as one kilo of bread per day. The level of living we consider in the United States as corresponding to poverty would be considered affluence today by most people in the world. The impossibility of a truly objective definition does not keep us from having an official United States government definition of *poverty* as "an amount equal to three times the estimated cost of a freely chosen diet that is estimated to be nutritionally adequate."[7] These numerical "poverty" limits, which are modified each year to allow for changes in the level of prices, are different for families of different sizes and hence embody an implicit scale of equivalence.[8]

The problem of the income unit is therefore two-fold: what unit to use and how to combine units of different sizes and compositions.

2. Income definition: Whatever the unit, what concept of income should be used? We have already considered the major problem raised by taxes and government subsidies. On a still broader conceptual level, two other issues that arise are the use of income versus consumption and labor income versus property income.

For problems involving utilization of productive resources, income as ordinarily understood is clearly the more appropriate concept. For problems involving welfare or levels of living, however, consumption seems clearly the more appropriate. There are a host of problems in this area that have never been explored, especially the different movements of the prices of items consumed at different income levels. Whatever may have happened over long periods of time to the incomes of the very richest persons in society relative to the incomes of the very poorest, there can be no doubt that there has been a major narrowing in their relative levels of consumption.

Consider the position of the very richest over history. Economic, techni-

---

7. *Nutritional adequacy* is in itself an arbitrary term. There is uncertainty about the "required" allowances as indicated by the changes that have been made from time to time in the recommended allowances by the National Research Council. However these are defined, not all families spending the same amount will meet them. The percentage of families meeting them rises with total spending on food but never reaches 100 percent. In the original determination of *nutritional adequacy*, the U.S. Department of Agriculture defined it as satisfied when 75 percent of the families achieved two-thirds of the National Research Council's allowances for each of eight specified nutrients. See Rose D. Friedman, *Poverty: Definition and Perspective* (Washington, D.C.: American Enterprise Institute, February, 1965).

8. The implicit scale of equivalence implies very large economies of scale and a rather curious pattern. For example, consider the sequence of an unrelated male individual less than sixty-five; a married couple with head under sixty-five; a similar couple with one, two, three, four children, all nonfarm. Designate the unrelated male individual as 1. Then the marginal value assigned to the additional members are .25 (i.e., the "low-income threshold" for the married couple is 1.25 times that for the unrelated male); .25 for the first child, .38 for the second, .33 for the third, .27 for the fourth.

cal, and scientific progress has benefited them only in two important respects: improvements in medicine and health care and improvements in transportation. For the rest, the vaunted modern improvements have availed them little. Running hot and cold water: the Roman patricians had slaves to carry water for their baths. Movies, television, radio: the Roman patricians could command the finest artists of their time to give private performances. And so on down the line.

To come closer to modern times, I once estimated on the basis of a visit to Thomas Jefferson's home in Monticello how much a person would have to be able to spend on consumption today to command the time of as many persons catering to his wants as Jefferson commanded. The sum ran into many millions of dollars a year, a sum that very few today can or do spend. Yet Jefferson was not a particularly wealthy man in his day when there was a drastically smaller population.

The problem raised by labor income versus property income is that property income is measured net of costs of earning the income including depreciation or return of capital, whereas labor income is measured gross of many costs (e.g., food, housing, and clothing that are both costs and a way of spending the income earned) and gross of depreciation or return of human capital. This latter problem is frequently mentioned but ordinarily only to put it to one side. I know no satisfactory treatment of it in work on the distribution of income.

On an empirical level, the key issue with respect to the definition of *income* is the treatment of nonmoney income, such as income in kind from home gardens or from the services of the husband or wife in the household or from consumption services received from children, or imputed income from owned home or other owned consumer durable goods. The incentive to receive income in a nonmoney form is clearly affected by its likely exclusion from some categories of taxes, hence its neglect—the typical practice—may well introduce a significant bias into measured distributions of income.

3. *Time unit:* In principle, we can conceive of a distribution of income as of a point in time, classifying flows of income per arbitrary time unit. The problem of time unit is then reduced to the problem of definition of income: Do we want to define income as the momentary rate of flow? As the rate of flow that can be maintained indefinitely? Maintained indefinitely in real terms or nominal terms?

In practice, the data tend to come as income receipts or consumption spending during a specified period: a day, a week, a month, or a year. Clearly, the results can differ greatly depending on the time unit used. To avoid seasonal effects, most estimated distributions of income are for income receipts during a one-year period. This clearly eliminates many arbitrary elements that would affect data for briefer periods, but also clearly is not fully satisfactory.

In the first place, the lifetime pattern of earnings depicted in Figure 13.2 means that persons who have precisely the same lifetime expectations will nonetheless have different incomes in a particular year because they are of a different age. Considerations of this kind call for classifying people by lifetime income rather than one year's income, which raises a host of conceptual and empirical problems—some of which will become apparent by asking what the meaning of such a concept is for a family rather than for a person. A more attractive alternative is to aim for a distribution of wealth, including both human and nonhuman wealth. Human wealth will be evaluated as the present value of expected future earnings, which can in principle (though hardly in practice) be calculated for each member of the family and summed. In practice, such distributions of wealth as have been constructed are only for nonhuman wealth.[9]

A second issue has to do with the effect of economic mobility on the interpretation of distributions of income. Consider two countries that have identical distributions of population by age, sex, family size, etc., and identical size distributions of annual income. Suppose in one country, every person stays in his relative position in his age-sex group year after year. In the second, there is much shifting about, much movement up and down, so that a person near the top of his group one year may be near the bottom the next. In short, transitory factors affecting income are important relative to permanent factors. If income were measured over a two-year period rather than a one-year period, the distribution in the first country would be more dispersed than in the second, since mobility would lead to averaging out in the second that does not occur in the first. And the longer the time period, the greater the difference.

I believe that there are wide differences of this kind among countries that render cross-country comparisons highly unreliable. For example, I suspect that relative to one another, Britain is more like the first country of the preceding paragraph and the United States more like the second and hence that distributions of annual income tend to understate the diversity of income in Britain compared to the United States.

Facts About Types of Income

Even if all of the issues raised in the preceding section were resolved satisfactorily—or at least acceptably—it would not be easy to pass from the functional to the personal distribution. Increasingly over time, indi-

9. One of the major issues for such distributions in the United States is how to handle as a component of individual wealth the present value of current and anticipated social security payments. See Martin Feldstein, "Social Security, Induced Retirement, and Aggregate Capital Accumulation," *Journal of Political Economy*, LXXXII (September/October, 1974), 905–26, and "Social Security and the American Economy," *Public Interest*, No. 40 (July, 1975).

vidual and family incomes have come to consist of several types of functional components: wages plus interest, dividends, rents, or entrepreneurial returns; government transfer payments, such as social security payments, unemployment benefits, food stamps; and so on in endless profusion. Moreover, each of these generic titles covers a wide variety of specific items. "Wages" or "wages and salaries" include payments received by low-paid domestic servants and high-paid chief executive officers of giant corporations. Interest, for example, includes the few dollars received by a low-income family whose only nonhuman wealth is a nest egg in a savings and loan association and the larger sum received by a wealthy holder of a sizable block of tax-exempt securities.

The common image that wages and salaries are the income of the "poor" and property income plus entrepreneurial returns are the income of the "rich" has much validity to it, but is oversimplified. To judge from income-tax data, wages and salaries are decidedly lower as a percentage of total income at high reported incomes than at intermediate income levels, and property income is decidedly higher—but interestingly enough, this is also true at low-income levels. However, there is a difference in the kind of property income received at the bottom and top of the income scale. At the bottom, property income is primarily in the form of interest and rents, as well, of course, as receipts from private pensions and social security—interest because of the importance of savings deposits at commercial and mutual savings banks and savings and loan associations and of government saving bonds; rents because ownership of residential property in the form of buildings with two or more dwelling units or of property housing small businesses requires much personal attention and hence is more attractive to persons with relatively little property and much time. At the top of the income scale, property income is primarily in the form of corporate dividends and capital gains.

Income from independent businesses is spread throughout the income scale. Its ratio to total income is bimodal as a function of total income, first rising with income, then declining, then rising, then finally declining again. At the bottom, the income comes from the millions of relatively small businesses—farms, mom-and-pop grocery stores, service stations, repair shops and so on. The average income of proprietors of such establishments is likely to be lower than the average income of persons who are primarily wage-earners. At the second mode are not only the large farmers and proprietors of substantial businesses but in even larger number independent professionals such as physicians, dentists, lawyer, accountants, and so on.

The variety of sources of income and the complex pattern with which they are distributed across the income and wealth scale is what makes it so difficult to infer the effect of a change affecting the functional distribution on the personal distribution, as the examples of the next section illustrate.

Two Examples

Rent Control: A by now ancient example is the effect of rent control. During World War II, general price control was imposed in the United States, including control on rents of dwelling units. Since then, rent control was abolished on a basis that permitted individual cities to continue controlling rents. New York was the only major city that did. However, in the interim, a number of localities have reintroduced rent control; and rent control on a nationwide basis was included in the general price freeze imposed by President Nixon on August 15, 1971, and the subsequent price control, which finally ended in 1974.

A frequent argument that was made in favor of rent control was that landlords are rich, tenants poor, and hence rent control is a way of redistributing income from rich to poor. For our purposes, let us put to one side the normative issue whether this result, if it were achieved, would justify rent control. Was it in fact achieved?

The facts in the preceding section already raise some doubts. Rent is a more important source of income to low-income families than to families of moderate and high incomes. Apparently, landlords are on the average poorer than tenants. But that, too, is too simple a conclusion. Rent paid is gross, rent reported as received is net. More important, rent receipts are for commercial as well as residential property, but rent control affected mostly residential property. More important still, much residential property is owned by corporations. Rents paid are converted into interest and dividend payments and are included in reported data under these headings rather than as rents. It is not implausible that high-income families receive a larger fraction of rents indirectly in these forms than low-income families.

One thing is clear from even these casual comments: no simple statement about the redistributive effects of rent control can be made that deserves much confidence. D. Gale Johnson investigated the issue in detail years ago and concluded, "I do not want to argue that the evidence presented indicates that landlords are poorer than tenants. But the data certainly do not indicate the contrary—that landlords have significantly higher incomes than tenants."[10]

Oil Prices: A more recent example is the effect of the quadrupling of oil prices by the OPEC cartel in the fall of 1973. Public discussion of United States policy with respect to oil has been replete with assertions about the income distributive effect of higher oil prices—almost invariably, assertions that the higher oil prices bear with special severity on low-income families. Of course, such assertions can be treated as truisms, simply expressing the view that anything harmful bears more severely on persons

10. D. Gale Johnson, "Rent Control and the Distribution of Income," *American Economic Review, Papers and Proceedings,* 41 (May 1951): 571–82.

with low than on persons with high incomes. But let us consider the proposition more seriously as expressing an empirical judgment that the effect
of the higher prices was to reduce the fraction of total income or consumption available to the 10 percent or 20 percent or some other percentage of
families with lowest incomes. For the country as a whole, the higher cost of
imported oil amounted to roughly 1.5 percent of the national income;
this was the "real cost" imposed on the nation, the amount transferred
from United States consumers to the owners of the foreign oil sources.
The assertion in question is then that the reduction in real income of
"low-income" families as a result of the higher price was more than 1.5
percent.

For one component, gasoline used for private passenger cars, the situation is clearly the reverse. The automobile is a luxury, in the sense that the
income elasticity of demand for automotive services is decidedly higher
than unity. The fraction of total consumption spending allocated to gasoline rises sharply with the size of total spending. Extra spending on gasoline as the result of higher gasoline prices reduces spending on other
things, which lowers their relative prices. On average, these "other things"
have a lower income elasticity than gasoline, so prices of things more important to low-income people go down relatively, offsetting some of the
negative effect of higher gasoline prices on them. For this component, the
higher oil prices clearly had a favorable *relative* effect on low-income
families.

For all other components, the situation is far less clear. Expenditures on
petroleum products for heating purposes are less income elastic and may
be inelastic, operating in the opposite direction. The higher price of gasoline used for commercial vehicles affects the relative prices of the products
into which the transportation services enter. Those products indirectly
using much gasoline will rise in price relatively to those using little. Is
there a systematic difference in the income elasticity of the products dif-
ferentially affected in this way? It would take a major research project to
answer such questions with any confidence. The same goes for tracing
through the ultimate incidence of the higher oil price on the costs of
generating electric power.

And so far, we have only considered one side of the picture: effects via
costs of items consumed. The other side is the effects on value of productive resources. Resources employed in the automobile industry and in other
industries especially adversely affected now face a lower relative demand,
resources employed in the coal industry and other industries providing direct or indirect substitutes for imported oil face a higher relative demand.
In which direction does this tend to redistribute income? Again it would
take a major research project to give a confident answer.

These examples could be multiplied. You will find it instructive to explore others, such as the redistribution effect of social security, of the graduated income tax, of environmental controls, and so on.

15

The Size Distribution of Income*

The traditional "theory of distribution" is concerned exclusively with the pricing of factors of production—the distribution of income among co-operating resources classified by their productive function. It has little to say about the distribution of income among the individual members of the society, and there is no corresponding body of theory that does. This absence of a satisfactory theory of the personal distribution of income and of a theoretical bridge connecting the functional distribution of income with the personal distribution is a major gap in modern economic theory.

The functional distribution of income has been treated as primarily a reflection of choices made by individuals through the market: the value of factors is derived from the value of the final products that they cooperate in producing; and the value of final products in turn is determined by choices of consumers among the alternatives technically available. The personal distribution of income, on the other hand, when it has been ana-

* These pages are reproduced from my essay, "Choice, Chance, and the Personal Distribution of Income," *The Journal of Political Economy*, Vol. 41, No. 4 (August 1953): 277–90. By permission of the publisher; copyright 1953 by the University of Chicago.

This is a revised version of a paper presented in May, 1952, at an International Conference on the Foundations and Applications of the Theory of Uncertainty held in Paris at the Centre d'Économétrie under the auspices of the Centre National de la Recherche Scientifique of the French government. A French translation of the original version, entitled "La Théorie de l'incertitude et la distribution des revenus suivant leur grandeur," appeared in *Colloques Internationaux du Centre National de la Recherche Scientifique*, Vol. 40: *Économétrie* (Paris: Centre National de la Recherche Scientifique, 1953): pp. 65–78.

lyzed at all, has been treated as largely independent of choices made by individuals through the market, except as these affect the price per unit of the factors of production. Differences among individuals or families in the amount of income received are generally regarded as reflecting either circumstances largely outside the control of the individuals concerned, such as unavoidable chance occurrences and differences in natural endowment and inherited wealth, or collective action, such as taxation and subsidies.

This sharp difference in the role assigned individual choice in two such closely related contexts seems hardly justified. Individual choice through the market can greatly modify the effects on the personal distribution of income both of circumstances outside the control of the individuals concerned and of collective actions designed to affect the distribution of income. Moreover, these collective actions are themselves primarily a manifestation of individual preferences, even if not of choice through the market.

Individual choice can affect the income distribution in two rather different ways. The first—that differences in money income may compensate for nonpecuniary advantages or disadvantages attached to the receipt of those incomes—has often been noticed, though its importance is typically underestimated and will not be dealt with further in this paper. For example, an unpleasant occupation must be more highly rewarded than more pleasant occupations if it is to attract persons to whom the latter are equally open; incomes in unattractive localities must be higher than those in attractive localities readily accessible to the same class of people if their inhabitants are not to leave them; and so on. In these cases, differences in money income are required to produce equality in real income.[1]

The second way that individual choice can affect the distribution of income has been less frequently noticed. The alternatives open to an individual differ, among other respects, in the probability distribution of income they promise. Hence his choice among them depends in part on his taste for risk. Let the same set of alternatives be available to members of two societies, one consisting of people who have a great aversion to risk; the other, of people who "like" risk. This difference in tastes will dictate different choices from the same alternatives. These will be reflected most clearly, though by no means exclusively, in a different allocation of resources to activities devoted to manufacturing the kind of risk attractive to individuals. For example, insurance will be a major industry in the first society, lotteries in the second; income and inheritance taxes will be highly progressive in the first society, less progressive or regressive in the second. The result will be different income distributions in the two societies; the

1. See George Garvy, "Inequality of Income: Causes and Measurement," in Conference on Research in Income and Wealth, *Studies in Income and Wealth,* Vol. 15 (National Bureau of Economic Research, 1952), for evidence on the possible importance of such differences in money income.

inequality of income will tend to be less in the first society than in the second. It follows that the inequality of income in a society may be regarded in much the same way as the kinds of goods that are produced, as at least in part—and perhaps in major part—a reflection of deliberate choice in accordance with the tastes and preferences of the members of the society rather than as simply an "act of God."

The following remarks illustrate and explore on an abstract level this relation between individual choice among alternatives involving risk and the distribution of individuals by size of income. For purposes of this exploratory discussion, I shall accept the expected-utility theory of choice: that is, I shall suppose that individuals choose among alternatives involving risk as if they knew the probability distribution of incomes attached to each alternative and were seeking to maximize the expected value of some quantity, called "utility," which is a function of income.[2] I shall take it for granted that utility is an increasing function of income.

The Isolated Individual

As the simplest case, consider a Robinson Crusoe entirely isolated from all other human beings. To avoid the problem of measuring income, suppose that he produces only a single product or, what is equivalent, that there is a set of relative "prices" or "values" for all products that can be used to express the total output in units of a single product.

At any moment, Robinson Crusoe has many courses of action open to him—that is, different ways of using his time and the resources on the island. He can cultivate the arable land intensively or extensively, make one or another kind of capital goods to assist in cultivation, hunt or fish or do both, and so on in infinite variety. Let him adopt some course of action and carry it out. The result will be some flow of income over time, say $I(t)$, where I stands for income per unit of time and t for time. At the moment he adopts the course of action, say t_0, $I(t)$ for $t > t_0$ is of course not precisely known—the actual result of the course of action adopted depends not only on what Robinson Crusoe does but also on such chance events as the weather, the number of fish in the neighborhood when he happens to fish, the quality of the seed he plants, the state of his health, and so on. We can take account of this uncertainty by supposing that a set of possible future income streams, each with known probability $p_{t_0} [I(t)]$ of occurring, corresponds to any course of action. Such a probability distribution of income streams we may call a *prospect*.

The prospects among which Robinson Crusoe can choose at any time t_0

2. See Milton Friedman and L. J. Savage, "The Utility Analysis of Choices Involving Risk," *Journal of Political Economy*, 56 (August 1948): 279–304, reprinted in American Economic Association, *Readings in Price Theory* (Chicago: Richard D. Irwin, 1952), pp. 57–96; and "The Expected-Utility Hypothesis and the Measurability of Utility," *Journal of Political Economy*, 60 (December 1952): 463–74.

clearly depend on his own past course of action. But this in turn can be viewed as the consequence of a similar choice at an earlier stage. So we can, if we wish, think of him as making a single decision at whatever point we start our analysis, say when he lands on the island, for the rest of his life. This degree of generality may not be desirable for all purposes; for some, it may be better to consider individual *moves* rather than entire *strategies,* in von Neumann's and Morgenstern's terminology. At our present stage of analysis, however, it will be well to eliminate all unnecessary complications. Adopting this point of view enables us to dispense with the subscript t_0, since there is only one set of prospects that is relevant, and each prospect contains future income streams for the same period, namely, from the initial starting point to the indefinite future.

As a further, albeit more questionable, simplification, we can replace each $I(t)$ by a single number, either by assuming that the $I(t)$ are all members of a one-parameter family, say all straight lines with the same slope, or by discounting future incomes back to the initial point at some given rate of interest, adding the discounted incomes to get the present value of each income stream, and assuming that, at this rate of interest, the individual is indifferent between any two streams with the same present value.[3] Either assumption permits each $I(t)$ to be replaced by a single number, say W (for wealth), that can be calculated without knowing the individual's utility function.

These simplifying assumptions mean that any prospect can be completely described by a cumulative probability distribution, say $P(W)$, giving the probability that the result of the course of action in question will be a value of wealth less than W. Let A′ be the set of all courses of action, a any particular course of action, and $P_a(W)$, the prospect corresponding to a.[4]

3. The reason this step is questionable, even if we waive the problem of determining the "right" interest rate, is that the utility attached by an isolated individual to a given and unchangeable income stream is a function solely of its present value only for a highly special form of utility function. For any different form, the time shape of the income stream affects the utility attached to it in a more complex way, so that two streams with the same present value do not have the same utility.

The discounting process can be justified in general only by introducing the possibility of converting income streams of any one time shape into income streams of any other desired time shape at a given intertemporal rate of substitution either by productive activity, for the isolated individual, or, more generally, by borrowing and lending in a free capital market at a market rate of interest. This justification is unobjectionable for income streams that are certain to be received. Our whole problem, however, centers precisely on streams whose receipt is uncertain, and, for these, the very notions of a free capital market and conversion of income streams at market rates of interest are surrounded with difficulties.

It would clearly be desirable therefore to relax this simplification in a fuller analysis of the problem than is attempted in this paper.

4. It should be noted that this description takes account of deliberate action by the individual to alter the probability distribution of returns: e.g., one course of action may involve devoting time to building storage space or engaging in other activity designed to reduce the chance of an abnormally low wealth because of premature starvation.

The assumption that utility is an increasing function of wealth (which in our present formulation replaces income) is alone enough to rule out some prospects. If

$$P_a(W) \le P_{a'}(W) \text{ for all } W$$

and

(1) $$P_a(W) < P_{a'}(W) \text{ for some } W,$$

then a is clearly preferable to a', regardless of the precise shape of the utility function of wealth.[5] Let the (reduced) set A consist of courses of action such that no pair of prospects corresponding to these courses of action satisfies equation 1. The choice among the set A then depends on more than the first derivative of the utility function.

Let U(W) be the utility function of Robinson Crusoe. He will then, on the expected-utility hypothesis, choose that prospect a for which

(2) $$\overline{U} = \int_{w\,=\,0}^{w\,=\,\infty} U(W)\,dP_a(W)$$

is a maximum. Beyond this restatement of the expected utility hypothesis, there is little that can be said about this special case on the present level of generality.

Suppose that there are many identical Robinson Crusoes faced with identical sets of action and associated prospects and completely isolated one from the other. All would, in principle, make the same choice, say prospect a'. If, further, the outcome of the actions of any one Robinson Crusoe (his realized W) were statistically independent of the outcome of the actions of any other Robinson Crusoe (the other's realized W), then $P_{a'}(W)$ would be the realized cumulative distribution of wealth among them. Income "inequality" among them would be partly a product of deliberate choice, and the amount of "inequality" would depend partly on the shape of the utility function common to them. If the utility function were a straight line, each Robinson Crusoe would choose the prospect with the highest expected income; if it were everywhere concave downward (diminishing marginal utility of income), he would be willing to sacrifice some expected income for decreased variance of income; it it were everywhere concave upward (increasing marginal utility of income), he would be willing to sacrifice some expected income for increased variance of income, and so on. Given a sufficiently large and varied set of prospects, the "inequality" of income among the Robinson Crusoes would be least in the second case and greatest in the third.[6]

5. This is an example of what Pierre Massé has designated in a similar context as *absolute preference*.

6. I am of course using *inequality* here in a loose sense, since no precise meaning is required for present purposes.

The realized W of any one Robinson Crusoe need not, however, be statistically independent of the realized W of others. For example, though each were ignorant of the existence of the others, all their islands might be in the same geographical area and subject to the same weather conditions. In this case, $P_{a'}$ (W) would not be the realized cumulative distribution of wealth among them, if we suppose each to make only one choice. At the extreme of complete dependence, all would realize the same wealth, so there might be complete equality even though the utility function were everywhere concave upward. In intermediate cases, the kind and degree of interdependence affects the shape of the realized distribution of income but not the general conclusion about the effect of the shape of the utility function on the degree of inequality.

Individuals in a Society: Redistribution Is Costless

Suppose the many identical Robinson Crusoes establish communication with one another. The considerations determining the course of action to be adopted by each are now radically changed, for it is now possible to produce new prospects by joint advance agreement among the Robinson Crusoes for a redistribution of the product obtained. Many arrangements common among individuals in our society involve this kind of redistribution, so that one need not assume collective action through "government." Private enterprises explicitly selling insurance or conducting lotteries are extreme and obvious examples. But the phenomenon is much more widespread: almost every enterprise in our society is in part an arrangement to change the probability distribution of wealth. For example, let one Robinson Crusoe set himself up as an entrepreneur guaranteeing "wages" to the others and taking the residue, but let each proceed to do what he otherwise would have done, so that the "entrepreneur" exercises none of the usual supervisory functions. The result is to change the set of prospects available to the individuals concerned. Indeed, a strong case can be made for regarding this function of "producing" new prospects, not by technical change or improvement, but by redistribution of the impact of uncertainty, as the "essential" entrepreneurial function in modern society.

In general, of course, communication changes the probability distribution of wealth corresponding to any course of action by the diffusion of knowledge and makes new courses of action available by the exchange of products, thereby giving scope to the division of labor and specialization of function. We may neglect these complications, however, since in the main they affect the attainable level of income rather than its distribution. We shall therefore assume that the mere establishment of communication or the exchange of goods does not change the set of probability distributions of income available to each Robinson Crusoe.

We cannot brush aside so blithely another complication: costs of administration and enforcement involved in redistributive arrangements. The most important of these costs is the effect of such arrangements on incentives. A man who carries insurance against the loss of his house by fire has less incentive to devote resources to preventing fire than if he himself bore the full cost of the loss. In our terminology, the course of action a and its associated probability distribution $P_a(W)$ may be achievable only if the Robinson Crusoe in question himself receives directly the resulting W. If a group agrees that each will follow the course of action a, pool the resulting product, and share it, say, equally, the actual realized wealth may be quite different from what it would have been if each had adopted a independently—that is, individuals would not in fact follow a. This is, of course, the basic reason why full insurance against loss is feasible only for hazards that are largely independent of individual action and why all attempts to divorce payment to individuals from their productive contribution have encountered great difficulty or completely failed.

We shall postpone this complication to the next section. In this one, we shall assume that redistributive arrangements involve no cost: that is, that the set of courses of actions A and associated prospects $P_a(W)$ is equally achievable whether individuals act separately or enter into redistributive arrangements, where W represents the wealth realized by an individual *before* redistribution, that is, the amount he can contribute to any redistributive pool. If we further assume that the realized W of any one Robinson Crusoe is statistically independent of the realized W of any other,[7] that the $P_a(W)$ are reasonably well behaved,[8] and that the number of Robinson Crusoes is sufficiently large, then the course of action adopted depends only on the expected value of the $P_a(W)$, and the inequality of the distribution of wealth among the identical individuals depends only on their tastes. For given independence and large numbers, there is little (in the limit, no) uncertainty about the wealth per person—the average or expected wealth—that will be realized by any common course of action. In consequence, it will pay to adopt the course of action for which the wealth per person is a maximum, since this will maximize the total to be divided, and then divide it among the Robinson Crusoes in the optimum manner. More formally, suppose a' is the course of action chosen under conditions of the preceding section, that it yields an expected wealth $\overline{W}_{a'}$, and that the course of action a" yields a higher expected wealth $\overline{W}_{a''}$. Suppose an agreement to be reached that each Crusoe will follow a", contribute the resulting product to a common pool, and then draw out a first return determined by a random mechanism that gives him a probability $P_{a'}(W)$ of getting less than W. The prospect of this first return alone is clearly as attractive to every Crusoe as a' is without a redistributive arrangement, and $\overline{W}_{a''}$

7. This is a more stringent restriction than is necessary. Its adoption, however, simplifies the discussion without loss of essential generality.

8. To satisfy the conditions required for the law of large numbers to hold true.

— $\overline{W}_{a'}$ times the number of Crusoes is now left in the common pool to provide an additional return, so a″ with an appropriate redistributive arrangement is clearly preferable to a′. By the same reasoning, it is clear that there always exists a redistributive arrangement that will make a prospect with a higher expected wealth preferable to any prospect with a lower expected wealth, whether or not the latter is accompanied by a redistributive arrangement. It follows that for the special case under consideration, the opportunities offered man by "nature" determine only the mean value of the realized distribution of wealth; the inequality of wealth is entirely a man-made creation.

Suppose the utility function of wealth is everywhere concave downward. The optimum distribution of wealth is then obviously egalitarian. The Robinson Crusoes will pool their wealth and each take out a prorata share. At the other extreme, suppose the utility function of wealth is everywhere concave upward. The optimum distribution of income is then obviously as unequal as possible. The Robinson Crusoes will pool their wealth, and each will get a lottery ticket giving an equal chance to win a single prize equal to the total wealth.

A more interesting and empirically relevant utility function to analyze is one that has the shape suggested by Savage and me to rationalize a few simple and widely accepted empirical generalizations about behavior under circumstances involving risk.[9] We suggested a function initially concave downward, then concave upward, and then finally concave downward, like the U(W) curve in Figure 15.1.

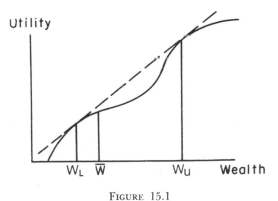

FIGURE 15.1

Let $\overline{W}$ be the maximum expected wealth (realized when each individual follows the course of action a″). Consider a prospect consisting of two values of W, say W_L and W_U, such that $W_U \geq \overline{W} \geq W_L$, and associated probabilities p_L and p_U such that $p_L W_L + p_U W_U = \overline{W}$. The expected utility corresponding to this prospect is given by the ordinate at $\overline{W}$ of the chord

9. Friedman and Savage, "The Utility Analysis of Choices Involving Risk."

connecting $U(W_L)$ and $U(W_U)$. It is obvious geometrically that if there is a line tangent to the utility function in Figure 15.1 at two points, and if $\overline{W}$ is between the abscissae of the points of tangency, which we may designate W_1 and W_2 with $W_2 > W_1$, then this expected utility is a maximum if W_L and W_U are equal to W_1 and W_2 respectively.[10] The associated probabilities p_L and p_U are then $(W_2 - \overline{W}) / (W_2 - W_1)$ and $(\overline{W} - W_1) / (W_2 - W_1)$, respectively. Call this prospect a_d (d for "double tangent").

Any more complicated prospect with the expected value $\overline{W}$ can always be expressed as a probability combination of one- or two-valued prospects, each with the same expected value $\overline{W}$. The expected utility of the more complicated prospect can therefore be expressed as the expected value of the expected utilities of the one- or two-valued prospects into which it can be decomposed, hence it cannot exceed the expected utility of the component one- or two-valued prospect with the highest expected value. It follows that a_d is the optimum prospect for each member of a society composed of individuals, each of whom has the utility function of Figure 15.1. Under our assumptions, it will also be the realized wealth distribution.

One rather remarkable feature about this result is that it remains valid, with one minor proviso, if we drop entirely the assumption made up to this point that the set of courses of action A and the associated prospects $P_a(W)$ are identical for all individuals.[11] Given our other assumptions, the *ex post* distribution of wealth depends only on the shape of the utility function and the maximum expected wealth per person for the society as a whole and not at all on differences in the prospects available to different Robinson Crusoes, provided only that for every Robinson Crusoe the expected wealth of the prospect with the highest expected wealth is between W_1 and W_2. To demonstrate this proposition, suppose that there are two groups, with the members of each having identical prospects, and that the maximum expected wealth for the first group, $\overline{W}^{(1)}$, is different from the maximum expected wealth for the second, $\overline{W}^{(2)}$. By the preceding analysis, the members of each group separately will pool their wealth, and each member will get in return a lottery ticket giving him a chance $(W_2 - \overline{W}^{(1)})/(W_2 - W_1)$ to W_1 and a chance $(\overline{W}^{(1)} - W_1)/(W_2 - W_1)$ to W_2. Suppose the first group contains a fraction $n^{(1)}$ of the total number of individuals, the second a fraction $n^{(2)}$ so that $n^{(1)}\overline{W}^{(1)} + n^{(2)}\overline{W}^{(2)} = \overline{W}$, the highest expected wealth for the society as a whole. The final result is that a fraction equal to

10. Ibid., pp. 289–91.

11. This is equally true for a utility function everywhere concave upward, which leads to complete inequality. It is not true for a utility function everywhere concave downward. With different prospects and such a utility function, each individual adopts the course of action that has the highest expected wealth, contributes the result to a common pool, and draws out an amount equal to this highest expected wealth, so the final distribution of wealth is given by the distribution of the maximum expected wealth among individuals and is no longer egalitarian.

(3)
$$n^{(1)} \frac{W_2 - \overline{W}^{(1)}}{W_2 - W_1} + n^{(2)} \frac{W_2 - \overline{W}^{(2)}}{W_2 - W_1} = \frac{W_2 - \overline{W}}{W_2 - W_1}$$

will realize a wealth of W_1, and the rest a wealth of W_2. But this is precisely the result that would have been reached if all had identical prospects, with a highest expected wealth of $\overline{W}$. More generally, the final result is that each individual adopts the course of action that has the highest expected wealth, contributes the result to a common pool, and receives in return a guarantee of a wealth W_1 plus a chance to win a single prize equal to $W_2 - W_1$, the size of the chance being equal to $(\overline{W}^{(i)} - W_1)/(W_2 - W_1)$ for the ith individual, where $W^{(i)}$ is the expected wealth contributed by him. The chance of ending up with a wealth W_2 thus varies from individual to individual according to the brightness of his prospects, but the final distribution of realized wealth is the same as if all had identical prospects.

Neither is this result greatly affected, though it is complicated, by dropping the assumption that the realized W's (before redistribution) are statistically independent. Consider the extreme case in which knowledge of the outcome for one individual implies complete knowledge of the outcome for all individuals. Suppose, first, that all possible values of W for all individuals and any a in the set A are between W_1 and W_2. Regardless of the course of action adopted, there will then be some single actual realized value after the event, and the preceding analysis shows that the individuals will pool their W's and redistribute the total through a lottery. The realized wealth distribution will therefore consist of two groups of individuals, each member of one receiving W_1, each member of the other receiving W_2. Only the fraction of all individuals who end up in each group depends on the actual outcome. In advance, with an appropriate agreement for redistribution, expected utility increases with expected wealth, so again it is best for all to adopt the course of action that promises the highest expected wealth. And again, differences among individuals in the prospects open to them do not affect the final result but only the number of lottery tickets each gets. If all possible values of W for the set A are not between W_1 and W_2, the a with the highest expected wealth may no longer be the optimum. But this much is still true: the advance arrangements will be such that if the actually realized W (before redistribution) is between W_1 and W_2, it will be redistributed so as to yield values of W_1 and W_2. In consequence, the final realized wealth distribution will under all circumstances be empty between W_1 and W_2.

The assumption that tastes (i.e., utility functions) of all individuals are identical can also be dropped without affecting our general conclusion that, so long as redistribution is costless, the inequality of wealth depends predominantly on the tastes of the members of the community and only secondarily, if at all, on the prospects available to them. Dropping this assumption does, however, change the more specific conclusion that the realized distribution of wealth will generally be two-valued. Let each individual separately have a utility function of the same general shape as that drawn in Figure 15.1 but let W_1 and W_2 (the abscissae of the points of tangency of the double tangent to the utility function) vary from individual to individual (these are the only two parameters of the function that are relevant for the present problem) and designate their values for the ith individual by $W_1^{(i)}$ and $W_2^{(i)}$. For each individual separately, the optimum redistributive arrangement is essentially the same as previously: a chance $(\overline{W}_2^{(i)} - W^{(i)})/(W_2^{(i)} - W_1^{(i)})$ of a wealth $W_1^{(i)}$, and a chance $(W^{(i)} - W_1^{(i)})/(W_2^{(i)} - W_1^{(i)})$ of a wealth $W_2^{(i)}$, where $\overline{W}^{(i)}$ is the maximum expected wealth obtainable by any course of action available to him. And there is nothing to prevent this arrangement from being adopted: each individual follows the course of action that promises the maximum expected wealth, contributes the resulting product to a common pool, and receives in return a lottery ticket giving him the above chances of receiving a wealth $W_1^{(i)}$ or $W_2^{(i)}$. Since each lottery ticket is actuarially "fair," the entire lottery is; and so long as the $P_a^{(i)}(W)$ are reasonably well behaved and the $W_2^{(i)}$ finite, the law of large numbers will still apply. So, with a sufficiently large number of individuals, the uncertainty for the lottery as a whole is negligible.[12] The realized wealth distribution in this case depends on the distribution of the $W_1^{(i)}$ and $W_2^{(i)}$ as well as on the maximum expected wealth. The effect of the difference in tastes is to introduce additional dispersion into the distribution of wealth that would be realized with identical tastes, the amount of the dispersion depending on the extent of divergence in tastes. As we shall see in the next section, the costs of redistribution have a very similar effect.

12. This redistributive arrangement can perhaps best be visualized concretely as consisting of two parts. (1) Each individual enters into an agreement to follow the course of action that promises the highest expected value, $\overline{W}^{(i)}$, to turn over the resulting product to a common pool, and to receive in return a guarantee of $\overline{W}^{(i)}$. He buys an insurance policy, as it were. (2) A single actuarially fair lottery offering a very large single prize is made available to the individual. He can buy any number of either whole or fractional tickets in this lottery. With such a lottery, each individual can construct any actuarially fair prize distribution he wants, subject only to the limitation that the maximum prize does not exceed the single prize offered. The number of different tickets he buys determines his chance of winning a prize; the fraction of each ticket he buys determines the size of the prize he wins if that ticket is the winning ticket. For example, if there are one million tickets in a lottery with a single prize of $1,000,000 so each ticket costs $1, he can have one chance in 200,000 of winning $100,000 by buying one-tenth of each of five tickets; one chance in 25,000 of winning $50,000 by buying one-twentieth of each of forty tickets, and so on. With a utility function like that in Figure 15.1, he will spend $\overline{W}^{(i)} - W_1^{(i)}$ on tickets; he will take the same fraction of each ticket he buys; and that fraction will be such as to yield a single prize of $W_2^{(i)} - W_1^{(i)}$. The only requirement in order that every individual be able to get his optimum prospect is that the prize offered in the lottery exceed the largest $W_2^{(i)} - W_1^{(i)}$.

Individuals in a Society: Redistribution Involves Cost

The significant costs of redistributive arrangements, particularly through their effects on "incentives," rule out some arrangements that would otherwise be desirable, with the result that the kinds of opportunities offered by "nature," the original set of prospects $P_a(W)$, affect the shape of the distribution of wealth and not merely its mean value. The effect is to produce something of a mixture between the conclusions of the first section for the isolated individual and of the second section for individuals in a society in which redistribution is costless.

Perhaps the simplest model that combines these two cases (and one that, as we shall see, is capable of generating distributions of wealth or income bearing at least a family resemblance to those actually observed) is to suppose that each individual's possible actions can be divided into two independent and noncompeting sets—one set of actions, say A_s, the results of which are not accessible to redistribution, the other, say A_r, the results of which can be redistributed without cost.[13] The individual then chooses one course of action from each set. Before redistribution, his realized wealth consists of two parts, W_s and W_r, after redistribution of W_s and, say W'_r so his final wealth is $W_s + W'_r$. Each individual is now concerned with the probability distribution of $W_s + W'_r$ not with either separately.

What is the optimum redistributive arrangement if the utility function has the shape of $U(W)$ in Figure 15.1 and, for simplicity, is the same for all individuals? It is now no longer possible to achieve the *optimum optimorum*—namely, the two-valued prospect of receiving either W_1 or W_2 with the highest expected value and appropriate probabilities. For, whatever redistributive arrangements are adopted, there is no way of averaging out or avoiding the risk attached to W_s if we suppose, as seems desirable, that W'_r does not depend on the realized W_s, though it may depend on the anticipated $P_{a_s} (W_s)$.[14] Clearly the best choice from A_r is still the one that has the highest expected wealth—since any desired redistribution of the W_r is available, there is nothing to be lost by making the total pie as large as possible. Beyond this, it is best to adjust both the choice from the set A_s and the redistributive arrangements so as to approximate as closely as possible the *optimum optimorum*.

---

13. The actual division between the two classes of actions will, of course, depend on tastes (i.e., utility functions), since the cost it pays to incur depends on the gains to be achieved by improved distribution. Nonetheless, the present assumption that a hard and fast division can be made in advance does not involve any great loss at the present level of analysis.

14. To suppose the opposite is essentially to revert to the case of the second section. For making W_r depend on realized W_s is equivalent to making W_s accessible to redistributive arrangements.

In order to say anything more specific about the optimum redistributive arrangements, it is almost certainly necessary to specify more precisely than we have so far done the characteristics of the set $P_{a_s}(W_s)$ and perhaps also of the utility function $U(W)$; it seems not impossible that there exists some $P_{a_s}(W_s)$ that would justify almost any kind of redistributive arrangement. I have not attempted an exhaustive analysis of this problem. But I conjecture that for a wide class of functions $P_{a_s}(W_s)$ and of utility functions $U(W)$, the optimum redistributive arrangement is identical with that of the second section, and that this is so even if the prospects differ from individual to individual.[15] Pending further analysis, I shall tentatively accept this conjecture and assume that the $P_{a_s}(W)$ and utility function $U(W)$ have the properties required to make it valid.

This redistributive arrangement can be described as the contribution of a sum by each individual, that is, the purchase of a share in a lottery, and his receiving in return some specified chance of receiving a designated sum, that is, some chance of a prize. The amount paid by each individual depends on his realized W_r and on the prospect he adopts from the set A_s—but not on the realized W_s, for this would contradict the assumption that W_s is not accessible to redistribution. If all individuals have identical sets of prospects, all will choose the same pair of prospects, and the sum paid will differ among individuals only because the realized W_r does. If, however, individuals have different sets of prospects, the amount paid depends on the particular prospect chosen from the set A_s, as well as on the realized

---

15. For example, suppose the set $P_{a_s}(W_s)$ is the same for all individuals, that every member of it is unimodal and symmetrical, with a mean value less than W_1, and that for some neighborhood around W_1 and W_2, the vertical difference between $U(W)$ and the double tangent is the same for $W_i + \Delta$ and $W_i - \Delta$ ($i = 1, 2$). Suppose further that the variance of W_s for each $P_{a_s}(W_s)$ is small compared to $W_2 - W_1$. Select any $P_{a_s}(W)$ which has a mean value $\overline{W}_s$ and combine it with a lottery involving pooling all W_r and receiving a chance $(W_2 - \overline{W}_s - \overline{W}_r)/(W_2 - W_1)$ of getting $W_1 - \overline{W}_s$ and a chance $(\overline{W}_s + \overline{W}_r - W_1)/(W_2 - W_1)$ of getting $W_2 - \overline{W}_s$. This breaks the original $P_{a_s}(W)$ into two distributions, one with its mode at W_1, the other at W_2 and combined in the proportions necessary to keep the total expected value unchanged. The expected utility of this arrangement deviates from the expected utility of the *optimum optimorum* by the expected value of the vertical differences between $U(W)$ and the double tangent. Given our assumptions, this deviation from the *optimum optimorum* is clearly less than for any alternative redistributive arrangement combined with the same $P_{a_s}(W)$, for any such arrangement would widen the variance of the two distributions at W_1 and W_2 or move their means away from W_1 and W_2 and thus increase the average value of these vertical differences. But if this is true for any $P_{a_s}(W)$ separately, it is true for the optimum $P_{a_s}(W)$.

The assumptions of the preceding paragraph are clearly stricter than are necessary. In particular, it seems likely that symmetry of the $P_{a_s}(W)$ is not necessary and that much milder restrictions on the utility function will do. Further, the $P_{a_s}(W)$ need not be the same for all individuals. Differences among them can be offset by differences in the contributions to the redistributive arrangement. All that is required is that each individual contribute $W_r^{(i)} - (W_1 - \overline{W}_s^{(i)})$ for a chance $(\overline{W}_s^{(i)} + \overline{W}_r^{(i)} - W_1)/(W_2 - W_1)$ of getting $W_2 - W_1$.

W_r, because the aim of the payment is to put each individual in the neighborhood of W_1 if he does not win a prize. In consequence, those who have prospects promising a relatively high value of W_s will keep a smaller amount from W_r (or pay more in addition to it) than those who have prospects promising a relatively small value of W_s. These differences in payment will be compensated by differences in the chance of winning a prize (that is, the number of lottery tickets), the former receiving a larger chance than the latter. The size of the prize will be the same for all and equal to $W_2 - W_1$, since its purpose is to put the winners in the neighborhood of W_2.

With this redistributive arrangement, the final realized wealth distribution is the probability sum of two wealth distributions. The courses of action adopted from the set A_s lead to some wealth distribution of the realized W_s, its exact form depending on the particular choices that are optimum,[16] the degree of interdependence among the W_s's realized by different individuals, and the differences among individuals in the prospects available to them. This distribution is now modified by the payments made for lottery tickets. Their effect is to shift the center of gravity of the distribution to W_1 and, in so far as the prospects available to the individuals differ, to reduce its variability, since the differences in the payments made by different individuals are designed to offset such differences in available prospects. Suppose the lottery now drawn and the winners and losers determined. This separates the wealth distribution into two distributions— one for winners and one for losers. These two distributions need not in general be the same, since individuals with generally better prospects have larger chances of winning, and since the wealth distribution yielded by generally better prospects may differ systematically from that yielded by other prospects in respects other than the mean value or whatever parameter of location determines the offsetting payments into the lottery. The distribution for the winners is now shifted by the payment of a prize of $W_2 - W_1$ to each winner, and the final distribution is the sum of the distributions for the losers and for the winners.

To illustrate, let $D(W)$ be the cumulative distribution of realized wealth after payments for lottery tickets but before distribution of the prizes; that is, $D(W)$ is the fraction of individuals with a wealth less than W at this stage. Assume that the distribution at this stage is independent of the agreed-on payment into the lottery, so that the distribution is the same for winners and losers. Let g be the fraction of individuals who are to win

16. Note that the choice from the set A_s that is optimum to an individual is affected by the existence of the redistributive arrangement. In particular, if the redistributive arrangement affects a large enough fraction of total anticipated wealth, it will never be worth sacrificing expected W_s to increase the variance of W_s, even though it would be in the absence of the redistributive arrangement. It may be worth sacrificing expected W_s to reduce the variance of W_s, even though it would not be in the absence of the redistributive arrangement.

prizes, and $W' = W_2 - W_1$ be the prize. Then the final wealth distribution is

(4) $$F(W) = (1 - g)D(W) + g\,D(W - W').$$

It may perhaps be worth noting explicitly that this distribution is the sum of two distributions, *not* the distribution of the sum of two random variables.

As noted in the preceding section, dropping the assumption of identical tastes does not fundamentally change these results. If there is some general similarity in tastes, the individual values of W_1 and W_2 will form two largely distinct distributions. This dispersion among the values of W_1 and W_2 is essentially added to the dispersion among the values of W_s and has the same general effect on the final distribution as an initially greater dispersion among the latter.

The relative importance of the two component distributions in equation 4, or a generalized version of it, depends on the fraction of winners, which in turn depends on the size of the mean realized wealth, $\overline{W}$, relative to W_1 and W_2. It seems reasonable that the shape and location of the utility curve is itself determined by the average wealth in the community and the distribution of wealth: we have so far treated the utility curve as simply given and as independent of the prospects available to the individuals or the realized wealth distribution, but clearly from a broader view than has been necessary for our purpose the utility curve and prospects must be regarded as interacting.[17] To fit the observed facts from which the particular shape of the utility curve in Figure 15.1 is inferred, the mean wealth in the community must be very much closer to W_1 than to W_2. This implies that g, the fraction of winners, is close to zero. If g is close to zero, the probability or frequency distribution derived by differentiating or differencing the cumulative distribution described by equation 4 is highly skewed, since the first component distribution, centered about W_1, is weighted much more heavily than the second, centered about W_2. In addition, the distribution may be unimodal, with its single mode in the neighborhood of W_1 and below $\overline{W}$; the second mode that the rising part of the second distribution tends to introduce in the neighborhood of W_2 may be swamped by the decline after W_1 in the much more heavily weighted first distribution. The effect of the second component distribution would then be to shift the mode of the combined distribution slightly to the right of the mode of the first distribution alone and to flatten and extend the tail of the distribution. The combined distribution would appear relatively peaked, with an unusually long tail in the direction of higher values of wealth. Now "considerable skewness, wide variability, and great peakedness . . . are the hallmarks of distributions of income from independent professional prac-

17. Some tentative suggestions along these lines are made in Friedman and Savage. "The Utility Analysis of Choices Involving Risk," Sec. 5*b*, pp. 298–99.

tice,"[18] and from other sources, as well as of observed distributions of wealth. And these are precisely the characteristics that the distributions derived from equation 4 can be expected to reveal when g is small. So the distribution function to which our theoretical analysis leads meets at least the initial test of being able to reproduce the more outstanding features of observed distributions of wealth and income.[19]

Of course, the fact that equation 4 is not patently inconsistent with observed distributions of wealth or income does not mean that it is consistent with them or that the model on which it is based isolates the central elements accounting for existing distributions of wealth or income. But, together with the plausibility of the theoretical structure, perhaps it does justify empirical study designed to see whether equation 4 in fact provides an adequate description of existing distributions of wealth or income.

Conclusion

The foregoing analysis is exceedingly tentative and preliminary: it contains conjectures that need to be checked, considers only highly simplified models, makes the drastic simplification of regarding the distribution of wealth as the result of a single choice and the subsequent unfolding of this choice under the impact of random events, and so on. Yet I think it goes far enough to demonstrate that one cannot rule out the possibility that a large part of the existing inequality of wealth can be regarded as produced by men to satisfy their tastes and preferences. It suggests that the link between differences in natural endowment or inherited wealth and the

18. Milton Friedman and Simon Kuznets, *Income from Independent Professional Practice* (New York: National Bureau of Economic Research, 1945), p. 62.

19. "Despite the great similarity among income distributions, none of the many attempts to discover a formula that describes them adequately has yet met with success. . . . The logarithmic normal curve is perhaps the closest approximation to the desired formula yet discovered, since it often fits the data rather well. However, it occasionally gives a poor fit; the small deviations from it when it does fit reasonably well do not seem randomly distributed, and it . . . is unable to represent negative income" (ibid., pp. 66–67). The final objection would be irrelevant for distributions of wealth defined to include all sources of possible future income, including human capital, since wealth so defined cannot be negative. It is not irrelevant if, as in most statistical studies, measured wealth includes only nonhuman sources of income. Similar comments apply to various definitions of income. My offhand impression is that the addition of a second logarithmic normal curve in the way suggested by equation 4 would tend to modify a single logarithmic normal curve in the direction suggested by the systematic deviations referred to above. And it might be that the sum of two distributions would give a good fit with arithmetic normal curves, so solving the negative wealth or income problem, since the second distribution introduces the skewness which makes the logarithmic transformation or its eqivalent essential when only one distribution is used. [It is an amusing example of scientific serendipity that the idea of using the sum of two probability distributions to approximate the income distribution occurred to me during World War II when, employed as a mathematical statistician on war research, I used such a sum to describe the distribution of the points of burst of a rocket equipped with a particular fuse. *Note added in 1975.*]

realized distribution of wealth or income is less direct and simple than is generally supposed and that many common economic and social arrangements—from the organizational form of economic enterprises to collectively imposed and enforced income and inheritance taxes—can be interpreted as, at least in part, devices for achieving a distribution of wealth in conformity with the tastes and preferences of the members of society. Finally, it has implications for normative judgments about the distribution of income and the arrangements producing it—inequalities resulting from deliberate decisions to participate in a lottery clearly raise very different normative issues than do inequalities imposed on individuals from the outside.

16

Profits

Few economic terms have been used in so many senses as the term *profits*. The one common element in the usage is a connection, however vague, with uncertainty. For our purposes, the main distinction is between the use of the term to refer to a return to a factor of production, as determined by the supply and demand for productive services, and to refer to a discrepancy between an anticipated and actual return, as determined by stochastic factors. The first use has been and may well still be the most common, but we shall reject it in favor of the second.

In the classical economic writings of Smith, Ricardo, and so on, the term *profits* referred to one of three categories of factor returns: "wages" as the return to human capital; "rent" as the return to nonhuman, nonreproducible capital (the "original and indestructible" qualities of the soil); and "profits of stock" as the return to nonhuman, reproducible capital. As time passed, this usage declined. The return to nonhuman, reproducible capital was increasingly referred to as interest or quasi-rent, and the word *profits* came to refer to the earnings of management, with special reference to the reward for bearing uncertainty.

The use of *profits* in this sense is closely related to "profit maximization" as a supposed principle underlying a market system, or more particularly, a free enterprise money exchange economy. The relation to uncertainty is the special importance attributed to the entrepreneur, the free enterpriser, in undertaking risky enterprises.

A rather different strand of usage is in the term *monopoly profits,* which refer to a special category of rents, or price-determined returns, distinguished from land rent by the institutional source of the inelasticity of supply of the corresponding factor of production (patent, license, or what-not). This is the usage that is perhaps least connected with uncertainty. It derives simply from the treatment of "profits" as the return to the entrepreneur, or residual income recipient, identified in this case with the beneficiary from whatever it is that limits entry and creates a monopoly.

In current popular usage, *profits* is treated as an accounting concept referring to the difference between receipts and contractual costs, as in *corporate profits*. Its functional counterpart depends on the accidental financial structure of the enterprise. For example, consider two otherwise identical corporations, one of which has obtained much of its capital by issuing fixed-interest securities, the other, all of its capital by issuing common stock. Let all other receipts and expenditures be identical for the two concerns. The same sum will then appear on the books of the first corporation as partly "interest paid" and partly "profits"; on the books of the second, as all "profits." Again, let the first rent the land it uses, the second own it. The sum entered on the first corporation's books as rent would be entered on the second as profits.

Whenever, as in the examples so far, the term *profits* is used to refer to a factor return, this usage is ambiguous, redundant, and misleading. It is ambiguous because, as in the examples just cited, it is always difficult to draw any clear line separating that factor return which is to be labeled *profits* from factor returns which are to be labeled something else: *wages, return on capital, interest, dividends,* etc. It is redundant because terms are already available to describe all factor returns. It is misleading because of the connotation that economic agents seek to maximize profits as distinct from other factor returns. We treat economic agents as seeking to maximize their utility, or better, their expected utility. An intermediate step is the attempt to maximize returns to the factors owned by the economic agents. Workers seek to maximize the return to their labor, just as owners of land seek to maximize the return to their land, and owners of other forms of capital the return to their capital. The residual income recipient seeks to maximize the expected return to the resources he owns. The fundamental principle of a free enterprise money exchange economy is more accurately described as maximization of returns than maximization of profits.

Obviously, the term *profits* will continue to be used loosely in business accounts, in national economic accounts, and in popular discussion to refer to a factor return. However, for the reasons cited, it seems undesirable to use the term in that way in technical economics, especially when there is another concept for which we need a term, and *profits* has the right connotations for that purpose.

The alternative is to follow the usage of Frank H. Knight in his classic book, *Risk, Uncertainty, and Profit,* and use the term *profits* to refer to the difference between an expected return and a realized return, as intimately connected with uncertainty, but as a consequence of uncertainty, not as a reward for submitting to uncertainty.

This usage can be exemplified most simply by a lottery. Let 1,000 people get together, each agree to chip in $1 and to participate in a strictly random drawing on the basis of which one person will win $1,000, and each of the others will get nothing. In advance, each has an expected return of $1. After the drawing, one person ends up with $1,000, which means in the terminology we are now using, with a profit of $999; 999 people end up with zero, which means with a profit of − $1 (i.e., a loss of $1). The incentive to participate in the lottery was the prospect of such an outcome but it is obviously meaningless to describe the participants as seeking to maximize *profits* in this usage of the term. No one could tell in advance what his profits would be; hence it could not be an incentive to behavior.

Complicate the problem by introducing costs of setting up the lottery. Let these be such that competition in offering the lotteries makes the equilibrium prize $900 instead of $1,000; i.e., the "costs" of conducting the lottery are $100; or the "equilibrium" price of the services of the conductors of the lottery are 10¢. Each purchaser of a ticket pays 10¢ for these services; the $100 total is paid for the consumption service of being able to participate in the lottery and is a factor return to the enterprise conducting the lottery. In advance, the expected return to each purchaser of a ticket is 90¢ in the form of the actuarial value of his possible prize, plus 10¢ in the consumption services of participation. *Ex post,* the winner has a return of $900.10, and a profit of $899.10; each loser has a return of 10¢ and a profit of −90¢.

This example carries over exactly to the market in general. An enterprise uses some factors of production on a contractual basis and guarantees a specified return to their owners. In the simplest case, the "entrepreneur" or the "residual income recipient" alone receives an uncertain return. He decides what to produce, how to produce it, and how much to produce on the basis of his anticipations about the probability distributions of costs and receipts if he does one thing rather than another, choosing that course of action that promises to yield the highest expected return to the resouces he owns (or more precisely, the highest expected utility from that return). After the event, he realizes some actual return. If the actual return exceeds his anticipated return, he realizes a positive profit; otherwise, he realizes a loss.

More generally, owners of most factors of production will be in this position. For example, a worker may be guaranteed a wage per hour without being guaranteed a definite number of hours of work per year, or he may be hired on a piece basis, or he may be on a "profit-sharing" arrangement. In each of these cases, he faces a probability distribution of returns and not a simple certain return. There will be a difference between his actual and his anticipated return. He will receive a profit or a loss.

Can we say, as in the simple lottery case, that the sum of profits and losses will be zero? By definition, that is true in advance of the anticipated distribution of profits and losses. But there is no necessity for it to be true after the event. The actual returns may on the average fall short of the anticipated returns: optimism prevailed and there is a net loss. And the converse can also be true. Indeed, Frank Knight conjectured that this situation was typical; that persons engaging in uncertain activities were generally optimistic and generally realized a loss.

The anticipated distribution of profits can affect behavior in advance, as we have seen in chapter 4 in analyzing behavior under uncertainty and in chapter 15 in analyzing the size distribution of income. It affects behavior, not because economic agents seek to maximize profits, but because they seek to maximize expected utility and do not regard the actuarial value of a probability distribution of income as the only relevant parameter determining expected utility.

The *ex post* distribution of profits and losses can affect future behavior by altering the anticipations of participants about the future probability distributions. This is the feature of behavior stressed in the "rational expectations" literature referred to in chapter 12.

In his seminal work, Frank Knight drew a sharp distinction between *risk,* as referring to events subject to a known or knowable probability distribution and *uncertainty,* as referring to events for which it was not possible to specify numerical probabilities. I have not referred to this distinction because I do not believe it is valid. I follow L. J. Savage in his view of *personal probability,* which denies any valid distinction along these lines. We may treat people as if they assigned numerical probabilities to every conceivable event (see chapter 4). Sometimes people will agree—we then may designate the probabilities "objective"; sometimes they will not—we then may designate the probabilities "subjective." But this classification is itself subject to change.

17

The Theory of Capital and the Rate of Interest

On an abstract level, it is instructive to view the economic system as one in which stocks of productive resources (capital) produce flows of productive services that are transformed into flows of final consumer services. The continuing flow problem is the allocation of the productive services to various uses, their combination in the process of transformation into consumer services, and the distribution of the consumer services among the ultimate consumers in the economy—problems 1, 2, 3, and 5 in Frank Knight's five-fold subdivision of the economic problem introduced in chapter 1. These are the problems that have been dealt with in the preceding chapters, which can be regarded as concerned primarily with the relative prices of different service flows.

In addition to the flow problem, there is Knight's problem number 4, "provision for maintenance and progress," or the management of the stocks of productive resources, of the sources of productive services. This is the subject matter of the theory of capital with which the present chapter deals.

In practice, of course, the flow problem and the stock problem are intertwined. For example, to keep the two completely separate, we must regard consumer purchases of bread and other foods as part of the stock problem, not the flow problem. The consumer is maintaining a stock of sources of productive services, namely, his inventory of food, combining the services they render with the services from the consumer capital he uses, such as a refrigerator, stove, etc., to produce the final service of nutrition. In a physical sense, the law of conservation of energy assures that no matter can be consumed, only transformed. All consumption is the consumption of services. The food inventory is different from the refrigerator or stove only in depreciating at a much more rapid rate in the process of producing nutritive services.

For many concrete problems, nothing is gained by carrying the analysis to this point. It is often useful to assimilate goods that depreciate rapidly with services proper. But it is important to recognize that this is what we are doing.

From the broadest point of view, capital includes all sources of productive services. There are three main categories of capital: (1) material, non-human capital, such as buildings, machines, inventories, land, and other natural resources; (2) human beings, including their knowledge and skills; and (3) the stock of money. The main distinction between human capital and the other items is that the existing institutional and social framework and imperfections in the capital market produce a different response of human capital to economic pressures and incentives than of nonhuman capital. The stock of money differs from the other two categories because the productive services rendered by money do not depend closely on the number of physical units there are, but primarily on the mere existence of a stock. Consider two societies that are alike except that in one there are twice as many pieces of paper, each labeled one dollar, as in the other. The only effect will be that nominal prices are twice as high in the first as in the second society. The total stream of services from the stock of money is the same in the two societies.

One of the most common examples of confusion between stocks and flows is the frequently made statement that capital becomes cheap (or dear) relative to labor, and hence capital is substituted for labor (or the reverse). The statement implies that the wage rate is comparable to the interest rate. However, the wage rate is comparable to the rent per machine per unit of time, both being dollars per physical unit per unit of time, and not to the interest rate, which is dollars per dollar (a pure number) per unit of time. Put differently, a rate of wages divided by rent of a machine is entirely in physical units; it shows the rate at which man-hours can be substituted for machine-hours by purchase on the market. It is clear what it means for this ratio to go up or down, and the ratio is unaffected by a proportional change in all prices. The ratio of the wage rate to the interest rate, on the other hand, is very different; it is not wholly in physical units, but in value terms. It shows the rate of substitution between man-hours and dollar-of-capital hours, as it were, and is therefore affected by a proportional change in all prices.

An example of the usual image of the substitution of capital for labor is the use of a man operating a mechanical backhoe to dig a ditch instead of a man with a hand shovel. What is really involved is a substitution of the labor used to build the backhoe for the labor used to wield the shovel, or of the human (and other) capital used to build the backhoe for the human (and other) capital used to build the hand shovel and to wield it. Skilled labor services—of the people who build the backhoe, the engineers who design it, etc.—are substituted for unskilled labor, because skilled labor has become cheaper relative to unskilled labor. In addition, the society may have become wealthier; it may have acquired more capital in total. This is not a substitution of capital for labor, but the acquisition of more capital, generally of both more human capital and more nonhuman capital. The use of some of the existing stock of capital in the form of the man operating a backhoe instead of the form of the man wielding the hand shovel, matched by a rearrangement of other capital elsewhere, is part of the management of the existing stock of capital—Knight's "provision for maintenance." The use of current productive services to add to the stock of capital (human and nonhuman) instead of for current consumption is part of the process of saving and investment—Knight's "provision for progress."

The key price in the theory of capital is conventionally a rate of interest. However, the reciprocal of the rate of interest is in some ways a more readily grasped, basic concept. It gives the price of a source of services in terms of the service flow. Consider a piece of land yielding $1 a year indefinitely and let "the" relevant interest rate be 5 percent. Then the price of the piece of land will be $20, or in terms used more frequently in Britain than in the United States, twenty-years' purchase. This brings out the key nature of the price: the number of years' service flow from a permanent source of services that it takes to buy the source itself. Note also that there are many equivalent forms of contract. In a world of certainty, leasing the piece of land for $1 a year would be precisely equivalent to buying the piece of land by borrowing $20 indefinitely at 5 percent, or by borrowing for one year at 5 percent, intending to borrow again the next year, and so on. In a world of uncertainty, however, these would not be equivalent, which produces the coexistence of different kinds of contractual arrangements and of many quoted prices for different intertemporal transactions.

Rates of interest affect a great many decisions, such as the following:

1. The time pattern of consumption, since the terms on which income streams of varying time patterns may be exchanged depend on the rate of interest.
2. The form in which assets are held. One special problem to which recent work in monetary theory has called attention is whether to hold wealth in money or other forms. This is merely an extension of the marginal principle—the proportions of different resources held should be such as to equalize the marginal return in all directions.
3. The character and structure of production.
4. The composition of the social output, i.e., the fraction of total output that will be investment and the fraction that will be consumption goods.

A decrease in the rate of interest raises the prices of sources of services and provides an incentive to produce sources of services.

5. The ratio of nonhuman wealth to total wealth and the size of contingency reserves. Since we are restricting ourselves here to relative price theory, we abstract from the possible short-run effects of the rate of interest on the level of activity.

The bewildering variety of intertemporal transactions and associated terms raises the basically arithmetic problem of how to distinguish between essential and nonessential differences in terms. We discuss this first, then turn to an analysis of the twin stock-flow problem (the pricing of stocks in terms of flows and the use of flows to add to stocks) for a particular item, using houses as an example; and finally generalize this stock-flow analysis to capital as a whole.

The Arithmetic of Interest Rates

In common parlance, the term *capital market* is used to refer to a market in which paper claims to income streams of different sizes and timings are purchased and sold. Though for our purposes, we shall want to use *capital* in a broader sense to correspond to the sources of productive services, the narrower sense is sufficient to illustrate the problems involved in comparing different income streams.

Consider, for example, the following contracts: (a) promise to pay $105 one year from date, (b) promise to pay $210 one year from date, and (c) promise to pay $525 one year from date. In all cases, for simplicity, neglect the possibility of default.

Suppose the market price for contract a is $100. We could describe that price as paying $1 for $1.05 a year from date. If the price of b were $200, of c, $500, we would say that all three are selling at the same price of $1 now for $1.05 a year from now, or at a (simple) interest rate of 5 percent per year for a one year loan.

Note that nothing in arithmetic or economics requires that the price of b be twice that of a and the price of c five times that of a. Just as there might be quantity discounts that make the price of a dozen shirts less than twelve times the price of one shirt, so there might be quantity discounts (or the reverse) that make the price of contract c less than (or more than) five times the price of contract a. (Incidentally, the need to include in the statements for the loan contracts the parenthetical alternatives illustrates the dualism of the intertemporal contracts. Is the lender buying future funds from the borrower in return for current funds, so he could expect to pay less than five times as much for five times as much next year? Or is the borrower buying current funds from the lender in return for future funds, so he could expect to pay less than five times as much for five times as much this year?

The first case leads to a higher interest rate for the larger transaction; the second to a lower interest rate for the larger transaction.) The point of reducing all the transactions to dollars a year from now for a dollar today is to be able to distinguish unessential differences from essential differences.

If there are essential differences in contracts like a, b, and c, the possibility of arbitrage arises: borrow at the terms that have the lower interest rates, lend at the terms that have the higher interest rates. This is one service of financial intermediation by such institutions as commercial banks, mutual savings banks, savings and loan associations, money market funds, etc. Such arbitrage, or financial intermediation, tends to limit essential differences to margins related to the costs that determine the supply of intermediation. In addition, it means that, as in every market in which there are middlemen, it may be necessary to distinguish between "buying" and "selling" prices for what appears to be the same contract. In general, we shall neglect this complication and speak of a single price.

Consider now a slightly different contract: (d) promise to pay $110.25 two years from date. Clearly this is a more complex situation. If its price is $100, it is a contract to pay $1.1025 two years from date for $1 today. This can be reduced to two identical one-year contracts like a. For example, it can be described as a contract promising to pay $1.05 next year for $1 this year, plus a linked contract promising to pay $1.05 two years from now for $1 next year ($1.05 \times 1.05 = 1.1025$). However, this decomposition is not unique. Contract d is also equivalent to a contract promising to pay $1.03 next year for $1 this year, plus a linked contract promising to pay $1.07038835 two years from now for $1 next year ($1.03 \times 1.07038835 = 1.1025$); and similarly to any other pair of linked contracts producing the same final product. Clearly, more than arithmetic is required to reduce contract d to the same terms as contracts a, b, and c.

The market will determine a price for contract d and a price for contract a, and from these two prices we can determine the separate price for two elementary contracts like a but for different years. For example, if the "two-year rate of interest compounded annually" is .05 (i.e., contract d sells for $100 currently), and the current "one-year rate of simple interest" is .05 (i.e., contract a sells for $100 also), then the (implicit) market rate of simple interest today for a one-year loan to begin a year from today is also .05. If, however, the current "one-year rate of simple interest" is $1.03 (i.e., contract a sells for $\frac{105}{1.03} = \$101.9417876$), then the (implicit) market rate of simple interest today for a one-year loan to begin a year from today is .07038835.

Note that in making this decomposition, we have had to beg the question of quantity discounts or premiums. Note too that it is entirely feasible for individuals to make the linked contracts separately if we neglect problems of default (and hence of collateral). By simultaneously buying contract d and selling contract a—that is, lending for a two-year term and borrowing for one year—an individual is today making a loan to begin a year from now. It follows that any contract for intertemporal payments can be reduced to a series of elementary one-year contracts like contract a differing in starting dates, for all of which there can in principle be implicit market prices. And, of course, there is nothing natural about one year. The elementary contract can be for one quarter or one month or one day. The limit is continuous compounding, so that contract a can be regarded as an infinite linked sequence of instantaneous contracts at a rate of interest of the natural logarithm of 1.05 or .04879. . . . .

It is possible to arbitrage between contracts for the same initial and terminal dates, such as a, b, and c, or like the elementary, one-year contracts for the same year. But there is in general no way of arbitraging between two elementary contracts for different time units in the sense of entering into financial purchase and sale contracts which cancel, and so involve no risk. For example, suppose that the price of contract a is $101.94 (rounding to two decimal places) and the price of contract d is $100, so that the one-year simple rate of interest is .03 for the current year and .07 for the next year. It looks as if it would be desirable to borrow this year to lend next year. That can be done by, for example, selling two contracts like a and buying one contract like d, which involves borrowing net this year and lending net next year. But if you go through the arithmetic of payments and receipts, you will find that there is no assured return. The outcome depends on what the one-year interest rate turns out to be next year. The only case in which financial arbitrage proper is possible is if future interest rates are negative, in which case it pays to lend short and borrow long. At worst, the proceeds of the loan can be held in cash (yielding a zero return) to pay off the long borrowing when it becomes due.[1]

Reducing all intertemporal contracts to a succession of elementary contracts is one way, and very likely the most general way, to reduce different contracts to a common basis in terms of which essential can be distinguished from unessential differences in prices or interest rates. However, for the exposition of the basic principles of capital theory, there is an alternative, less general way that is more satisfactory.

The alternative way is to convert all patterns of intertemporal payments into constant, permanent income streams. This method was adopted by Frank Knight and also by John Maynard Keynes, in defining his concept of the *marginal efficiency of investment*. It is also the method that is used in the financial pages of newspapers in reporting the "yield to maturity" of fixed income securities.

Consider the generalized contract: (e) promise to pay R_1 (for receipts) at

---

1. The reason for emphasis on "financial" arbitrage proper is, of course, because of the distinction between "real" and "nominal" yield.

the end of one year from now; R_2, at the end of two years, ... R_n at the end of n years.

Suppose this contract is selling on the market for an amount W (for wealth). Then we can write

(1)
$$W = \frac{R_1}{1+r} + \frac{R_2}{(1+r)^2} + \frac{R_3}{(1+r)^3} + \ldots + \frac{R_n}{(1+r)^n},$$

i.e., the market value is the discounted value of the payment stream.[2] If W and $R_1, R_2, \ldots R_n$ are known, then the value of r that satisfies this equatio is the "internal rate of return." This formula is for discontinuous data. Still more generally, let R(t) be payments promised at time t. Then the capital value at time 0 can be written

(2)
$$W = \int_0^\infty e^{-\rho t} R(t) dt,$$

where ρ is a rate of interest compounded continuously.[3] The permanent income stream equivalent to contract e is then rW, if we use annual compounding, or ρW, if we use continuous compounding.

It will help to understand more fully what is involved in the discounting process, if we spell it out in gory detail. The essence of the process that converts a finite income stream into a permanent income stream is the division of each receipt into two parts: income and a depreciation allowance (which may be positive or negative). Take the discontinuous example of equation 1. The receipt at the end of year one is to be regarded as

Income for year 1	rW
Depreciation allowance	$R_1 - rW$.

The capital value at the outset of the next year, say W_1, is then

(3)
$$W_1 = R_1 - rW + \frac{R_2}{1+r} + \frac{R_3}{(1+r)^2} + \ldots + \frac{R_n}{(1+r)^{n-1}}.$$

If we replace W by its value from equation (1) and collect like terms we have:

$$W_1 = R_1\left(1 - \frac{r}{1+r}\right) + R_2\left[\frac{1}{1+r} - \frac{r}{(1+r)^2}\right] + \ldots + R_n\left[\frac{1}{(1-r)^{n-1}} - \frac{r}{(1-r)^n}\right]$$

(4)
$$= \frac{R_1}{1+r} + \frac{R_2}{(1+r)^2} + \ldots + \frac{R_n}{(1+r)^n} = W,$$

2. Note that some of the values of R can be negative. E.g., equation 1 may be used for a contract that requires the purchaser to pay additional amounts for some years, as in the example of a purchaser of an unfinished building.

3. More generally still, the value of ρ can be allowed to vary, giving

(2a)
$$W = \int_0^\infty e^{-\int_0^t \rho(\tau) d\tau} R(t) dt,$$

where $\rho(\tau)$ is a continuous rate applicable to time τ. However, for given W and R(t), there is no unique $\rho(\tau)$, as was indicated in the text earlier.

establishing the proposition that rW is the income that can be consumed while keeping the capital value constant. To continue the process for future years, the depreciation allowance must be assumed to earn income at the rate r, the common discount rate.

The great virtue of this way of converting all intertemporal contracts into a comparable form is that it obviates all problems of dating. A contract is described by two numbers: total capital value and permanent income, or even more simply, by one number, yield per dollar of capital value. Of course, this does not mean that the yield may not differ depending on other characteristics of the contract, such as size, maturity of payments, etc., but at least unessential differences are eliminated.

Another virtue of this approach is that it brings out the possibility of converting income streams of one time shape into income streams of another. If a particular income stream is of one shape and the market rates of interest are constant over time, it can always be converted into any other time shape by appropriate borrowing and lending or accumulation and decumulation of depreciation allowances. Hence all that matters for describing the opportunities of the owner of the income stream is the permanent income stream to which it is equivalent.

These virtues for our subsequent theoretical presentation are paid for by a number of serious disadvantages. For one thing, as is clear from our earlier discussion, this mode of summarizing intertemporal contracts suppresses the simultaneous coexistence of different rates of interest for different future dates—an extremely important feature of actual capital markets and one to which an enormous amount of theoretical and empirical economic research has been devoted, especially in the past decade or so.

A second defect is that this mode of summarization fosters the incorrect view that a contract (or investment project) that yields a higher internal rate is preferable to one that yields a lower internal rate. This is correct, if the time pattern of receipts of the two projects are identical. It is not correct, if the time patterns of receipts are not identical and if there is a market rate of interest at which the project can be financed. For example, consider the following two projects:

	Initial cost	Receipts at end of	
		Year 1	Year 2
(f)	100	110	—
(g)	100	—	118.81

Project f has an internal rate of return of 10 percent, project g of 9 percent, both compounded annually. Is project f preferable to project g? That depends on the conditions. *If* it is known now that at the end of year one another project identical to f will be available, then two such successive projects will yield $121 in year two, which is clearly preferable to $118.81. What we have done is to convert the two into projects with the same time pattern of receipts. Suppose, however, that the agent in question can borrow or lend at 5 percent in the market in general and has these two projects available to him as well. In that case, project f will have a present value of \$104.76 $\left[\dfrac{110}{1.05}\right]$, project g of \$107.76, and clearly g is preferable to f. Of course, under our assumptions so far, the agent would be well advised to undertake both projects, as well as any others that have an internal rate above 5 percent. However, that may not be possible for the two projects described, since they may be alternatives, for example, correspond to different ways of building a house.

This is very far indeed from a full discussion of the principles that are relevant in choosing among investment projects, but it does bring out the important point that the objective of an economic agent engaged in undertaking projects involving converting current resources into a future income stream cannot in general be described as maximizing the internal rate of return. The agent's objective is better described as maximizing a present value calculated at an appropriate external rate of return. For an enterprise in an active capital market, that external rate of return is given by the market. For the opposite extreme, a Robinson Crusoe deciding how to use his resources, the present value he is to be interpreted as maximizing is a present value of utility, and the rate of return external to the project he considers is given by his utility function, which reveals the rate at which he is willing to substitute future income for current income.

One final comment on the arithmetic of interest rates. There is nothing in that arithmetic that requires interest rates to be positive. For example, consider a contract selling for \$100 that promises to pay \$90 one year hence. The internal rate of return is −10. There is something in economics that prevents negative interest rates from being more than an occasional curiosity. (This used to occur in Illinois annually at a date on which personal property tax was levied. The base included demand deposits of corporations in Illinois but not certain other financial assets. Corporations on that date would be willing to lend for brief periods at a negative rate to avoid the tax.) For nominal rates, the economic consideration is the near-zero cost of holding on to cash.[4] For real returns, the economic consideration is the existence of economically permanent assets, as we shall see more fully later.

The Relation Between Stocks and Flows: The Price of Stocks in Terms of Flows

In order to keep distinct the problem of the pricing of stocks in terms of flows and the use of flows to add to or subtract from stocks, let us start by analyzing a fixed stock that is permanent, so that it requires no mainte-

---

4. Even in this case, the willingness of people to pay fees for safety-deposit boxes in bank vaults to hoard cash is an example of a negative interest rate.

nance expense, and that cannot be added to. A concrete example that comes close to meeting these conditions would be the stock of Old Master paintings. They cannot be added to (except by counterfeiting), but they do require maintenance expenditures, in the form of protection from theft and destruction, and occasional cleaning. However, to keep the same example for both stock-flow problems, let us take the hypothetical example of dwelling units that are homogeneous and fixed in number, say by a legal prohibition of building any additional ones. As to maintenance expenditures, we may simply assume that the stock of dwelling units is maintained physically intact and that in drawing the demand curve for dwelling units, the rent per dwelling unit is the net rent over and above the resource costs of maintaining the dwelling units intact.

On these assumptions, Figure 17.1 gives the demand curve for the services

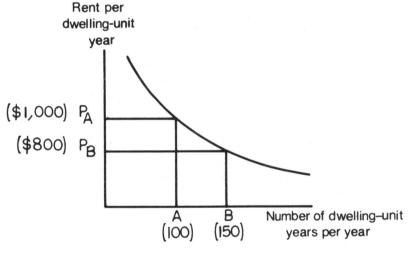

FIGURE 17.1

rendered by the dwelling unit. If there are A (say 100) dwelling-unit years available per unit of time, say per year, the demand price is R_A, say $1,000, per dwelling-unit year. Total rent paid would be $A \cdot R_A$, say $100,000, per year. If there are B (150) dwelling-unit years available, the demand price is R_B ($800), so the total rent paid per year would be $B\ R_B = $ ($120,000) per year.

The question now is, what is the demand curve, not for the services of the dwelling units but for the dwelling units themselves? If there is an exogenous market interest rate determined somehow independently of the housing market, the answer is simple. The dwelling unit will sell for the capitalized value of the permanent income stream it yields (recall that we have defined the rent as net of maintenance costs), or, if r is the rate of interest, for $\frac{R}{r}$. The demand curve drawn in Figure 17.2 will be a duplicate of the demand curve in Figure 17.1 except that the scales will be different: number of dwelling units rather than number of dwelling-unit years per

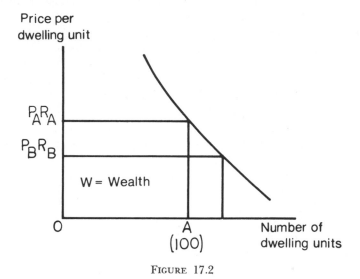

FIGURE 17.2

year on the horizontal axis; the rent multiplied by the reciprocal of the interest rate on the vertical axis; or; if the interest rate is, say, .05, the vertical scale in Figure 17.2 will be twenty times the vertical scale on Figure 17.1.[5]

But to assume that there is an exogenous interest rate simply begs the basic question that we are interested in. Let us suppose, therefore, that dwelling units are the only sources of income streams that can be appropriated and purchased and sold—that is, we are letting dwelling units represent all nonhuman capital. In that case, the interest rate must be determined simultaneously with the rent per dwelling unit. Letting the interest rate be endogenous does not alter Figure 17.1, given our explicit assumption that dwelling units cannot be added to and will not be subtracted from, and the implicit assumption that the stock of other sources of productive services is constant as well. For those assumptions rule out the use of current income, i.e., the services of the stock of productive assets, for any purpose other than current consumption. Hence the demand for dwelling units is simply a question of the allocation of a fixed total stream of con-

5. As drawn, the horizontal scales would be numerically identical. But this is misleading. Suppose the horizontal scale of Figure 17.1 had been "number of dwelling-unit years per month." Then the horizontal scale on Figure 17.2 would be twelve times the horizontal scale on Figure 17.1, since one dwelling unit can provide only one-twelfth of a dwelling-unit year per month.

sumption services among alternative uses. Once we permit the use of current productive services to add to the stock of capital, or the using up of current capital to add to the flow of consumption services, it will not be possible to treat the demand for dwelling services as independent of the determination of the rate of interest.

Figure 17.3 shows the demand curve that is relevant to the determination of the rate of interest. The horizontal axis gives the number of dollars per year generated by dwelling units. It corresponds to the area of the rectangles in Figure 17.1—in our example to $100,000 corresponding to point A. The vertical axis shows the price of a dollar per year. The demand for dollars per year has nothing to do with the utility derived from housing services—which is embodied in Figure 17.1. It depends rather on the utility people attach to having a stock of nonhuman wealth as a reserve for emergencies.

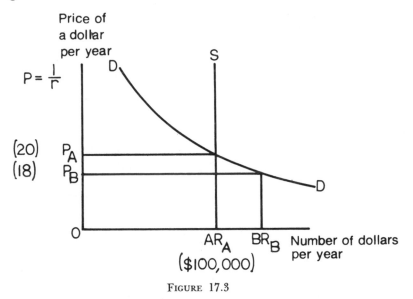

FIGURE 17.3

Consider the attitudes of individuals in the society to various prices for permanent income streams. If the price of a dollar a year were "low," few or no individuals would be willing to sell permanent income streams (i.e., a "source"), and many would be willing to buy permanent income streams. Many people would be willing to give up current consumption in order to acquire a permanent income stream. Under our assumptions, there is no way society as a whole can do this; the willingness to do so simply means that at this price people would be trying to buy more than AR_A dollars of permanent income streams that are available and so would bid up the price of a permanent income stream. If the price of a dollar a year were "high," on the other hand, owners of permanent income streams would be induced to sell them—few would be interested in buying them—and the community as a whole would be seeking to convert sources of permanent income streams into current consumption. But it cannot do so under our assumptions; its willingness to do so would mean that the price would be bid down. There is some intermediate price, say OP_A, at which this market will be in equilibrium, in the sense that at this price society as a whole makes no attempt to get rid of or add to sources of income: the number some people want to sell is equal to the number others want to buy. The locus of prices like OP_A (DD) for different hypothetical supplies of income streams is then a demand curve for income streams in our hypothetical society. The product of OP_A times AR_A is the total amount of wealth or the total value of all the dwelling units in our hypothetical society.

If the concept of capital were all-inclusive, including human as well as nonhuman capital, there is no reason to expect the demand curve for permanent income streams to have a negative rather than a positive slope. Perhaps the most reasonable presumption is that it would be infinitely elastic. For in such a society, income (Y) is equal to rW, where r is the interest rate and W is wealth, since all wealth has been capitalized. $\frac{1}{r}$, the number of time units of income that must be paid to buy a source of a permanent income stream, is then the ratio of wealth to income. This ratio of wealth to income has the dimension of time and is free from absolute units of any other kind. Why should the desired value of this ratio depend on the absolute level of either the numerator or denominator? Indeed, what standard of comparison is there by which to regard one level of wealth as "large" or "small" except *relative* to another or *relative* to income; or one level of income as "large" or "small" except *relative* to another or *relative* to wealth? But if the community desires to maintain a fixed ratio of wealth to income regardless of the absolute level of income, this implies a horizontal demand curve for permanent income streams.

If the concept of capital is not all-inclusive and refers to nonhuman wealth, and if we assume that people still wish to maintain a constant ratio between wealth and income (but in this case a constant ratio between nonhuman wealth and total income), then $\frac{W_{N\,H}}{Y_H + rW_{N\,H}} = K$ where $W_{N\,H}$ is the value of nonhuman wealth and Y_H is the income from human wealth. The fixed stock, given by AR_A, is defined by $rW_{N\,H}$. Call this Y_p. Substituting $\frac{Y_p}{r}$ for $W_{N\,H}$ in the preceding expression gives $\frac{Y_p\frac{1}{r}}{Y_H + Y_p} = K$ or $\frac{1}{r} = \frac{K(Y_H + Y_p)}{Y_p}$ which defines a negatively sloping demand curve for permanent income streams, for a given income from human capital. More generally, whether the desired ratio of wealth to income is a constant or not, there is in this case reason to expect a negatively sloping demand curve. For in this case an increase in nonhuman wealth, with a given income from human wealth, raises the ratio of nonhuman wealth to human wealth and the ratio of non-human wealth to income and so may be expected to lower the importance that individuals attach to nonhuman wealth *relative* to the importance they attach either to human wealth or to income.

The derivation of the demand curve for dwelling units in Fig. 17.2 is now straightforward. For any given number of dwelling units, say A, find the rent as given by the demand curve in Figure 17.1, multiply the two to-gether to get the total number of dollars per year, enter that in the demand curve of Figure 17.3 to get the price of a dollar per year, and multiply that by the rent per dwelling unit to get the price per dwelling unit for that number of dwelling units. The demand curve in Figure 17.2 for the stock of dwelling units is clearly a hybrid depending on two completely different sets of considerations: on the one hand, the relative utility attached to housing services compared to other consumption services; on the other, the relative utility attached to future versus current income and to a reserve of nonhuman wealth.

The demand for permanent income streams summarized in Figure 17.3 is one side of a coin of which the other is the supply of capital. Owners of wealth supply capital and demand permanent income streams. Entrepre-neurs building dwelling units—for a moment let us suspend the assump-tion that no new dwelling units can be built—demand capital and supply permanent income streams. It is natural to express the supply curve of capital as in Figure 17.4, with the interest rate viewed as the price and the

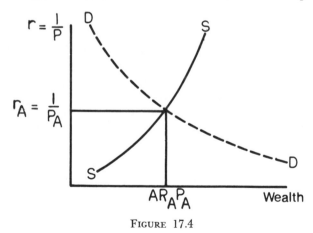

FIGURE 17.4

stock of wealth as the quantity supplied. Note the relation between the curves in Figures 17.3 and 17.4. If the demand curve in Figure 17.3 has an elasticity of unity, that would mean that total wealth would be a constant regardless of the interest rate, which would translate into a vertical supply curve in Figure 17.4. For the supply curve in Figure 17.4 to slope positively, as seems natural, the demand curve in Figure 17.3 must be elastic. If the demand curve in Figure 17.3 were inelastic, the supply curve in Figure 17.4 would slope negatively, at the extreme being a rectangular hyperbola with elasticity equal to -1. The vertical supply curve in Figure 17.3 translates in Figure 17.4 into a unit elasticity rectangular hyperbola demand curve for capital.[6]

The two ways of looking at the determination of the interest rate bring out an essential ambiguity in the concept of a constant stock of capital. Suppose that the number of dwelling units and the demand for their services are fixed so that the number of dollars per year yielded by them is also fixed, i.e., the supply curve in Figure 17.3 is vertical. Now suppose the demand curve in Figure 17.3 were to shift upwards, as a result, say, of an increase in the demand for an emergency reserve. The price of a dollar a year would go up, and so would the wealth value of the unchanged physical stock of capital yielding an unchanged flow of services. In one sense, the stock of capital has remained unchanged; in another sense, it has risen. Much confusion has arisen as a result of the failure to keep these two senses clearly distinct. One virtue of the form of presentation in Figure 17.3 is precisely that it brings this point out very sharply.

For simplicity, let us suppose that the supply curve of capital in Figure 17.4 slopes positively, as seems reasonable, so the demand curve of permanent income streams in Figure 17.3 has an elasticity greater than unity in absolute value. We can then describe fairly simply the relation between the hybrid demand curve for dwelling units in Figure 17.2 and the two demand curves in Figures 17.1 and 17.3 on which it depends. Suppose the demand for housing services has unit elasticity. Then regardless of the number of dwelling units, total rents will be the same, which means that so will the supply curve in Figure 17.3 (and the demand curve in Figure 17.4), which means so will the interest rate. The demand for dwelling units will then also have an elasticity of unity. Increasing the physical stock of capital does not change the value attached to the flow of services from that stock, and hence does not change the wealth value of the stock. If the demand for housing services is elastic, a larger physical stock of houses will yield a higher total rent and hence a lower price per dollar of income. The value of the stock of housing will tend to increase because of the larger flow of rents but will tend to decrease because of the lower price of a dollar of rent. Our assumption that the demand curve in Figure 17.3 is elastic assumes

6. Note that even if the supply curve in Figure 17.4 slopes negatively, at its extreme it only approaches the rectangular hyperbola; hence, there is always a stable equilibrium in Figure 17.4.

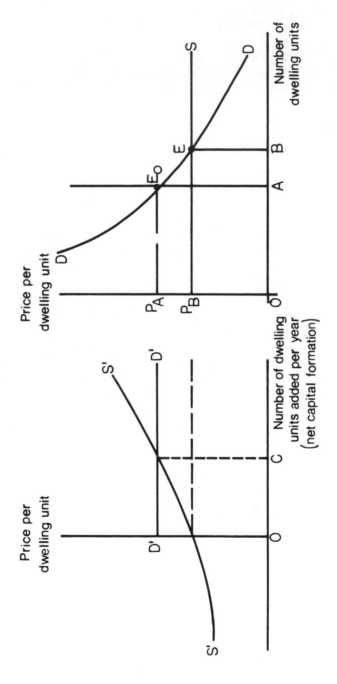

FIGURE 17.5

that the first effect will more than balance the second, so the demand curve for dwelling units in Figure 17.2 will be elastic also, but less elastic than that for housing services. Likewise, if the demand for housing services is inelastic, the demand for dwelling units will also be inelastic, but less so than for housing services because a larger stock of houses, by lowering the total rents, will raise the price of a dollar of rent.

The Relation Between Stocks and Flows: The Use of Flows to Alter Stocks

We can now turn to the second stock-flow problem, the use of flows to alter stocks. To explore this problem, let us drop the assumption that the stock of dwelling units is fixed. Instead, we shall suppose that new dwelling units can be built, and old ones wear out, but we shall continue to assume that all dwelling units are homogeneous regardless of age so that we can continue to speak of *the* rent of a dwelling unit. Presumably, there will be some level of activity in the building industry that will just serve to maintain the stock of dwelling units intact. A higher level of building means an increase in the stock of dwelling units—positive net capital formation in the language of national income accounting; a lower level of building means a decrease in the stock of dwelling units—negative net capital formation.[7]

The right-hand panel of Figure 17.5 reproduces the stock demand curve for dwelling units from Figure 17.2. The left-hand panel gives a simple, and as we shall see, highly special representation of the conditions of supply of new dwelling units. The supply curve S'S' of additional dwelling units extends to negative values on the horizontal axis, because the total stock can decline as well as rise. The supply curve is shown as rising throughout be-

---

7. One pitfall in this way of putting the matter should be made explicit because it explains why the widely used figures on gross capital formation and gross national product are conceptually arbitrary. If dwelling units were like the fabled "one-hoss shay," requiring no maintenance over a finite period during which they gave homogeneous housing services and then collapsed, it would be straightforward to count the total number of houses built each year and to specify the number that had to be built to maintain the stock of dwelling units intact. In practice, this is clearly not the case. There are alternative ways of maintaining the stock of dwelling units intact: by maintaining existing dwelling units and by letting them deteriorate and building new ones. How draw the line? Which expenditures should be regarded as ongoing current expenditures of operation, and which expenditures, as making good capital consumption and hence as includable in "gross capital formation"? The line is arbitrary both in concept and in practice. (In practice, it is defined by the durability of the items produced, the line being drawn at items having an expected durability of three years. Items that have an expected durability longer than that are treated as capital items, the production of which enters into gross capital formation; items that have a shorter expected durability are treated on an inventory basis and only net changes in stocks included in gross capital formation.) On the other hand, *net* capital formation is a logically rigorous concept, referring to the change in the stock of capital, though it is extremely difficult to measure accurately in practice.

cause the greater the rate of decline, the smaller the building industry, the greater the rate of rise, the larger the building industry, and, for simplicity, we assume rising costs throughout.

The special feature, to which we shall have to return, is that the supply curve is drawn as independent of the stock of houses, yet the stock of houses determines the size of the building industry at the point at which the supply curve cuts the vertical axis. A rationalization for such a special assumption is that long-run costs in the housing industry are constant, so the *stock* supply curve in the right-hand panel (SS) is horizontal. However, maintaining the industry at a high enough level to add to the stock of housing raises costs, because it is understood to be a temporary position; hence resources have to be compensated for entering the industry on that basis. Similarly, maintaining the industry at a low enough level to reduce the stock of housing lowers costs, because that too is understood to be a temporary position, and some resources are willing to accept temporarily lower returns because of better, long-run prospects. Even this argument suggests that while supply curves for different stocks of housing might cut the vertical axis at the same point, they might not have the same slope.

The stock demand curve DD in the right-hand panel also embodies a highly special assumption, namely, that the demand curve does not depend on the rate at which dwelling units are being added to the stock. We have already noted at least one reason why that is a dubious assumption, namely that if current resources are being used to add to the stock of housing, total current consumption will be less, which will affect the demand curve for housing services in Figure 17.1.

We shall return to these complications later. For the moment, let us carry through the analysis of the special case described in Figure 17.5. If we start from an initial stock of A dwelling units, the short-run supply of dwelling units is inelastic at A, and the price for existing houses would have to be P_A to equate demand and supply. If a new dwelling unit can be built for less than P_A, clearly it would be preferable to build new dwelling units rather than to buy existing ones. The amount of new building will therefore expand up to the point (designated by C in Figure 17.5) at which the supply price of new dwelling units equals the price of existing dwelling units. Output of new dwelling units will be at the *rate* of OC.

Note that the stock demand DD and short-run supply curve $S'S'$ are for a moment of time, which is why a fixed stock is consistent with any *rate* of addition to the stock of dwelling units, just as you can be at a particular point in your car at a specific time, even though the car is travelling at high speed. However, you will not stay at that point. Similarly, at the point of time for which the stock is A and the price is P_A, the stock of dwelling units is being added to at the rate of OC, hence the point E_0 is strictly a temporary equilibrium position. As time passes, the equilibrium point will slide down DD to the stable equilibrium position E at which the stock is OB and the price P_B. This is a stable equilibrium position because P_B is the long-run supply price of new housing, the price at which net output is zero.

Had the initial stock of houses exceeded OB, the initial price would have been below P_B, net output would have been negative, and the equilibrium point would have slid up DD until it came to rest at E.

The time it takes to go from one point to the other depends of course on the shape and exact numerical specification of $S'S'$, the supply curve of new dwelling units. The steeper that curve through the common intersection with the vertical axis, the slower the approach to equilibrium, and conversely.

We have seen how a fixed, positively sloping supply curve ($S'S'$) for new dwelling units implies an infinitely elastic stock supply curve (SS). The counterpart is that a fixed, negatively sloping stock demand curve (DD) implies an infinitely elastic flow demand curve for new dwelling units ($D'D'$), but one which changes over time. As the equilibrium position slides down DD from E_0 to E, the flow demand curve falls, always remaining infinitely elastic, until it coincides with the horizontal line through OP_B, where it comes to rest.

An infinitely elastic flow demand curve seems highly implausible as a theoretical matter, though of course it could be a reasonable empirical approximation for an item for which current production is very small compared to the stock.[8] It seems highly implausible because the price someone would be willing to pay for an existing dwelling unit would not be independent of the rate of flow of new dwelling units for two reasons. First, because, as we have seen, the diversion of resources to producing new dwelling units lowers total consumption currently, which can be expected to shift the demand curve for housing services in Figure 17.1 to the left, thus lowering current rental values. Second, because the prospective increase in the stock of houses would tend to lower the price of houses, ultimately to OP_B, as a result of the effect of the larger stock of houses on rental values and on the price of permanent income streams. Anyone who currently purchased a house at OP_A, knowing that the stock of houses was increasing, would have to look forward to bearing a future capital loss. Clearly, that prospect would reinforce the first effect. We were able to neglect these effects in discussing Figure 17.2 because that demand curve was drawn for a set of alternative, stationary worlds. But in a world in which the stock of houses is changing, the present value of a rental stream must allow for changing future rents and interest rates.

We can take these complications into account, as in Figure 17.6 by treat-

---

8. For example, suppose houses have an average useful life of fifty years and that we can approximate them by the one-horse shay model. If the stock is constant, gross output per year will be 2 percent of the stock and doubling current output will add only 2 percent to the stock after a year. Even if stock demand were highly elastic, the price would fall only a little over a year.

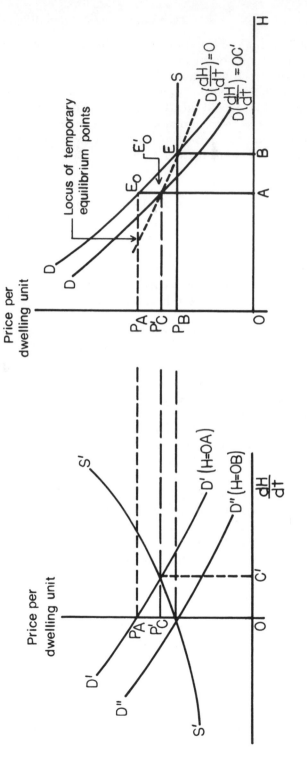

FIGURE 17.6

ing DD as valid only for alternative stocks of houses, each corresponding to a zero flow $\left(\dfrac{dH}{dt} = 0\right)$. This means that on the flow side, OP_A is the demand price only for $\dfrac{dH}{dt} = 0$. The larger the flow of new dwelling units, for the given initial stock of OA, the lower the demand price for both the stock and the flow. If D'D' in Figure 17.6 is the flow demand for new dwelling units, then the temporary equilibrium price is $P_{C'}$, and C' is the rate of flow. On the right-hand side for stocks, we can express this effect by drawing a separate stock demand curve for a rate of flow equal to C'. For every stock of dwelling units, the demand price will be less when $\dfrac{dH}{dt} = C'$ than when it is zero. Between the two curves drawn in Figure 17.6 there are, of course, an infinite number of others for rates of flow between 0 and C' and, similarly, still lower curves would correspond to higher rates of flow and curves above DD $\left(\dfrac{dH}{dt} = 0\right)$ to negative rates of flow.[9]

Point E'_0 is now the equilibrium position. But it is obviously only a momentary one. Net output of dwelling units is positive, so the stock of housing is growing; the short-run stock supply curve moves to the right. As it does, the flow demand curve in the left-hand panel of Figure 17.6 shifts downward, its intersection on the vertical axis linked to the demand price on the stock demand curve for $\dfrac{dH}{dt} = 0$. The process continues until the stock of dwelling units is OB, at which point the flow demand and supply curves intersect on the vertical axis. Net output is zero, and a full equilibrium is attained at E with the price of housing equal to P_B.[10]

So long as we stick to the assumption that the long run stock supply curve is horizontal and the short-run flow supply curve positively sloping and independent of the stock, the price of dwelling units must be higher than the long-run price whenever output is growing and lower whenever output is falling. That is, the locus of temporary equilibrium points in the right-hand panel of Figure 17.6 must be downward sloping as it is there drawn. However, just as we have generalized the stock and flow demand curves, it is desirable to generalize the stock and flow supply curves, as in Figure 17.7. If the long-run stock supply curve is positively sloped, as in the right-hand panel of Figure 17.7, then the flow supply curve can no

---

9. In principle, the stock demand curves for nonzero rates of flow depend on the whole anticipated future course of net additions to the stock of dwelling units and not solely on the current rate of flow. Treating them as a function of the current rate of flow implicitly assumes that the alternative future time paths of additions to the stock of dwelling units are a one-parameter family.

10. Obviously, the whole analysis is readily modified for a world in which the stock of housing is growing at a steady rate along with resources in general.

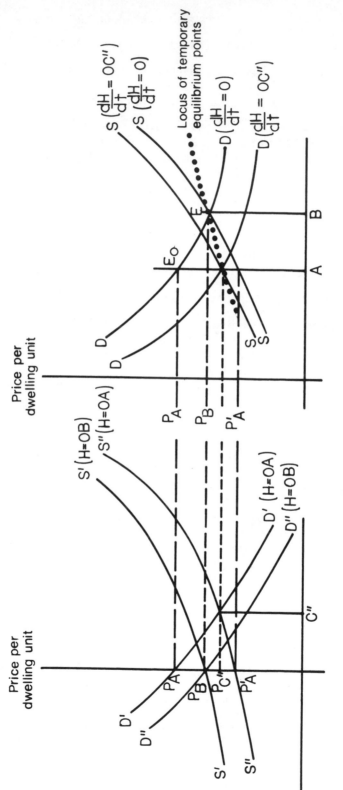

FIGURE 17.7

longer be independent of the stock of houses. The flow supply curve S'S', which cuts the vertical axis at P_B is valid only when the stock is OB. If the stock is OA, the flow supply curve must cut the vertical axis in the left-hand panel of Figure 17.7 at P'_A, the stock supply price of the smaller stock of dwelling units OA.

Note that the positive slope of the long-run stock supply curve in Figure 17.7 is mirrored in the left-hand panel in the points of intersection of the flow supply curves with the vertical axis, not in the slopes of the flow supply curve. The positive slope of the long-run stock supply curve reflects the rising costs attached to maintaining stationary building industries of different sizes. These rising costs reflect the need to change the proportions of factors in the industry and to attract resources less suited to the industry, the usual reasons for positively sloping, long-run supply curves. The positive slopes of the flow supply curves in the left-hand panel reflect a different, though not unrelated, set of effects, namely, the costs associated with *temporarily* expanding or contracting the building industry to above or below its usual size.

From the stock demand and supply curves in the right-hand panel, we know that the price must be between the demand price P_A and the supply price P'_A, which correspond to zero net output. If it were P_A, the price of a dwelling unit would exceed the cost of building one, and builders would have an incentive to add to the stock of dwelling units, so that is not an equilibrium position. If it were P'_A, the price of a dwelling unit would just correspond to the cost of building one, so builders would have no incentive to add to the stock, but owners and potential owners of dwelling units would want to own a larger stock at that price and so would tend to bid up the price, hence that is not an equilibrium position. As the rate of addition to the stock increases, the demand price falls and the supply price rises, as shown by the flow demand curve (D'D') and flow supply curve (S''S'') in the left-hand panel of Figure 17.7 for a stock of OA. Just where the temporary equilibrium price will be depends on the elasticity of these flow curves. I have drawn them in Figure 17.7 in such a way as to produce an equilibrium price, $P_{C''}$, which is less than the long-run equilibrium price, in order to illustrate the possibility drawn in the right-hand panel that the temporary equilibrium price will rise, rather than fall, in the process of going from the initial stock of OA to the final stock of OB. But of course this is not necessary. Let the flow demand curve be flatter and the flow supply curve be steeper and the temporary equilibrium price could be above the final equilibrium price as it was in our earlier example.

Just as, in Figure 17.6, we were led to draw different stock demand curves for different rates of flow, so we are now led in Figure 17.7 to draw different stock supply curves for different rates of flow. The temporary equilibrium position at a price of $P_{C''}$ is at the intersection of the stock supply curve for the rate of flow of C'' and the corresponding stock demand

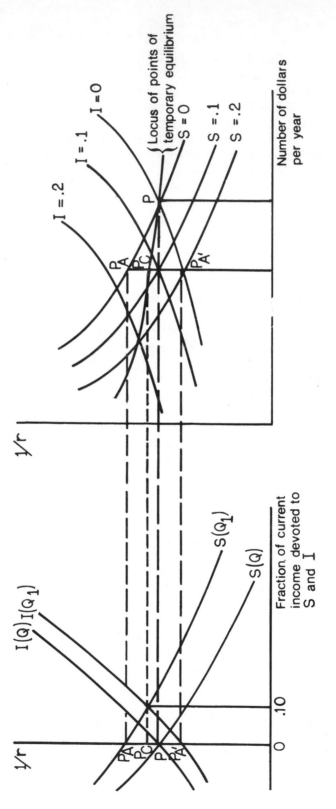

FIGURE 17.8

curve (which is lower than the one drawn in Figure 17.6 for $\frac{dH}{dt} = OC'$ because $\frac{dH}{dt}$ is here larger). As the stock increases, the stock demand curve rises, the stock supply curve falls; the flow demand curve falls and the flow supply curve rises, until ultimately the two stock curves intersect at point E, and the two flow curves intersect on the vertical axis of the left-hand panel at a net output of zero and a price of P_B.

Generalization of the Stock-Flow Analysis

The generalization of the example of dwelling units to capital in general and the determination of the interest rate is straightforward. Instead of starting with the stock demand curve for dwelling units in Figure 17.2, we start with the stock demand for permanent income streams in Figure 17.3. Instead of introducing the supply curve for building dwelling units, we introduce the costs of providing dollars of permanent income not alone by building dwelling units but by any addition to the stock of sources of productive services or consumption services. This shift transfers the effect of an increase in the capital stock on the prices of the services it yields from the demand side to the supply side, since a decline in rents, for example, as the stock of houses increases, now shows up as a higher cost of providing a dollar of income since more physical dwelling units need to be built to produce the same permanent income stream. And as we saw earlier, the demand curve for income streams in Figure 17.3 does not depend on the demand curve for the services of dwelling units in Figure 17.1. But that is the only change of substance. As a result, Figure 17.8, which summarizes the situation for capital in general, is a direct counterpart of Figure 17.7, except for changes in labelling and except that, to illustrate a different possibility, the locus of points of temporary equilibrium in the right-hand panel is downward sloping.

In Figure 17.8, S stands for saving, I for investment. The long-run stock demand curve for permanent income streams corresponds to savings equal zero $(S = 0)$; the long-run stock supply curve, to investment equals zero $(I = 0)$. We have expressed savings and investment as fractions of income, to make them independent of units. If society has a stock of capital denoted by Q_1, then it cannot be on either the supply curve with $I = 0$ or the demand curve with $S = 0$. If it were on the former, owners of resources would try to buy more sources than are available and so raise their price; if it were on the latter, producing enterprises would be seeking to offer for sale more sources than are demanded and so lower their price. Somewhere between P_A and P_B, at a price here designated as P_C, is a price at which quantity of additional sources demanded is equal to the quantity of additional sources supplied. The demand price is lower because of the lessened desirability of additional sources relative to current consumption as the fraction of income devoted to buying sources increases; the supply price is higher because of the increased cost of producing additional sources as the fraction of productive services devoted to producing sources instead of current consumption increases. In the particular case on the graph, the demand price and supply price are equal when .1 of productive services are being devoted to producing additional sources and .1 of income to buying additional sources; i.e., $S = I = .1$. At this point, the stock of sources is growing. Thus point P_C is a temporary position, implying a movement along the line drawn through P_C and P in the direction of P.

Suppose we used an all-inclusive concept of capital. Then just as we saw earlier that we could expect the stock demand curve for permanent income streams to be infinitely elastic, we could also expect the stock supply curve for permanent income streams to be infinitely elastic. To use Knight's terminology, we should expect no diminishing returns from investment. The height of this curve would be determined by whatever happens to be the cost of producing a capital source capable of yielding a dollar a year indefinitely (the reciprocal of the marginal productivity of capital, according to one interpretation of that ambiguous term). The figure corresponding to Figure 17.8 might then look like Figure 17.9. All the

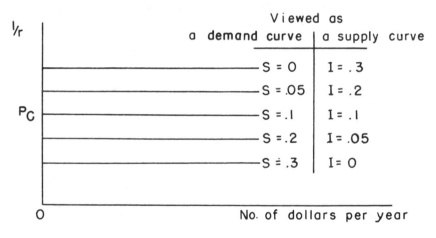

FIGURE 17.9

curves could be horizontal, so any horizontal curve would correspond to a demand curve for some level of savings and a supply curve for some level of investment. If the demand curve for $S = 0$ is above the supply curve for $I = 0$, as in this diagram, the picture describes an indefinitely progressive state—there is no level of capital stock that will be consistent with stationary state equilibrium. As the figure is drawn, a kind of "moving equilibrium" emerges, in which the price of a dollar a year is P_C, investment and saving proceed indefinitely at a rate of .1 of income, and the stock of capital continuously grows.

We shall now translate the preceding analysis into terms of wealth. Instead of talking about the demand for and supply of permanent income streams in terms of the price of a permanent income stream, we shall talk about the demand for and supply of capital values with the rate of interest as the independent variable. The chief advantage of the previous mode of expression (which is also the chief disadvantage of the present mode of expression) is the presentation of a constant stock of capital. Of the two ways of measuring the stock of capital, one of them is affected by the interest rate and the other is not. If capital stock is measured in terms of capitalized value of the permanent income stream, this measure will vary inversely with the rate of interest. A given set of sources yields a given income stream, and a constant stock of capital yielding a constant permanent income stream will be represented by a rectangular hyperbola. On the other hand, if we measure the stock of capital in terms of the permanent income streams it yields, this measure will not be affected by the interest rate, and hence this measure of the stock of capital will be a vertical line.

To get the demand for and supply of capital values using this second approach, we must remember that the demand for capital will be the demand of producing enterprises—what was formerly regarded as the supply of permanent income streams. The supply of capital will be the supply on the part of savers of capital sums—what was formerly regarded as the demand for income streams. Again, it is to be noted that these two curves refer to stocks and do not measure rates of flow per unit of time. The intersection of the two curves, as in Figure 17.10, will give us the long-run, stationary

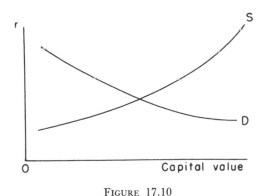

FIGURE 17.10

equilibrium stock of capital and rate of interest. As before, the curves have the shapes they do have because the concept of capital used is not all-inclusive. Consider the demand curve in this terminology that corresponds to the previous supply curve. Following the Knightian argument, we see that because the capital concept is restricted by institutional or other reasons, diminishing returns accrue to investment. The more inclusive concept of capital with no diminishing returns would imply an infinitely elastic demand for capital. The height of the demand curve or the rate of interest would be determined by the "marginal productivity of capital." Similarly, if we assume that people wish to maintain a certain constant ratio of wealth to income and if all income is derived from wealth (i.e., no distinction is necessary between human and nonhuman wealth), the supply curve would be infinitely elastic. The height of the supply curve is given by $\frac{1}{K}$ where K is $\frac{W}{Y}$.

In any particular stage in society there exists a stock of capital that may not be the equilibrium stock. The curve in Figure 17.11 labelled Q_1 is a

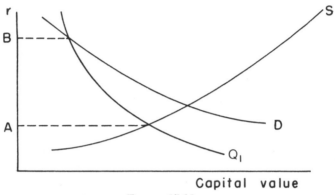

FIGURE 17.11

rectangular hyperbola and represents the capital value of a stock of capital yielding a permanent income stream of Q_1. If producing enterprises had no incentive to change this stock of capital at any interest rate—i.e., had no incentive to pay interest on a larger stock of capital—the Q_1 curve would represent the demand for capital. In a given state of technology, the incentive for producing enterprises to increase the stock of capital is greater the lower the rate of interest. Hence the lower the rate of interest, the higher the D curve should be relative to the Q_1 curve. If the rate of interest were at B, producing enterprises would have no incentive to try to increase the stock of capital on which they are paying interest. However, savers would have an incentive to seek to lend more. Likewise, if the rate of interest were at A, savers would have no incentive to lend more, but producing enterprises would have an incentive to borrow more. Savers will force the rate of interest below its level at B; investors will force the rate of interest above its level at A.

Therefore, the rate of interest can be at neither A nor B. Where it will be depends on the propensities of people to save and invest, i.e., on the savings and investment curves as in Figure 17.12. These curves determine the rate at which society moves away from the stock of capital corresponding to Q_1 to the equilibrium stock. As before, the demand curves for capital

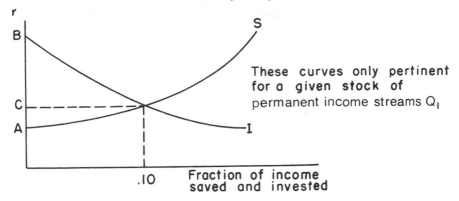

FIGURE 17.12

in Figure 17.11 consist of a locus of the combination of r and capital sums for which investment would be zero. Likewise, the supply curve of capital is the locus of combinations of r and capital sums for which savings would be zero. These two behavior functions enable us to define the long-run value of the equilibrium stock of capital. On the other hand, the savings and investment functions that are drawn in Figure 17.12 relating r to the rates of flow of savings and investment as percentages of national income, are drawn for given stocks of capital. These curves enable us to trace the dynamic path to long-run equilibrium.

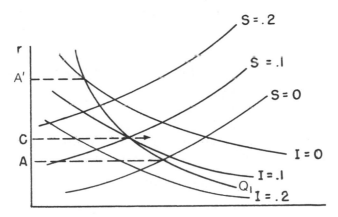

FIGURE 17.13

This can all be summarized in Figure 17.13, which is the counterpart of Figure 17.8. The S = 0 and I = 0 curves represent the supply of and demand for capital values. The intersection of these curves tells us about long-run equilibrium. The other curves have to do with direction. They give the various combinations of capital values and interest rates that must occur in order to maintain different rates of flow of savings and investment. We have assumed society to possess a given stock of capital whose value is represented by the rectangular hyperbola Q_1, so the interest rate must lie between A′ and A; from the savings and investment functions which obtain when society has this given stock of capital, we have determined that the rate of interest would be C with a rate of investment and saving of .1. This rate of interest C and rate of investment and saving of .1 are temporary, because as the stock of capital of society grows, there will be a new rate of saving and investment and a new rate of interest, leading eventually to the stable equilibrium position designated by P.

This analysis can be summarized in the form of a system of simultaneous equations. Let W = total real wealth of the kind being considered,

r = interest rate,

Y_w = income per unit time from W (so that $Y_w = rW$),

I = "investment" per unit time, and

S = "savings" per unit time.

For producing enterprises, there will be a relation showing the rate of interest corresponding to each value of wealth and investment, say

$$(5) \qquad\qquad r = f(W, I).$$

This can be viewed as a demand curve for "capital," i.e., as showing the maximum amount of wealth on which producing enterprises would be willing to pay a rate of interest r when a fraction I of current productive services is being used to add to the capital stock. Or it can be viewed as a supply curve of permanent income streams, showing the minimum price $\frac{1}{r}$ at which producing enterprises would keep available permanent income streams of an amount rW when they are using a fraction I of current productive services to produce income streams.

For owners of resources, there will be another relation showing the supply of "capital" or the demand for income streams, say

$$(6) \qquad\qquad r = g(W, S).$$

In the short run, we suppose Y_w fixed, say at Y_{w_0}. Short-run equilibrium is then given by equations 5 and 6 plus

$$(7) \qquad\qquad S = I$$

$$(8) \qquad\qquad rW = Y_w$$

$$(9) \qquad\qquad Y_w = Y_{w_0}$$

This is a system of five equations in the five unknowns, r, W, S, I, Y_w.

In the long run, the relevant system is equations 5 and 6 plus

(10) $S = 0$

(11) $I = 0$

(12) $Y_w = rW.$

This is a system of five equations in the same five unknowns.

A Negative Equilibrium Interest Rate

As long as we restrict ourselves to a barter economy, nothing we have said so far imposes very many restrictions on the shape of the $S = 0$, $I = 0$ curves. In particular, it is possible for the curves to intersect at a negative rate of interest, as in Figure 17.14. This would mean that society would be

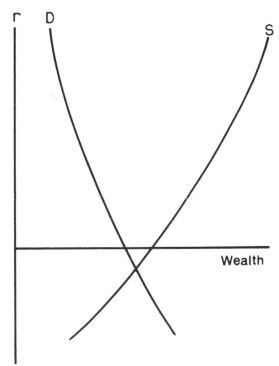

FIGURE 17.14

in long-run equilibrium with a given stock of capital at a negative rate of interest.

What conditions must be satisfied in order for a result such as this to occur? Consider first the S curve, showing the stock of wealth of the limited kind that is appropriable and capable of purchase and sale and that ultimate wealth-holders are willing to hold at various rates of interest. Suppose that the rate of interest were zero—that is, that there were no way of holding wealth that would yield a return. No wealth-holders would then hold wealth as a source of current (pecuniary) income. But individuals and families would still want to hold wealth as a reserve against emergencies. Clearly, that would remain true even if wealth imposed costs rather than gave returns. For example, suppose the only way people could hold wealth was in the form of stocks of foodstuffs, which imposed carrying costs in the form of making good deterioration and wastage. People would clearly still want to hold some wealth in that form to protect themselves against fluctuations in the supply of food. The wealth-value shown by the stock supply curve in Figure 17.14 for negative interest rates corresponds to such holdings. Of course, the actual stock held would not be constant year after year, so the amount depicted is to be treated as the average value over a considerable period.[11]

In practice, negative returns on capital to wealth-holders could arise not only from such physical circumstances as those just exemplified but also from capital taxes that converted before-tax, positive returns into after-tax, negative returns.

Let us now consider the demand curve. At first, this seems to conflict with our earlier analysis that described a fixed stock of capital in the sense of a constant stream of permanent income as generating a unit elastic demand curve for wealth. The constant income stream would be the maximum total amount that the producing enterprises holding the capital would be willing to pay as interest on the wealth value of the capital. How can the demand curve be less elastic than that? Clearly, it cannot be if there is any capital source yielding an economically permanent income stream. Let there be one acre of land yielding an economically permanent stream of rent of $1 a year, and its capital value would approach infinity as the rate of interest became lower and lower. Putting it differently, if there is any way of producing an economically permanent income stream of any size at any finite cost—say by filling in swamps—it will be profitable, at a low enough interest rate, to borrow that sum to produce that stream.

Note the stress on *economically* permanent. As in the discussion of the supply of capital, there may be no economically permanent source of income for physical reasons. The only capital sources capable of being produced, appropriated, and transferred might be inventories of depreciating foodstuffs. Alternatively, there may be sources of physically or technically permanent income streams, like land areas, but taxation or other institutional arrangements like ownership rights of limited duration may make them not economically permanent.

---

11. Also, the yield is negative in physical terms, in terms of own-interest rate, but not in utility terms, since the reserves are used to supplement deficient production when their utility value is high and are replenished when production is ample and hence its utility value is low.

The essential condition, therefore, for the long-run equilibrium interest rate to be negative is that there exist no capital item included in the category of wealth to which Figure 17.14 applies that can yield an economically permanent income stream. The negative interest rate corresponds to the owners of wealth paying caretakers to maintain the wealth intact. In order for such a situation to persist, the owners of wealth must have some other source from which to get the sums they pay (the negative interest rate times the value of wealth). There must exist some forms of capital (human capital, nontransferable, nonhuman capital) that yield a permanent income stream. Otherwise, the society could not be stationary. It would simply run down. A negative equilibrium interest rate is therefore not conceivable for an all-inclusive concept of capital.

The conditions required for the long-run stationary state interest rate to be negative are highly special. It is nonetheless worth spelling them out, because a negative equilibrium interest rate is very closely connected with Keynes's proposition that there may not be a long-run stationary state equilibrium at full employment. One insightful way of interpreting that proposition consists of the following sub-propositions:

1. In a nonmonetary, barter economy, the equilibrium interest rate may be negative.
2. In a monetary economy, the market interest rate cannot be negative.
3. Therefore, in a monetary economy, it may not be possible to reach full equilibrium.

The preceding analysis shows that 1 is correct, though only under very special conditions. We have already seen, in discussing the arithmetic of interest rates, the sense in which 2 is correct. But 3 is a non sequitur from 1 and 2 unless the equilibrium interest rate in a monetary economy is the same as in a nonmonetary economy. But that is not the case. The contrast that Keynes drew between "market" and equilibrium rates is misleading. Neither can be negative in the kind of money economy that underlay his analysis. In order to see why that is so we must introduce money explicitly into our analysis.

Introduction of Money

Once money is introduced into an economy, it is essential to distinguish between the *nominal* interest rate—the number of dollars per dollar after maintaining the dollar amount of capital intact—and the *real* interest rate —the number of dollars per dollar after maintaining the real amount of capital intact. For continuous compounding, the real interest rate is the nominal rate minus the rate of change of prices:

(13)
$$\rho = r - \frac{1}{P}\frac{dP}{dt},$$

where ρ is the real interest rate, r the nominal rate, and $\dfrac{1}{P}\dfrac{dP}{dt}$ the instantane-

ous rate of change of prices. For monetary analysis, it is essential to dis-

tinguish between the realized real rate, which treats $\dfrac{1}{P}\dfrac{dP}{dt}$ as the actual

rate of price change, and the anticipated real rate, which treats $\dfrac{1}{P}\dfrac{dP}{dt}$ as the

anticipated rate of change of prices. But for our purposes of analyzing
stationary state equilibrium, we may neglect this distinction and treat the
realized and anticipated real rates as identical.

For simplicity, we shall first consider alternative stationary states in

each of which the price level is stable so $\dfrac{1}{P}\dfrac{dP}{dt} = 0$. This is the case im-

plicitly considered by Keynes and most of his followers. We shall then introduce the possibility of changing prices. We shall throughout regard
money as the counterpart of currency or its equivalent, i.e., as an asset that
pays zero nominal interest.

Once we introduce money, the nominal rate of interest can never be
negative, since the costs of simply holding cash are essentially zero. Hence
if the rate of interest approached zero, people would hold all their wealth
in the form of money. In terms of the preceding section, money now becomes a form of wealth that yields a permanent income stream of zero and
so dominates any form of wealth that yields a negative permanent income
stream.

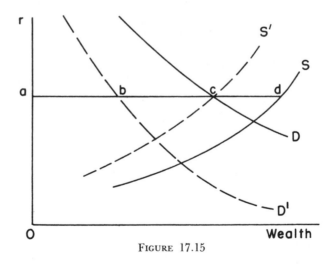

FIGURE 17.15

Figure 17.15 incorporates this feature into our long-run stationary equilibrium diagram. The S curve in Figure 17.15 is the supply curve of capital
(for S = 0) previously defined. The S' curve shows the amount of each cor-

responding level of wealth that owners of resources would desire to hold in forms other than money, so the horizontal distance between the S′ and S curves measures the amount that owners of resources would want to hold in the form of money. The S′ curve then gives the supply of wealth available for "renting" to productive enterprises at each interest rate, and its intersection with the demand curve (for I = 0) previously defined gives the long-run equilibrium position (c in Figure 17.15).

However, producing enterprises would use part of the wealth on which they pay interest to finance the holding of cash. These "business balances" are indicated in Figure 17.15 by the horizontal distance between the D and D′ curves. In equilibrium, then, bd is the equilibrium "real" amount of money of which cd is held directly by owners of resources and bc as "working" capital by producing enterprises. The equilibrium price level is then whatever is necessary to make the real value of the existing nominal quantity of money equal to bd. This assertion is one way of stating compactly the quantity theory of money.

We can now see why, once money is introduced into the system, the equilibrium rate of interest cannot be negative. In Figure 17.16, the S and

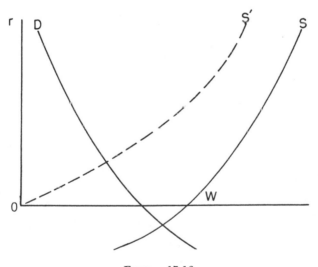

Figure 17.16

D curves, reproduced from Figure 17.14, intersect at a negative interest rate. This intersection gives the equilibrium solution for a barter economy. But once money is introduced, equilibrium is given by the intersection of the S′ curve and the D curve, and the S′ curve necessarily cuts the D curve at a positive interest rate so long as the cost of holding money can be regarded as zero. This is one way to state the essence of the so-called Pigou effect, which demonstrated the non sequitur in Keynes's proposition 3.

If the price level is not constant, we can no longer use r as in Figures 17.15 and 17.16 to refer to both the nominal and the real interest rate. Suppose prices are rising at a constant rate so that the nominal rate exceeds the real rate. This will affect all of the curves in Figure 17.16. Whereas before the nominal and real return from holding a dollar of cash was zero, now it is negative. Hence for a given real rate (say Oa of Figure 17.15), assets yielding that real rate are more attractive relative to cash. This will be true for both ultimate wealth-holders and for business enterprises, so the distances bc and cd in Figure 17.15 will both contract as in Figure 17.17, which reproduces the curves from Figure 17.15 and adds the

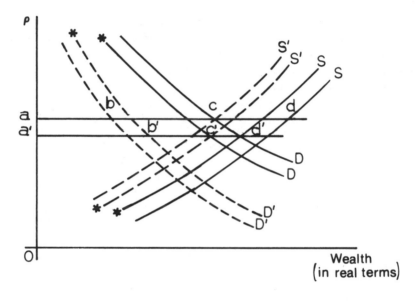

FIGURE 17.17

curves designated by an asterisk relevant to the new situation with prices rising. Both business enterprises and ultimate wealth-holders will be induced to substitute real wealth for cash balances, so both curves D' and S' will move to the right. However, the collection of wealth is now less productive for business enterprises and yields less utility for ultimate wealth-holders, so both curves D and S will shift to the left. The new equilibrium real rate is now defined by the intersection of the D and S' curves designated by an asterisk and is lower than the earlier real rate. However, the decline in the real rate must be less than the rate of change of prices, because it is produced by the simultaneously higher nominal rate. As a theoretical proposition, nothing more can be said about the division of the price rise between a higher nominal rate and a lower real rate. As an empirical proposition, the major effect appears to be on the nominal rate, the real rate being essentially unchanged. The implication is that the demand and supply curves D′ and S′ are highly elastic or that the real quantity of money is small compared to the total wealth value of all capital.

Figure 17.17 contains the essence of what has sometimes been labelled the *Mundell effect*.[12]

If prices were falling at a constant rate, the effects would be reversed: the real interest rate would be higher than with constant prices and the nominal rate lower.[13]

A digression will help relate this analysis to the more usual discussion of the Keynesian proposition about the possibility that there may not exist an equilibrium at full employment of resources. For such an equilibrium to exist, the amount business enterprises want to add to the stock of capital, net capital formation, or net investment, must, Keynes argued, be equal to the amount ultimate wealth-holders want to add to their stock of wealth, net savings, when all resources are employed. But suppose the yield on capital is so low that business enterprises do not want to invest as much as the community wants to save at full employment. In a barter economy, that would be resolved, Keynes implicitly argues, by a negative interest rate. But in a money economy, the nominal rate cannot be negative. The conflict will be resolved by a reduction in employment that will reduce the amount people desire to save to the amount enterprises desire to invest.

But this situation, Keynes recognizes, is not a stable equilibrium: the unemployed resources will compete for employment, driving down their nominal prices. However, he argues, there is no end to this process; lower nominal costs mean lower nominal prices, mean lower nominal values of investment and savings, but do not introduce any force eliminating the initial discrepancy between the amount business enterprises want to add to productive capital and the community wants to add to its wealth. Hence he introduced price and wage rigidity as a *deus ex machina* to stop the indefinite decline in prices and wages.

Pigou argued that the public's desire is not ultimately to save but to have a desired stock of wealth, that there exists a stock supply curve of capital as in our figures corresponding to S = 0. For a given nominal quantity of money (which is what Keynes assumed), the wealth value of that quantity of money can be anything whatsoever depending on the price level. For a "high" price level, its wealth value will be low, for a "low" price level, its wealth value will be high. In terms of Figure 17.16, there always exists a price level that will make the wealth value of money balances equal to OW. At this price level, the desired stock of wealth will be attained and desired saving at full employment will be zero; hence even if

12. From Robert Mundell, "Inflation and Real Interest," *Journal of Political Economy*, 71 (June 1963): 280–83.

13. See Milton Friedman, "The Optimum Quantity of Money," in *The Optimum Quantity of Money and Other Essays* (Chicago: Aldine, 1969).

desired investment is zero, there is no conflict. The equilibrium rate of interest is at least zero in a money economy.

This argument is entirely valid for a fixed nominal quantity of money and alternative levels of prices: there always exists a low enough price level to sate the community with wealth, or a high enough price level to reduce the real value of money balances to whatever fraction of total wealth the community (ultimate wealth-holders plus business enterprises) wishes to hold in that form.

For a fixed nominal quantity of money, there is an even more far-reaching answer to Keynes's propositions that renders them invalid even if the public had an insatiable desire to add to (nonhuman) wealth while there was a limit to the physical productivity of capital. That answer derives from distinguishing income defined as the value of productive resources from income defined as the sum of what individuals separately regard their incomes as being. The latter includes not only payments for productive services but also capital gains or losses. Suppose the Keynesian dilemma were to arise, and prices and wages started falling. Declining prices would add to the real value of wealth. Holders of cash would realize capital gains. Incomes as they perceived them would exceed the value of productive resources. Consumption would equal the value of productive resources, so net investment by entrepreneurs would be zero, yet wealth-holders could be saving at any desired rate. There always exists, with a fixed nominal quantity of money, a rate of price decline sufficiently great to reconcile at full employment the desires of producing enterprises to invest and of wealth-holders to save, no matter how stubborn both are.

This answer is not incorporated in our diagrams because the underlying assumptions contradict the notion that there exists a supply curve of wealth that has a finite desired level of wealth for an interest rate of zero.

Figure 17.17 shows that the Pigovian argument can readily be extended to encompass a changing nominal quantity of money and an associated changing price level. The stationary picture it depicts for a positive rate of price rise corresponds to a rate of monetary growth equal to the rate of price rise. For that rate of growth of prices and money there exists at each point of time a price level and a real interest rate that will simultaneously equate the nominal amount of money available to the nominal quantity demanded and the amount of wealth on which producing enterprises are willing to pay interest to the amount of wealth ultimate wealth-holders want to hold in interest-bearing form.

Finally, the more far-reaching argument that depends on the rate of price change rather than the level of prices can also be extended to encompass a changing quantity of money. If wealth-holders stubbornly insist on saving at full employment more than producing enterprises wish to invest, then prices must fall sufficiently more rapidly than the quantity of money is falling to enable the wealth-holders to achieve their objectives in the form of increasing real value of cash balances.

The Pigovian and the more far-reaching answer to Keynes's proposition have been extremely important on a theoretical level in assuring that there is no basic flaw in our theoretical analysis. But I hasten to add that in my opinion neither corresponds to effects that are empirically important in the kind of economic fluctuations that actual economies experience.

A Final Note on an All-Inclusive Concept of Capital

The concept of stationary state equilibrium has a highly unrealistic ring in a world that has been accustomed to economic growth over centuries. Hence it is worth stressing that the stationary state character of our analysis derives from our considering mostly only one class of sources of productive services and implicitly assuming other sources of productive services (human capital in the main) as fixed in amount. The equilibrium is stationary only relative to that fixed amount.

If the quantity of other resources grows, then all our curves for a partial concept of capital keep shifting to the right, so the stationary state equilibrium becomes a moving equilibrium as in many so-called growth models.

Still more fundamentally, if we regard the quantity of other resources as altering in response to economic considerations by more indirect means than market purchase and sale, we can shift to an all-inclusive concept of capital as we did briefly in Fig. 17.9. It will help bring out the implications of the all-inclusive concept of capital to express the $S = 0$ and $I = 0$ curves of Fig. 17.9 in terms of interest rate and wealth rather than, as there, in terms of number of years' purchase and income streams. This is done in Fig. 17.18 for an expanding economy.

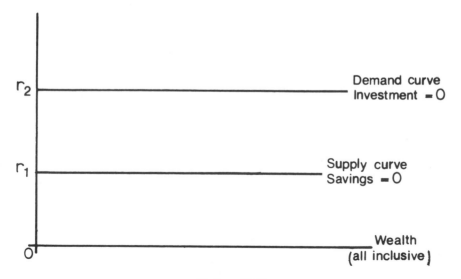

FIGURE 17.18

Note that the supply curve of capital includes the part of the vertical axis below r_1, the demand curve, the part above r_2. At any (real) interest rate above r_1, there is no limit to the amount of wealth the community would be willing to accumulate in all forms, though of course at each point of time there is a limit to how rapidly they would be willing to accumulate it. At any (real) interest rate below r_2, there is no limit to the amount of sources of productive services on which it would be worth paying that interest, though of course there is a limit on how rapidly it would be worth producing the additional sources. In this conception, r_1 deserves to be called *the internal rate of discount* or *time preference;* r_2 deserves to be called *the marginal productivity of capital.* There is nothing that requires the internal rate of discount and the marginal productivity of capital to be a numerical constant for all levels of wealth, as in the special case depicted in Fig. 17.18, but, as noted earlier, there is no presumption as to whether they will be higher or lower for higher quantities of capital. So long as the marginal productivity of capital is higher than the internal rate of discount, the economy will be growing.

If r_2 were less than r_1, the economy would be declining, and a similar figure could be drawn for such an economy.

Appendix A:
Reading Assignments

Notes

1. It is assumed that students are familiar with material equivalent to that contained in George Stigler, *Theory of Price,* or Kenneth Boulding, *Economic Analysis.*

2. *Supplementary books* (recommended but not required; some contain reprints of articles referred to below):

American Economic Association. *Readings in Price Theory.* Homewood, Ill.: Irwin, 1952.

————. *Readings in the Theory of Income Distribution.* Homewood, Ill.: Irwin, 1951.

Becker, Gary S. *Economic Theory.* New York: Knopf, 1971.

Breit, W., and Hochman, H., eds. *Readings in Microeconomics.* Paperback. 2d ed. New York: Holt, Rinehart & Winston, 1971.

Hirshleifer, J. *Investment, Interest, and Capital.* Englewood Cliffs, N.J.: Prentice Hall, 1970. Esp. part 1.

Stigler, G. J. *Production and Distribution Theories.* New York: Macmillan, 1941.

3. Readings marked with an asterisk (*) are recommended, not required.

Introductory and Methodological

Knight, F. H. *The Economic Organization.* 1st published ed., 1951; reprint ed., New York: Augustus M. Kelley, 1967. Esp. pp. 3–37.

Keynes, J. N. *The Scope and Method of Political Economy.* 1st ed., 1891; reprint of 1917 ed., New York: Augustus M. Kelley, 1973. Chapters 1 and 2.

Friedman, M. "The Methodology of Positive Economics," pp. 3–43, in M. Friedman, *Essays in Positive Economics.* Chicago: University of Chicago Press, 1953.

Hayek, F. A. "The Use of Knowledge in Society." *American Economic Review* 35 (September 1945): 519–30; reprinted in F. A. Hayek, *Individual-*

ism and Economic Order. Chicago: University of Chicago Press, 1948. Pp. 77–91.

Theory of Demand

Marshall, A. *Principles of Economics.* 1st ed., 1890; 8th ed., London: Macmillan, 1930. Book 3, chapters 2–4; Book 5, chapters 1 and 2.

Friedman, M. "The Marshallian Demand Curve." *Journal of Political Economy* 57 (December 1949): 463–95; reprinted in Friedman, *Essays in Positive Economics,* pp. 47–99.

Schultz, H. *The Meaning of Statistical Demand Curves.* Chicago: n.p., 1930. Pp. 1–10.

Working, E. J. "What Do Statistical 'Demand Curves' Show?" *Quarterly Journal of Economics* 41 (1927): 212–27; reprinted in A.E.A., *Readings in Price Theory,* pp. 97–115.

Knight, F. H. *Risk, Uncertainty and Profit.* 1st ed., 1921; Harper Torchbook ed., New York: Harper & Row, 1965. Chapter 3.

*Becker, G. S. "Irrational Behavior and Economic Theory." *Journal of Political Economy* 70 (February 1962): 1–13.

Stigler, G. J. "Economics of Information." *Journal of Political Economy* 69 (June 1961): 213–25; reprinted in G. J. Stigler, *The Organization of Industry.* Homewood, Ill.: Irwin, 1968. Pp. 171–90.

*Alchian, A. A. "Information Cost, Pricing, and Resource Development," pp. 27–52, in E. S. Phelps et al., *Microeconomic Foundations of Employment and Inflation Theory.* New York: Norton, 1969.

Theory of Consumer Choice

*Allen, R. G. D. "The Nature of Indifference Curves." *Review of Economic Studies* 1 (1933–34): 110ff.

Hicks, J. R. *Value and Capital.* Oxford: Clarendon Press, 1939; 2d ed., 1946. Part 1 (pp. 11–52).

*———. *A Revision of Demand Theory.* Oxford: Clarendon Press, 1956.

*Samuelson, P. A. *Foundations of Economic Analysis.* Cambridge: Harvard University Press, 1947; 2d ed., 1958.

*Wold, H. *Demand Analysis.* New York: Wiley, 1953. Chapter 1.

*Friedman, M. *A Theory of the Consumption Function.* National Bureau of Economic Research Series, no. 63. Princeton: Princeton University Press, 1957.

*Stigler, G. J. "The Early History of Empirical Studies of Consumer Behavior." *Journal of Political Economy* 62 (April 1954): 95–113.

*Slutsky, E. "On the Theory of the Budget of the Consumer," pp. 27–56, in A.E.A., *Readings in Price Theory.*

Mosak, J. L. "On the Interpretation of the Fundamental Equation of

Value Theory," pp. 69–74, in O. Lange et al., *Studies in Mathematical Economics and Econometrics*. Chicago: University of Chicago Press, 1942.

*Wallis, W. A., and Friedman, M. "The Empirical Derivation of Indifference Functions," pp. 175–89, in Lange et al., *Studies in Mathematical Economics and Econometrics*.

Houthakker, H. "The Present State of Consumption Theory." *Econometrica* 29 (October 1961): 204–40.

*Lancaster, K. "A New Approach to Consumer Theory." *Journal of Political Economy* 74 (April 1966): 132–57.

*Becker, G. S. "A Theory of the Allocation of Time." *Economic Journal* 75 (September 1965): 493–515.

*Friedman, M., and Savage, L. J. "The Utility Analysis of Choices Involving Risk." *Journal of Political Economy* 56 (August 1948): 270–304; reprinted in A.E.A., *Readings in Price Theory*, pp. 57–96.

Friedman, M., and Savage, L. J. "The Expected-Utility Hypothesis and the Measurability of Utility." *Journal of Political Economy* 60 (December 1952): 463–74.

Alchian, A. A. "The Meaning of Utility Measurement." *American Economic Review* 43 (March 1953): 26–50.

Supply and the Economics of the Individual Firm

Marshall, A. *Principles of Economics*. Book 5, chapters 3–5, 12; Appendix H.

*Robinson, J. *The Economics of Imperfect Competition*. 1st ed., 1933; 2d ed., London: Macmillan, and New York: St. Martin's Press, 1964. Chapter 2.

Clark, J. M. *Studies in the Economics of Overhead Costs*. Chicago: University of Chicago Press, 1923; 2d ed., 1931. Chapter 9.

Viner, J. "Cost Curves and Supply Curves." *Zeitschrift für Nationaloekonomie*, Book 3 (September 1931), pp. 23–46; reprinted in A.E.A., *Readings in Price Theory*, pp. 193–232.

Apel, H. "Marginal Cost Constancy and Its Implications." *American Economic Review* 38 (December 1948): 870–85.

Smith, C. "Survey of the Empirical Evidence on the Economies of Scale," pp. 213–30, in *Business Concentration and Price Policy*. A Conference of the Universities-National Bureau Committee for Economic Research. Princeton: Princeton University Press, 1955.

Stigler, G. J. "The Economies of Scale." *Journal of Law and Economics* 1 (October 1968): 54–71.

Chamberlin, E. H. *The Theory of Monopolistic Competition*. Cambridge: Harvard University Press, 1933; 8th ed., 1962. Chapter 3, sections 1, 4, 5, 6; chapter 5.

*Harrod, R. F. "Doctrines of Imperfect Competition." *Quarterly Journal of Economics* 48 (May 1934): 442–61, section 1.

Stigler, G. J. "Monopolistic Competition in Retrospect," pp. 12–24, and "Competition in the United States," pp. 46–65, in G. J. Stigler, *Five Lectures on Economic Problems*. London and New York: Longmans, Green, 1949.

*Triffin, R. *Monopolistic Competition and General Equilibrium Theory*. Cambridge: Harvard University Press, 1940. Esp. part 2.

Harberger, A. C. "Monopoly and Resource Allocation." *American Economic Review,* Suppl., 44 (May 1954): 77–87.

Robinson, E. A. G. *The Structure of Competitive Industry*. 1st ed., 1931; rev. Cambridge Economic Handbook, no. 7, Chicago: University of Chicago Press, 1958.

*Stigler, G. J. "The Statistics of Monopoly and Merger." *Journal of Political Economy* 64 (February 1956): 35–40.

*————. "The Kinky Oligopoly Demand Curve and Rigid Prices." *Journal of Political Economy* 55 (October 1947): 432–49; reprinted in A.E.A., *Readings in Price Theory*, pp. 410–39, and in Stigler, *The Organization of Industry*, pp. 208–34.

*————. "A Theory of Oligopoly." *Journal of Political Economy* 72 (February 1964): 44–61; reprinted in Stigler, *The Organization of Industry*, pp. 39–63.

Archibald, G. C. "Chamberlin versus Chicago." *Review of Economic Studies* 29 (October 1961): 1–28.

*Robinson, E. A. G. *Monopoly*. 1st ed., 1941; Cambridge Economic Handbook, no. 11, Cambridge: Cambridge University Press, and London: Nisbet, 1955.

*Plant, Arnold. "The Economic Theory Concerning Patents for Invention." *Economica,* N.S., 1 (February 1934): 30–51.

*Dennison, S. R. "The Problem of Bigness." *Cambridge Journal* 1 (November 1947): 109–25.

Theory of Distribution

Marshall, A. *Principles of Economics*. Book 4, chapters 1–3; Book 5, chapter 6.

Clark, J. B. *The Distribution of Wealth*. 1st ed., 1899; reprint ed., New York: Kelley & Millman, 1956. Preface; chapters 1, 7, 8, 11–13, 23.

Mill, J. S. *Principles of Political Economy*. 1st ed., 1848; reprint of 7th ed., New York: Augustus M. Kelley, 1965. Book 2, chapter 14.

Hicks, J. R. *The Theory of Wages*. London: Macmillan, 1932; 2d ed., 1963. Chapters 1–6.

Smith, A. *The Wealth of Nations*. 1st ed., 1776; reprint of the 1904 E. Cannan ed., New Rochelle, N.Y.: Arlington House, 1966. Book 1, chapter 10.

Marshall, A. *Principles of Economics*. Book 6, chapters 1–5.

*Friedman, M., and Kuznets, S. *Income from Independent Professional Practice*. New York: National Bureau of Economic Research, 1945. Preface, pp. v–x; chapter 3, section 3, pp. 81–95; chapter 4, section 2, pp. 118–37; appendix, sections 1 and 3, pp. 142–51 and 155–61.

*Stigler, G. J. *Domestic Servants in the United States, 1900–1940*. N.B.E.R. Occasional Paper, no. 24. New York: National Bureau of Economic Research, 1946.

Becker, G. S. *Human Capital: A Theoretical and Empirical Analysis*. New York: Columbia University Press for the National Bureau of Economic Research, 1964. Chapters 2–3.

*————. *Human Capital and the Personal Distribution of Income: An Analytical Approach*. Ann Arbor: University of Michigan, 1967.

Lewis, H. G. *Unionism and Relative Wages in the U.S.* Chicago: University of Chicago Press, 1963. Esp. chapter 5.

Reder, M. W. "A Partial Survey of the Theory of Income Size Distribution," pp. 205–53, in Lee Soltow, ed., *Six Papers on the Size Distribution of Wealth and Income*. N.B.E.R. Studies in Income and Wealth, no. 33. New York and London: Columbia University Press for the National Bureau of Economic Research, 1969.

*Friedman, D. *Laissez Faire in Population*. New York: Population Council, 1972.

Economic Report of the President transmitted to the Congress February 1974. Washington, D.C.: U.S. Government Printing Office, 1974. Chapter 5, "Distribution of Income."

Theory of Capital and of Profit

Fisher, I. *The Nature of Income and Capital*. New York and London: Macmillan, 1906. Chapters 1, 2, 4, 7, 11–15.

Knight, F. H. "Interest," in *Encyclopedia of the Social Sciences*, vol. 8 (1932); reprinted in F. H. Knight, *Ethics of Competition*. 1st ed., 1935; reprint ed., Freeport, N.Y.: Books for Libraries, 1969. Pp. 251–76.

Keynes, J. M. *The General Theory of Employment, Interest and Money*. London: Macmillan, 1936. Chapters 11–14.

Lerner, A. P. "On the Marginal Product of Capital and the Marginal Efficiency of Investment." *Journal of Political Economy* 61 (February 1953): 1–14.

Clower, R. W. "Productivity, Thrift, and the Rate of Interest." *Economic Journal* 64 (March 1954): 107–15.

*Solow, R. M. *Capital Theory and the Rate of Return*. Amsterdam: North Holland, 1963. Lectures 1 and 2.

*Weston, J. F. "A Generalized Uncertainty Theory of Profit." *American Economic Review* 40 (March 1950): 40–60.

————. "The Profit Concept and Theory: A Restatement." *Journal of Political Economy* 52 (April 1954): 152–70.

Theory of General Equilibrium

Cassel, G. *Fundamental Thoughts in Economics.* New York: Harcourt, Brace & Co., 1925. Chapters 1–3.

————. *The Theory of Social Economy.* Translated by J. McCabe. New York: Harcourt, Brace & Co., 1924; new rev. ed. translated by S. L. Barron for the same publisher, 1932. Chapter 4.

Walras, L. *Elements of Pure Economics.* Translated by William Jaffé. 1st French ed., 1874; English translation of rev. ed., Homewood, Ill.: Irwin for the American Economic Association and the Royal Economic Society, 1954. Part 3, lessons 11 and 12.

Hicks, J. R. "Mr. Keynes and the 'Classics': A Suggested Interpretation." *Econometrica* 5 (April 1937): 147–59.

Modigliani, F. "Liquidity Preference and the Theory of Interest and Money." *Econometrica* 12 (January 1944): 45–88. Esp. part 1, sections 1–9 and 11–17; and part 2, section 21.

*Pigou, A. C. "The Classical Stationary State." *Economic Journal* 53 (December 1943): 343–51.

————. "Economic Progress in a Stable Environment." *Economica,* N.S., 14 (August 1947): 180–90; reprinted in American Economic Association, *Readings in Monetary Theory.* Philadelphia: The Blakiston Co., 1951. Pp. 241–51.

Patinkin, D. "Price Flexibility and Full Employment." *American Economic Review* 38 (September 1948): 543–64; reprinted in A.E.A., *Readings in Monetary Theory,* pp. 252–83.

Hahn, F. H., and Matthews, R. C. O. "The Theory of Economic Growth: A Survey." *Economic Journal* 74 (December 1964): 779–902.

Phelps, E. S. "The Golden Rule of Accumulation: A Fable for Growthman." *American Economic Review* 51 (September 1961): 638–43.

Denison, E. F. *The Sources of Economic Growth in the U.S.* New York: Committee for Economic Development, 1962.

Appendix B: Problems

Part I: Pricing of Final Products and Industrial Organization

POINT RATIONING PLUS PRICE RATIONING

Assume that a comprehensive system of point rationing is superimposed on a money price system. Each consumer is given an equal number of points, although money incomes are very unequal. Point prices exist for every commodity for which a money price exists, and a consumer must pay both points and money to purchase a commodity. To simplify the analysis, assume throughout that the points are dated (that is, they can be used only during a specific period); and that fixed and known quantities of various commodities are available in each period.

1. Indicate (on an indifference diagram or in any other manner) how to determine the quantity of each good that an individual would purchase, given money prices, point prices, his money income, and his point income (a) if it is illegal to transfer points from one person to another and consumers conform to this requirement, and (b) if points may legally be bought and sold for money. In this case, take as given to the individual consumer also the price of points in terms of money.

2. If the only thing the government fixed were the number of points each individual receives, and it were to allow the money prices, point prices, and price of points in terms of money to be determined on the market, there would not be a unique set of values of these variables that would establish equilibrium, because the number of variables would be greater than the number of conditions. Explain this statement. Suppose the government tries to remove the indeterminacy by assigning values to some variables on the basis of criteria other than clearing the market. How many variables could the government so set and still have a determinate equilibrium? Does it matter which variables the government sets?

3. It has been argued that every consumer will gain if nontransferable points, case 1a, were made freely transferable into money, case 1b. Do you think this correct? Discuss.

MEDICAL CARE FINANCED BY TAXATION

Suppose a plan for medical insurance were adopted under which individuals paid for medical care in the form of taxes levied on them in the same manner as other taxes. Assume that no additional fee is charged, so that patients may call on physicians of their own choice at any time without specific charge, and that no drastic changes were made in the organization of medical practice. Assume also, for 1, 2, 3, and 4 below, that the number of physicians is the same as before the system was adopted. As an economist,

1. What would you expect to be the reaction of patients? Explain in terms of demand curves.

2. What would you expect to be the reaction of physicians if each physician were paid a flat fee by the state for each patient-visit? Would the reaction be different if the physician were paid an annual lump-sum salary? If so, how?

3. What variable might be expected to produce an equilibrium? How would it operate?

4. What conflict would arise between the reactions of patients and physicians? Would the conflict be affected by the manner in which physicians were paid? Can you suggest any means for resolving the conflict, subject to the limitation of a given number of physicians?

5. Suppose the conflict were resolved by an adjustment in the number of physicians, the state paying whatever was required to get the necessary number and the entire cost being financed by taxes. What kind of adjustment would be required? *If* you accept individuals' judgments as final and as the sole consideration, and *if* you neglect entirely any effects on the distribution of income, what, if anything, can you say about the effect of the change in the manner of handling medical service on the efficiency of allocation of resources? State your answer in terms of the relevant rates of substitution.

6. Why the two "if" clauses in 5?

SEARS, ROEBUCK & CO., ALLSTATE, AND DIVERSIFICATION

It is widely argued that entrepreneurs engaged in a number of different activities somehow have a "competitive advantage" over entrepreneurs engaged in only one, even if no technical economies are achieved by combining the activities. This general argument and the supposed advantage take many different forms: sometimes it is that one activity provides a "guaranteed" market for another activity; sometimes that one activity provides financing or capital for another; sometimes that a monopoly in one line confers an advantage in another. An example of this reasoning is contained in a report by the *Chicago Daily News* financial columnist on November 20, 1951, that Sears, Roebuck had completed an arrangement with Kaiser-

Frazer to market an automobile under the name of "Allstate." The columnist commented, "also there is the Allstate Insurance Company, a wholly owned subsidiary, which would benefit heavily through liability and other policies written in connection with the sales of an Allstate automobile. . . . Some of the gossip around Detroit has been to the effect that the Allstate would have Sears batteries and tires and certain other Sears accessories as original equipment—which would mean more business for these departments of the company."

(1) The key question is, of course, whether the financial incentive to Sears to market an automobile is greater because it owns the subsidiary companies than it would be if it did not own them. You will find it helpful in answering this question to consider first two intermediate questions: (2) Given that Sears does own the subsidiary companies and that it is going to market an automobile under its name, is it in its own interests to require that the car be equipped with accessories produced by its companies? (3) Is it in its own interests to require that cars it sells be insured by its own insurance company?

In answering questions 1, 2, and 3, consider separately two cases: (a) the subsidiary companies can be regarded as operating under highly competitive conditions, and (b) the subsidiary companies can be regarded as having a monopoly of the products they produce. Do the conclusions depend on the assumption made about competitive conditions? Assume throughout that there are no "technical" economies from combining the various activities.

THE ECONOMICS OF TIE-IN SALES

Very frequently, two items that could be sold separately are in fact sold jointly and one or the other or both of the items cannot be purchased separately. Such arrangements have come to be called "tie-in sales" or "compulsory tie-in sales." There appear to be three sets of circumstances under which making a tie-in sale compulsory will either not decrease the returns to the firm in question or will be a means of increasing the returns: (1) If there are economies in producing and/or selling the two items jointly— in this case, joint sales may well become so much the rule that there is no loss in making them compulsory, though there seems no reason why firms should not be willing to sell the items separately at prices the sum of which is greater than the price of the items purchased jointly. (2) If the firm has a monopoly on at least one of the items and can use the tie-in arrangement as a device for price discrimination, i.e., for charging different prices to different purchasers. (3) If there is a fixed price (e.g., a legal maximum price) that can be evaded by requiring the purchaser to buy a non-price-fixed item.

Each of the following is an example of a tie-in arrangement. Under which one of the above headings does each case come? Explain in detail in each case how the existence of the tie-in can be explained and what economic function it performs. You may find it helpful to preface your discussion of the individual cases with a statement of the general principles of price discrimination. Under what circumstances should a firm discriminate in price among its customers? What determines the optimum prices to charge?

1. New shoes are always (or essentially) sold with shoelaces. The shoelaces can be bought separately, but it is difficult if not impossible to buy the shoes separately.

2. Frequently, manufacturers of razor-blades will make an offer of a "free" razor with a certain number of blades. This is a tie-in, since in effect the purchaser is required to buy blades plus razor. The offers are generally made only if the given firm's blades are the only ones that fit its "free" razor. Try to explain these arrangements without invoking irrationality on the part of purchasers.

3. Mimeograph machines, at least in the early days, were sold to customers subject to the requirement that the customers buy the ink and the mimeograph stencils from the company that held the patent on the machine, although this company had no patent on these items.

4. Motion-picture producers have used "block-booking" extensively. Block-booking is an arrangement whereby a theater operator must buy the use of a number of pictures as a "block"; he cannot decide to buy one picture in the block and not others. It will be simplest to suppose that only two pictures are involved, say A and B. Why should the producer require their joint purchase? Why not sell each at the most profitable price for each?

5. Persons subletting apartments in New York City frequently require tenants to purchase furniture from them.

6. Advertisements for tobacco, etc. are frequently painted on the sides of barns instead of on specially constructed billboards. Some companies consistently pay the farmer for the use of his property by painting his entire barn rather than by paying money. Why "tie" the two together? Why doesn't the advertising company pay the farmer in money, which the farmer can then use for painting the barn or for any other purpose he wishes?

7. The International Business Machines company rents its tabulating and computing machines to users. The rental is typically expressed per shift per unit time (week, month, etc.). In its rental contracts, the company insists that users buy the tabulating cards used with the machines from I. B. M.[1] Why should the company insist on tying together the rental of the machines and the purchase of the cards? Assume, for purposes of your answer, that equally good cards can be produced by any of a large number of potential producers (this is probably correct). What considerations determine the optimum price to charge for the cards? (An interesting ques-

---

1. These practices have been modified in recent years as a result of antitrust actions.

tion—which, while not part of your assignment, is closely related to it—is why I. B. M. rents rather than sells the machines.)

8. The Political Economy Club is holding a party for which it is selling tickets of admission. The price is $1.25 per person and $2.00 per couple (presumably subject to the limitation that a couple contain one person of each sex). Why the special price for the tied-in sale? Under what circumstances will it increase returns? What considerations should determine the optimum price?

THE ECONOMICS OF INTERNAL PRICING

A general class of monopoly problems concerns the terms on which firms sell to closely connected firms and to unrelated firms. To put it abstractly, firms A and B are owned by the same person. Firm A produces a product X that is used by Firm B in its process of production and that Firm A also sells on the open market. In the interests of the common owner, what is the optimum pricing policy for Firm A? Under what circumstances, if any, should it charge the same price to Firm B as to other buyers? Different prices? What criteria should it use in setting the price? Consider only the long-run solution.

A few examples will illustrate some of the various forms under which this problem arises.

1. In many patent cases, objection is raised to the "competitive advantage" that the owner of a patent is alleged to have in manufacturing the item covered by the patent, even though the owner of the patent freely licenses it to others at a fixed fee. In terms of our example, Firm A owns the patent and the product X is the license to use the patent. The complaint presumably is that Firm A charges a zero license fee to its own manufacturing subsidiary, a positive fee to others, and that this gives it a "competitive advantage." The analytical question at issue is whether the patent owner will maximize his revenue by charging the same or a different fee (internal price) to his own manufacturing subsidiary than to others.

2. In an antitrust suit against General Motors, U.S. Rubber, and Du-Pont, the complaint included the charge, "DuPont has required all three corporations to grant 'systematic secret rebates and preferential prices' in selling to one another, while they have sold the same products to outsiders at higher prices."

3. General Motors has repeatedly instructed its automobile divisions to buy their parts where they can get them cheapest, whether from GM subsidiaries or not, and has instructed its parts subsidiaries to sell them where they can get the highest price. This is equivalent to insisting on identical prices.

4. Some of the gasoline companies are reputed to sell gasoline to their own filling stations, who market it as a branded gas, at a higher price than they sell the same gasoline to independent filling stations who market it

as an unbranded gas. This is equivalent to charging a higher internal than external price.

THE ECONOMICS OF TOLL ROADS

A considerable number of toll highways have been constructed (e.g., the Pennsylvania, New Jersey, Ohio, and Indiana turnpikes) and more are under construction. Almost all, if not all, are being constructed under governmental rather than private auspices. They generally charge fees roughly proportional to the number of miles driven on them.[2] Generally also, there are service facilities—gas, food, etc.—at a limited number of locations along the highway designated by the governmental authority in charge. These service facilities are generally operated by private enterprises licensed to do so by the governmental authorities and no other service facilities are permitted. Two classes of economic problems thus arise: first, the setting of tolls; second, the licensing of service facilities.

1. The setting of tolls

a. The gasoline tax is a form of toll for roads in general. What is the distinguishing feature of the new toll highways that makes an explicit toll feasible or desirable for them but not for the usual road?

b. Suppose a private enterprise constructed and operated a particular toll road. On what principle would it set prices? What structure of prices for short and long distances do you think would emerge, taking account of the facts of the situation? How would its method of price setting be connected with the kind of road it decided to construct (e.g., its capacity)?

c. Let a governmental body now operate the road. Assume that it does not seek to maximize net financial revenue from the road but rather to "maximize social welfare." On what principle should it set prices? How should it determine whether it is worth building a particular road and what size (in the sense of capacity) to make it? How do you think the structure of prices for long and short distances would compare with that under b?

2. The service facilities

For simplicity and concreteness, restrict the following discussion to gas stations. Restrict it also to case 1c, operation of the road by a governmental authority. The principles involved will apply also to other service facilities.

a. Assume, first, that the number and location of gas stations on the road is definitely fixed in advance; second, that for all practical purposes, the users of the road have no alternative to buying gas at these stations if they

2. This problem was written before the interstate highway system was authorized. The law establishing that system prohibited tolls but permitted the retention of pre-existing tolls. A natural expansion of this problem is to analyze the economic effects and desirability of the prohibition of tolls.

buy any gas at all on their trip. (In fact, of course, there are gas stations at or close to all exits and it is possible to get off the road and back on again.) Suppose the license to operate the facilities is simply auctioned off to the single highest bidder and that no restrictions are imposed on the prices he charges. Would this policy be consistent with the objective assumed in 1c? If not, why not? What restrictions, if any, should the authority impose on the licensees to achieve this objective?

b. Limitation of the number of facilities is generally justified on grounds of the expense of providing access to and egress from the facilities without slowing down traffic on the road. Suppose the authority were to grant a license to anyone who would pay the costs of providing access and egress. Would this lead to the "correct" number of facilities? Would it obviate the necessity of imposing any restrictions suggested under 2a?

CARTELS

This problem is concerned with the economic theory of cartels. For this purpose, a *cartel* is defined as an agreement among some or all producers of a product that is restricted to the price at which the product is sold and the output of each member. It is assumed that the members of the cartel would operate independently in its absence. These specifications are designed to exclude from the problem changes in cost conditions, or in methods of production, as a reason for or result of collusive arrangements.

1. Suppose that (a) a cartel is in existence; (b) entry into the cartel is effectively prevented; and (c) no nonmember can produce (e.g., because the cartel is governmentally organized and enforced).

Describe the optimum price and output position of the cartel and the optimum distribution of output among the members. Does the latter differ from the distribution that would exist at the same price in the absence of the cartel? If so, how?

2. Alter b in the preceding case by making entry free to all and assume that each entrant gets a (nontransferable) quota equal to his fraction of the "productive capacity" of the industry, defined, e.g., in terms of "rated capacity" of blast furnaces or the like.

Describe the long-run equilibrium position of the industry for any fixed price. Can you define an *optimum long-run price* for the industry?

Consider the short-run situation at the time the cartel is formed. How does it differ from the long-run situation? Can you say anything about the optimum short-run price for the cartel? What factors determine the duration and effects of the transition from the short- to the long-run position?

3. Alter c in case 1 by assuming that on establishment of the cartel, all producers are members of it, but the cartel cannot prevent new firms from being established and producing.

Describe the long-run equilibrium position of the industry. How does it differ from case 2?

In the short-run, when the cartel is formed, the members can get "monopoly returns" by raising the price. What, if anything, is the long-run offset to these short-run gains? What considerations determine the size of the short-run gains? The size of the long-run costs?

4. Do the considerations of the preceding case suggest to you a "theory" of cartel formation? Of the circumstances that are favorable and unfavorable to the formation of cartels?

5. The U.S. Steel Company was formed in 1901 and can for our purposes be regarded as a cartel largely satisfying the conditions of case 3. It then accounted for about two-thirds of the industry's output; it now accounts for about one-third of the industry's output. Can you interpret this episode in terms of the theory arrived at under point 4?

EASTMAN KODAK, A.T.&T., AND THE PRICING OF MULTIPLE PRODUCTS

1. An executive in a firm manufacturing cameras expressed the view that his firm was at a competitive disadvantage relative to Eastman-Kodak. Kodak, he said, "could sell its cameras for less because it makes so much from the sales of film," whereas his company is solely in the camera-producing business.

Evaluate his analysis, with special attention to the conditions, if any, under which it would be in Kodak's own interest to "sell its cameras for less because it makes so much from the sale of film." Explain precisely what you interpret the words to mean.

2. American Telephone and Telegraph Company is a common carrier with respect to long-distance telephone communications. In this connection, it currently leases wires to firms that wish to have private telephone communication among different plants or offices or the like.

A new method of long-distance radio communication using microwaves has been developed that promises to be a cheaper substitute for long-distance lines and that can be installed and operated by firms on their own. Individual firms are now applying to the Federal Communications Commission for licenses to install and use such microwave equipment. A.T.&T. is requesting the commission to interpret its current franchise, which applies to long-distance telephone communication, as covering the new method as well and to prevent private firms from installing their own equipment.

A.T.&T. argues (1) that it is more efficient to have a single common carrier than many private installations; and (2) that even though it might be equally or more efficient for some individual firms to have their own installations, permitting them to do so would take away from A.T.&T. the "cream" of their business and thus require them to charge higher rates on other services. Evaluate these arguments.

3. The argument of the camera manufacturer and the second of A.T.

& T.'s argument have much in common. Are they the same? Or are they different?

1. Commercial banks are now prohibited from paying interest to their depositors on demand deposits. In recommending a continuation of this prohibition in a published report, The Commission on Money and Credit wrote, "This legislation was adopted to reduce competition for deposits among commercial banks and thereby to relieve pressure for increased earnings which led to imprudent loans and investments" (*Money and Credit*, p. 167). Evaluate the economic validity of the quoted argument, i.e., could the measure be expected to have the implied effects? If so, how? If not, why not?

2. Some concerns selling products in which bank financing plays a large role follow the practice of keeping sizable, inactive demand deposits at banks that finance or might finance their customers, explicitly for the purpose of getting the bank to push their product or their services instead of competing ones. How is this practice linked to the prohibition of the payment of interest on demand deposits? Would you expect the practice to exist in the absence of the prohibition? Justify your answer.

ALCOA: THE SECONDHAND MARKET AND MONOPOLY POSITION

In an antitrust case against the Aluminum Company of America (Alcoa) decided before World War II when Alcoa was the only American producer of primary ingots, Judge Learned Hand argued that Alcoa could be regarded as having essentially a complete monopoly on aluminum despite the existence of a highly competitive market in secondary or reclaimed aluminum (made from scrap) accounting for about one-third of the total aluminum used for fabrication. He justified this conclusion on the grounds that all secondary aluminum derives ultimately from primary aluminum produced earlier and hence that Alcoa indirectly controlled the quantity of scrap available through its control of the output of primary aluminum.

To state Hand's conclusion in a precise form in which it can be demonstrated to be true or false, assume that Alcoa has a complete monopoly of primary aluminum, that aluminum for fabrication comes from primary aluminum and secondary aluminum, and that primary aluminum and secondary aluminum are perfect substitutes. Consider two alternative situations: (1) secondary aluminum is refined and sold by a large number of firms under competitive conditions; (2) Alcoa has a complete monopoly of the refining of secondary aluminum as well as of the production of primary aluminum. Hand's conclusion then is that the price of aluminum would be the same in cases (1) and (2), i.e., that Alcoa would find it in its own interests to charge the same price in either case.

Even in this simplified form, the problem of determining whether and under what conditions Hand is right or wrong is extremely difficult. The easiest way I know to get an answer is not to attack this problem directly but instead to analyze the following mock problems that contain its essential features.

a. There is a durable good, say, a milling machine, which company X alone manufactures. This milling machine wears out in precisely ten years, but is as good as new until it wears out. It cannot be repaired or in any other way made to last more than ten years, and its life does not depend on rate of use. Company X contemplates either (i) selling machines outright, in which case there will be a competitive second hand market or (ii) retaining ownership in the machines and renting them out.

Show how to determine the ultimate optimum long-run position for company X in both cases (i.e., neglect the initial stage of building up its market) and prove that its optimum output is the same in the two cases. Assume perfect capital markets, perfect foresight on its part and its customers' part, etc.

b. Change the preceding case by supposing that the life of milling machines can be prolonged by spending money repairing or servicing them, and assume that the repairing or servicing can be obtained competitively. Prove that the company's optimum output will now be different in cases (i) and (ii), and indicate in which case the total number of machines in existence will be larger, and hence the net rental value lower.

c. Explain how these mock problems are connected to the Alcoa problem and what the answers to them imply for the Alcoa problem.

RECIPROCITY IN BUSINESS PURCHASING

Analyze the business practice discussed in the accompanying excerpt from a *Wall Street Journal* article of December 4, 1973.

Under what circumstances, if any, would you expect such a practice to be in the self-interest of the participating companies? How would you suggest testing your explanation?

"Dear Red," wrote FMC Corp. Chairman Paul Davies to Ford Motor Co. Vice President Irving Duffy. "This is just a note to express . . . appreciation . . . for the good news we had that your company had decided to purchase part of your Nashville requirements for soda ash from our company."

"Effective as of now wherever possible," Mr. Davies continued, "our people are to purchase Ford products. . . . I believe our salesmen and service fleet that we own amounts to 600 to 800 cars. . . . As . . . you know, our two company chauffeured cars are Lincolns which we buy new each year and the Davies' family have only Lincolns."

This promise of orders for automobiles in return for the purchase of soda ash, used in making auto window glass, is business "reciprocity"—you buy from me and I'll buy from you. The practice is as old as business itself. It is found at every level of business—from giant corporations down to the grocer who has his delivery truck serviced at the gas station whose owner shops at his market.

A Government Attack

Despite its antiquity and universality, however, reciprocity—especially that involving big companies—is drawing mounting criticism. The chief sources of the criticism are the Justice Department and the Federal Trade Commission. In some instances, the agencies have charged in suits, reciprocity may amount to an illegal restraint of trade, particularly if coupled with coercion. Mr. Davies' "Dear Red" letter came to light in a Government suit aimed at blocking FMC's acquisition of American Viscose Corp. assets, partly on the ground that it would create opportunities for illegal reciprocity.

The firms that have been targets of the Federal attack deny any wrongdoing, and many companies appear to take the view that reciprocity is a perfectly acceptable way of doing business as long as the practice does not force any firm to buy goods at higher-than-normal prices or to accept unsatisfactory products or services.[3]

AMERICAN ECONOMIC ASSOCIATION TIE-IN

The American Economic Association publishes two journals: *The American Economic Review* and the *Journal of Economic Literature*. It offers to nonmembers a joint subscription to the two for $30 a year.

1. Prove that the AEA's net revenue from subscriptions could be raised by offering subscriptions to each journal separately, *in addition to* a joint subscription (i.e., at prices that might add up to more than $30).

2. Under what conditions, if any, would this (a) also be true, (b) no longer be true, if the separate prices were required to add up to $30 (i.e., in effect, if joint subscriptions were abolished)?

For simplicity, the question is restricted to nonmembers, though obviously the same questions arise for members (who pay $20 a year and get both journals). For simplicity also, assume that costs are completely separable, i.e., that it would cost the AEA precisely as much to service two separate subscriptions, one for each journal, as it now does to service a single joint subscription.

AUTOMOBILE SAFETY REQUIREMENTS

It has been argued that the automobile industry is irrational to object to the requirements for safety belts, pollution equipment, etc., on cars because these requirements have the effect of giving the automobile firms captive customers. Every purchaser of a car must also buy safety belts, and

---

3. "Swapping Business," *The Wall Street Journal*, December 4, 1973. Reprinted with permission of *The Wall Street Journal*, © Dow Jones & Company, Inc. (1973). All Rights Reserved.

it must buy that belt from the firm from which it buys the car. Hence, automobile producers are given a monopoly position with respect to the required items.

Under what conditions, if any, is the argument valid? Invalid?

DEVALUATION AND U.S. PRICES

Let West Germany be a proxy for the non-U.S. world. Assume it to have a single currency, the mark. We are going to analyze the effect on the price of soybeans in the United States and West Germany of a 25 percent change in the dollar price of the mark from, say, 31¢ per mark to 38.75¢ per mark. To simplify, consider only the partial effects in the soybean market, neglecting the reflex influence from that market to the foreign exchange market.

1. Assume that (a) the U.S. is the sole producer of soybeans; (b) the stock for the 1972–73 crop year is given; (c) there are no restrictions on international trade in soybeans (they can be exported from or imported into the U.S. or West Germany without quotas, tariffs, etc.); and (d) at the 31¢ price per mark, the U.S. market price would be $4 per bushel; and half the crop would be sold in the U.S., half in West Germany.

What additional information do you need to estimate the effect of the rise in the price of the mark on U.S. price and U.S. consumption, and on mark price and German consumption? Make specific assumptions about the additional information and calculate specific numerical estimates.

2. Same as 1, except that assumption (a) is replaced by: (a)′ the U.S. produces a minor fraction of the total world crop of soybeans, and (d)′ refers to the U.S. crop, not the world crop.

GASOLINE RATIONING

There is much talk about the rationing of gasoline. Some proposed schemes are as follows:

1. Each family will be assigned coupons entitling it to a specified number of gallons of gasoline per week (say fifteen gallons) at a fixed price of, say, 45¢ per gallon, will be permitted to buy or sell coupons, and will be permitted to buy additional gasoline in the free market at the market price without coupons.
2. Same as 1, except that no purchases without coupons are permitted and the price is fixed at 45¢ a gallon. Size of allotment is determined so that all coupons can be honored.
3. Same as 1, except that coupons are distributed per car rather than per family, but for the same total amount of gasoline.
4. Rationing is solely by price, but a tax is imposed equal to the excess of price over 45¢.
5. Free market solution.

Analyze the determination of the market price of the coupons for cases 1 and 2.

Prove that, to a first approximation, the total quantity of gasoline available will be the same under plan 1 and plan 2. Why "to a first approximation"? What will be the relation between the price of coupons under plan 2 and the tax under plan 4?

How will amount of gasoline available under 1 compare with amount under 2? Under 5? How will the free market price of gasoline under 1 compare with the price, including price of coupon, under 2, and with market price under 5?

How and why will results differ under plan 1 from under plan 2?

PATENT LICENSING AND MONOPOLY

The accompanying article from *The Wall Street Journal* raises a number of questions.

The Federal Trade Commission said its antitrust settlement with Xerox Corp. should enable competitors to challenge the company's dominance in the office-copier field.

By unanimous vote, the agency accepted a previously described consent agreement requiring Xerox to license competitors to use its more than 1,700 copier patents and some future patents. In addition, the Stamford, Conn., concern agreed to make available to all domestic competitors, except International Business Machines Corp., much of its manufacturing expertise on a royalty-free basis.

"The central purpose of the consent order is to eliminate the fundamental sources of Xerox's total dominance of the multibillion-dollar office-copier industry—its vast patent portfolio, its manufacturing know-how," according to an FTC staff description of the settlement.

"We would expect to see Xerox's market share significantly whittled down," said James T. Halverson, director of the FTC's Bureau of Competition. "I will be dissatisfied if Xerox's market position isn't significantly diminished over the next 10 years," he added.

However, one competitor, SCM Corp., quickly challenged the validity of Mr. Halverson's expectations. And Xerox itself has recently said patents were of declining importance to its position in the copier industry.

Increased Competition

The increased competition should "ultimately result in lower prices and greater consumer choice" in the office-copier field, Mr. Halverson said. Despite competition from IBM, Litton Industries Inc., SCM, and Minnesota Mining & Manufacturing Co., Xerox currently controls about 85% of the plain-paper copier market, according to the FTC. The copier market is divided between machines that use plain paper—about 70% of the total business—and machines that use treated or coated paper.

The FTC said that several other large companies, such as Eastman Kodak Co., are potential entrants into the market.

Because a number of concerns want to compete with Xerox, "it's much more important to get relief now" through a settlement, than to wait the six or seven years it would take to complete litigation of the FTC's 1973 antitrust complaint, Mr. Halverson said.

The complaint charged Xerox with dominating the office-copier industry by engaging in unfair market and patent practices and by foreclosing foreign subsidiaries from competing with Xerox in the U.S.

Xerox declined to comment on the commissioners' decision to accept the settlement, beyond referring to a statement by C. Peter McColough, Xerox's chairman and chief executive, when the proposed terms were announced. Mr. McColough said then: "The proposed settlement would be in the best interests of Xerox shareholders and employes."

In the prospectus for last week's sale of $400 million in notes and debentures, Xerox stated: "Although patents in the field of xerography were of material significance to the company's business during its early development, they are now of lessening importance. In the future, patents are not expected to be as important as the company's capability in developing, manufacturing and marketing new and improved products."

Sharing Patents

The settlement requires Xerox to share its patents and know-how, which the FTC said "have constituted barriers to entry into the office-copier market and have precluded effective competition," so that other companies may, essentially, copy Xerox's machines.

Xerox; Rank Xerox Ltd., a British joint venture with Rank Organisation Ltd., and Fuji Xerox Co., a Japanese joint venture of Rank Xerox, must grant world-wide licenses to all their current copier patents. They must grant similar licenses to patents issued within the next six years.

A competitor may receive licenses for up to three patents without paying royalties, which will enable some companies to enter the industry without any patent-licensing cost, the FTC said. Competitors would have to pay a royalty of up to 0.5% of product revenue for each of the next three patents licensed per product, with additional patents royalty-free.

Xerox could require "cross licenses" of patents from competitors, but only after the competing company had used them exclusively for four years. "Thus, competitors who cross-license their patents to Xerox will reap the substantial benefits of being first into the market with a new product," the FTC staff explained.

Xerox also agreed to disclose such things as blueprints, drawings, manuals, production methods and specifications to domestic competitors, except IBM.

Another important provision requires Xerox to establish independent price plans for machines with different usage patterns. Under the company's machine-utilization plan, it leases a range of machines with different capabilities to large users at package rates, according to the FTC. This made it difficult for competitors with less than a full line to compete.

In addition, Xerox agreed to refrain for 10 years from:

—Acquiring competitors or patents, with some exceptions.

—Prohibiting employes from going to work for other companies.

—Announcing or taking orders for new copier models more than six months before expected commercial availability.

Despite its scope, the settlement is sure to provoke controversy. After Xerox disclosed terms of the settlement last month, one competitor, SCM, criticized the "gross inadequacy" of the terms, and a number of Wall Street security analysts called the proposed settlement a victory for Xerox. The agency asked for public comment on the proposed settlement by Jan. 13, 1975. After that, the agency may finally accept or reject the settlement.

In agreeing to the settlement, Xerox didn't concede any wrongdoing.

Controversy on Settlement

In New York, SCM, which had denounced the terms of the proposed settlement in a letter to the commissioners, said it would file formal objections. "It would be naive to believe that the proposed order will have any real impact on Xerox's technology position," Richard Sexton, vice president and general counsel of SCM, declared.

SCM has been pressing its own civil monopoly suit against Xerox since July 1973.

The provision requiring Xerox licensees to grant patent licenses back to Xerox would "further entrench" Xerox's technology lead, Mr. Sexton insisted Friday. He contended that the proposed order "does almost nothing about Xerox's restrictive marketing practices or its monopoly profits" and objected that it doesn't affect "the cartel agreement" under which Xerox and the two foreign units allegedly "divide up the world."

Mr. Sexton asserted again that the FTC would have been better advised to "admit defeat" and dismiss the complaint without a consent order.

In Armonk, N.Y., an IBM spokesman said he couldn't say whether IBM would object to or comment formally on the settlement. It is an unusual feature that IBM, a potentially formidable competitor for Xerox, is excluded by name from two provisions of the proposed order.

Xerox has sued IBM for patent infringement, and IBM has attacked Xerox's patents in counterclaims.

Several other copier manufacturers are involved in patent litigation with Xerox. One of them, Nashua Corp., Nashua, N.H., previously said it didn't consider the proposed FTC-Xerox settlement "appropriate."[4]

1. The article implies that Xerox did not license patents before. Assume for the sake of the problem that that is true. Then why did it not?

    a. Prove that in the ordinary case of a patent for a product, it is in the patent owner's own interest to license the patent freely at an appropriate price, show how to derive that price, and the division of output between direct production by patent owner and licensed production.

    b. At first glance, it may seem that the interest of Xerox in developing new technology changes the situation. Does it or does it not?

4. "Xerox Accord in Patent Case Cleared by FTC," *The Wall Street Journal,* November 18, 1974. Reprinted with permission of *The Wall Street Journal,* © Dow Jones & Company, Inc. (1974). All Rights Reserved.

c. Do you have any other suggested explanations for the assumed failure of Xerox to license patents?

2. Was it in Xerox's interest to foreclose "foreign subsidiaries from competing with Xerox in the U.S."? If they could successfully compete, wouldn't Xerox benefit from the extra profits they got that way just as much as or more than from the profits of the American company? How do you explain this alleged practice?

3. What features of the copier business will be affected in the long run by the decree? What will the effects be?

Part 2: Distribution

THE INCIDENCE OF THE CORPORATE INCOME TAX

Suppose the federal government were to raise the rate of the corporation income tax, while at the same time reducing other taxes so as to keep total revenues unchanged. For the purposes of this problem, assume that the corporation income tax is a flat rate tax on the net income of incorporated enterprises and that net income is computed in the usual fashion by subtracting expenses, including interest on debt, from gross income.

1. Appraise the effects of this change in taxation on the allocation of resources among alternative uses. Be as concrete as you possibly can in your discussion, naming specifically the areas or kinds of areas favored or disfavored, commenting on the effects, if any, on wages of particular kinds of employees, etc. Abstract from any effect of the tax change on the general level of income, prices, and employment.

2. Dividends paid to stockholders are not currently allowed as a deduction in computing net income subject to tax. How would your answer be changed if dividend income were to be allowed as a deduction in computing the additional tax, i.e., the additional tax were to be levied on retained earnings alone?

INCOMES IN NORTH AND SOUTH AND DISCRIMINATION BY RACE

Available evidence tentatively indicates that (1) average income of white families living in the same size of city is roughly the same in the North and the South; (2) the wage rate of a white worker in any given occupation is higher in the North than in the South for cities of the same size; (3) property income is roughly of equal importance for white families in the North and the South.

For purposes of this question, accept these as correct statements of fact. Can you suggest any way of reconciling the apparent contradiction among them? Presumably, any reconciliation will turn on the larger fraction of blacks and greater discrimination against them in the South than in the North.

Spell out your suggestion in detail, explaining the theoretical links, if any, between the higher fraction of blacks and greater discrimination, on the one hand, and the indicated results on the other. Indicate how the validity of your suggestion could be tested.

MORTGAGE GUARANTEES

The U.S. Government currently guarantees a large fraction of mortgages on newly constructed houses through the Federal Housing Administration and the Veterans Administration. The government guarantee naturally makes these more attractive than nonguaranteed mortgages and so leads to their being available at a lower rate of interest. In 1957, there was a decline in residential building. Representatives of the industry suggested that one means of stimulating building would be to extend the government guarantee to mortgages on existing houses. They claimed that the higher costs of mortgages on such houses inhibited their sale and thus prevented individuals currently owning houses from coming into the market for new houses.

1. Analyze the effect that the enactment of this proposal would have on the rate of construction of residential housing. Do *not* discuss the desirability as a matter of public policy of either the existing guarantees or the proposed extension.

2. Does the government guarantee of these mortgages, and similar guarantee programs, involve any cost to the government other than the cost of making good the losses on defaulted obligations and the administrative costs of operating the programs? If so, what?

OPTIMUM BUILDING HEIGHTS

In the course of discussing why buildings in New York City have been higher than he thinks is most economic, Lewis Mumford writes "... probably because there is a big difference between putting up a building for immediate profit and putting up one for permanent income. A building that can mean a big reward for the builder who overcrowds a site can mean a low income for the man who buys it from him as an investment."

Later, in the same article, he writes, "... when the early planners drew up the building ordinances, they did not take into account the rather low land values that prevailed in the all-but-virgin midtown area (low land values make low buildings economically feasible)." (*New Yorker,* October 23, 1954, pp. 118 and 120.)

Discuss the economics of these quotations.

WAGES AND PRODUCTIVITY

The desirability of linking wages to "productivity" is a recurrent theme in discussions of inflation, as exemplified by the following exchange reported in the transcript of President Eisenhower's press conference of February 25, 1959:

Newspaper man: ". . . Senator Kefauver has proposed that the steel industry forego a price increase if the steel union limits its wage demands to an amount equal to the average increase in productivity. I'd like to know what you think about that proposal?"

President Eisenhower: ". . . I have always urged that wage increases should be measured by increases in productivity, and I think that there would be no inflationary effects if they were measured by that criterion."

Analyze this proposal, not in terms of its effect on inflation, a topic outside the area covered by this course, but in terms of relative price and wage theory. In your analysis, discuss the meaning of "productivity," the sense or senses in which wages are always linked to productivity and the sense or senses in which they need not be, the effect of linking wages to "productivity" in these latter senses, on the employment and return to labor of various kinds, and the effect of linking prices to wages on the output and distribution of commodities.

LICENSING TAXICABS

New York City licenses taxicabs in two classes: for operation by companies with fleets and for operation by independent driver-owners each having only one cab. It also, of course, fixes the rates that taxis charge. For many years now, no new licenses have been issued in either class. There is an unofficial market in the "medallions" that signify the possession of a license. A medallion for an independent cab in 1959 sold for about $17,000 in this market.

1. Discuss the factors determining the price of a medallion. For concreteness, conjecture at the numerical values of the various components that together can be summarized in a present value of $17,000.

2. What factors would determine whether a change in the fare fixed by the city would raise or lower the price of a medallion?

3. Cab drivers, whether hired by companies or owners of their own cabs, seem unanimous in opposing any increase in the number of cabs licensed. They argue that an increase in the number of cabs, by increasing competition for customers, would drive down what they regard as an already unduly low return to drivers. Is their economics correct? Who would benefit and who would lose from an expansion in the number of licenses issued at a nominal fee?

WAGES AND EMPLOYMENT

1. "Under conditions of perfect competition . . . whenever there is an excess supply of anything, the price of that thing will fall. Consequently, if there were perfect competition in all markets, . . . the existence of unemployment would imply excess supply, . . . and wages would fall" (William G. Bowen, *Wage Behavior in the Postwar Period* [Princeton University Press, 1960, p. 4]). Of course, there is no way to define unambiguously *zero unemployment,* so we may interpret *the existence of unemployment*

to mean that unemployment is above normal, and interpret *normal* rather arbitrarily, since the ambiguity of this concept is not one of the points at issue in this problem. (For example, in his empirical work for the postwar period, Bowen uses 4.3 percent unemployment as an admittedly arbitrary dividing line.)

Consider changes in employment over a business cycle, roughly schematized in the accompanying chart, which distinguishes the period of fall-

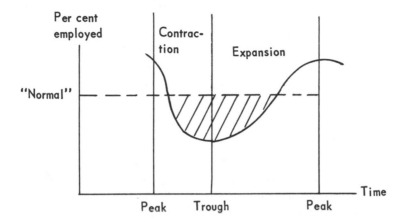

ing employment (contraction) from that of rising employment (expansion) and also the period when employment is below normal (the shaded area) from the period when employment is above normal.

On the basis of the quoted analysis, which is perfectly consistent with the loose way we draw demand and supply curves for labor (and other commodities) in class, wage rates would be expected to fall during the shaded period and rise during the remainder. Of course, wage rates generally rise throughout the cycle, so we might translate this expectation into a less rapid rise (or absolute fall) during the shaded period and a more rapid rise during the remainder. Yet in fact, as is well known and as Bowen again documents, this is not the case; wages rise less rapidly during a period that comes closer to coinciding with the contraction phase of the cycle than with the "below normal" period and begin to reverse their acceleration and rise more rapidly at or shortly after the trough.

This phenomenon cannot, I believe, be attributed to monopoly. The same phenomenon is found in a wide range of labor markets, even those that would generally be regarded as competitive (and, indeed, in highly competitive product markets). In any event, for this problem assume that monopoly is not the explanation.

Can you restate the relevant theory more carefully and precisely than is usually done, so as to explain why (a) "of course, wage rates generally rise throughout the cycle," and (b) why the rate of change of employment seems to be an important variable explaining the rate of change of wages rather than or in addition to the level of employment?

2. "The relationship between unemployment and the rate at which money wages rise is the key empirical relation" (ibid., p. 5). In the recent rash of discussion of so-called cost-push inflation, this statement has been almost taken for granted. It has led Phillips in England to relate empirically over a long period the rate of change of wages to the level of unemployment (he reported a fairly good empirical relation) and Bowen to do the same for the United States (he reports a poor relation).

This statement is, of course, derived from the analysis of the first quotation and like the immediate implications for cyclical behavior suggested by that analysis is seriously defective, and for very similar reasons. Considerations derived from price theory give no reason to expect any systematic, long-term relation between the percentage of the labor force unemployed and the rate at which money wages rise. Explain why not.

THE "WASTELAND" OF BOOK PUBLISHING

There has been much recent discussion about the quality of television programs, partly centering about then Commissioner Newton Minow's description of television programming as a "wasteland." Criticism can be and is on two different levels: (1) that the public is not getting the programs it wants and is willing to pay for—i.e., that the market is working poorly; (2) that the public is getting what it wants but that the public's tastes are vulgar.

With respect to argument 1, the key issue is the method of pricing for programs. Currently, the costs are met by advertisers who sponsor programs.

One argument for the present method of financing television is that once a program is produced, it costs nothing for an additional viewer to see it; hence the social optimum is obtained when the price the viewer must pay is equal to the marginal cost is equal to zero. This same argument can be applied to book publishing. For a particular book, the marginal cost of producing another copy is only direct manufacturing costs, which are generally only a small fraction of the price charged for the book. Does it follow that the present method of pricing books involves a socially unnecessary loss? If so, what measures would you expect publishers to take as a consequence?

One way to avoid such a loss would be to use a method of financing in the publishing of books like that used in television. That is, suppose a law were passed saying that it shall be illegal to charge a specific price for a particular book; that books may be published and distributed only if they are distributed without specific charge, the expenses being paid by foundations or contributions (educational television) or by firms using the cover or jacket or pages in the book to advertise their product.

Analyze what effect you would expect this change to have on (1) the total volume of resources used in writing and publishing books, (2) the kinds of books that would be published—let your imagination roam and be as specific as you can, (3) the average return to authors of books, and (4) the distribution of returns among authors. Would publishing become a "wasteland"? Is the analogy valid? Discuss whether there are any essential differences between television and books that would make the analysis of the one medium inapplicable to the other.

ORWELL ON THE ECONOMICS OF PUBLISHING

Analyze the following venture by George Orwell into economics:

The Penguin books are splendid value for sixpence, so splendid that if the other publishers had any sense they would combine against them and suppress them. It is, of course, a great mistake to imagine that cheap books are good for the book trade. Actually it is just the other way about. If you have, for instance, five shillings to spend and the normal price of a book is half-a-crown, you are quite likely to spend your whole five shillings on two books. But if books are sixpence each you are not going to buy ten of them, because you don't want as many as ten; your saturation point will have been reached long before that. Probably you will buy three sixpenny books and spend the rest of your five shillings on seats at the "movies." Hence the cheaper books become, the less money is spent on books. This is an advantage from the reader's point of view and doesn't hurt trade as a whole, but for the publisher, the compositor, the author, and the bookseller it is a disaster. . . .

If the other publishers follow suit, the result may be a flock of cheap reprints that will cripple the lending libraries (the novelist's foster-mother) and check the output of new novels. This would be a fine thing for literature, but it would be a very bad thing for trade, and when you have to choose between art and money—well, finish it for yourself. (From "Review of Penguin Books," by George Orwell, published in *New English Weekly*, 5 March 1936, as reprinted in *The Collected Essays, Journalism and Letters of George Orwell*, I, 165–67.)

OIL ROYALTIES

In discussing the North Sea Oil Boom, *Newsweek* wrote: "To be sure, the stakes are high. Both capital costs and operating costs in the North Sea may be ten times those in the Mideast, where oil seems to gush forth at each poke in the sand. But Mideast royalties are so high that the companies are gladly spending record sums to battle North Sea waves and drill at harrowing depths of 500 feet and more."

What determines the royalties? (1) Give an *analytical* answer assuming no collusion among the Mideast countries. (2) How would you alter your answer to allow for collusion?

LAND PRICES

For most Americans, land-price inflation costs more than it is worth. For the homeowner, a rise in the value of his house is purely theoretical profit until he sells, but the land spiral meanwhile helps raise the price of almost everything that he must buy. Packing plants, bakeries, supermarkets, movie theaters, filling stations, widget makers—all pass on to their customers the rising prices—and taxes—that their owners must pay for the land on which they set up shop.

Food prices are jacked up by the land boom in two ways. The rising price of farm land is reflected directly in the cost of crops. The land boom also turns farm land into lots for houses, roads, and stores, thus removing it from food production while food demand keeps growing. Between 1960 and 1970, developers bought as much as 3,000,000 acres of crop land out of America's total 1.1 billion acres of farm land. In some areas, the land surge practically forces farmers to sell out.

Analyze this quotation from *Time Magazine*. How do you reconcile it with the view underlying Henry George's single tax proposal that the rent of land is price-determined rather than price-determining?

STOCKS VERSUS FLOWS

1. The sharp rise in the price of oil in October 1973 produced a sharp decline in the demand for large cars relative to small cars.

2. According to a newspaper story,

In recent testimony . . . , Dr. Malcolm C. Todd, president of the A.M.A., said that if doctors can't get adequate malpractice coverage they can't practice medicine.

"When premium rates double, triple, and quadruple, physicians and hospitals protest, but we pay," he said. "And we pass the additional costs along in the form of higher fees and higher rates, because we have no other choice. The ultimate payer—the real loser—is the public, the individual patient."

Assume that the rises in the price of both oil and malpractice insurance were unanticipated and that both will prove permanent. Show that the two price rises can be regarded as giving rise to special cases of the same problem in capital theory. Give a formal analysis of both in terms of stocks and flows.

In particular, what would you expect to be the time pattern of the price of large cars relative to small cars? The time pattern of production? The time pattern of medical prices and medical incomes? Of the provision of medical services?

MEDICAL MALPRACTICE INSURANCE

Evaluate the economic analysis in the following quotation. Expand it to indicate the effect of higher medical malpractice costs on the number of physicians. Pay special attention to the time pattern of effects, making use of the formal stock-flow apparatus in doing so.

"And physicians, who must bear the direct costs of malpractice actions, are not comforted by the thought that they *may* be able to pass those costs on in the form of higher fees for their services.*

---

* "... In general it is safe to say that too much has been made of the ability of physicians and insurance companies to pass on the costs of increased malpractice losses. To the extent that these losses arise out of incidents in past years, there is no way for either physicians or insurance companies to recoup these 'sunk costs' by charging higher rates for future services ..." (From Richard A. Epstein, "Medical Malpractice: The Case for Contract," *American Bar Foundation Research Journal*, No. 1 [1976], p. 88.)

Index